DAVID BUSCH'S
CANON® EOS® 70D

GUIDE TO DIGITAL SLR PHOTOGRAPHY

David D. Busch

Cengage Learning PTR

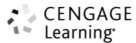

Professional • Technical • Reference

Australia, Brazil, Japan, Korea, Mexico, Singapore, Spain, United Kingdom, United States

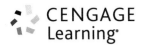

David Busch's Canon® EOS® 70D Guide to Digital SLR Photography
David D. Busch

Publisher and General Manager, Cengage Learning PTR:
Stacy L. Hiquet

Associate Director of Marketing:
Sarah Panella

Manager of Editorial Services:
Heather Talbot

Senior Marketing Manager:
Mark Hughes

Executive Editor:
Kevin Harreld

Project Editor:
Jenny Davidson

Series Technical Editor:
Michael D. Sullivan

Interior Layout Tech:
Bill Hartman

Cover Designer:
Mike Tanamachi

Indexer:
Katherine Stimson

Proofreader:
Sara Gullion

© 2014 David D. Busch

For product information and technology assistance, contact us at
Cengage Learning Customer & Sales Support, 1-800-354-9706

For permission to use material from this text or product,
submit all requests online at **cengage.com/permissions**
Further permissions questions can be emailed to
permissionrequest@cengage.com

Library of Congress Control Number: 2013953472

ISBN-13: 978-1-285-76526-6

ISBN-10: 1-285-76526-5

Cengage Learning PTR
20 Channel Center Street
Boston, MA 02210
USA

Cengage Learning is a leading provider of customized learning solutions with office locations around the globe, including Singapore, the United Kingdom, Australia, Mexico, Brazil, and Japan. Locate your local office at: **international.cengage.com/region**

Cengage Learning products are represented in Canada by Nelson Education, Ltd.

For your lifelong learning solutions, visit **cengageptr.com**

Visit our corporate website at **cengage.com**

Printed in the United States of America
1 2 3 4 5 6 7 15 14 13

For Cathy

Acknowledgments

Once again thanks to the folks at Cengage Learning PTR, who have pioneered publishing digital imaging books in full color at a price anyone can afford. Special thanks to executive editor Kevin Harreld, who always gives me the freedom to let my imagination run free with a topic, as well as my veteran production team including project editor Jenny Davidson and technical editor Mike Sullivan. Also thanks to Bill Hartman, layout; Katherine Stimson, indexing; Sara Gullion, proofreading; Mike Tanamachi, cover design; and my agent, Carole Jelen, who has the amazing ability to keep both publishers and authors happy. I'd also like to thank the Continent of Europe, without which this book would have a lot of blank spaces where illustrations are supposed to go.

About the Author

With more than a million books in print, **David D. Busch** is the #1 selling author of camera-specific photography books, and the originator of popular series like *David Busch's Pro Secrets* and *David Busch's Quick Snap Guides.* He has written dozens of hugely successful guidebooks for Canon digital SLR models, including the all-time bestsellers for the many Canon models, additional user guides for other camera models, as well as many popular books devoted to dSLRs, including *Mastering Digital SLR Photography, Third Edition* and *Digital SLR Pro Secrets.* As a roving photojournalist for more than 20 years, he illustrated his books, magazine articles, and newspaper reports with award-winning images. He's operated his own commercial studio, suffocated in formal dress while shooting weddings-for-hire, and shot sports for a daily newspaper and upstate New York college. His photos and articles have been published in *Popular Photography, Rangefinder, Professional Photographer,* and hundreds of other publications. He's also reviewed dozens of digital cameras for Ziff-Davis online and print publications.

When About.com named its top five books on Beginning Digital Photography, debuting at the #1 and #2 slots were Busch's *Digital Photography All-In-One Desk Reference for Dummies* and *Mastering Digital Photography.* During the past year, he's had as many as five of his books listed in the Top 20 of Amazon.com's Digital Photography Bestseller list—simultaneously! Busch's 200-plus other books published since 1983 include bestsellers like *David Busch's Quick Snap Guide to Using Digital SLR Lenses.* His advice has been featured on National Public Radio's *All Tech Considered.*

Busch is a member of the Cleveland Photographic Society (www.clevelandphoto.org), which has operated continuously since 1887. Visit his website at http://www.dslrguides.com/blog. There you'll find news, tips, and an errata page with typo alerts from sharp-eyed readers.

Contents

Chapter 3
Canon EOS 70D Roadmap   39

PART II: MASTERING YOUR TOOLS

Chapter 4
Nailing the Right Exposure   65

Chapter 5
Mastering the Mysteries of Autofocus   109

Chapter 6
Live View and Movies   133

Chapter 7
Advanced Shooting   173

PART III: CONFIGURING YOUR CANON EOS 70D

Chapter 8
Customizing with the Shooting and Playback Menus   203

Chapter 9
Customizing with the Set-up Menu and My Menu   263

PART IV: ENHANCING YOUR CANON EOS 70D

Chapter 10
Working with Lenses   299

Chapter 11
Working with Light   333

Chapter 12
Working with Wireless Flash   377

Chapter 13
Downloading, Editing, and Printing Your Images   405

Chapter 14
Troubleshooting and Prevention   419

Index   439

Preface

If you've invested in a camera as sophisticated as the Canon EOS 70D, you're looking for more than good pictures—you demand *outstanding* photos. After all, the 70D boasts 20.2 megapixels of resolution and a pioneering autofocus system that provides fast focus whether you are shooting movies, live view stills, or taking conventional photographs using the optical viewfinder. But your gateway to pixel proficiency is dragged down by the slim little book included in the box as a manual. You know everything you need to know is in there, somewhere, but you don't know where to start. In addition, the camera manual doesn't offer much information on photography or digital photography. Nor are you interested in spending hours or days studying a comprehensive book on digital SLR still photography that doesn't necessarily apply directly to your 70D.

What you need is a guide that explains the purpose and function of the 70D's basic controls, how you should use them, and *why*. Ideally, there should be information about file formats, resolution, exposure, and special autofocus modes available, but you'd prefer to read about those topics only after you've had the chance to go out and take a few hundred great pictures with your new camera. Why isn't there a book that summarizes the most important information in its first two or three chapters, with lots of illustrations showing what your results will look like when you use this setting or that?

Now there is such a book. If you want a quick introduction to the 70D's focus controls, wireless flash synchronization options, how to choose lenses, or which exposure modes are best, this book is for you. If you can't decide on what basic settings to use with your camera because you can't figure out how changing ISO or white balance or focus defaults will affect your pictures, you need this guide.

Introduction

The Canon EOS 70D continues to blaze new trails for cameras at its price level, including a sophisticated 19-point autofocus module like that found on much more expensive dSLRs, and a new Dual Pixel CMOS AF system for live view and movie-making modes that is currently found in no other digital SLR, regardless of price. To sweeten the deal, the company added *new* features, like built-in Wi-Fi capabilities. Your new 20.2-megapixel camera is loaded with capabilities that few would have expected to find in a mid-level dSLR.

Nor will you easily outgrow this camera. It's got enough resolution for the most demanding applications, improved autofocus, and lots of customization options. Canon must love serious photographers, because it seems to work extra hard to give them incredible value for their money.

But once you've confirmed that you made a wise purchase decision, the question comes up, *how do I use this thing?* All those cool features can be mind numbing to learn, if all you have as a guide is the manual furnished with the camera. Help is on the way. I sincerely believe that this book is your best bet for learning how to use your new camera for still photography, and for learning how to use it well.

If you're a Canon EOS 70D owner who's looking to learn more about how to use this great camera, you've probably already explored your options. There are DVDs and online tutorials—but who can learn how to use a camera by sitting in front of a television or computer screen? Do you want to watch a movie or click on HTML links, or do you want to go out and take photos with your camera? Videos are fun, but not the best answer.

There's always the manual furnished with the 70D. It's compact and filled with information, but there's really very little about *why* you should use particular settings or features, and its organization may make it difficult to find what you need. Multiple cross-references may send you flipping back and forth between two or three sections of the book to find what you want to know. The basic manual is also hobbled by black-and-white line drawings and tiny monochrome pictures that aren't very good examples of what you can do.

Also available are third-party guides to the 70D, like this one. I haven't been happy with some of these guidebooks, which is why I wrote this one. The existing books are often skimpy (one guide has only 150 pages actually devoted to the 70D); others are illustrated by black-and-white photos or are too generic to do much good. Photography instruction is useful, but it needs to be related directly to the Canon EOS 70D as much as possible.

I've tried to make *David Busch's Canon EOS 70D Guide to Digital SLR Photography* different from your other 70D learn-up options. The roadmap sections use larger, color pictures to show you where all the buttons and dials are, and the explanations of what they do are longer and more comprehensive. I've tried to avoid overly general advice, including the two-page checklists on how to take a "sports picture" or a "portrait picture" or a "travel picture." Instead, you'll find tips and techniques for using all the features of your Canon EOS 70D to take *any kind of picture* you want. If you want to know where you should stand to take a picture of a quarterback dropping back to unleash a pass, there are plenty of books that will tell you that. This one concentrates on teaching you how to select the best autofocus mode, shutter speed, f/stop, or flash capability to take, say, a great sports picture under any conditions.

However, as you explore the pages of this book, you'll see that, in addition to serving as a supplement to the operator's manual furnished with the camera, I attempt to relate every feature, control, and option to actual picture-taking situations, and, still photography in general, at every opportunity. Some readers who visit my blog have told me that the 70D is such an advanced camera that few people really need the kind of basics that so many camera guides concentrate on. "Leave out all the basic photography information!" On the other hand, I've had many pleas from those who are trying to master digital photography as they learn to use their 70D, and they've asked me to help them climb the steep learning curve.

Rather than write a book for just one of those two audiences, I've tried to meet the needs of both. You veterans will find plenty of information on getting the most from the camera's features, and may even learn something from an old hand's photo secrets. I'll bet there was a time when you needed a helping hand with some confusing photographic topic. And those who are looking to learn about photography and their camera will find just what you need in this book, too.

EMPHASIS ON STILL PHOTOGRAPHY

However, if you're looking for extensive and exhaustive coverage of this camera's video capture capabilities, you'll need a full book from another author if you need to explore that aspect. This is primarily a book devoted to *still* photography, and, given the 70D's extensive feature set, already runs more than 100 pages longer than most of my other camera guides. I've devoted extra attention to topics that really deserve it, such as autofocus and wireless flash, and I urge budding Spielbergs to explore the mysteries of time codes and codecs in books that can explore their intricacies in depth. I'll get you started, however, with a chapter that does look at the basics of live view and movie making.

Who Am I?

After spending years as the world's most successful unknown author, I've become slightly less obscure in the past few years, thanks to a horde of camera guidebooks and other photographically oriented tomes. You may have seen my photography articles in *Popular Photography* magazine. I've also written about 2,000 articles for magazines like *Petersen's PhotoGraphic* (which is now defunct through no fault of my own), plus *Rangefinder, Professional Photographer*, and dozens of other photographic publications. But, first, and foremost, I'm a photojournalist and commercial photographer and made my living in the field until I began devoting most of my time to writing books.

Although I love writing, I'm happiest when I'm out taking pictures, which is why I invariably spend several days each week photographing landscapes, people, close-up subjects, and other things. I spend a month or two each year traveling to events, such as Native American "powwows," Civil War re-enactments, county fairs, ballet, and sports (baseball, basketball, football, and soccer are favorites). Just before beginning work on this book, I took 11 days for a visit to Europe, strictly to shoot photographs of the people, landscapes, and monuments that I've grown to love. I can offer you my personal advice on how to take photos under a variety of conditions because I've had to meet those challenges myself on an ongoing basis.

Like all my digital photography books, this one was written by someone with an incurable photography bug. My first Canon SLR was a Pellix back in the 1960s, and I've used a variety of newer models since then. I've worked as a sports photographer for an Ohio newspaper and for an upstate New York college. I've operated my own commercial studio and photo lab, cranking out product shots on demand and then printing a few hundred glossy 8 × 10s on a tight deadline for a press kit. I've served as a photo-posing instructor for a modeling agency. People have actually paid me to shoot their weddings and immortalize them with portraits. I even prepared press kits and articles on photography as a PR consultant for a large Rochester, N.Y., company, which shall remain nameless. My trials and travails with imaging and computer technology have made their way into print in book form an alarming number of times.

As you can see, like you, I love photography for its own merits, and I view technology as just another tool to help me get the images I see in my mind's eye. But, also like you, I had to master this technology before I could apply it to my work. This book is the result of what I've learned, and I hope it will help you master your Canon digital SLR, too. If you want some of the basic information in this book condensed into a camera-bag-friendly, spiral-bound, lay-flat package, check out my *Compact Field Guide*. I also have other books that might help you.

David Busch's Compact Field Guide for the Canon EOS 70D

While most readers enjoy poring over the wealth of information I provide in my full-size guides, many of you have asked for a condensed version with just the basic operational and settings information, in a compact size that can be slipped in a camera bag. Well, you can throw away your cheat sheets and command cards. My *Compact Field Guide* for your 70D is a spiral-bound, lay-flat, full-color book with all the information you need when on the go. Unlike a laminated command card, my field guide tells you what each control, menu item, and option does—and why you should or should not use it. If you like my "big book" and want to get the most from your 70D, you need this compact guide, too.

David Busch's Guide to Canon Flash Photography

Although I cover photography with Canon Speedlites in several chapters of this book, those who are looking for more detailed instructions for using the latest Canon strobes will want to check out my new guide to Canon flash photography. It provides tips on using wireless flash, multiple units, and lists the steps you need to follow to activate the essential features of the most recent Canon Speedlites, including the new 600EX-RT.

Quick Snap Guide to Digital SLR Photography

Consider this a prequel to the book you're holding in your hands. It might make a good gift for a spouse or friend who may be using your 70D, but who lacks even basic knowledge about digital photography, digital SLR photography, and Canon EOS photography. It serves as an introduction that summarizes the basic features of digital SLR cameras in general (not just the 70D), and what settings to use and when, such as continuous autofocus/single autofocus, aperture/shutter priority, EV settings, and so forth. The guide also includes recipes for shooting the most common kinds of pictures, with step-by-step instructions for capturing effective sports photos, portraits, landscapes, and other types of images.

David Busch's Quick Snap Guide to Using Digital SLR Lenses

A bit overwhelmed by the features and controls of digital SLR lenses, and not quite sure when to use each type? This book explains lenses, their use, and lens technology in easy-to-access, two- and four-page spreads, each devoted to a different topic, such as depth-of-field, lens aberrations, or using zoom lenses.

David Busch's Quick Snap Guide to Lighting

This book tells you everything you need to know about using light to create the kind of images you'll be proud of. It's not Canon-specific, and doesn't include any details on using any of the Canon-dedicated flash units, but the information you'll find applies to any digital SLR photography.

Mastering Digital SLR Photography, Third Edition

This book is an introduction to digital SLR photography, with nuts-and-bolts explanations of the technology, more in-depth coverage of settings, and whole chapters on the most common types of photography. While not specific to the 70D, this book can show you how to get more from its capabilities. I've added six brand new chapters and the latest technology secrets in this new version.

David Busch's dSLR Movie Shooting Compact Field Guide

Although this book is not specific to Canon cameras, it takes up where my 70D guidebooks leave off in offering additional techniques and tips for shooting your best video ever. Movie shooting is an entirely different discipline from still photography, and deserves an entire book—or two—of its own. My movie-oriented *Compact Field Guide* belongs in your camera bag.

In closing, I'd like to ask a special favor: let me know what you think of this book. If you have any recommendations about how I can make it better, visit my website at www.dslrguides.com/blog, click on the E-Mail Me tab, and send your comments, suggestions on topics that should be explained in more detail, or, especially, any typos. (The latter will be compiled on the Errata page you'll also find on my website.) I really value your ideas, and appreciate it when you take the time to tell me what you think! Some of the content of the book you hold in your hands came from suggestions I received from readers like yourself. If you found this book especially useful, tell others about it. Visit http://www.amazon.com/dp/1285765265 and leave a positive review. Your feedback is what spurs me to make each one of these books better than the last. Thanks!

Part I

Getting Started with Your Canon EOS 70D

This first part of the book, consisting of just three short chapters, is designed to familiarize you with the basics of your Canon EOS 70D as quickly as possible, even though I have no doubt that you've already been out shooting a few hundred (or thousand) photographs with your pride and joy.

After all, inserting a memory card, mounting a lens, stuffing a charged battery into the base, and removing the lens cap to fire off a shot or two isn't rocket science. Even the rawest neophyte can rotate the Mode Dial (located at top left on the camera body) to the P (Programmed auto) position or select Scene Intelligent Auto (marked with a green A+ icon) and then point the 70D at something interesting and press the shutter release. Presto! A pretty good picture will pop up on the color LCD on the back of the camera. It's easy!

But in digital photography, there is such a thing as *too* easy. If you bought a 70D, you certainly had no intention of using the camera as a point-and-shoot snapshooter. After all, the 70D is a tool suitable for the most advanced photographic pursuits, with an extensive array of customization possibilities. As such, you don't want the camera's operation to be brainless; you want *access* to the advanced features to be easy.

You get that easy access with the Canon 70D. However, you'll still need to take the time to learn how to use these features, and I'm going to provide everything you need to know in these first three chapters to begin shooting:

- **Chapter 1, "Thinking Outside of the Box":** This is a "Meet Your 70D" introduction, where you'll find information about what came in the box with your camera and, more importantly, what *didn't* come with the camera that you seriously should consider adding to your arsenal. I'll also cover some things you might not have known about charging the 70D's battery, choosing a memory card, setting the time and date, and a few other pre-flight tasks. This is basic stuff, and if you're a Canon veteran, you can skim over it quickly. A lot of this first chapter is intended for EOS newbies, and even if you personally don't find it essential, you'll probably agree that there was some point during your photographic development (so to speak) that you wished this information was spelled out for you. There's no extra charge!

- **Chapter 2, "Canon EOS 70D Quick Start":** Here, you'll find a Quick Start aimed at those who may not be old hands with Canon cameras having this level of sophistication. The 70D has some interesting new features, including one of the most advanced autofocus systems ever seen in a mid-level camera body (and which deserves an entire chapter of its own later in this book). But even with all the goodies to play with and learning curve still to climb, you'll find that Chapter 2 will get you shooting quickly with a minimum of fuss.

- **Chapter 3, "Canon EOS 70D Roadmap":** This is a Streetsmart Roadmap to the Canon EOS 70D. Confused by the tiny little diagrams and multiple cross-references for each and every control that send you scurrying around looking for information you know is buried somewhere in the small and inadequate manual stuffed in the box? This chapter uses multiple large full-color pictures that show every dial, knob, and button, and explain the basics of using each in clear, easy-to-understand language. I'll give you the basics up front, and, even if I have to send you deeper into the book for a full discussion of a complex topic, you'll have what you need to use a control right away.

Once you've finished (or skimmed through) these three chapters, you'll be ready for Part II, which explains how to use the most important basic features, such as the 70D's exposure controls, nifty new autofocus system, and the related tools that put live view and movie-making tools at your fingertips. Then, you can visit Part III, the advanced tools section, which explains all the dozens of setup options that can be used to modify the capabilities you've learned to use so far, how to choose and use lenses, and introduces the EOS 70D's built-in flash and external flash capabilities. I'll wind up this book with Part IV, which covers image software, printing, and transfer options and includes some troubleshooting that may help you when good cameras (or film cards) go bad.

1

Thinking Outside of the Box

Whether you subscribe to the "my camera is just a tool" theory, or belong to the "an exquisite camera adds new capabilities to my shooting arsenal" camp, picking up a new Canon EOS 70D is a special experience. Those who simply wield tools will find this camera as comforting as an old friend, a solid piece of fine machinery ready and able to do their bidding as part of the creative process.

Other photographers see the 70D's low-light capabilities (up to H, the equivalent of ISO 25600), its 7 frames-per-second continuous shooting, sensational touch screen, and 20.2-megapixels of resolution, and gain a sense of empowerment. Add in the "dual pixel" sensor with phase detect autofocus capabilities in Live View and Movie modes (more on *that* in Chapter 5), and you have a truly revolutionary digital SLR. *Here* is a camera with fewer limitations and more capabilities for exercising renewed creative vision. In either case, using less mawkish terms, the 70D is one of the coolest cameras Canon has ever offered. Whether you're upgrading from another brand, from another Canon model (like one of the "lesser" models), or your 70D is your first digital camera and/or single lens reflex, welcome to the club.

But, now that you've unwrapped and recharged the beast, mounted a lens, and fueled it with a memory card, what do you *do* with it? That's where this chapter—and the chapters that follow—should come in handy. Like many of you, I am a Canon user of long standing. And, like other members of our club, I had to learn at least some aspects of my newest EOS camera for the very first time at some point. Experienced pro, or Canon newbie, you bought this book because you wanted to get the most from a very powerful tool, and I'm here to help.

Depending on your path to the camera, the Canon EOS 70D is either the company's most ambitious consumer camera (two full models more advanced than the EOS SL1/100D or T5i/700D) or most affordable advanced camera, which are both distinctions that I find almost meaningless in the greater scheme of things. I know consummate professionals who produced amazing images with an original Digital Rebel and experienced wedding photographers who still evoke the most romantic photos from an ancient Canon 30D. In the right hands, the 70D is a professional camera capable of professional photographs. But whether your *images* are of professional quality, both technically and inspirationally, depends on what's between your ears, and how you apply it. The goal of this book is to provide you with the information you need to put your brain cells together with Canon's electro-mechanical components to work productively.

There's a lot to learn, but you don't have to master every detail all at once. Some of the other camera guides I've seen winnow this information down to about one-third as many pages. Indeed, I find it odd that those guidebooks use the same basic template for more advanced cameras as for a resolutely amateur-level model like the very basic SL1. A camera like the 70D has a lot more depth than that, and deserves the in-depth coverage you'll find here.

Whether you've already taken a dozen or twelve hundred photos with your new camera, now that you've got that initial creative burst out of your system, you'll want to take a more considered approach to operating the camera. This chapter and the next are designed to get your camera fired up and ready for shooting as quickly as possible. After all, the 70D is not a point-and-shoot camera, even though it does boast easy-to-use "Basic Zone" options that include several fully automatic modes, plus "scene" modes for portraits, close-ups, landscapes, sports, or other types of subjects.

So I'm going to provide a basic pre-flight checklist that you need to complete before you really spread your wings and take off. You won't find a lot of detail in these first two chapters. Indeed, I'm going to tell you just what you absolutely *must* understand, accompanied by some interesting tidbits that will help you become acclimated to your 70D. I'll go into more depth and even repeat some of what I explain here in later chapters, so you don't have to memorize everything you see. Just relax, follow a few easy steps, and then go out and begin taking your best shots—ever.

Even if you're a long-time Canon shooter, I hope you won't be tempted to skip this chapter or the next one. I realize that you probably didn't purchase this book the same day you bought your camera and that, even if you did, the urge to go out and take a few hundred—or thousand—photos with your new camera is enticing. As valuable as a book like this one is, nobody can suppress their excitement long enough to read the instructions before initiating play with a new toy.

No matter how extensive your experience level is, you don't need to fret about wading through a manual to find out what you must know to take those first few tentative snaps. I'm going to help you hit the ground running with this chapter, which will help you set up your camera and begin shooting in minutes. Because I realize that some of you may already have experience with Canon cameras similar to the 70D, each of the major sections in this chapter will begin with a brief description of what is covered in that section, so you can easily jump ahead to the next if you are in a hurry to get started.

First Things First

This section helps get you oriented with all the things that come in the box with your Canon EOS 70D, including what they do. I'll also describe some optional equipment you might want to have. If you want to get started immediately, skim through this section and jump ahead to "Initial Setup" later in the chapter.

The Canon EOS 70D comes in an impressive gray-and-red box filled with stuff, including connecting cords, booklets, CDs, and lots of paperwork. The most important components are the camera and lens (if you purchased your 70D with a lens), battery, battery charger, and, if you're the nervous type, the neck strap. You'll also need a memory card, as one is not included. If you purchased your EOS 70D from a camera shop, as I did, the store personnel probably attached the neck strap for you, ran through some basic operational advice that you've already forgotten, tried to sell you a memory card, and then, after they'd given you all the help you could absorb, sent you on your way with a handshake.

Perhaps you purchased your 70D from one of those mass merchandisers that also sell washing machines and vacuum cleaners. In that case, you might have been sent on your way with only the handshake, or, maybe, not even that if you resisted the efforts to sell you an extended warranty. You save a few bucks, but don't get the personal service a professional photo retailer provides. It's your choice. There's a third alternative, of course. You might have purchased your camera from a mail order or Internet source, and your 70D arrived in a big brown (or purple/red) truck. Your only interaction when you took possession of your camera was to scrawl your signature on an electronic clipboard.

In all three cases, the first thing to do is carefully unpack the camera and double-check the contents with the checklist on one end of the box, helpfully designated with a CONTENTS heading. The box should include a Digital Camera EOS 70D, Wide Strap EW-EOS70D, Battery Charger LC-E6 or LC-E6E, Battery Pack LP-E6, Interface Cable IFC-200U, and three software/instructional CD-ROMs, all described in more detail below. You also got several instruction manuals for the camera and Wi-Fi functions, and some other paperwork. It's likely that the camera was accompanied by a lens, as well, and that the contents I've listed above will vary slightly depending on when and where you bought the camera.

While this level of setup detail may seem as superfluous as the instructions on a bottle of shampoo, checking the contents *first* is always a good idea. No matter who sells a camera, it's common to open boxes, use a particular camera for a demonstration, and then repack the box without replacing all the pieces and parts afterwards. Someone might actually have helpfully checked out your camera on your behalf—and then mispacked the box. It's better to know *now* that something is missing so you can seek redress immediately, rather than discover two months from now that the video cable you thought you'd never use (but now *must* have) was never in the box.

At a minimum, the box should have the following:

- **Canon EOS 70D digital camera.** This is hard to miss. The camera is the main reason you laid out the big bucks, and it is tucked away inside a nifty bubble-wrap envelope you should save for protection in case the 70D needs to be sent in for repair.

- **Rubber eyecup Ef.** This slide-on soft-rubber eyecup should be attached to the viewfinder when you receive the camera. It helps you squeeze your eye tightly against the window, excluding extraneous light, and also protects your eyeglasses (if you wear them) from scratching.

- **Body cap.** The twist-off body cap keeps dust from entering the camera when no lens is mounted. Even with automatic sensor cleaning built into the 70D, you'll want to keep the amount of dust to a minimum. The body cap belongs in your camera bag if you contemplate the need to travel with the lens removed.

- **Lens (if purchased).** The 70D may come in a kit with the Canon Zoom Lens EF-S 18-135mm f/3.5-5.6 IS STM lens, or the new EF-S 18-55mm f/3.5-56 IS STM lens introduced at the same time as the camera. You may purchase it with another lens. I would have purchased mine as a body only, because I already have an extensive collection of Canon lenses, but I wanted to check out the new STM version of the venerable 18-55mm kit lens. (The pioneering original Digital Rebel came with the original version in 2003—more than a decade ago!) The lens will come with a lens cap on the front, and a rear lens cap aft.

- **Battery pack LP-E6 (with cover).** The power source for your 70D is packaged separately. You'll need to charge this 7.2V, 1120mAh (milliampere hour) battery before using it. It should be charged as soon as possible (as described next) and inserted in the camera. Save the protective cover. If you transport a battery outside the camera, it's a good idea to reattach the cover to prevent the electrical contacts from shorting out.

- **Battery charger LC-E6 or LC-E6E.** One of these two battery chargers will be included.

- **Wide strap EW-EOS70D.** Canon provides you with a suitable neck strap, emblazoned with Canon advertising. While I am justifiably proud of owning a fine Canon camera, I prefer a low-key, more versatile and secure strap from UPstrap (www.upstrap.com). If you carry your camera over one shoulder, as many do, I particularly recommend the UPstrap shown in Figure 1.1. That patented non-slip pad offers reassuring traction and eliminates the contortions we sometimes go through to keep the camera from slipping off. I know several photographers who refuse to use anything else. If you do purchase an UPstrap, be sure you mention to photographer-inventor Al Stegmeyer that I sent you hence. You won't get a discount, but Al will get yet another confirmation of how much I like his neck straps.

- **Interface cable IFC-130U.** You can use this USB cable to transfer photos from the camera to your computer, although I don't recommend that mode, because direct transfer uses a lot of battery power. You can also use the cable to upload and download settings between the camera and your computer (highly recommended), and to operate your camera remotely using the software included on the CD-ROM. It can also be used to link the camera to PictBridge compatible printers. This cable is a standard one that works with the majority of digital cameras—Canon and otherwise—so if you already own one, now you have a spare.

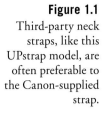

Figure 1.1
Third-party neck
straps, like this
UPstrap model, are
often preferable to
the Canon-supplied
strap.

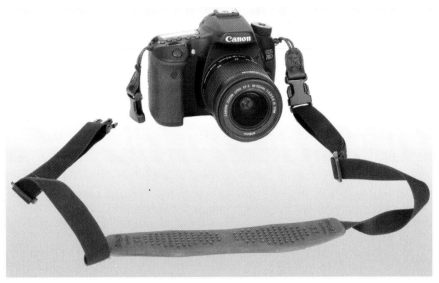

- **EOS Digital Solution Disc CD.** The disc contains useful software that will be discussed in more detail in Chapter 13.

- **Software instruction manual CD.** While the software itself is easy to use, if you need more help you'll find it in the PDF manuals included on this CD.

- **Camera Instruction Manual CD-ROM.** Contains a much more detailed camera instruction manual in PDF format, along with electronic versions of the Wi-Fi Function Instruction Manual and Quick Reference Guides. Even if you have this book, you'll probably want to check the PDF user's guide that Canon provides from time to time, if only to check the actual nomenclature for some obscure accessory, or to double-check an error code. If you have a smart phone with sufficient free memory, copy the PDF files to your phone for access with your favorite PDF reader. Otherwise, if you have an old SD card that's too small to be usable on a modern dSLR (I still have some 128MB and 256MB cards), you can store the PDF on that. An even better choice is to put the manual on a low-capacity USB "thumb" drive, which you can buy for less than $10. You'll then be able to access the reference anywhere you are, because you can always find someone with a computer that has a USB port and Adobe Acrobat Reader available. You might not be lucky enough to locate a computer with an SD card reader.

- **Printed instruction manuals.** These include a set of brief instruction manuals and guides for the camera's basic features.

- **Warranty and registration card.** Don't lose these! You can register your Canon 70D by mail, although you don't really need to in order to keep your warranty in force, but you may need the information in this paperwork (plus the purchase receipt/invoice from your retailer) should you require Canon service support.

Don't bother rooting around in the box for anything beyond what I've listed previously. There are a few things Canon classifies as optional accessories, even though you (and I) might consider some of them essential. Here's a list of what you *don't* get in the box, but might want to think about as an impending purchase. I'll list them roughly in the order of importance:

- **Memory card.** First-time digital camera buyers are sometimes shocked that their new tool doesn't come with a memory card. Why should it? The manufacturer doesn't have the slightest idea of how much storage you require, or whether you want a slow/inexpensive card or one that's faster/more expensive, so why should they pack one in the box and charge you for it? For an 20-megapixel camera, you really need one that's a minimum of 8GB in size.

- **Extra LP-E6 battery.** Even though you might get 440 shots from a single battery, it's easy to exceed that figure in a few hours of shooting sports at 7 fps. Batteries can unexpectedly fail, too, or simply lose their charge from sitting around unused for a week or two. Buy an extra (I own four, in total), keep it charged, and free your mind from worry.

- **Add-on Speedlite.** One of the best uses for your Canon 70D's built-in electronic flash is as a remote trigger for an off-camera Speedlite such as the 600EX-RT, or the more affordable 320EX and 270EX II strobes, which were designed especially for cameras in this class. Your flash can function as the main illumination for your photo, or softened and used to fill in shadows. If you do much flash photography at all, consider an add-on Speedlite as an important accessory.

- **Stereo AV Cable AVC-DC400ST.** Use this cable to view your camera's LCD output on a larger television screen, monitor, or other device with a yellow RCA composite input jack. Unlike the cables for previous models, this one allows stereo sound output. Canon stopped providing it in the box with the camera, so it's now an optional purchase, for about $25.

- **AC Adapter Kit ACK-E6.** This includes the AC Adapter AC-E6 and DC Coupler DR-E6, which are used together to power the 70D independently of the batteries. There are several typical situations where this capability can come in handy: when you're cleaning the sensor manually and want to totally eliminate the possibility that a lack of juice will cause the fragile shutter and mirror to spring to life during the process; when indoors shooting tabletop photos, portraits, class pictures, and so forth for hours on end; when using your 70D for remote shooting as well as time-lapse photography; for extensive review of images on your television; or for file transfer to your computer. These all use prodigious amounts of power, which can be provided by this AC adapter. (Beware of power outages and blackouts when cleaning your sensor, however!)

- **Angle Finder C right angle viewer.** This handy accessory fastens in place of the standard rubber eyecup and provides a 90-degree view for framing and composing your image at right angles to the original viewfinder, useful for low-level (or high-level) shooting. (Or, maybe, shooting around corners!)

- **HDMI cable HTC-100.** You'll need this optional cable if you want to connect your camera directly to an HDTV for viewing your images. Not everyone owns a high-def television, and Canon saved the holdouts a few bucks (actually, close to $80) by not including one (or charging for it).
- **Battery Grip BG-E14.** This add-on vertical grip/battery pack can be outfitted with two LP-E6 batteries or six AA batteries for longer shooting life, and an extra shutter release and control dial for convenient shooting with the camera in a vertical orientation.

Initial Setup

This section helps you become familiar with the important controls most used to make adjustments. You'll also find information on charging the battery, setting the clock, mounting a lens, and making diopter vision adjustments. If you're comfortable with all these things, skim through and skip ahead to the next section.

The initial setup of your Canon EOS 70D is fast and easy. Basically, you just need to charge the battery, attach a lens, and insert a memory card. I'll address each of these steps separately, but if you already feel you can manage these setup tasks without further instructions, feel free to skip this section entirely. You should at least skim its contents, however, because I'm going to list a few options that you might not be aware of.

Battery Included

Your Canon EOS 70D is a sophisticated hunk of machinery and electronics, but it needs a charged battery to function, so rejuvenating the LP-E6 lithium-ion battery pack furnished with the camera should be your first step. A fully charged power source should be good for approximately 1,300 shots without flash, or 920 shots when using flash for 50 percent of the exposures, based on standard tests defined by the Camera & Imaging Products Association (CIPA) document DC-002.

A BATTERY AND A SPARE

My experience is that the CIPA figures are often a little optimistic, so it's probably a good idea to have a spare battery on hand. I always recommend purchasing Canon brand batteries (for less than $50) over less-expensive third-party packs. My reasoning is that it doesn't make sense to save $20 on a component for an advanced camera, especially since batteries (from Canon as well as other sources) have been known to fail in potentially harmful ways. Canon, at least, will stand behind its products, issue a recall if necessary, and supply a replacement if a Canon-brand battery is truly defective. A third-party battery supplier that sells under a half-dozen or more different product labels and brands may not even have an easy way to get the word out that a recall has been issued.

If your pictures are important to you, always have at least one spare battery available, and make sure it is an authentic Canon product.

All rechargeable batteries undergo some degree of self-discharge just sitting idle in the camera or in the original packaging. Lithium-ion power packs of this type typically lose a small amount of their charge every day, even when the camera isn't turned on. Li-ion cells lose their power through a chemical reaction that continues when the camera is switched off. So, it's very likely that the battery purchased with your camera is at least partially pooped out, so you'll want to revive it before going out for some serious shooting.

There are many situations in which you'll be glad you have that spare battery:

- **Remote locales.** If you like to backpack and will often be far from a source of electricity, rechargeable cells won't be convenient. They tend to lose some charge over time, even if not used, and will quickly become depleted as you use them. You'll have no way to recharge the cells, lacking a solar-powered charger that might not be a top priority for your backpacking kit.

- **Unexpected needs.** Perhaps you planned to shoot landscapes one weekend, and then are given free front-row tickets to a Major League Baseball game. Instead of a few dozen pictures of trees and lakes, you find yourself shooting hundreds of images of Nick Swisher and company, which may be beyond the capacity of the single battery you own. If you have a spare battery, you're in good shape.

- **Unexpected failures.** I've charged up batteries and then discovered that they didn't work when called upon, usually because the rechargeable cells had passed their useful life, the charger didn't work, or because of human error. (I *thought*, I'd charged them!) That's one reason why I always carry three times as many batteries as I think I will need.

- **Long shooting session.** Perhaps your niece is getting married, and you want to photograph the ceremony, receiving line, and reception. Several extra batteries will see you through the longest shooting session.

Power Options

Several battery chargers are available for the Canon EOS 70D. Purchasing an additional charging device offers more than some additional features: You gain a spare that can keep your camera running until you can replace your primary power rejuvenator. Here's a list of your power options:

- **LC-E6E.** This is the standard charger for the 70D and charges a single battery, but requires a cord (see Figure 1.2). That can be advantageous in certain situations. For example, if your power outlet is behind a desk or in some other semi-inaccessible location, the cord can be plugged in and routed so the charger sits on your desk or another more convenient spot. The cord itself is a standard one that works with many different chargers and devices (including the power supply for my laptop), so I purchased several of them and

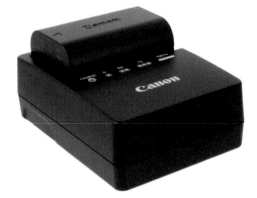

Figure 1.2 A flashing status light (not shown) indicates that the battery is being charged.

leave them plugged into the wall in various locations. I can connect my 70D's charger, my laptop computer's charger, and several other electronic components to one of these cords without needing to crawl around behind the furniture. The cord itself draws no "phantom" power when it's not plugged in to a charger.

- **LC-E6.** This charger may be the most convenient for some, because of its compact size and built-in wall plug prongs that connect directly into your power strip or wall socket and require no cord. This charger, as well as the LC-E6E, has a switching power module that is fully compatible with 100V to 240V 50/60 Hz AC power, so you can use it outside the US with no problems. When I travel to Europe, for example, I take my charger and an adapter to convert the plug shape for the European sockets. No voltage converter is needed.

- **AC Adapter Kit ACK-E6.** This device consists of AC Adapter AC-E6 and DC Coupler DR-E6, and allows you to operate your 70D directly from AC power, with no battery required. Studio photographers need this capability because they often snap off hundreds of pictures for hours on end and want constant, reliable power. The camera is probably plugged into a flash sync cord (or radio device), and the studio flash are plugged into power packs or AC power, so the extra tether to this adapter is no big deal in that environment. You also might want to use the AC adapter when viewing images on a TV connected to your 70D, or when shooting remote or time-lapse photos.

- **Car Battery Charger CBC-E6/CB-570 cable.** This is a charger that can juice up your battery when connected to your auto's 12V power source. The vehicle battery option allows you to keep shooting when in remote locations that lack AC power. Personally, I use a more flexible alternative. I purchased a Bestek 300w/3.1A power inverter that converts my vehicle's power to 110V, and has two AC and two USB charging outlets. I can use that compact device with *any* AC charger, and revitalize my iPad, iPhone, or Kindle at the same time. At about $27 on Amazon, it's roughly $100 cheaper than Canon's car charger. That makes a capability that most people (other than campers and survivalists) won't use very often a bit more affordable.

- **Battery Grip BG-E14.** This accessory holds two LP-E6 batteries (another reason to own a spare, or two), which, Canon says, will double the camera's shooting capacity. It can also be equipped with six AA cells with the BGM-E14A battery holder. It adds another shutter release, Main Dial, AE Lock/FE Lock, and AF point selection controls for vertically oriented shooting.

Charging the Battery

When the battery is inserted into the LC-E6 charger properly (it's impossible to insert it incorrectly), a Charge light begins blinking orange-red that indicates the battery is at least partially depleted. When the device completes the charge, the Full Charge lamp glows green, approximately two hours later. When the battery is charged, remove it from the charger, flip the lever on the bottom of the camera, and slide the battery in. (See Figure 1.3.) To remove the battery, you must press a white lever, which prevents the pack from slipping out when the door is opened.

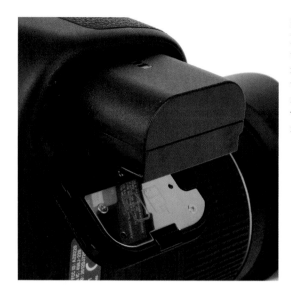

Figure 1.3
Insert the battery in the camera; it only fits one way. Press the white button to release the battery when you want to remove it.

Final Steps

Your Canon EOS 70D is almost ready to fire up and shoot. You'll need to select and mount a lens, adjust the viewfinder for your vision, and insert a memory card. Each of these steps is easy, and if you've used any Canon EOS camera in the past, you already know exactly what to do. I'm going to provide a little extra detail for those of you who are new to the Canon or digital SLR worlds.

Mounting the Lens

As you'll see, my recommended lens mounting procedure emphasizes protecting your equipment from accidental damage, and minimizing the intrusion of dust. If your 70D has no lens attached, select the lens you want to use and loosen (but do not remove) the rear lens cap. I generally place the lens I am planning to mount vertically in a slot in my camera bag, where it's protected from mishaps, but ready to pick up quickly. By loosening the rear lens cap, you'll be able to lift it off the back of the lens at the last instant, so the rear element of the lens is covered until then.

After that, remove the body cap by rotating the cap toward the shutter release button. You should always mount the body cap when there is no lens on the camera, because it helps keep dust out of the interior of the camera, where it can settle on the mirror, focusing screen, the interior mirror box, and potentially find its way past the shutter onto the sensor. (While the 70D's sensor cleaning mechanism works fine, the less dust it has to contend with, the better.) The body cap also protects the vulnerable mirror from damage caused by intruding objects (including your fingers, if you're not cautious).

Once the body cap has been removed, remove the rear lens cap from the lens, set it aside, and then mount the lens on the camera by matching the alignment indicator on the lens barrel (red for EF lenses and white for EF-S lenses) with the red or white dot on the camera's lens mount (see Figure 1.4). Rotate the lens away from the shutter release until it seats securely. (You can find out more about the difference between EF and EF-S lenses in Chapter 10.) Set the focus mode switch on the lens to AF (autofocus). If the lens hood is bayoneted on the lens in the reversed position (which makes the lens/hood combination more compact for transport), twist it off and remount with the edge facing outward (see Figure 1.5). A lens hood protects the front of the lens from accidental bumps, stray fingerprints, and reduces flare caused by extraneous light arriving at the front element of the lens from outside the picture area.

Figure 1.4
Match the white dot on EF-S lenses with the white dot on the camera mount to properly align the lens with the bayonet mount. For EF lenses, use the red dots.

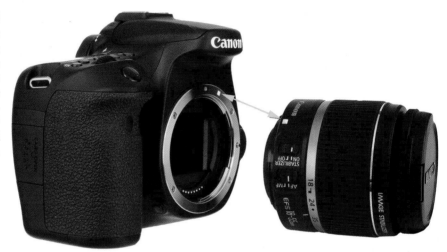

Figure 1.5
A lens hood protects the lens from extraneous light and accidental bumps.

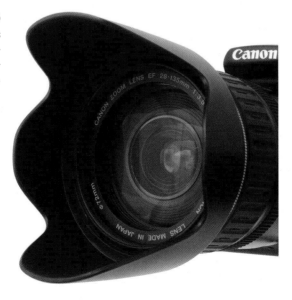

Adjusting Diopter Correction

Those of us with less than perfect eyesight can often benefit from a little optical correction in the viewfinder. Your contact lenses or glasses may provide all the correction you need, but if you are a glasses wearer and want to use the EOS 70D without your glasses, you can take advantage of the camera's built-in diopter adjustment, which can be varied from –3 to +1 correction. Press the shutter release halfway to illuminate the indicators in the viewfinder, then rotate the diopter adjustment knob next to the viewfinder (see Figure 1.6) while looking through the viewfinder until the indicators appear sharp.

If the available correction is insufficient, Canon offers 10 different Dioptric Adjustment Lens Series E correction lenses for the viewfinder window. If more than one person uses your 70D, and each requires a different diopter setting, you can save a little time by noting the number of clicks and

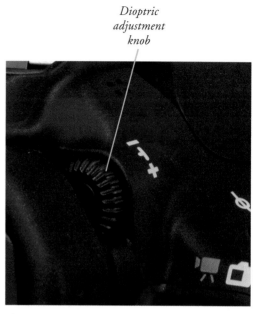

Dioptric adjustment knob

Figure 1.6 Viewfinder diopter correction from –3 to +1 can be dialed in.

direction (clockwise to increase the diopter power; counterclockwise to decrease the diopter value) required to change from one user to the other. There are 18 detents in all.

Inserting a Memory Card

You can't take photos without a memory card inserted in your EOS 70D (although there is a Release Shutter without Card entry in Shooting 1 menu that enables/disables shutter release functions when a memory card is absent—learn about that in Chapter 8). So, your final step will be to insert a memory card. Slide the door on the right side of the body toward the back of the camera to release the cover, and then open it. (You should only remove the memory card when the camera is switched off, but the 70D will remind you if the door is opened while the camera is still writing photos to the memory card.)

Insert the memory card with the label facing the back of the camera, as shown in Figure 1.7, oriented so the edge with the connectors goes into the slot first. Close the door, and your pre-flight checklist is done! (I'm going to assume you remember to remove the lens cap when you're ready to take a picture!) When you want to remove the memory card later, push it inward to make the memory card pop out.

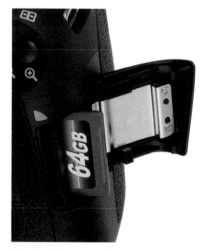

Figure 1.7 Insert the memory in the slot with the label facing the back of the camera.

Formatting a Memory Card

There are three ways to create a blank memory card for your 70D, and two of them are at least partially wrong. Here are your options, both correct and incorrect:

- **Transfer (move) files to your computer.** When you transfer (rather than copy) all the image files to your computer from the memory card (either using a direct cable transfer or with a card reader, as described later in this chapter), the old image files are erased from the card, leaving the card blank. Theoretically. This method does *not* remove files that you've labeled as Protected (choosing the Protect Images function in the Playback menu) nor does it identify and lock out parts of your memory card that have become corrupted or unusable since the last time you formatted the card. Therefore, I recommend always formatting the card, rather than simply moving the image files, each time you want to make a blank card. The only exception is when you *want* to leave the protected/unerased images on the card for a while longer, say, to share with friends, family, and colleagues.

- **(Don't) Format in your computer.** With the memory card inserted in a card reader or card slot in your computer, you can use Windows or Mac OS to reformat the memory card. Don't! The operating system won't necessarily arrange the structure of the card the way the 70D likes to see it (in computer terms, an incorrect *file system* may be installed). The only way to ensure that the card has been properly formatted for your camera is to perform the format in the camera itself. The only exception to this rule is when you have a seriously corrupted memory card that your camera refuses to format. Sometimes it is possible to revive such a corrupted card by allowing the operating system to reformat it first, then trying again in the camera.

- **Set-up menu format.** To use the recommended method to format a memory card, turn on the camera, press the MENU button, rotate the Main Dial (located on top of the camera, just behind the shutter release button), choose the Set-up 1 menu (which is represented by a wrench icon with a single dot next to it), use the up/down multi-controller directional buttons (the buttons immediately above and below the SET button in the center of the control pad) to navigate to the Format entry, and press the SET button to access the Format screen. Press the left/right multi-controller directional buttons (located to the left and right of the SET button) again to select OK and press the SET button one final time to begin the format process.

LOW LEVEL FORMAT

You can also press the Trash button, located in the lower-right corner of the back of the camera, to mark the Low level format box on the Format screen. This tells the 70D to perform an additional, more thorough, formatting of the card after the initial format is finished. The low level format serves to remove data from all writable portions of your memory card while locking out "bad" sectors, and can be used to restore a memory card that is slowing down as it "trips" over those bad sectors. This extra step takes a bit longer than a standard reformat, and need not be used every time you format your card.

Powering Up/Setting Date and Time

Rotate the On/Off switch on top of the camera to the On position. Automatic sensor cleaning takes place (unless you specifically disable this action) as the 70D powers up. The camera will remain on or in a standby mode until you manually turn it off. After a period of idling (which you can adjust from 1 to 30 minutes, or disable, in the Set-up 2 menu), the 70D goes into the standby mode to save battery power. Just tap the shutter release button to bring it back to life. The automatic sensor cleaning operation does not occur when exiting standby mode.

The first time you use the 70D, it may ask you to enter the time and date. (This information may have been set by someone checking out your camera on your behalf prior to sale.) Just follow these steps, using the controls shown in Figure 1.8.

NOTE

I'm introducing you to the keys/dials/wheels navigational controls first in this Quick Start, but most functions can be selected (often more quickly) using the 70D's touch screen. I'll explain how to use the touch screen in Chapter 2.

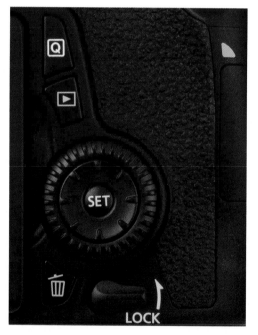

Figure 1.8
These controls are used to navigate menus.

1. Press the MENU button, located in the upper-left corner of the back of the 70D.

2. Rotate the Main Dial (near the shutter release button on top of the camera) until the Set-up 2 menu is highlighted. It's marked by a wrench with two dots next to it, as shown in Figure 1.9.

3. Use the up/down multi-controller directional buttons to move the highlighting down to the Date/Time/Zone entry, and press the SET button.

4. You can rotate the Quick Control Dial (the large wheel located to the right of the back LCD monitor) to select, in turn, the month, day, year, hour, minutes, and seconds.

5. When each setting is highlighted, press the SET button, then rotate the Quick Control Dial to adjust the value up or down. A pair of up/down pointing triangles appears above the value. Press SET again to confirm.

6. Repeat Step 5 to adjust the other date and time parameters, as shown in Figure 1.10.

Figure 1.9
Choose the Date/Time/Zone entry from the Set-up 2 menu.

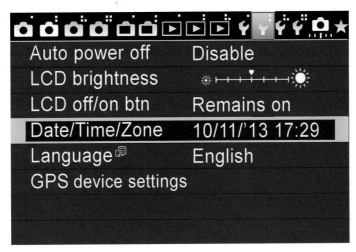

Figure 1.10
Adjust the date, time, and format used to display the date.

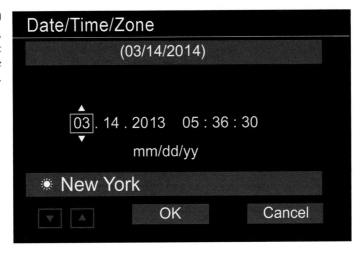

7. Scroll to the date format line located under the Date/Time listing, press SET, and use the same procedure to adjust the way dates are displayed (that is, mm/dd/yy, yy/mm/dd, or dd/mm/yy).

8. Scroll down to the Daylight Savings icon and turn that option on or off, as appropriate, and then finish by moving to the Time Zone field and selecting the city in your current zone.

9. When all parameters are entered, highlight OK and press SET to confirm and exit.

Your Canon EOS 70D is ready to go. If you need a quick start for its basic operation, jump ahead to Chapter 2.

REACH OUT AND TOUCH SOMETHING

The EOS 70D is one of the first advanced cameras with a touch-screen LCD. When menus are on the screen, you can tap choices to select them, slide your finger across the screen to scroll among menus and change sliding scales, and perform other functions. I'll explain how to use the touch screen in more detail in Chapter 2.

2

Canon EOS 70D Quick Start

Now it's time to fire up your EOS 70D and take some photos. The easy part is turning on the power—that Off-On switch on the left side, just east of the Mode Dial. Turn on the camera, and, if you mounted a lens and inserted a fresh battery and memory card—as I prompted you in the last chapter—you're ready to begin. You'll need to select a shooting mode, metering mode, focus mode, and, if need be, elevate the 70D's built-in flash.

Navigating the Menus

While you'll find complete instructions for using every menu option the 70D offers in Chapters 8 and 9, the next few chapters will often ask you to use the camera's menu system to make adjustments. The 70D often provides several different ways of performing an action, and menu navigation is one of them. The traditional way is to use the physical controls:

- **Access menus.** You can produce the 70D's main menus by pressing the MENU button, located at the far-left corner of the back of the camera (and shown at left in Figure 2.1).

- **Navigate among menus.** Use the Quick Control Dial or the directional buttons in the center of the Quick Control Dial (seen in the middle in Figure 2.1) to move within the menu system. Press SET to activate your choice or confirm selection.

- **Main Dial.** This dial (shown at right in Figure 2.1) can often be used to move highlighting left and right, say, to scroll among the main menu heading tabs.

- **Quick Control button.** The Quick Control button (Q button) (shown in upper center in Figure 2.1) produces a Quick Control menu (described later), which offers fast access to many adjustments.

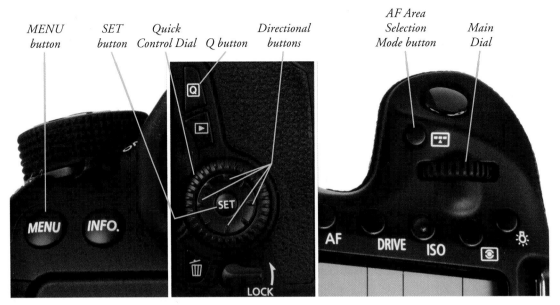

Figure 2.1 Your basic controls include the MENU button (left); Quick Control Dial, directional keys, and Q button (center); and Main Dial (right).

Mastering the Touch Screen

When a main menu, adjustment screen, or the Quick Control menu is displayed, you will probably elect to use the 70D's touch screen to make your changes. Optionally, you can resort to the physical controls that provide the equivalent functions, including the available buttons and directional key navigational buttons. However, I think that once you become familiar with the speed with which the touch screen allows you to make these adjustments, you'll be reluctant to go back to the "old" way of doing things.

The 70D's touch screen is *capacitive* rather than *resistive*, making it more like the current generation of smart phones than earlier computer touch-sensitive screens. The difference is that your camera's LCD responds to the electrical changes that result from *contact* rather than the force of *pressure* on the screen itself. That means that the screen is able to interpret your touches and taps in more complex ways. It "knows" when you're using two fingers instead of one, and can react to multi-touch actions and gestures, such as swiping (to scroll in any direction), and pinching/spreading of fingers to zoom in and out. Since you probably have been using a smart phone for a while, these actions have become ingrained enough to be considered intuitive. Virtually every main and secondary function or menu operation can be accessed from the touch screen. However, if you want to continue using the buttons and dials, the 70D retains that method of operation.

TIP: YOUR CHOICE

Throughout this book, I may not explicitly say "tap the screen (or use the button)" for every single operation, in order to simplify descriptions and avoid extra verbiage. I'm assuming that once you master the touch screen using the information in this section, you'll make your own choice and use whichever method you prefer.

Here's what you need to know to get started:

- **Enable/Disable touch features.** As I'll explain in Chapter 9, you can enable or disable touch operation in the Set-up 3 menu under the Touch Control entry, and turn the click sound the touch feature makes on or off using the Beep setting in the Shooting 1 menu.

- **Tap to select.** Tap (touch the LCD screen briefly) to select an item, including a menu heading or icon. Any item you can tap will have a frame or box around it. Figure 2.2 shows the taps needed to select a menu tab and specific entry within that menu.

- **Drag/swipe to select.** Many functions can be selected by touching the screen and then sliding your finger to the right or left until the item you want is highlighted. For example, instead of tapping, you can slide horizontally along the main menu's tabs to choose any Shooting, Playback, Custom, or My Menu tab, and slide vertically to choose an individual menu entry.

- **Drag/swipe to adjust scales.** Screens that contain a sliding scale (say, to make an image brighter or darker) can be adjusted by dragging. Figure 2.3 shows how you can drag along the LCD Brightness scale to select a value or, alternatively, tap the left/right arrow icons to either side of the scale. (Note that you can also press the left/right directional keys if you prefer.)

- **Drag/swipe to scroll among images.** In Playback mode, as you review your images you can drag your finger left and right to advance from one image to another, much as you might do with a smart phone or tablet computer. This is probably the coolest use for the touch screen. Figure 2.4 shows you can use either one finger to scroll or two fingers to jump among playback images.

Figure 2.2
Tap menu tabs or entries to select them.

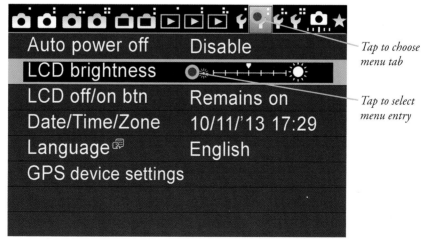

Tap to choose menu tab

Tap to select menu entry

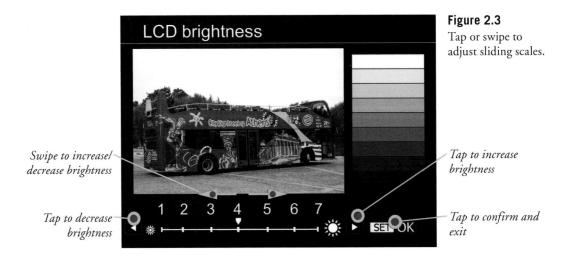

Figure 2.3
Tap or swipe to adjust sliding scales.

Swipe to increase/decrease brightness

Tap to increase brightness

Tap to decrease brightness

Tap to confirm and exit

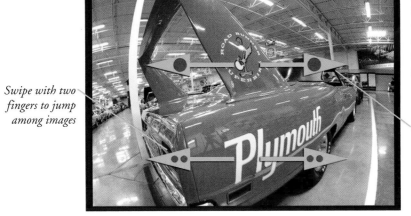

Figure 2.4
Swipe left or right with one finger to scroll among images; swipe with two fingers to jump.

Swipe with two fingers to jump among images

Swipe with one finger to scroll among images

■ **Pinch to reduce/enlarge.** During playback, you can use two fingers to "pinch" the screen to zoom out from single-frame display to multiple thumbnails, and spread those two fingers apart to zoom in again to a single frame and magnified image—also very cool and intuitive. (See Figure 2.5.)

■ **Avoid "protective" sheets, moisture, sharp implements.** The LCD uses capacitive technology to sense your touch, rather than pressure sensitivity. LCD protectors or moisture can interfere with the touch functions, and styluses or sharp objects (such as pens) won't produce the desired results. I have, in fact, used "skins" on my 70D's LCD with good results (even though the screen is quite rugged and really doesn't need protection from scratches), but there is no guarantee that all such protectors will work for you.

Figure 2.5
Spread two fingers apart to enlarge/ zoom in, or pinch two fingers together to zoom out/view thumbnails.

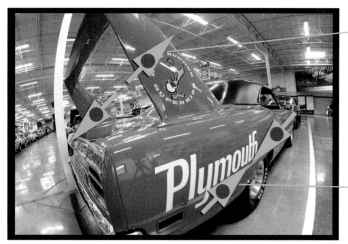

Spread two fingers apart to enlarge/zoom in

Pinch two fingers together to reduce/zoom out

As I noted, the choice of whether to use the traditional buttons or touch screen is up to you. I've found that with some screens, the controls are too close together to be easily manipulated with my wide fingers. The touch screen can be especially dangerous when working with some functions, such as card formatting. In screens where the icons are large and few in number, such as the screen used to adjust LCD brightness, touch control works just fine. Easiest of all is touch operation during Playback. It's a no-brainer to swipe your finger from side to side to scroll among images and pinch/ spread to zoom out and in.

Selecting a Shooting Mode

The following sections show you how to choose Scene, semi-automatic, or automatic shooting (exposure) modes; select a metering mode (which tells the camera what portions of the frame to evaluate for exposure); and set the basic autofocus functions. If you understand how to do these things, you can skip ahead to "Other Functions."

You can choose a shooting method from the Mode Dial located on the top left of the Canon EOS 70D. (See Figure 2.6.) There are Basic Zone automatic and Scene shooting modes, in which the camera makes virtually all the decisions for you (except when to press the shutter). The camera also offers four Creative Zone modes, which allow you to provide input over the exposure and settings the camera uses. You'll find a complete discussion of both Basic Zone and Creative Zone modes in Chapter 4.

Turn your camera on by flipping the power switch (located to the right of the Mode Dial) to On. Next, you need to select which shooting mode to use. If you're very new to digital photography, you might want to set the camera to Scene Intelligent Auto (the green frame on the Mode Dial) or P (Program mode) and start snapping away. Either mode will make all the appropriate settings for you for many shooting situations.

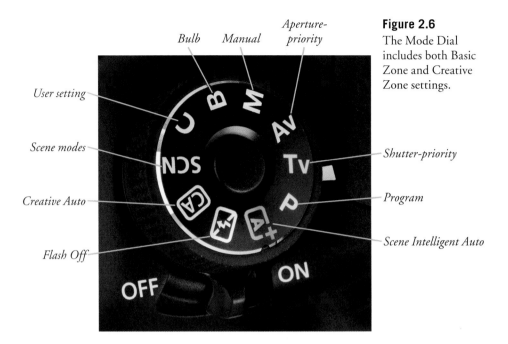

User setting

Scene modes

Creative Auto

Flash Off

Bulb   Manual   Aperture-priority

Shutter-priority

Program

Scene Intelligent Auto

Figure 2.6
The Mode Dial includes both Basic Zone and Creative Zone settings.

- **Scene Intelligent Auto/Full Auto.** In this mode, marked with a green A+ icon, the EOS 70D makes all the exposure decisions for you, and will pop up the flash if necessary under low-light conditions.

- **Flash Off.** This mode is like Scene Intelligent Auto with the flash disabled. You'll want to use it in museums and other locations where flash is forbidden or inappropriate. It otherwise operates exactly like the Auto setting but disables the pop-up internal flash unit.

- **CA.** This Creative Auto mode is basically the same as the Full Auto option, but, unlike the other Basic Zone modes, allows you to change the brightness and other parameters of the image. The 70D still makes most of the decisions for you, but you can make some simple adjustments using the Creative Auto setting screen that appears when you press the Quick Control button. You can find instructions for using this mode and the other shooting modes in Chapter 4, and a brief summary below.

With the dial in the SCN position, you can also select any of seven additional Special Scene modes. Turn the Mode Dial to the SCN position, then press the Q button (or tap the Q icon in the lower left of the LCD monitor screen). You can then rotate the Quick Control Dial or Main Dial to choose one of the following Scene modes:

- **Portrait.** Use this mode when you're taking a portrait of a subject standing relatively close to the camera and want to de-emphasize the background, maximize sharpness, and produce flattering skin tones.

- **Landscape.** Select this mode when you want extra sharpness and rich colors of distant scenes.

■ **Close-up.** This mode is helpful when you are shooting close-up pictures of a subject from about one foot away or less.

■ **Sports.** Use this mode to freeze fast-moving subjects.

■ **Night Portrait.** Choose this mode when you want to illuminate a subject in the foreground with flash, but still allow the background to be exposed properly by the available light. Be prepared to use a tripod or an image-stabilized (IS) lens to reduce the effects of camera shake. (You'll find more about IS and camera shake in Chapter 10.)

■ **Handheld Night Scene.** The 70D takes four continuous shots and combines them to produce a well-exposed image with reduced camera shake.

■ **HDR Backlight Control.** The 70D takes three continuous shots at different exposures and combines them to produce a single image with improved detail in the highlights and shadows.

If you have more photographic experience, you might want to opt for one of the Creative Zone modes. These, too, are described in more detail in Chapter 4. These modes let you apply a little more creativity to your camera's settings. These modes are indicated on the Mode Dial by the letters M, Av, Tv, and P, plus B.

■ **M (Manual).** Select when you want full control over the shutter speed and lens opening, either for creative effects or because you are using a studio flash or other flash unit not compatible with the 70D's automatic flash metering.

■ **Av (Aperture-priority).** Choose when you want to use a particular lens opening, especially to control sharpness or how much of your image is in focus. The 70D will select the appropriate shutter speed for you. Av stands for *aperture value.*

■ **Tv (Shutter-priority).** This mode (Tv stands for *time value*) is useful when you want to use a particular shutter speed to stop action or produce creative blur effects. The 70D will select the appropriate f/stop for you.

■ **P (Program).** This mode allows the 70D to select the basic exposure settings, but you can still override the camera's choices to fine-tune your image.

■ **B (Bulb).** When the shutter release button is held down, or activated by a remote control, the shutter remains open until you release it, allowing you to take exposures longer than the 30 seconds allowed in the other Creative Zone modes.

■ **C (Custom).** This is not an exposure mode, even though it appears on the Mode Dial. Instead, it is a "memory" slot that stores a particular group of camera settings that you want quick access to. I'll show you how to save settings in the C slot in Chapter 9.

You can change some settings when the shooting settings display is shown on the screen (press the INFO. button to the left of the viewfinder window if you want to make the display visible). Press the Quick Control button and then tap the touch screen or use the directional keys to navigate to the setting you'd like to adjust. (See Figure 2.7.) The available adjustments change, depending on what Basic Zone or Creative Zone exposure mode you're using. (See Figure 2.8 for a typical Creative Zone shooting settings display.)

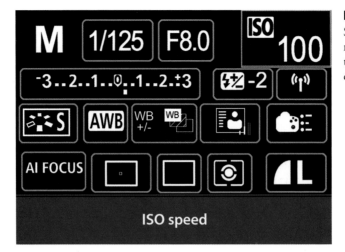

Figure 2.7
Some settings can be made quickly when the shooting settings display is visible.

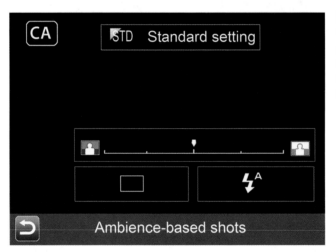

Figure 2.8
You can tweak the settings of the Creative Auto mode using this screen of options.

TWEAKING SETTINGS WITH CREATIVE AUTO

"Ambience" is a new, Picture-Style-like feature, available to let you tweak settings when using Basic Zone modes, including Creative Auto. I'll explain all the options in Chapter 4, but you can begin using Ambience now.

If you've set the Mode Dial to CA, when you press the Quick Control button, a screen like the one shown in Figure 2.8 appears. One of nine "ambience" options can be selected by pressing the left/right/up/down directional keys. Your choices are Standard Setting, Vivid, Soft, Warm, Intense, Cool, Brighter, Darker, or Monochrome, plus Standard Setting. Once your ambience is selected, the up/down directional keys let you highlight an intensity for that kind of ambience (for example, more vivid or less vivid), plus background/foreground blur, and drive/flash settings. Choose the parameter you want to modify, and press the left/right buttons to make the change.

Choosing a Metering Mode

You might want to select a particular metering mode for your first shots, although the default Evaluative metering (which is set automatically when you choose a Basic Zone mode) is probably the best choice as you get to know your camera. To change metering modes when using a Creative Zone mode, you'll need to press the Metering button on top of the camera or use the Q button. The options are shown in Figure 2.9.

- **Evaluative metering.** The standard metering mode; the 70D attempts to intelligently classify your image and choose the best exposure based on readings from 63 different zones in the frame, with emphasis on the autofocus points.

- **Partial metering.** Exposure is based on a central spot, roughly 7.7 percent of the image area.

- **Spot metering.** Exposure is calculated from a smaller central spot, about 3.0 percent of the image area.

- **Center-weighted averaging metering.** The 70D meters the entire scene, but gives the most emphasis to the central area of the frame.

You'll find a detailed description of each of these modes in Chapter 4.

Figure 2.9
Metering modes
(left to right):
Evaluative,
Partial, Spot,
Center-weighted.

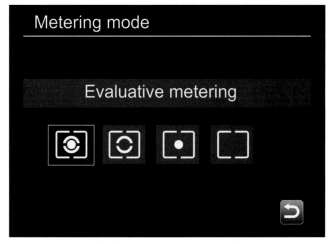

Choosing a Focus Mode

You can easily switch between automatic and manual focus by moving the AF/MF switch on the lens mounted on your camera. However, if you're using a Creative Zone shooting mode, you'll still need to choose an appropriate focus mode. (You can read more on selecting focus parameters in Chapter 5.) If you're using a Basic Zone mode, the focus method is set for you automatically.

To set the focus mode, you must first have set the lens to the AF position (instead of the manual focus MF position). Then press the AF button on the top of the camera to produce the selection screen shown in Figure 2.10. Choose the focus mode you want and select SET to confirm your focus mode. The three choices available in Creative Zone modes are as follows:

- **One-Shot.** This mode, sometimes called *single autofocus*, locks in a focus point when the shutter button is pressed down halfway, and the focus confirmation light glows in the viewfinder. The focus will remain locked until you release the button or take the picture. If the camera is unable to achieve sharp focus, the focus confirmation light will blink. This mode is best when your subject is relatively motionless. Portrait, Night Portrait, and Landscape Basic Zone modes use this focus method exclusively.

- **AI Servo.** This mode, sometimes called *continuous autofocus*, sets focus when you partially depress the shutter button, but continues to monitor the frame and refocuses if the camera or subject is moved. This is a useful mode for photographing sports and moving subjects. The Sports Basic Zone mode uses this focus method exclusively.

- **AI Focus.** In this mode, the 70D switches between One-Shot and AI Servo as appropriate. That is, it locks in a focus point when you partially depress the shutter button (One-Shot mode), but switches automatically to AI Servo if the subject begins to move. This mode is handy when photographing a subject, such as a child at quiet play, that might move unexpectedly. The Flash Off Basic Zone mode uses this focus method.

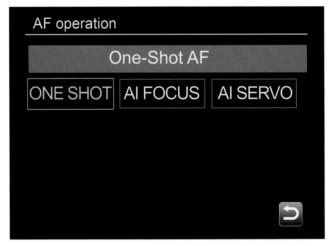

Figure 2.10
Set AF mode.

Selecting an AF Area Selection Mode

The Canon EOS 70D uses nineteen different focus points to calculate correct focus. In any of the Basic Zone shooting modes, the focus point is selected automatically by the camera. In the Creative Zone modes, you can allow the camera to select the focus point automatically, or you can specify which focus point should be used. There are three AF Area Selection modes, which I'll explain in detail in Chapter 5. They are as follows:

- **Single-point AF (Manual Selection).** You can choose one AF point for focus.
- **Zone AF (Manual Zone Selection).** Select any of five different focus zones, each with multiple focus points.
- **19-point Automatic Selection AF.** The camera will choose the focus point for you. This mode is always used in Basic Zone exposure modes.

To get up and running with this Quick Start, you should set the 70D to 19-point Automatic Selection AF mode. If you want to choose an individual point or zone yourself, skip ahead to Chapter 5 after you've finished reading this chapter. For now, just follow these steps:

1. Make sure the lens AF/MF switch is set to AF.
2. Tap the shutter release to activate the focus system.
3. Press the AF Area Selection Mode button shown earlier in Figure 2.1. The current focus selection indicators will be highlighted in red.
4. Continue pressing, if necessary, until the 19-point Automatic Selection AF icon has an up-pointing triangle underneath it, as seen in Figure 2.11.

Figure 2.11
Select the 19-point automatic selection AF mode.

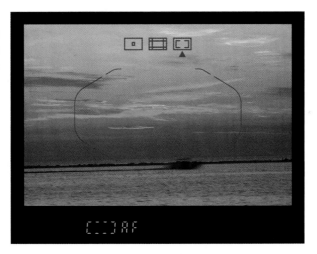

Other Settings

There are a few other options, such as ISO, using the self-timer, or working with flash. Use these right away if you're feeling ambitious, but don't feel ashamed if you postpone using these features until you've racked up a little more experience with your EOS 70D.

Adjusting ISO

If you like, you can custom-tailor ISO sensitivity setting. To start out, it's best to set ISO to ISO 100 or ISO 200 for daylight photos, and ISO 400 for pictures in dimmer light. You can adjust ISO now by pressing the ISO button (shown earlier in Figure 2.1) and then navigating with the touch screen or either Main Dial or Quick Control Dial until the setting you want appears on the LCD.

Using the Self-Timer

If you want to set a short delay before your picture is taken, you can use the self-timer. Press the Drive button on top of the camera, and rotate the Main Dial or QCD until the Self-timer: 10-sec/Remote control (which also can be used with the optional and RC-6 infrared remote controls) or Self-timer: 2 sec/remote is highlighted (see Figure 2.12). Select SET to confirm your choice, and a self-timer icon will appear on the shooting settings display on the back of the 70D. Press the shutter release to lock focus and start the timer. The self-timer lamp will blink and the beeper will sound (unless you've silenced it in the menus) until the final two seconds, when the lamp remains on and the beeper beeps more rapidly.

Canon recommends slipping off the eyepiece cup and replacing it with the viewfinder cap, in order to keep extraneous light from reaching the exposure meter through the viewfinder "back door." I usually just shade the viewfinder window with my hand (if I'm using the self-timer to reduce camera shake for a long exposure) or drape a jacket or sweater over the back of the camera (if I'm scurrying to get into the picture myself).

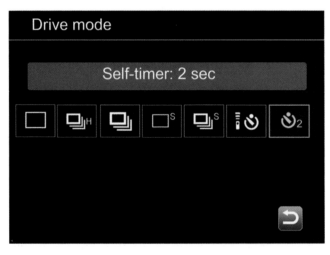

Figure 2.12
The drive modes include (left to right) Single Shooting, High Speed Continuous Shooting (7 shots/second); Low-Speed Continuous Shooting (3 shots/second); Silent Single Shooting; Silent Continuous Shooting (3 shots/second); Self-timer: 10-sec/Remote Control; and Self-timer: 2 sec.

Using the Built-in Flash

Working with the EOS 70D's built-in flash as well as external flash units deserves a chapter of its own, and I'm providing two (see Chapters 11 and 12). But the built-in flash is easy enough to work with that you can begin using it right away, either to provide the main lighting of a scene or as supplementary illumination to fill in the shadows. The 70D will automatically balance the amount of light emitted from the flash so that it illuminates the shadows nicely, without overwhelming the highlights and producing a glaring "flash" look. (Think *Baywatch* when they're using too many reflectors on the lifeguards!)

The 70D's flash has a power rating of 12/39.4 (meters/feet) at ISO 100, using the GN (guide number) system that dates back to the film era and before electronic flash units had any sort of automatic features. In plain terms, the flash's rating means that the unit is powerful enough to allow proper illumination of a subject that's 10 feet away at f/4 at the *lowest* ISO (sensitivity) setting of your camera. Boost the ISO (or use a wider f/stop) and you can shoot subjects that are located at a great distance. For example, at ISO 800, the 70D's flash is good enough for a subject at 20 feet using f/5.6 or, alternatively, you can expose that scene at the original 10 feet distance at f/11. Ordinarily, the 70D takes care of all these calculations for you. If you need a bigger blast of light, you can add one of the Canon external flash units, described in Chapter 11.

The flash will pop up automatically when using any of the Basic Zone modes except for Landscape, Sports, or No Flash modes. In Creative Zone modes, just press the flash button (marked with a lighting bolt as shown in Figure 2.13).

Figure 2.13
The pop-up electronic flash can be used as the main light source, or for supplemental illumination.

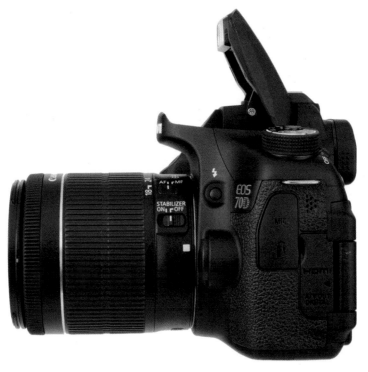

When using these modes, the flash functions in the following way:

■ **P (Program mode).** The 70D selects a shutter speed from 1/60th to 1/250th second and appropriate aperture automatically.

■ **Tv (Shutter-priority mode).** You choose a shutter speed from 30 seconds to 1/250th second, and the 70D chooses the lens opening for you, while adjusting the flash output to provide the correct exposure.

■ **Av (Aperture-priority mode).** You select the aperture you want to use, and the camera will select a shutter speed from 30 seconds to 1/250th second, and adjust the flash output to provide the correct exposure. In low light levels, the 70D may select a very slow shutter speed to allow the flash and background illumination to balance out, so you should use a tripod.

■ **M (Manual mode).** You choose both shutter speed (up to 1/250th second) and aperture, and the camera will adjust the flash output to produce a good exposure based on the aperture you've selected.

You can read about flash exposure compensation, red-eye reduction options, and other built-in flash features in Chapter 11.

Taking a Picture

This final section of the chapter guides you through taking your first pictures, reviewing them on the LCD, and transferring your shots to your computer.

Just press the shutter release button halfway to lock in focus at the selected autofocus point. When the shutter button is in the half-depressed position, the exposure, calculated using the shooting mode you've selected, is also locked.

Press the button the rest of the way down to take a picture. At that instant, the mirror flips up out of the light path to the optical viewfinder (assuming you're not using Live View mode, discussed in Chapter 6), the shutter opens, the electronic flash (if enabled) fires, and your 70D's sensor absorbs a burst of light to capture an exposure. In fractions of a moment, the shutter closes, the mirror flips back down restoring your view, and the image you've taken is escorted off the CMOS sensor chip very quickly into an in-camera store of memory called a buffer, and the EOS 70D is ready to take another photo. The buffer continues dumping your image onto the Secure Digital card as you keep snapping pictures without pause (at least until the buffer fills and you must wait for it to get ahead of your continuous shooting, or your memory card fills completely).

Reviewing the Images You've Taken

The Canon EOS 70D has a broad range of playback and image review options, including the ability to jump ahead 10 or 100 images at a time. I'll cover them in more detail in Chapter 3. For now, you'll want to learn just the basics.

Here is all you really need to know at this time, as shown in Figure 2.14, with the touch screen options shown earlier in Figures 2.4 and 2.5.

■ **Display image.** Press the Playback button (marked with a blue right-pointing triangle just below the Q button) to display the most recent image on the LCD in full-screen Single Image mode. If you last viewed your images using the thumbnail mode (described later in this list), the Index display appears instead.

■ **View additional images.** Use the left and right directional keys or swipe the touch screen left or right to view the next or previous image. Use a two-finger swipe to jump quickly among the images.

■ **View image information.** Press the INFO. button repeatedly to cycle among overlays of basic image information, detailed shooting information, or no information at all.

■ **Zoom in on an image.** When an image is displayed full-screen on your LCD, magnify the image by spreading two fingers apart on the touch screen, or reduce the image to thumbnails by pinching two fingers together on the touch screen. You can also press the Magnify button repeatedly to zoom in. The Magnify button is located in the upper-right corner of the back of the camera, marked with a blue magnifying glass with a plus sign in it. The Index/Reduce button, located to the left of the Magnify button, zooms back out. Press the Playback button to exit magnified display.

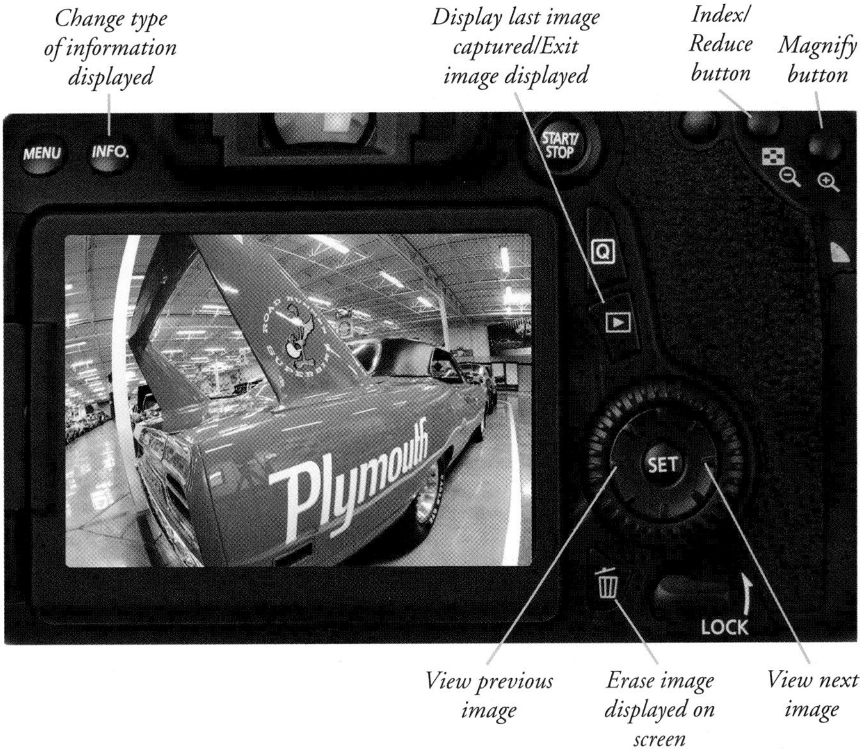

Figure 2.14
Review your images.

Change type of information displayed

Display last image captured/Exit image displayed

Index/ Reduce button

Magnify button

View previous image

Erase image displayed on screen

View next image

■ **Scroll around in a magnified image.** Use the left/right/up/down directional keys or swipe the touch screen to scroll around within a magnified image. If you're using the touch screen, tap the "Return" arrow icon to go back to a single-image display.

■ **View thumbnail images.** You can also rapidly move among a large number of images using the Index mode described in the section that follows this list. The Index/Reduce button in full-frame view switches from single image display to display of four or nine reduced-size thumbnails. To change from a larger number of thumbnails to a smaller number (from nine to four to single image, for example), press the Magnify button until the display you want appears. You can also tap the highlighted image on the touch screen to view a full-screen rendition of that thumbnail.

■ **Jump forward or back.** You can set the jump increment in the Playback 2 menu. (I'll explain all the jump options in Chapter 3.) Once a jump increment has been selected, you can leap forward or back that number of pictures by rotating the Main Dial or by swiping the touch screen from left to right with *two* fingers. If using the Main Dial, turn it counterclockwise to review images from most recent to oldest, or clockwise to start with the first image on the memory card and cycle forward to the newest, using the jump size you've selected.

Cruising Through Index Views

You can navigate quickly among thumbnails representing a series of images using the 70D's Index mode. Here are your options.

■ **Display thumbnails.** Press the Playback button to display an image on the color LCD. If you last viewed your images using Index mode, an Index array of four or nine reduced-size images appears automatically (see Figure 2.15). If an image pops up full-screen in single-image mode, press the Index/Reduce button once to view four thumbnails, or twice to view nine thumbnails. You can switch between four, nine, and single images by pressing the Index/Reduce button to see more/smaller versions of your images, and the Magnify button to see fewer/larger versions of your images.

■ **Navigate within a screen of index images.** In Index mode, use the up/down/left/right directional keys or the touch screen to move the blue highlight box around within the current index display screen. Swipe the scroll bar at the right of the touch screen to scroll down or up.

■ **View more index pages.** To view additional index pages, rotate the Main Dial. The display will leap ahead or back by the jump increment you've set in the Playback 2 menu (as described in Chapter 8), 10 or 100 images, by index page, by date, or by folder.

■ **Check image.** When an image you want to examine more closely is highlighted, press the Magnify button or tap the thumbnail on the touch screen until the single image version appears full-screen on your LCD.

Figure 2.15
Review thumbnails
of four or nine
images using Index
review.

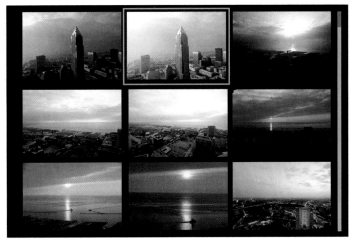

Transferring Photos to Your Computer

The final step in your picture-taking session will be to transfer the photos you've taken to your computer for printing, further review, or image editing. Your 70D allows you to print directly to PictBridge-compatible printers and to create print orders right in the camera, plus you can select which images to transfer to your computer.

For now, you'll probably want to transfer your images either by using a cable transfer from the camera to the computer or by removing the memory card from the 70D and transferring the images with a card reader. The latter option is usually the best, because it's typically much faster and doesn't deplete the battery of your camera. However, you can use a cable transfer when you have the cable and a computer, but no card reader (perhaps you're using the computer of a friend or colleague, or at an Internet café).

To transfer images from the camera to a Mac or PC computer using the USB cable:

1. Turn off the camera.
2. Pry back the rubber cover that protects the 70D's USB port (located closest to the LCD monitor), and plug the USB cable furnished with the camera into the USB port. (See Figure 2.16.)
3. Connect the other end of the USB cable to a USB port on your computer.
4. Turn the camera on. Your installed software usually detects the camera and offers to transfer the pictures, or the camera appears on your desktop as a mass storage device, enabling you to drag and drop the files to your computer.

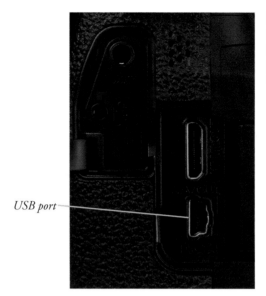

Figure 2.16
Images can be trans-
ferred to your com-
puter using a USB
cable.

USB port

To transfer images from a memory card to the computer using a card reader:

1. Turn off the camera.

2. Slide open the memory card door, and press on the card, which causes it to pop up so it can be removed from the slot.

3. Insert the memory card into your memory card reader. Your installed software detects the files on the card and offers to transfer them. The card can also appear as a mass storage device on your desktop, which you can open, and then drag and drop the files to your computer.

3

Canon EOS 70D Roadmap

One thing that surprises new owners of the Canon EOS 70D is that the camera has a total of 496 buttons, dials, switches, levers, latches, and knobs bristling from its surface. Okay, I lied. Actually, the real number is closer to two dozen controls and adjustments, just among the physical components and not counting the virtual controls on the touch screen. But that's still a lot of components to master, especially when you consider that many of these controls serve double-duty to give you access to multiple functions.

Traditionally, there have been two ways of providing a roadmap to guide you through this maze of features. One approach uses two or three tiny 2 × 3-inch black-and-white line drawings or photos impaled with dozens of callouts labeled with cross-references to the actual pages in the book that tell you what these components do. You'll find this tactic used in the pocket-sized manual Canon provides with the 70D, and most of the other third-party guidebooks as well. Deciphering one of these miniature camera layouts is a lot like being presented with a world globe when what you really want to know is how to find the capital of Belgium.

I originated a more useful approach in my field guides, providing you, instead of a satellite view, a street-level map that includes close-up, full-color photos of the camera from several angles (see Figure 3.1), with a smaller number of labels clearly pointing to each individual feature. And, I don't force you to flip back and forth among dozens of pages to find out what a particular component does. Each photo is accompanied by a brief description that summarizes the control, so you can begin using it right away. Only when a particular feature deserves a lengthy explanation do I direct you to a more detailed write-up later in the book.

So, after I explain how to use the ISO button to change the sensitivity of the 70D, I *will* provide a cross-reference to a longer explanation later in the book that clarifies noise reduction, ISO, and its effects on exposure. I think this kind of organization works best for a camera as sophisticated as the 70D, because producing 100 page chapters that include all the basics *plus* all the background for each feature simply isn't practical. I'll always give you what you need to get started.

By the time you finish this chapter, you'll have a basic understanding of every control and what it does. I'm not going to delve into menu functions here—you'll find a discussion of your Set-up, Shooting, and Playback menu options in Chapters 8 and 9. Everything here is devoted to the button pusher and dial twirler in you.

Front View

When we picture a given camera, we always imagine the front view. That's the view that your subjects see as you snap away, and the aspect that's shown in product publicity and on the box. The frontal angle is, for all intents and purposes, the "face" of a camera like the 70D. But, not surprisingly, most of the "business" of operating the camera happens *behind* it, where the photographer resides. The front of the 70D actually has very few controls and features to worry about. Five of them are readily visible in Figure 3.1:

■ **Shutter release.** Angled on top of the hand grip is the shutter release button. Press this button down halfway to lock exposure and focus (in One-Shot mode and AI Focus with nonmoving subjects). The 70D assumes that when you tap or depress the shutter release, you are ready to take a picture, so the release can be tapped to activate the exposure meter or to exit from most menus.

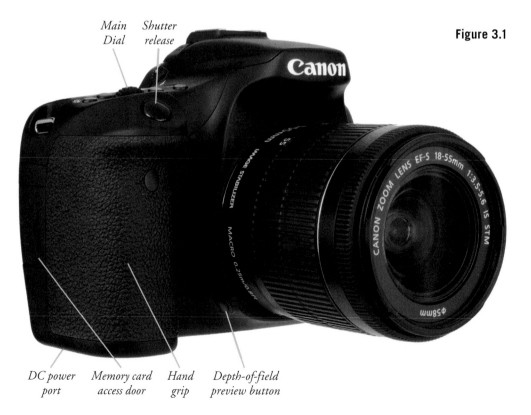

Main Dial   Shutter release

Figure 3.1

DC power port   Memory card access door   Hand grip   Depth-of-field preview button

- **Main Dial.** This dial is used to change shooting settings. When settings are available in pairs (such as shutter speed/aperture), this dial will be used to make one type of setting, such as shutter speed. The other setting, say, the aperture, is made using an alternate control, such as spinning the Quick Control Dial on the back of the camera.

- **Memory card access door.** Slide this panel toward the back of the camera to gain access to the memory card.

- **Depth-of-field preview button.** This button, adjacent to the lens mount, stops down the lens to the aperture that will be used to take the picture, so you can see in the viewfinder how much of the image is in focus. The view grows dimmer as the aperture is reduced.

- **Hand grip.** This provides a comfortable handhold, and also contains the 70D's battery.

- **DC power port.** You'll find an opening to allow the cable from the DC power pack to pass through to the battery compartment under this small rubber door in the side of the camera.

When viewed from the front with the lens removed, you can see more components, as shown in Figure 3.2:

- **Red-eye reduction/self-timer lamp.** This LED provides a blip of light shortly before a flash exposure to cause the subjects' pupils to close down, reducing the effect of red-eye reflections off their retinas. When using the self-timer, this lamp also flashes to mark the countdown until the photo is taken.

- **Remote control sensor.** The sensor behind this window receives signals from the optional Canon infrared remote controls. The RC-6 release gives the choice of triggering the camera immediately, or with the two-second delay. Note that the sensor is on the hand grip and thus would be blocked if you happened to be holding the 70D when trying to take a picture. In practice, of course, the camera will be mounted on a tripod or supported in some other way when using the remote control. The remote control generally must be used from in front of the camera for the sensor to detect its signal.

- **Lens bayonet mount.** This sturdy component mates with the matching bayonet mount on the lens to secure it to the camera body.

- **Index mark for EF lenses.** Match the round red bump on the lens with this mark to align EF-series lenses for mounting.

- **Index mark for EF-S lenses.** Match the raised white square on the lens with this mark to align EF-S-series lenses for mounting.

- **Electrical contacts.** Mates with matching contacts on the rear of the lens to provide two-way communication between the camera and the lens's operational features, such as image stabilization, autofocus, and aperture.

- **Lens release button/locking pin.** Press this button to retract the lens release locking pin so the lens can be rotated toward the shutter release and removed.

Figure 3.2

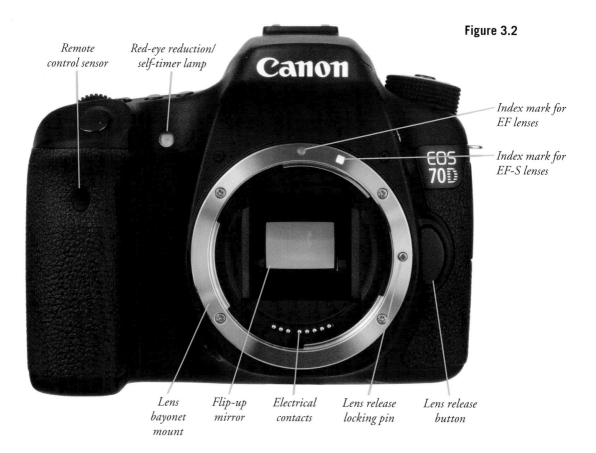

Remote control sensor

Red-eye reduction/ self-timer lamp

Index mark for EF lenses

Index mark for EF-S lenses

Lens bayonet mount

Flip-up mirror

Electrical contacts

Lens release locking pin

Lens release button

- **Flip-up mirror.** This partially silvered reflective component directs most of the light that passes through the lens upward toward the focus screen, exposure metering system, and viewfinder eyepiece. Some illumination is directed downward to the 19-point autofocus system in the floor of the mirror chamber.

You'll find more controls on the other side of the 70D, shown in Figure 3.3.

- **Flash button.** This button releases the built-in flash in Creative Zone modes so it can flip up (see Figure 3.4) and start the charging process. If you decide you do not want to use the flash, you can turn it off by pressing the flash head back down.
- **Lens switches.** Canon autofocus lenses have a switch to allow changing between automatic focus and manual focus, and, in the case of IS lenses, another switch to turn image stabilization on and off.
- **Neck strap mount.** This is one of two neck strap mounts (the other is on the other side of the camera).
- **Port covers.** These flip-away panels protect the connector ports underneath.

Figure 3.3

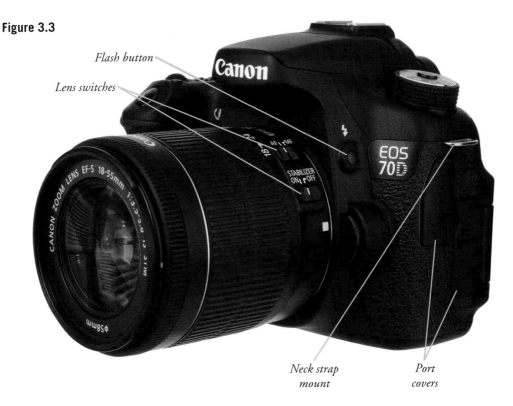

Flash button

Lens switches

Neck strap
mount

Port
covers

Figure 3.4

Pressing the Flash
button (which has
an arrow/lightning
bolt symbol) pops
up the built-in flash
unit and starts the
charging process.

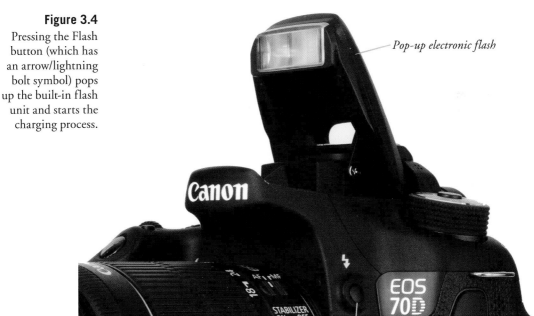

Pop-up electronic flash

Flash
button

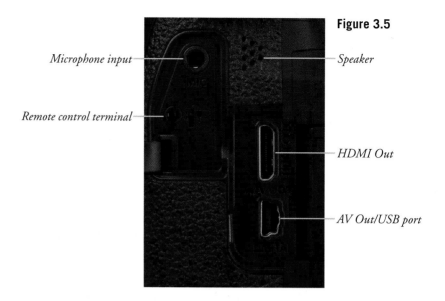

Figure 3.5

The main feature on this side of the 70D is a pair of flexible covers that protect the four connector ports underneath from dust and moisture. The four connectors, shown along with the camera's internal speaker in Figure 3.5, are as follows:

- **Microphone input.** Plug a stereo microphone into this jack.
- **Remote control terminal.** You can plug various Canon remote release switches, timers, and wireless controllers into this connector.
- **AV Out/USB port.** Plug in the USB cable furnished with your 70D and connect the other end to a USB port in your computer to transfer photos. Or, connect the optional AV cable and connect your camera to a television to view your photos on a large screen. Note that some previous models used two separate ports with different connectors for this pair of functions. They were combined to make room for the HDMI port.
- **HDMI port.** Use a Type C HDMI cable (not included in the box with your camera) to direct the video and audio output of the 70D to a high-definition television (HDTV) or HD monitor.
- **Speaker.** Sounds emanating from your camera emerge from this speaker.

The Canon EOS 70D's Business End

The back panel of the 70D (see Figure 3.6) bristles with nearly a dozen different controls, buttons, and knobs. That might seem like a lot of controls to learn, but you'll find, as I noted earlier, that it's a lot easier to press a dedicated button and spin a dial than to jump to a menu every time you want to change a setting.

Figure 3.6

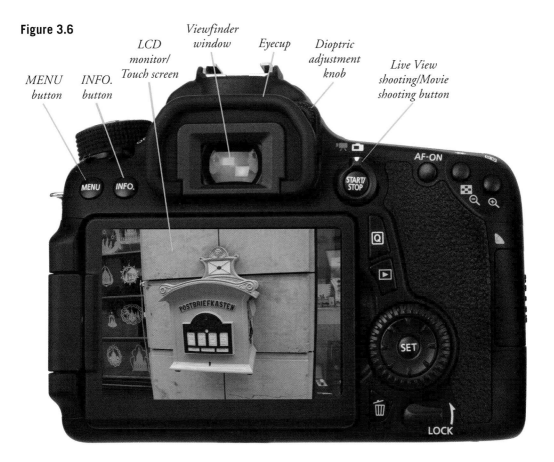

You can see the controls clustered on the top back edge of the 70D in the figure. The key buttons and components and their functions are as follows:

■ **LCD monitor/Touch screen.** This is the three-inch display that shows your Live View preview image review after the picture is taken, shooting settings display before the photo is snapped, and all the menus used by the 70D. A significant feature is the swiveling LCD, which can be folded with the display screen facing inward to protect it or reversed into the normal position, flipped out, swiveled, or even turned around to allow you to view yourself while shooting self-portraits. (See Figure 3.7.)

■ **MENU button.** Summons/exits the menu displayed on the rear LCD of the 70D. When you're working with submenus, this button also serves to exit a submenu and return to the main menu.

Figure 3.7

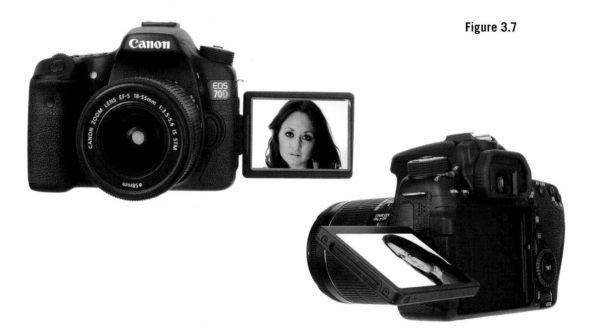

- **INFO. button (Shooting mode).** When pressed, cycles among Electronic Level, Camera Settings, and Shooting Functions screens, and Off (no information displayed). You can disable any of these (except Off) using the INFO. Button Display Options entry in the Set-up 3 menu, as described in Chapter 9. Electronic Level allows you to orient the camera; use the Camera Settings screen to review the current settings. When the Shooting Functions screen is visible, you can adjust the values of many settings by pressing the Quick Control button. Choose Off when you want a blank screen and no distractions or to save power.

  - **Electronic level.** This readout includes indicators that show the amount of horizontal rotation of the camera (along the axis passing through the center of the lens). Front/back tilt is not displayed. (See Figure 3.8.) This feature can be disabled if you find it distracting. An additional electronic level can be activated for the viewfinder in the Shooting 1 menu, as described in Chapter 8.

  - **Camera settings.** Shows a list of basic settings for the camera, including color space, white balance information, and the actual number of free shots remaining on your memory card. (Up to 9999; the counter on the top-panel LCD can display no more than 999 shots remaining.) (See Figure 3.9.)

  - **Shooting functions.** Displays the current shooting settings of the camera, including shutter speed, aperture, ISO sensitivity, battery status, and image quality settings. (See Figure 3.10.) Press the Q button on the back of the camera, and the Quick Control screen appears, as described in the sidebar that follows.

- **INFO. button (Live View/Movie mode).** When pressed repeatedly while using Live View or Movie mode, the INFO. button cycles among a slightly different set of informational screens. I'll show you those screens, and how to use them, in Chapter 6, which shows you how to use Live View mode and shoot video clips with your EOS 70D.

- **INFO. button (Playback mode).** In Playback mode, while reviewing images, pressing the INFO. button cycles among basic display of the image; a detailed display with a thumbnail of the image, shooting parameters, and a brightness histogram; and a display with less detail but with separate histograms for brightness, red, green, and blue channels. I'll show you the screens with the histograms—and how to use the histograms—in Chapter 4.

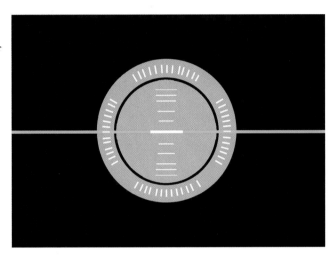

Figure 3.8
The outer ring shows the amount of horizontal rotation. When the bar turns from red to green, the camera is level.

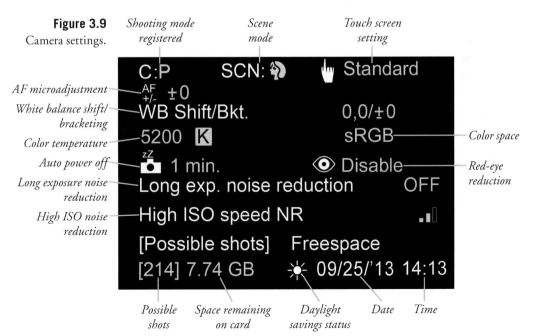

Figure 3.9
Camera settings.

Shooting mode registered — Scene mode — Touch screen setting

AF microadjustment
White balance shift/ bracketing
Color temperature
Auto power off
Long exposure noise reduction
High ISO noise reduction

Color space
Red-eye reduction

Possible shots — Space remaining on card — Daylight savings status — Date — Time

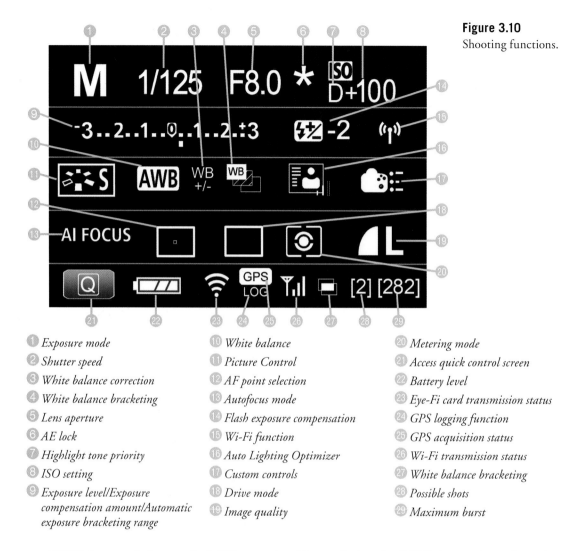

Figure 3.10
Shooting functions.

① Exposure mode
② Shutter speed
③ White balance correction
④ White balance bracketing
⑤ Lens aperture
⑥ AE lock
⑦ Highlight tone priority
⑧ ISO setting
⑨ Exposure level/Exposure compensation amount/Automatic exposure bracketing range

⑩ White balance
⑪ Picture Control
⑫ AF point selection
⑬ Autofocus mode
⑭ Flash exposure compensation
⑮ Wi-Fi function
⑯ Auto Lighting Optimizer
⑰ Custom controls
⑱ Drive mode
⑲ Image quality

⑳ Metering mode
㉑ Access quick control screen
㉒ Battery level
㉓ Eye-Fi card transmission status
㉔ GPS logging function
㉕ GPS acquisition status
㉖ Wi-Fi transmission status
㉗ White balance bracketing
㉘ Possible shots
㉙ Maximum burst

- **INFO. button (other modes).** When setting Picture Styles, the INFO. button is used to select a highlighted Picture Style for modification. When trimming an image, the INFO. button selects the orientation.

- **Viewfinder eyepiece.** You can frame your composition by peering into the viewfinder. It's surrounded by a soft rubber eyecup frame that seals out extraneous light when pressing your eye tightly up to the viewfinder, and it also protects your eyeglass lenses (if worn) from scratching.

- **Dioptric adjustment knob.** Use of this knob to adjust the viewfinder sharpness was explained in Chapter 1.

- **Live View/Movie button.** Press this button to activate/deactivate live view. To shoot movies, turn the power switch on top of the camera to the Movie position, and then press this button to start/stop video/audio recording.

The most-used controls reside on the right side of the 70D (see Figure 3.11). There are 11 buttons in all, many of which do double-duty to perform several functions. I've divided them into two groups; here's the first set of controls, found in the upper half of the panel:

■ **AF-ON button.** Press this button to activate the autofocus system without needing to partially depress the shutter release. This control, used with other buttons, allows you to lock exposure and focus separately. Lock exposure by pressing the shutter release halfway, or by pressing the AE Lock button; autofocus by pressing the shutter release halfway, or by pressing the AF-ON button. Functions of this button will be explained in more detail in Chapter 5.

■ **Index/Reduce/AE/FE (Autoexposure/Flash exposure) lock button.** This button, which has a * label above it, has several functions, which differ depending on the AF point and metering mode. You can find more about these variations, available in Creative Zone modes only, in Chapter 4.

Shooting mode. The button locks the exposure or flash exposure that the camera sets when you partially depress the shutter button. In Evaluative exposure mode, exposure is locked at the AF point that achieved focus. In Partial, Spot, or Center-weighted modes, exposure is locked at the AF center point. The exposure lock indication (*) appears in the viewfinder and on the shooting settings display. If you want to recalculate exposure with the shutter button still

Figure 3.11

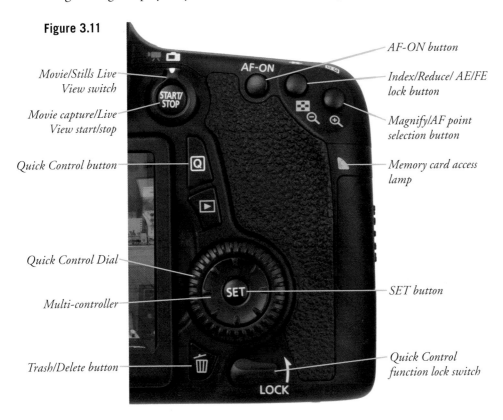

Movie/Stills Live View switch

Movie capture/Live View start/stop

Quick Control button

Quick Control Dial

Multi-controller

Trash/Delete button

AF-ON button

Index/Reduce/ AE/FE lock button

Magnify/AF point selection button

Memory card access lamp

SET button

Quick Control function lock switch

partially depressed, press the * button again. The exposure will be unlocked when you release the shutter button or take the picture. To retain the exposure lock for subsequent photos, keep the * button pressed while shooting.

When using flash, pressing the * button fires an extra pre-flash that allows the unit to calculate and lock exposure prior to taking the picture. The characters FEL will appear momentarily in the viewfinder, and the exposure lock indication and a flash indicator appear. (See the description of the viewfinder display later in this chapter.)

Playback mode: Press this button to switch from single-image display to nine-image thumbnail index. (See Figure 3.12.) Move highlighting among the thumbnails with the touch screen, multi-controller pad, or Main Dial. To view a highlighted image, press the Magnify button.

In Playback mode, when an image is zoomed in, press this button to zoom out, or use the touch screen.

- **Magnify/AF point selection button.** In Shooting mode, this button activates autofocus point selection. (See Chapter 4 for information on setting autofocus/exposure point selection when using Creative Zone exposure modes.) In Playback mode, if you're viewing a single image, this button zooms in on the image that's displayed. If thumbnail indexes are shown, pressing this button switches from nine thumbnails to four thumbnails, or from four thumbnails to a full-screen view of a highlighted image.

- **Quick Control (Q) button.** Press this button to produce the Quick Control screen, which gives you access to many features when in Shooting mode. When you're reviewing images in Playback, a different Quick Control screen pops up that allows you to protect or rate images, change jump method, resize, or perform other functions.

- **Quick Control Dial (QCD).** Used to select shooting options, such as f/stop or exposure compensation value, or to navigate through menus. It also serves as an alternate controller for some functions set with other controls, such as AF point.

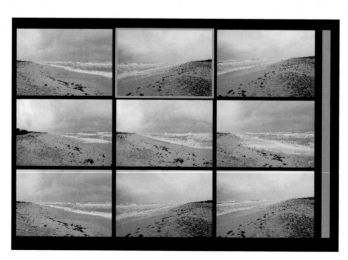

Figure 3.12
The Index/Reduce button changes the playback display from single image to four or nine thumbnails.

- **Multi-controller.** This thumbpad, located inside the Quick Control Dial, can be shifted up, down, side to side, and diagonally for a total of eight directions. It can be used for several functions, including AF point selection, scrolling around a magnified image, trimming a photo, or setting white balance correction.

- **SET button.** Located in the center of the cross key cluster, this button is used to confirm a selection or activate a feature, similarly to the SET icon on the touch screen.

- **Multi-function lock switch.** Set in the upward position, it prevents the Main Dial, QCD, and multi-controller from changing a setting. If you try to use one of these locked controls, an L warning will be displayed in the optical viewfinder and the LCD panel; in the Shooting Settings display, Lock will be shown. You can select which of the three are locked out using the Multi Function Lock entry in the Custom Functions III 02 (Operation/Others) menu. Choose any combination of one, two, or all three controls to freeze with this lock switch.

- **Playback button.** Displays the last picture taken. Thereafter, you can move back and forth among the available images by pressing the left/right multi-controller pad to advance or reverse one image at a time, or the Main Dial to jump forward or back using the jump method you've selected. (See the section below for more on jumping.) To quit playback, press this button again. The 70D also exits playback mode automatically when you press the shutter button (so you'll never be prevented from taking a picture on the spur of the moment because you happened to be viewing an image).

- **Erase button.** Press to erase the image shown on the LCD during Playback mode. A menu will pop up displaying Cancel and Erase choices. Use the left/right multi-controller pad to select one of these actions, then press the SET button to activate your choice.

- **Memory card access lamp.** When lit or blinking, this lamp indicates that the memory card is being accessed.

ON THE LEVEL

The 70D has three different display modes for the electronic level, using the back-panel LCD monitor and viewfinder. The INFO. button produces the electronic level on the LCD monitor in both still shooting and Live View/Movie shooting modes (the level display is switched off once movie capture actually begins, however).

You can also view two slightly different leveling displays in the optical viewfinder. The one that can be viewed during shooting is shown in Figure 3.13. That viewfinder Electronic Level must be activated in the Shooting 1 menu as described in Chapter 8. Five different icons are overlaid on the viewfinder screen (Figure 3.13, right), showing when the camera is level, tilted one degree, or tilted two degrees or more in either direction. The viewfinder level can be used in both horizontal and vertical shooting orientations. It's best suited for hand-held shooting. A second viewfinder level using the AF points as indicators can be displayed when leveling a camera mounted on a tripod.

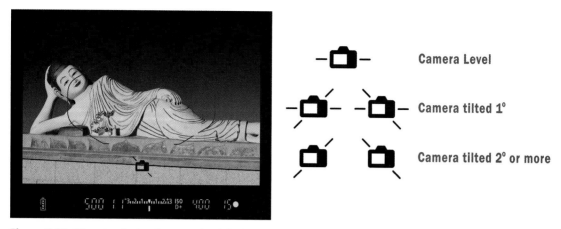

Figure 3.13 The viewfinder electronic level for hand-held photography.

Jumping Around

When a photo you've taken is displayed on the color LCD, you can move forward or backward one image at a time or "jump" ahead or back in different increments by rotating the Main Dial. As you jump, an overlay appears on the screen briefly showing the size of the leap you're making. (See Figure 3.14.)

As I'll describe in Chapter 8, you can specify the exact increment using the Image Jump with Dial entry in the Playback 2 menu. Your options are as follows:

- **1 image.** Rotating the Main Dial one click or swiping jumps forward or back one image.
- **10 images.** Rotating the Main Dial one click or swiping jumps forward or back ten images.
- **100 images.** Rotating the Main Dial one click or swiping jumps forward or back one hundred images.

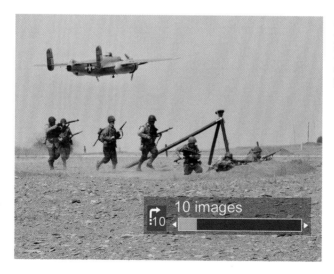

Figure 3.14
Rotate the Main Dial to jump ahead or back during image playback.

- **Display by Date.** Rotating the Main Dial one click or swiping jumps forward or back to the first image taken on the next or previous calendar date.

- **Display by Folder.** Rotating the Main Dial one click or swiping jumps to the next folder on your memory card.

- **Display Movies only.** Tells the 70D to jump only among movie images when using a card that contains both video clips and still images. This option is useful when you prefer to view only one kind of file.

- **Display Stills only.** Specifies jumping only between still images when using a card that has both video clips and still images.

- **Display by Image Rating.** As explained in Chapter 8, you can rate a particular movie or still photo by applying from one to five stars, using the Rating menu entry in the Playback 2 menu. This Jump choice allows you to select a rating rank, and then jump among photos with that rating applied.

Going Topside

The top surface of the Canon EOS 70D has a few frequently accessed controls of its own. The key controls, shown in Figure 3.15, are as follows:

- **Mode Dial.** Rotate this dial to switch among exposure modes, and to choose the camera user setting (C). You'll find these modes and options described in more detail in Chapter 8 (where I show you how to register your settings in the C "slot").

- **Mode Dial lock release.** You'll need to depress this button to free the Mode Dial to rotate.

- **Sensor focal plane.** Precision macro and scientific photography sometimes requires knowing exactly where the focal plane of the sensor is. The symbol on the side of the pentaprism marks that plane.

- **Flash hot shoe.** Slide an electronic flash into this mount when you need a more powerful Speedlite. A dedicated flash unit, like those from Canon, can use the multiple contact points shown to communicate exposure, zoom setting, white balance information, and other data between the flash and the camera. There's more on using electronic flash in Chapter 11.

- **LCD illuminator button.** Press this button to turn on the amber LCD panel lamp that backlights the LCD status panel for about six seconds, or to turn it off if illuminated. The lamp will remain lit beyond the six-second period if you are using the Mode Dial or other shooting control.

- **AF button.** Press once and then rotate the Main Dial or Quick Control Dial to change between One-Shot, AI Focus, and AI Servo autofocus modes (you'll find more about those modes in Chapter 5).

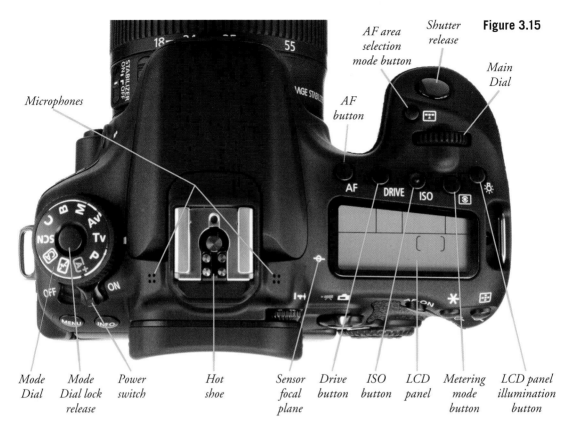

Figure 3.15

Microphones · AF area selection mode button · Shutter release · Main Dial · AF button

Mode Dial · Mode Dial lock release · Power switch · Hot shoe · Sensor focal plane · Drive button · ISO button · LCD panel · Metering mode button · LCD panel illumination button

- **DRIVE button.** Press once and then change Drive mode settings rotating the Main Dial or Quick Control Dial. Your options include single shooting, high speed continuous (up to 7 fps), low speed continuous shooting (up to 3 fps), single silent shooting, silent continuous shooting (at up to 3 fps), and 10- or 2-second self-timer/remote control.

- **ISO.** Press and rotate the Main Dial or Quick Control Dial to choose an ISO setting. You can press the INFO. button when this button is active to quickly change to Auto ISO mode. You'll find more about ISO options in Chapter 4.

- **Metering mode button.** Rotate the Main Dial or Quick Control Dial after pressing this button to change between Evaluative, Partial, Spot, or Center-weighted metering.

- **Monochrome LCD status panel.** The LCD panel provides information about the status of your camera and its settings, including exposure mode, number of pictures remaining, battery status, and many other settings. I'll illustrate all these in the next section.

- **Main Dial.** This dial is used to make many shooting settings. When settings come in pairs (such as shutter speed/aperture in Manual shooting mode), the Main Dial is used for one (for example, shutter speed), while the Quick Control Dial is used for the other (aperture). When an image is on the screen during playback, this dial also specifies the leaps that skip a particular number of images during playback of the shots you've already taken. Jumps can be 1 image, 10 images, 100 images, jump by date, or jump by screen (that is, by screens of thumbnails when using Index mode), date, or folder. (Jump method is selected in the Playback 2 menu, as described in Chapter 8.) This dial is also used to move among tabs when the MENU button has been pressed, and is used within some menus (in conjunction with the Quick Control Dial) to change pairs of settings.

■ **Shutter release button.** Partially depress this button to lock in exposure and focus. Press all the way to take the picture. Tapping the shutter release when the camera has turned off the autoexposure and autofocus mechanisms reactivates both. When a review image is displayed on the back-panel color LCD, tapping this button removes the image from the display and reactivates the autoexposure and autofocus mechanisms.

■ **Microphones.** The stereo microphones record the audio track of your HDTV movies. You can plug an external stereo mic into a port on the side.

LCD Panel Readouts

The top panel of the EOS 70D (see Figure 3.16) contains an amber-colored (when backlit) monochrome LCD readout that displays status information about most of the shooting settings. All of the information segments available are shown in Figure 3.17. I've color-coded the display to make it easier to differentiate them; the information does *not* appear in color on the actual 70D. Many of the information items are mutually exclusive (that is, in the autofocus area at upper left, only one of the possible settings illustrated will appear).

Some of the items on the status LCD also appear in the viewfinder, such as the shutter speed and aperture (pictured in the middle of the display in blue in the figure), and the exposure level (in yellow at the bottom).

Figure 3.16

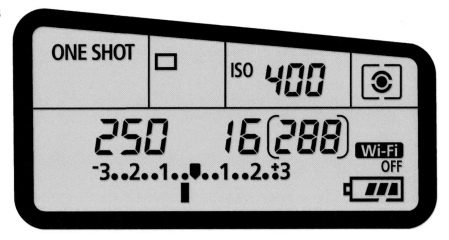

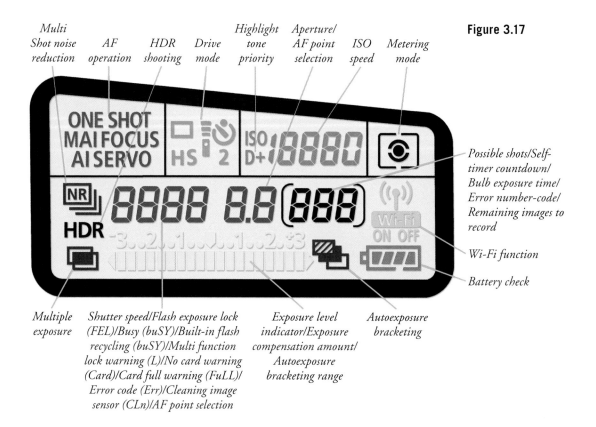

Figure 3.17

Multi Shot noise reduction

AF operation

HDR shooting

Drive mode

Highlight tone priority

Aperture/ AF point selection

ISO speed

Metering mode

Possible shots/Self-timer countdown/ Bulb exposure time/ Error number-code/ Remaining images to record

Wi-Fi function

Battery check

Multiple exposure

Shutter speed/Flash exposure lock (FEL)/Busy (buSY)/Built-in flash recycling (buSY)/Multi function lock warning (L)/No card warning (Card)/Card full warning (FuLL)/ Error code (Err)/Cleaning image sensor (CLn)/AF point selection

Exposure level indicator/Exposure compensation amount/ Autoexposure bracketing range

Autoexposure bracketing

Underneath Your 70D

There's not a lot going on with the bottom panel of your 70D. You'll find a tripod socket, which secures the camera to a tripod, and is also used to lock on the optional BG-E14 battery grip, which provides more juice to run your camera to take more exposures with a single charge. It also adds a vertically oriented shutter release, Main Dial, AE Lock/FE Lock, and AF point selection controls for easier vertical shooting. To mount the grip, slide the battery door latch to open the door, then push gently toward the outside edge of the camera to free the hinge pins from their sockets. That will let you remove the battery door. Then slide the grip into the battery cavity, aligning the pin on the grip with the small hole on the other side of the tripod socket. Tighten the grip's tripod socket screw to lock the grip onto the bottom of your 70D. Figure 3.18 shows the underside view of the camera.

Figure 3.18

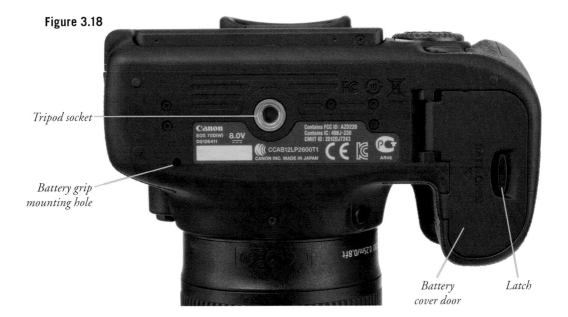

Tripod socket

Battery grip
mounting hole

Battery
cover door

Latch

Lens Components

The typical lens, like the ones shown in Figures 3.19 and 3.20, has seven or eight common features. Not every component appears on every lens. The lens on the left, for example, lacks the distance scale and distance indicator that the lens on the right has. Lenses that lack image stabilization will not have a stabilization switch.

- **Filter thread.** Lenses have a thread on the front for attaching filters and other add-ons. Some also use this thread for attaching a lens hood (you screw on the filter first, and then attach the hood to the screw thread on the front of the filter).
- **Lens hood.** Shields the front element of the lens from extraneous light arriving from outside the image area, and serves as protection.
- **Lens hood bayonet.** This is used to mount the lens hood for lenses that don't use screw-mount hoods (the majority).
- **Zoom ring.** Turn this ring to change the zoom setting.
- **Zoom scale.** These markings on the lens show the current focal length selected.
- **Focus ring.** This is the ring you turn when you manually focus the lens.
- **Distance scale.** This is a readout that rotates in unison with the lens's focus mechanism to show the distance at which the lens has been focused. It's a useful indicator for double-checking autofocus, roughly evaluating depth-of-field, and for setting manual focus guesstimates.

- **Infrared focus adjustment.** IR illumination doesn't focus at the exact same plane as visible light, so if you're shooting infrared photos, move the focus ring to line up to the appropriate focal length opposite the distance determined by normal focusing.

- **Autofocus/manual switch.** Allows you to change from automatic focus to manual focus.

- **Image stabilization switch.** Lenses with IS include a separate switch for adjusting the stabilization feature.

- **EF-S/EF mounting index.** EF-S lenses have a raised white square, while EF lenses have a raised red bump; line up these indexes with the matching white and red indicators on the camera lens mount to attach the lens.

- **Electrical contacts.** On the back of the lens (see Figure 3.20) are electrical contacts that the camera uses to communicate focus, aperture setting, and other information.

- **Lens mount.** This mount is used to attach the lens to a matching bayonet on the camera body.

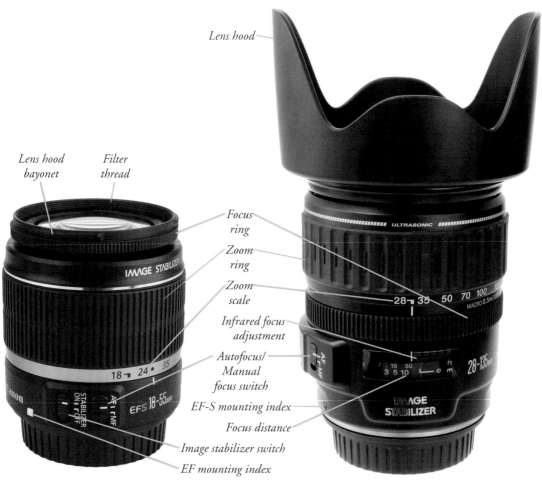

Figure 3.19

Figure 3.20

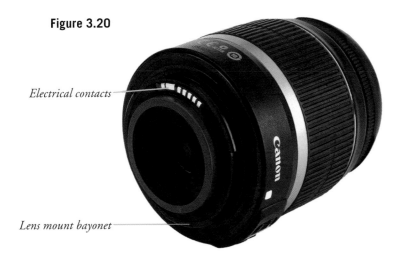

Electrical contacts

Lens mount bayonet

Looking Inside the Viewfinder

Much of the important shooting status information is shown inside the viewfinder of the 70D. As with the displays shown on the color LCD, not all of this information will be shown at any one time. Figure 3.21 shows what you can expect to see. I'll explain all of these readouts later in this book, with those pertaining to exposure in Chapter 4, and those relating to flash in Chapter 11. These readouts include:

- **Spot metering reference circle.** Shows the circle that delineates the metered area when Spot metering is activated. (The reference circle is visible at all times, even when you're not using Spot metering.)

- **Autofocus zones.** Shows the areas used by the 70D to focus. The camera can select the appropriate focus zone for you, or you can manually select one or all of the zones, as described in Chapter 4.

- **Autoexposure lock.** Shows that exposure has been locked. This icon also appears when an automatic exposure bracketing sequence is in process.

- **Flash-ready indicator.** This icon appears when the flash is fully charged. It also shows when the flash exposure lock has been applied for an inappropriate exposure value.

- **Flash status indicator.** Appears along with the flash-ready indicator. The H is shown when high-speed (focal plane) flash sync is being used. The * appears when flash exposure lock or a flash exposure bracketing sequence is underway.

- **Flash exposure compensation.** Appears when flash EV changes have been made.

- **Shutter speed/aperture readouts.** Most of the time, these readouts show the current shutter speed and aperture. This pair can also warn you of memory card conditions (full, error, or missing), ISO speed, flash exposure lock, and a buSY indicator when the camera is busy doing other things (including flash recycling).

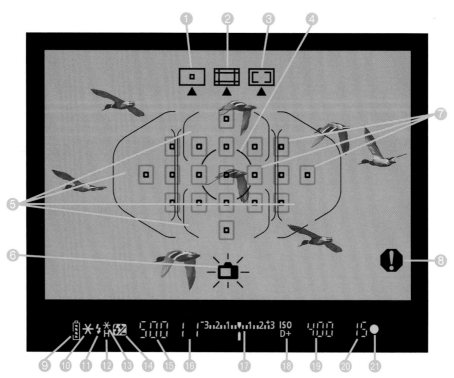

Figure 3.21

① *Single-point AF (manual selection)*

② *Zone AF (Manual selection)*

③ *19-point automatic selection*

④ *Spot metering circle*

⑤ *AF zones*

⑥ *Electronic level*

⑦ *AF points*

⑧ *Warning symbol*

⑨ *Battery check*

⑩ *AE lock/Autoexposure bracketing in progress*

⑪ *Flash ready/Improper flash exposure lock warning*

⑫ *Flash exposure lock/Flash exposure bracketing in progress*

⑬ *High-speed sync*

⑭ *Flash exposure compensation*

⑮ *Shutter speed/Flash exposure lock (FEL)/buSY/Built-in flash recycling (buSY)/Multi function lock warning (L)/No card/card error (Card)/Card full (FuLL)/ Error code (Err)/AF point selection*

⑯ *Aperture/AF point selection*

⑰ *Exposure level indicator/Exposure compensation amount/ Autoexposure bracketing range/ Red-eye reduction lamp-on indicator*

⑱ *Highlight tone priority*

⑲ *ISO speed*

⑳ *Maximum burst/Number of remaining exposures*

㉑ *Focus confirmation light*

■ **Exposure level indicator.** This scale shows the current exposure level, with the bottom indicator centered when the exposure is correct as metered. The indicator may also move to the left or right to indicate under- or overexposure (respectively). The scale is also used to show the amount of EV and flash EV adjustments and the number of stops covered by the current automatic exposure bracketing range, and is used as a red-eye reduction lamp indicator.

■ **ISO sensitivity.** This useful indicator shows the current ISO setting value. Those who have accidentally taken dozens of shots under bright sunlight at ISO 1600 because they forgot to change the setting back after some indoor shooting will treasure this addition.

■ **Maximum burst available.** Changes to a number to indicate the number of frames that can be taken in continuous mode using the current settings.

■ **Focus confirmation.** This green dot appears when the subject covered by the active autofocus zone is in sharp focus.

■ **Highlight tone priority.** Shows status of this feature, which allows the 70D to adjust the rendition of the lighter tones in an image to provide full detail, possibly at the expense of shadow detail.

■ **Electronic level.** Shows the degree of tilt when the camera is held horizontally or vertically.

Part II

Mastering Your Tools

Even if you've learned the fundamentals and controls of the Canon EOS 70D, there is lots of room to learn more and master the features of the camera so you can use them to their fullest. Even if you're getting great exposures a high percentage of the time, you can fine-tune tonal values and use your shutter speed, aperture, and ISO controls creatively. Your camera's high-performance autofocus system may zero in on your subject in most situations—but you still need to be able to tell the camera *what* to focus on, and *when*. Other tools at your disposal let you freeze an instant of time, create multiple exposures on a single frame, and improve your images in other imaginative ways. The chapters in this part will help you move your photography to the next level by understanding exposure, mastering the mysteries of autofocus, and using the 70D's advanced features.

> This part of the book contains the core chapters that will help you improve your images by nailing the best exposure every time, using the (often confusing, sometimes conflicting) features of the camera's advanced autofocus system and exploring some advanced techniques like trap focus, stacked focus, and in-camera HDR.

- **Chapter 4, "Nailing the Right Exposure":** This chapter explores all your options for fine-tuning exposure with the Canon 70D. You'll learn when to use—and not use—each of the camera's metering modes, how to work with histograms, and the rationale for choosing the built-in HDR feature—or whether to capture high dynamic range images "manually." I'm also going to explode the myth of the 18 percent gray card.

- **Chapter 5, "Mastering the Mysteries of Autofocus":** As autofocus features like the 70D's new "hybrid" AF system are added, this useful capability often becomes more confusing, even for veteran photographers. I'm going to show you exactly how autofocus works so you can better understand the strengths and limitations of each mode. You'll discover how to select the mode that will give you tack-sharp focus time after time, and learn how to use fine-tuning (with the included focus chart) to correct lenses with front- and back-focus problems.

- **Chapter 6, "Live View and Movies":** This is your introduction to shooting in Live View mode and capturing movies, with complete descriptions of the 70D's shooting features, along with tips on better video.

- **Chapter 7, "Advanced Shooting":** Here you'll find discussions of some more advanced techniques, including how to make people "invisible" with long exposures, getting the most from the 70D's continuous shooting capabilities, and some clever ways to create multiple exposures.

4

Nailing the Right Exposure

As you learn to use your 70D creatively, you're going to find that the right settings—as determined by the camera's exposure meter and intelligence—need to be *adjusted* to account for your creative decisions or to fine-tune the image for special situations.

For example, when you shoot with the main light source behind the subject, you end up with *back-lighting*, which results in an overexposed background and/or an underexposed subject. The 70D recognizes backlit situations nicely, and can properly base exposure on the main subject, producing a decent photo. Features like Highlight Tone Priority and the Auto Lighting Optimizer can fine-tune exposure to preserve detail in the highlights and shadows.

But what if you *want* to underexpose the subject, to produce a silhouette effect? Or, perhaps, you might want to flip up the 70D's built-in flash unit to fill in the shadows on your subject. The more you know about how to use your 70D, the more you'll run into situations where you want to creatively tweak the exposure to provide a different look than you'd get just following the camera's automatic or semi-automatic recommendations.

This chapter shows you the fundamentals of exposure, so you'll be better equipped to override the 70D's default settings when you want to, or need to. After all, correct exposure is one of the foundations of good photography, along with accurate focus and sharpness, appropriate color balance, freedom from unwanted noise and excessive contrast, as well as pleasing composition.

The 70D gives you a great deal of control over all of these, although composition is entirely up to you. You must still frame the photograph to create an interesting arrangement of subject matter, but all the other parameters are basic functions of the camera. You can let your 70D set them for you automatically, you can fine-tune how the camera applies its automatic settings, or you can make them yourself, manually. The amount of control you have over exposure, sensitivity (ISO settings), color balance, focus, and image parameters like sharpness and contrast make the 70D a versatile tool for creating images.

In the next few pages, I'm going to give you a grounding in one of those foundations, and explain the basics of exposure, either as an introduction or as a refresher course, depending on your current level of expertise. When you finish this chapter, you'll understand most of what you need to know to take well-exposed photographs creatively in a broad range of situations.

Getting a Handle on Exposure

This section explains the fundamental concepts that go into creating an exposure. If you already know about the role of f/stops, shutter speeds, and sensor sensitivity in determining an exposure, you might want to skip to the next section, which explains how the 70D calculates exposure.

In the most basic sense, exposure is all about light. Exposure can make or break your photo. Correct exposure brings out the detail in the areas you want to picture, providing the range of tones and colors you need to create the desired image. Poor exposure can cloak important details in shadow, or wash them out in glare-filled featureless expanses of white. However, getting the perfect exposure requires some intelligence—either that built into the camera or the smarts in your head—because digital sensors can't capture all the tones we are able to see. If the range of tones in an image is extensive, embracing both inky black shadows and bright highlights, we often must settle for an exposure that renders most of those tones—but not all—in a way that best suits the photo we want to produce.

As the owner of a Canon 70D, you're probably well aware of the traditional "exposure triangle" of aperture (quantity of light, light passed by the lens), shutter speed (the amount of time the shutter is open), and the ISO sensitivity of the sensor—all working proportionately and reciprocally to produce an exposure. The trio is itself affected by the amount of illumination that is available to work with. So, if you double the amount of light, increase the aperture by one stop, make the shutter speed twice as long, or boost the ISO setting 2X, you'll get twice as much exposure. Similarly, you can increase any of these factors while decreasing one of the others by a similar amount to keep the same exposure.

Working with any of the three controls involves trade-offs. Larger f/stops provide less depth-of-field, while smaller f/stops increase depth-of-field (and potentially at the same time can *decrease* sharpness through a phenomenon called *diffraction*). Shorter shutter speeds do a better job of reducing the effects of camera/subject motion, while longer shutter speeds make that motion blur more likely. Higher ISO settings increase the amount of visual noise and artifacts in your image, while lower ISO settings reduce the effects of noise. (See Figure 4.1.)

Exposure determines the look, feel, and tone of an image, in more ways than one. Incorrect exposure can impair even the best-composed image by cloaking important tones in darkness, or by washing them out so they become featureless to the eye. On the other hand, correct exposure brings out the detail in the areas you want to picture, and provides the range of tones and colors you need to create the desired image. However, getting the perfect exposure can be tricky, because digital sensors can't capture all the tones we are able to see. If the range of tones in an image is extensive,

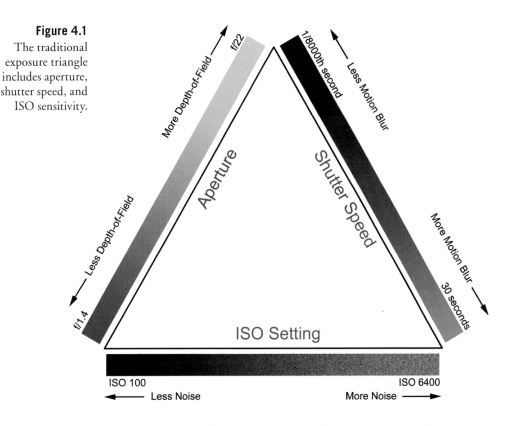

Figure 4.1

The traditional exposure triangle includes aperture, shutter speed, and ISO sensitivity.

embracing both inky black shadows and bright highlights, the sensor may not be able to capture them all. Sometimes, we must settle for an exposure that renders most of those tones—but not all—in a way that best suits the photo we want to produce. You'll often need to make choices about which details are important, and which are not, so that you can grab the tones that truly matter in your image. That's part of the creativity you bring to bear in realizing your photographic vision.

For example, look at two bracketed exposures presented in Figure 4.2. For the image at left, the highlights (chiefly the clouds at upper left and the top-left edge of the skyscraper) are well exposed, but everything else in the shot is seriously underexposed. The version on the right, taken an instant later with the tripod-mounted camera, shows detail in the shadow areas of the buildings, but the highlights are completely washed out. The camera's sensor simply can't capture detail in both dark areas and bright areas in a single shot.

With digital camera sensors, it's tricky to capture detail in both highlights and shadows in a single image, because the number of tones, the *dynamic range* of the sensor, is limited. The solution, in this particular case, was to resort to a technique called High Dynamic Range (HDR) photography, in which the two exposures from Figure 4.2 were combined in an image editor such as Photoshop, or a specialized HDR tool like Photomatix (about $100 from www.hdrsoft.com). The resulting shot is shown in Figure 4.3. I'll explain more about HDR photography later in this chapter. For now, though, I'm going to concentrate on showing you how to get the best exposures possible without resorting to such tools, using only the features of your Canon 70D.

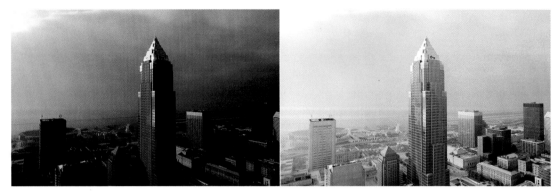

Figure 4.2 At left, the image is exposed for the highlights, losing shadow detail. At right, the exposure captures detail in the shadows, but the background highlights are washed out.

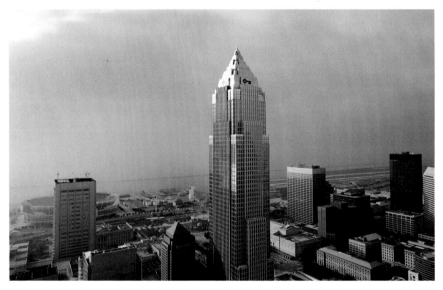

Figure 4.3
Combining the two exposures produces the best compromise image.

To understand exposure, you need to understand the six aspects of light that combine to produce an image. Start with a light source—the sun, an interior lamp, or the glow from a campfire—and trace its path to your camera, through the lens, and finally to the sensor that captures the illumination. Here's a brief review of the things within our control that affect exposure.

- **Light at its source.** Our eyes and our cameras—film or digital—are most sensitive to that portion of the electromagnetic spectrum we call *visible light*. That light has several important aspects that are relevant to photography, such as color and harshness (which is determined primarily by the apparent size of the light source as it illuminates a subject). But, in terms of exposure, the important attribute of a light source is its *intensity*. We may have direct control over intensity, which might be the case with an interior light that can be brightened or dimmed. Or, we might have only indirect control over intensity, as with sunlight, which can be made to appear dimmer by introducing translucent light-absorbing or reflective materials in its path.

- **Light's duration.** We tend to think of most light sources as continuous. But, as you'll learn in Chapter 11, the duration of light can change quickly enough to modify the exposure, as when the main illumination in a photograph comes from an intermittent source, such as an electronic flash.

- **Light reflected, transmitted, or emitted.** Once light is produced by its source, either continuously or in a brief burst, we are able to see and photograph objects by the light that is reflected from our subjects toward the camera lens; transmitted (say, from translucent objects that are lit from behind); or emitted (by a candle or television screen). When more or less light reaches the lens from the subject, we need to adjust the exposure. This part of the equation is under our control to the extent we can increase the amount of light falling on or passing through the subject (by adding extra light sources or using reflectors), or by pumping up the light that's emitted (by increasing the brightness of the glowing object).

- **Light passed by the lens.** Not all the illumination that reaches the front of the lens makes it all the way through. Filters can remove some of the light before it enters the lens. Inside the lens barrel is a variable-sized diaphragm that dilates and contracts to vary the size of the aperture and control the amount of light that enters the lens. You, or the 70D's autoexposure system, can control exposure by varying the size of the aperture. The relative size of the aperture is called the *f/stop* (see Figure 4.4).

- **Light passing through the shutter.** Once light passes through the lens, the amount of time the sensor receives it is determined by the 70D's shutter, which can remain open for as long as 30 seconds (or even longer if you use the Bulb setting) or as briefly as 1/8,000th second.

- **Light captured by the sensor.** Not all the light falling onto the sensor is captured. If the number of photons reaching a particular photosite doesn't pass a set threshold, no information is recorded. Similarly, if too much light illuminates a pixel in the sensor, then the excess isn't recorded or, worse, spills over to contaminate adjacent pixels. We can modify the minimum and maximum number of pixels that contribute to image detail by adjusting the ISO setting. At higher ISOs, the incoming light is amplified to boost the effective sensitivity of the sensor.

Figure 4.4
Top row (left to right): f/2, f/2.8, f/4, f/5.6; bottom row: f/8, f/11, f/16, f/22.

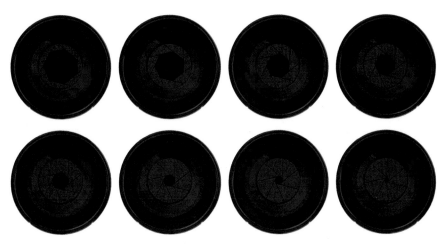

F/STOPS AND SHUTTER SPEEDS

If you're *really* new to more advanced cameras (and I realize that many soon-to-be-ambitious photographers do purchase the 70D as their first digital SLR), you might need to know that the lens aperture, or f/stop, is a ratio, much like a fraction, which is why f/2 is larger than f/4, just as 1/2 is larger than 1/4. However, f/2 is actually *four times* as large as f/4. (If you remember your high school geometry, you'll know that to double the area of a circle, you multiply its diameter by the square root of two: 1.4.)

Lenses are usually marked with intermediate f/stops that represent a size that's twice as much/half as much as the previous aperture. So, a lens might be marked f/2, f/2.8, f/4, f/5.6, f/8, f/11, f/16, f/22, with each larger number representing an aperture that admits half as much light as the one before, as shown in Figure 4.4.

Shutter speeds are actual fractions (of a second), but the numerator is omitted, so that 60, 125, 250, 500, 1,000, and so forth represent 1/60th, 1/125th, 1/250th, 1/500th, and 1/1,000th second. To avoid confusion, Canon uses quotation marks to signify longer exposures: 2", 2"5, 4", and so forth representing 2.0, 2.5, and 4.0-second exposures, respectively.

These factors—the quantity of light produced by the light source, the amount reflected or transmitted toward the camera, the light passed by the lens, the amount of time the shutter is open, and the sensitivity of the sensor—all work proportionately and reciprocally to produce an exposure. That is, if you double the amount of light that's available, increase the aperture by one stop, make the shutter speed twice as long, or boost the ISO setting 2X, you'll get twice as much exposure. Similarly, you can increase any of these factors while decreasing one of the others by a similar amount to keep the same exposure.

Most commonly, exposure settings are made using the aperture and shutter speed, followed by adjusting the ISO sensitivity if it's not possible to get the preferred exposure; that is, the one that uses the "best" f/stop or shutter speed for the depth-of-field (range of sharp focus) or action stopping we want (produced by short shutter speeds, as I'll explain later). Table 4.1 shows equivalent exposure settings using various shutter speeds and f/stops.

Table 4.1 Equivalent Exposures

Shutter Speed	f/stop	Shutter Speed	f/stop
1/30th second	f/22	1/1,000th second	f/4
1/60th second	f/16	1/2,000th second	f/2.8
1/125th second	f/11	1/4,000th second	f/2
1/250th second	f/8	1/8,000th second	f/1.4
1/500th second	f/5.6		

When the 70D is set for P (Program) mode, the metering system selects the correct exposure for you automatically, but you can change quickly to an equivalent exposure by locking the current exposure, and then spinning the Main Dial until the desired *equivalent* exposure combination is displayed. You can use this standard Program Shift feature more easily if you remember that you need to rotate the dial toward the *left* when you want to increase the amount of depth-of-field or use a slower shutter speed; rotate to the *right* when you want to reduce the depth-of-field or use a faster shutter speed. The need for more/less DOF and slower/faster shutter speed are the primary reasons you'd want to use Program Shift. I'll explain Program mode exposure shifting options in more detail later in this chapter.

In Aperture-priority (Av) and Shutter-priority (Tv) modes, you can change to an equivalent exposure using a different combination of shutter speed and aperture, but only by either adjusting the aperture in Aperture-priority mode (the camera then chooses the shutter speed) or shutter speed in Shutter-priority mode (the camera then selects the aperture). I'll cover all these exposure modes and their differences later in the chapter.

How the 70D Calculates Exposure

Your Canon 70D calculates exposure by measuring the light that passes through the lens and is bounced up by the mirror to sensors located near the focusing surface, using a pattern you can select (more on that later) and based on the assumption that each area being measured reflects about the same amount of light as a neutral gray card that reflects a "middle" gray of about 12- to 18-percent reflectance. (The photographic "gray cards" you buy at a camera store have an 18-percent gray tone, which does represent middle gray; however, your camera is calibrated to interpret a somewhat darker 12-percent gray; I'll explain more about this later.) That "average" 12- to 18-percent gray assumption is necessary, because different subjects reflect different amounts of light. In a photo containing, say, a white cat and a dark gray cat, the white cat might reflect five times as much light as the gray cat. An exposure based on the white cat will cause the gray cat to appear to be black, while an exposure based only on the gray cat will make the white cat appear washed out.

This is more easily understood if you look at some photos of subjects that are dark (they reflect little light), those that have predominantly middle tones, and subjects that are highly reflective. The next few figures show some images of actual cats (actually, the *same* cat rendered in black, gray, and white varieties through the magic of Photoshop), with each of the three strips exposed using a different cat for reference.

Correctly Exposed

The three pictures shown in Figure 4.5 represent how the black, gray, and white cats would appear if the exposure were calculated by measuring the light reflecting from the middle, gray cat, which, for the sake of illustration, we'll assume reflects approximately 12 to 18 percent of the light that strikes it. The exposure meter sees an object that it thinks is a middle gray, calculates an exposure based on that, and the feline in the center of the strip is rendered at its proper tonal value. Best of

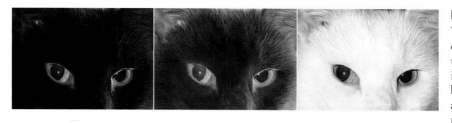

Figure 4.5
When exposure is calculated based on the middle-gray cat in the center, the black-and-white cats are rendered accurately, too.

all, because the resulting exposure is correct, the black cat at left and white cat at right are rendered properly as well.

When you're shooting pictures with your 70D, and the meter happens to base its exposure on a subject that averages that "ideal" middle gray, then you'll end up with similar (accurate) results. The camera's exposure algorithms are concocted to ensure this kind of result as often as possible, barring any unusual subjects (that is, those that are backlit, or have uneven illumination). The 70D has four different metering modes (described next), each of which is equipped to handle certain types of unusual subjects, as I'll outline.

Overexposed

The strip of three images in Figure 4.6 shows what would happen if the exposure were calculated based on metering the leftmost, black cat. The light meter sees less light reflecting from the black cat than it would see from a gray middle-tone subject, and so figures, "Aha! I need to add exposure to brighten this subject up to a middle gray!" That lightens the black cat, so it now appears to be gray.

But now, the cat in the middle that was *originally* middle gray is overexposed and becomes light gray. And the white cat at right is now seriously overexposed, and loses detail in the highlights, which have become a featureless white.

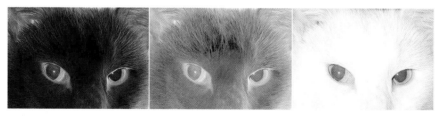

Figure 4.6
When exposure is calculated based on the black cat at the left, the black cat looks gray, the gray cat appears to be a light gray, and the white cat is seriously overexposed.

Underexposed

The third possibility in this simplified scenario is that the light meter might measure the illumination bouncing off the white cat, and try to render that feline as a middle gray. A lot of light is reflected by the white kitty, so the exposure is *reduced*, bringing that cat closer to a middle gray tone. The cats that were originally gray and black are now rendered too dark. Clearly, measuring the gray cat—or a substitute that reflects about the same amount of light—is the only way to ensure that the exposure is precisely correct. (See Figure 4.7.)

Figure 4.7
When exposure is calculated based on the white cat on the right, the other two cats are underexposed.

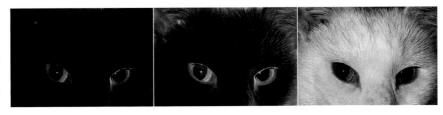

As you can see, the ideal way to measure exposure is to meter from a subject that reflects 12 to 18 percent of the light that reaches it. If you want the most precise exposure calculations, if you don't have a gray cat handy, the solution is to use a stand-in, such as the evenly illuminated gray card I mentioned earlier. But, because the standard Kodak gray card reflects 18 percent of the light that reaches it and, as I said, your camera is calibrated for a somewhat darker 12-percent tone, you would need to add about one-half stop *more* exposure than the value metered from the card.

Another substitute for a gray card is the palm of a human hand (the backside of the hand is too variable). But a human palm, regardless of ethnic group, is even brighter than a standard gray card, so instead of one-half stop more exposure, you need to add one additional stop. That is, if your meter reading is 1/500th of a second at f/11, use 1/500th second at f/8 or 1/250th second at f/11 instead. (Both exposures are equivalent.) You can use exposure compensation (described later in this chapter) to add the half or full stop of exposure in either case.

If you actually wanted to use a gray card, place it in your frame near your main subject, facing the camera, and with the exact same even illumination falling on it that is falling on your subject. Then, use the Spot metering function (described in the next section) to calculate exposure. Of course, in most situations, it's not necessary to make the (technically correct) adjustment from the gray card/human hand reading. Your camera's light meter will do a good job of calculating the right exposure that's close enough for practical purposes, especially if you use the exposure tips in the next section. But, I felt that explaining exactly what is going on during exposure calculation would help you understand how your 70D's metering system works.

WHY THE GRAY CARD CONFUSION?

Why are so many photographers under the impression that cameras and meters are calibrated to the 18-percent "standard," rather than the true value, which may be 12 to 14 percent, depending on the vendor? The most common explanation is that during a revision of Kodak's instructions for its gray cards in the 1970s, the advice to open up an extra half stop was omitted, and a whole generation of shooters grew up thinking that a measurement off a gray card could be used as-is. The proviso returned to the instructions by 1987, it's said, but by then it was too late. Next to me is a (c)2006 version of the instructions for KODAK Gray Cards, Publication R-27Q, and the current directions read (with a bit of paraphrasing from me in italics):

- For subjects of normal reflectance increase the indicated exposure by 1/2 stop.
- For light subjects use the indicated exposure; for very light subjects, decrease the exposure by 1/2 stop. (*That is, you're measuring a cat that's lighter than middle gray.*)
- If the subject is dark to very dark, increase the indicated exposure by 1 to 1-1/2 stops. (*You're shooting a black cat.*)

Choosing a Metering Method

To calculate exposure automatically, you need to tell the 70D *where* in the frame to measure the light (this is called the *metering method*) and *what controls* should be used (aperture, shutter speed, or both) to set the exposure. That's called *exposure mode* (and includes Program (P), Shutter-priority (Tv), Aperture-priority (Av), or Manual (M) options, plus Auto and Creative Auto. I'll explain all these next.)

But first, I'm going to introduce you to the four metering methods. You can select any of the four if you're working with P, Tv, Av, or M exposure modes; if you're using Auto or Creative Auto, Evaluative metering is selected automatically and cannot be changed.

1. Press the Metering Mode button on the top of the camera. You can also press the Q button or tap the Q icon on the shooting settings screen to access the Quick Control menu, where a Metering Mode icon resides. (The Metering Mode button is a *lot* faster.)

2. Use the touch screen or left/right multi-controller buttons to highlight Evaluative, Partial, Spot, or Center-weighted.

   - **Evaluative.** When you're not using live view, the 70D slices up the frame into 63 different zones, shown as blue rectangles in Figure 4.8. (In live view, the 70D works with 315 different areas of the sensor.) The zones used are linked to the autofocus system (the 19 autofocus zones are also shown in the figure). The camera evaluates the measurements, giving extra emphasis to the metering zones that indicate sharp focus to make an educated guess about what kind of picture you're taking, based on examination of thousands of different real-world photos. For example, if the top sections of a picture are much lighter than the bottom portions, the algorithm can assume that the scene is a landscape photo with lots of sky. This mode is the best all-purpose metering method for most pictures. See Figure 4.9 for an example of a scene that can be easily interpreted by the Evaluative metering mode.

- **Partial.** This is a *faux* spot mode, using roughly 19 percent of the image area to calculate exposure, which, as you can see in Figure 4.10, is a rather large spot, represented by the larger blue circle, roughly 7.7 percent of the viewfinder at the center. (In live view, this area is larger, amounting to 10.3 percent of the sensor area.) The status LCD icon is shown in the upper-left corner. Use this mode if the background is much brighter or darker than the subject, as in Figure 4.11.

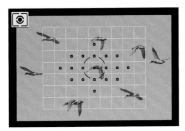

Figure 4.8 Evaluative metering uses 63 zones marked by blue rectangles, linked to the autofocus points shown as red brackets.

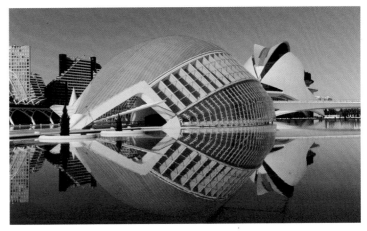

Figure 4.9 An evenly lit scene like this one can be metered effectively using the Evaluative metering setting.

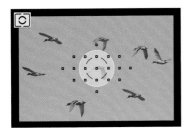

Figure 4.10 Partial metering uses a center spot that's roughly nine percent of the frame area.

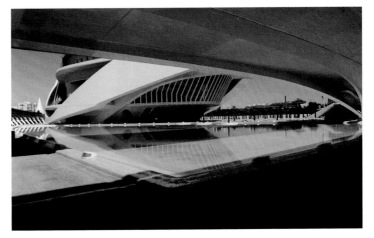

Figure 4.11 Partial metering allowed measuring exposure from the central area of the image, while giving less emphasis to the darker areas at top and bottom.

- **Spot.** This mode confines the reading to a limited area in the center of the viewfinder, as shown in Figure 4.12, making up only 3.0 percent of the image (2.6 percent in live view). This mode is useful when you want to base exposure on a small area in the frame, such as a spotlight performer on stage (see Figure 4.13), surrounded by a black background. If that area is in the center of the frame, so much the better. If not, you'll have to make your meter reading and then lock exposure by pressing the shutter release halfway, or by pressing the AE Lock button.

- **Center-weighted.** In this mode, the exposure meter emphasizes a zone in the center of the frame to calculate exposure, as shown in Figure 4.14, on the theory that, for most pictures, the main subject will be located in the center. Center-weighting works best for portraits, architectural photos, and other pictures in which the most important subject is located in the middle of the frame, as in Figure 4.15. As the name suggests, the light reading is *weighted* toward the central portion, but information is also used from the rest of the frame. If your main subject is surrounded by very bright or very dark areas, the exposure might not be exactly right. However, this scheme works well in many situations if you don't want to use one of the other modes.

3. Choose SET to confirm your choice.

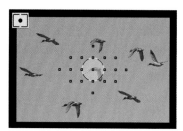

Figure 4.12 Spot metering calculates exposure based on a center spot that's only 4 percent of the image area.

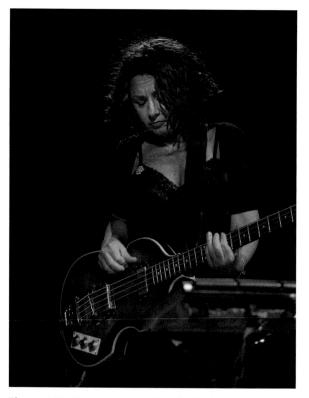

Figure 4.13 Spot metering allowed calculating exposure exclusively from the performer's face.

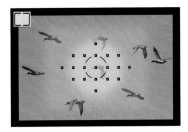

Figure 4.14 Center-weighted metering calculates exposure based on the full frame, but emphasizes the center area.

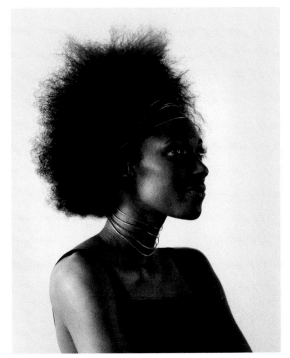

Figure 4.15 Center-weighted metering calculated the exposure for this shot from the large area in the center of the frame, with less emphasis on the bright, window-lit area behind the subject.

Choosing an Exposure Method

You'll find four Creative Zone methods for choosing the appropriate shutter speed and aperture: Program (P), Shutter-priority (Tv), Aperture-priority (Av), and Manual (M). To select one of these modes, just spin the Mode Dial (located at the top-right side of the camera) to choose the method you want to use. You can also select from the Basic Zone exposure methods, which provide much less control.

Your choice of which exposure method is best for a given shooting situation will depend on things like your need for lots of (or less) depth-of-field, a desire to freeze action or allow motion blur, or how much noise you find acceptable in an image. Each of the 70D's exposure methods emphasizes one of those aspects of image capture or another. This section introduces you to all of them.

Basic Zone Exposure Methods

When using Basic Zone modes, you have little control over exposure. In any of these modes, the 70D sets Evaluative metering for you, and chooses the shutter speed and aperture automatically. Indeed, when using Scene modes, you can't change any of the other shooting settings (other than image quality).

In Scene Intelligent Auto mode, the 70D selects an appropriate ISO sensitivity setting, color (white) balance, Picture Style, color space, noise reduction features, and use of the Auto Lighting Optimizer. (All of these will be discussed in Chapter 8.)

In Creative Auto mode, the 70D makes most of the exposure decisions for you (just as in Scene Intelligent Auto mode), but allows you to make some adjustments, in a round-about way. In terms of exposure adjustments, what you can do is adjust the f/stop used by telling the 70D whether you want the background more blurred or less blurred. Because the Basic Zone modes don't provide extensive exposure control, I'll continue the description of the adjustments you *can* make at the end of this chapter.

Aperture-Priority

In Av mode, you specify the lens opening used, and the 70D selects the shutter speed. Aperture-priority is especially good when you want to use a particular lens opening to achieve a desired effect. Perhaps you'd like to use the smallest f/stop possible to maximize depth-of-field in a close-up picture. Or, you might want to use a large f/stop to throw everything except your main subject out of focus, as in Figure 4.16. Maybe you'd just like to "lock in" a particular f/stop smaller than the maximum aperture because it's the sharpest available aperture with that lens. Or, you might prefer

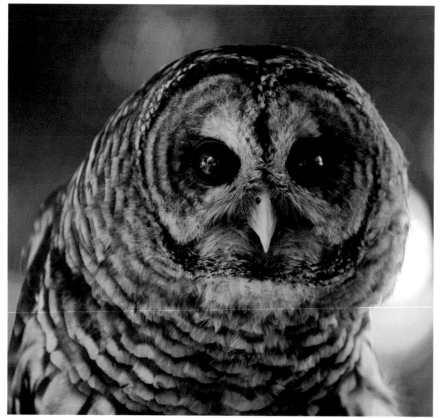

Figure 4.16

Use Aperture-priority to "lock in" a large f/stop when you want to blur the background.

to use, say, f/2.8 on a lens with a maximum aperture of f/1.4, because you want the best compromise between speed and sharpness.

Aperture-priority can even be used to specify a *range* of shutter speeds you want to use under varying lighting conditions, which seems almost contradictory. But think about it. You're shooting a soccer game outdoors with a telephoto lens and want a relatively high shutter speed, but you don't care if the speed changes a little should the sun duck behind a cloud. Set your 70D to Av, and adjust the aperture until a shutter speed of, say, 1/1,000th second is selected at your current ISO setting. (In bright sunlight at ISO 400, that aperture is likely to be around f/11.) Then, go ahead and shoot, knowing that your 70D will maintain that f/11 aperture (for sufficient DOF as the soccer players move about the field), but will drop down to 1/750th or 1/500th second if necessary should the lighting change a little.

A blinking 30 or 8000 shutter speed in the viewfinder indicates that the 70D is unable to select an appropriate shutter speed at the selected aperture and that over- and underexposure will occur at the current ISO setting. That's the major pitfall of using Av: you might select an f/stop that is too small or too large to allow an optimal exposure with the available shutter speeds. For example, if you choose f/2.8 as your aperture and the illumination is quite bright (say, at the beach or in snow), even your camera's fastest shutter speed might not be able to cut down the amount of light reaching the sensor to provide the right exposure. Or, if you select f/8 in a dimly lit room, you might find yourself shooting with a very slow shutter speed that can cause blurring from subject movement or camera shake. Aperture-priority is best used by those with a bit of experience in choosing settings. Many seasoned photographers leave their 70D set on Av all the time.

When to use Aperture-priority:

- **General landscape photography.** The 70D is a great camera for landscape photography, of course, because its 20MP of resolution allows making huge, gorgeous prints, as well as smaller prints that are filled with eye-popping detail. Aperture-priority is a good tool for ensuring that your landscape is sharp from foreground to infinity, if you select an f/stop that provides maximum depth-of-field.

  If you use Av mode and select an aperture like f/11 or f/16, it's your responsibility to make sure the shutter speed selected is fast enough to avoid losing detail to camera shake, or that the 70D is mounted on a tripod. One thing that new landscape photographers fail to account for is the movement of distant leaves and tree branches. When seeking the ultimate in sharpness, go ahead and use Aperture-priority, but boost ISO sensitivity a bit, if necessary, to provide a sufficiently fast shutter speed, whether shooting handheld or with a tripod.

- **Specific landscape situations.** Aperture-priority is also useful when you have no objection to using a long shutter speed, or, particularly, *want* the 70D to select one. Waterfalls are a perfect example. You can use Av mode, set your camera to ISO 100, use a small f/stop, and let the camera select a longer shutter speed that will allow the water to blur as it flows. Indeed, you might need to use a neutral-density filter to get a sufficiently long shutter speed. But Aperture-priority mode is a good start.

■ **Portrait photography.** Portraits are the most common applications of selective focus. A medium large aperture (say, f/5.6 or f/8) with a longer lens/zoom setting (in the 85mm-135mm range) will allow the background behind your portrait subject to blur. A *very* large aperture (I frequently shoot wide open with my 85mm f/1.2 lens) lets you apply selective focus to your subject's *face*. With a three-quarters view of your subject, as long as their eyes are sharp, it's okay if the far ear or their hair is out of focus.

■ **When you want to ensure optimal sharpness.** All lenses have an aperture or two at which they perform best, providing the level of sharpness you expect from a camera with the resolution of the 70D. That's usually about two stops down from wide open, and thus will vary depending on the maximum aperture of the lens. My 85mm f/1.2 is good wide open, but it's even sharper at f/2.8 or f/4; I shoot my 70-200mm f/2.8 wide open at concerts, but, if I can use f/4 instead, I'll get better results. Aperture-priority allows me to use each lens at its very best f/ stop.

■ **Close-up/Macro photography.** Depth-of-field is typically very shallow when shooting macro photos, and you'll want to choose your f/stop carefully. Perhaps you need the smallest aperture you can get away with to maximize DOF. Or, you might want to use a wider stop to emphasize your subject, as I did with the photo of the owl in Figure 4.16. Av mode comes in very useful when shooting close-up pictures. Because macro work is frequently done with the 70D mounted on a tripod, and your close-up subjects, if not living creatures, may not be moving much, a longer shutter speed isn't a problem. Aperture-priority (Av mode) can be your preferred choice.

Shutter-Priority

Shutter-priority (Tv) is the inverse of Aperture-priority: you choose the shutter speed you'd like to use, and the camera's metering system selects the appropriate f/stop. Perhaps you're shooting action photos and you want to use the absolute fastest shutter speed available with your camera; in other cases, you might want to use a slow shutter speed to add some blur to a ballet photo that would be mundane if the action were completely frozen (see Figure 4.19, later in this section). Shutter-priority mode gives you some control over how much action-freezing capability your digital camera brings to bear in a particular situation, as you can see in Figure 4.17.

You'll also encounter the same problem as with Aperture-priority when you select a shutter speed that's too long or too short for correct exposure under some conditions. I've shot outdoor soccer games on sunny Fall evenings and used Shutter-priority mode to lock in a 1/1,000th second shutter speed, which triggered the blinking warning, even with the lens wide open.

Like Av mode, it's possible to choose an inappropriate shutter speed. If that's the case, the maximum aperture of your lens (to indicate underexposure) or the minimum aperture (to indicate overexposure) will blink.

Figure 4.17
Lock the shutter at a slow speed to introduce a little blur into an action shot, seen here in the sticks, hands, and faces of the hockey players.

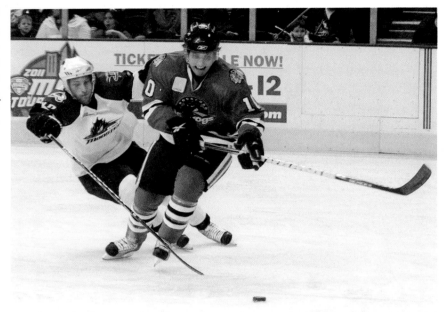

When to use Shutter-priority:

- **To reduce blur from subject motion.** Set the shutter speed of the 70D to a higher value to reduce the amount of blur from subjects that are moving. The exact speed will vary depending on how fast your subject is moving and how much blur is acceptable. You might want to freeze a basketball player in mid-dunk with a 1/1000th second shutter speed, or use 1/250th second to allow the spinning wheels of a motocross racer to blur a tiny bit to add the feeling of motion.

- **To add blur from subject motion.** There are times when you want a subject to blur, say, when shooting waterfalls with the camera set for a one- or two-second exposure in Shutter-priority mode.

- **To add blur from camera motion when *you* are moving.** Say you're panning to follow a pair of relay runners. You might want to use Shutter-priority mode and set the 70D for 1/60th second, so that the background will blur as you pan with the runners. The shutter speed will be fast enough to provide a sharp image of the athletes.

- **To reduce blur from camera motion when *you* are moving.** In other situations, the camera may be in motion, say, because you're shooting from a moving train or auto, and you want to minimize the amount of blur caused by the motion of the camera. Shutter-priority is a good choice here, too.

■ **Landscape photography handheld.** If you can't use a tripod for your landscape shots, you'll still probably want the sharpest image possible. Shutter-priority can allow you to specify a shutter speed that's fast enough to reduce or eliminate the effects of camera shake. Just make sure that your ISO setting is high enough that the 70D will select an aperture with sufficient depth-of-field, too.

■ **Concerts, stage performances.** I shoot a lot of concerts with my 70-200mm f/2.8 lens, and have discovered that, when image stabilization is taken into account, a shutter speed of 1/180th second is fast enough to eliminate the effects of camera shake from handholding the 70D with this lens, and also to avoid blur from the movement of all but the most energetic performers. I use Shutter-priority and set the ISO so the camera will select an aperture in the f/4-5.6 range.

Program Mode

Program mode (P) uses the 70D's built-in smarts to select the correct f/stop and shutter speed using a database of picture information that tells it which combination of shutter speed and aperture will work best for a particular photo. If the correct exposure cannot be achieved at the current ISO setting, the shutter speed or aperture indicator in the viewfinder will blink, indicating under- or overexposure. You can then boost or reduce the ISO to increase or decrease sensitivity.

The 70D's recommended exposure can be overridden if you want. Use the EV setting feature (described later, because it also applies to Tv and Av modes) to add or subtract exposure from the metered value. And, as I mentioned earlier in this chapter, you can change from the recommended setting to an equivalent setting (as shown in Table 4.1) that produces the same exposure, but using a different combination of f/stop and shutter speed. To accomplish this:

■ Press the shutter release halfway to lock in the current base exposure, or press the AE Lock button (*) on the back of the camera (in which case the * indicator will illuminate in the viewfinder to show that the exposure has been locked).

■ Spin the Main Dial to change the shutter speed (the 70D will adjust the f/stop to match).

Your adjustment remains in force for a single exposure; if you want to change from the recommended settings for the next exposure, you'll need to repeat those steps.

When to use Program mode priority:

■ **When you're in a hurry to get a grab shot.** The 70D will do a pretty good job of calculating an appropriate exposure for you, without any input from you.

■ **When you hand your camera to a novice.** Set the 70D to P, hand the camera to your friend, relative, or trustworthy stranger you meet in front of the Eiffel Tower, point to the shutter release button and viewfinder, and say, "Look through here, and press this button."

■ **When no special shutter speed or aperture settings are needed.** If your subject doesn't require special anti- or pro-blur techniques, and depth-of-field or selective focus aren't important, use P as a general-purpose setting. You can still make adjustments to increase/decrease depth-of-field or add/reduce motion blur with a minimum of fuss.

Manual Exposure

Part of being an experienced photographer comes from knowing when to rely on your 70D's automation (including Scene Intelligent Auto, Creative Auto, or P mode), when to go semi-automatic (with Tv or Av), and when to set exposure manually (using M). Some photographers actually prefer to set their exposure manually, as the 70D will be happy to provide an indication of when its metering system judges your settings provide the proper exposure, using the analog exposure scale at the bottom of the viewfinder and on the status LCD.

Manual exposure can come in handy in some situations. You might be taking a silhouette photo and find that none of the exposure modes or EV correction features give you exactly the effect you want. For example, when I shot the ballet dancer in Figure 4.18 in front of a mostly dark background highlighted by an illuminated curtain off to the right, there was no way any of my 70D's exposure modes would be able to interpret the scene the way I wanted to shoot it, even with Spot metering, which didn't have a narrow enough field-of-view from my position. So, I took a couple test exposures, and set the exposure manually using the exact shutter speed and f/stop I needed. You might be working in a studio environment using multiple flash units. The additional flash are triggered by slave devices (gadgets that set off the flash when they sense the light from another flash, or, perhaps from a radio or infrared remote control). Your camera's exposure meter doesn't compensate for the extra illumination, and can't interpret the flash exposure at all, so you need to set the aperture manually.

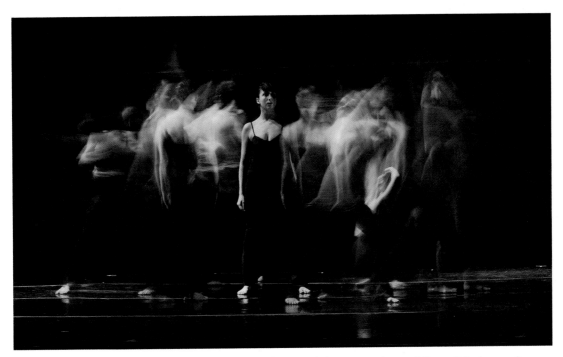

Figure 4.18 Manual exposure allows selecting both f/stop and shutter speed, especially useful when you're experimenting, as with this shot of ballet dancers.

Because, depending on your proclivities, you might not need to set exposure manually very often, you should still make sure you understand how it works. Fortunately, the 70D makes setting exposure manually very easy. Just set the Mode Dial to M, turn the Main Dial to set the shutter speed, and rotate the Quick Control Dial to adjust the aperture. Press the shutter release halfway or press the AE Lock button, and the exposure scale in the viewfinder shows you how far your chosen setting diverges from the metered exposure.

When to use Manual exposure:

- **When working in the studio.** If you're working in a studio environment, you generally have total control over the lighting and can set exposure exactly as you want. The last thing you need is for the 70D to interpret the scene and make adjustments of its own. Use M, and shutter speed, aperture, and (as long as you don't use ISO-Auto) the ISO setting are totally up to you.

- **When using non-dedicated flash.** External Canon dedicated flash units are cool, and can even be used to coordinate use of your 70D's internal flash. But if you're working with a non-compatible flash unit, particularly studio flash plugged into a PC/X sync adapter mounted on the hot shoe, the camera has no clue about the intensity of the flash, so you'll have to dial in the appropriate aperture manually.

- **If you're using a handheld light meter.** The appropriate aperture, both for flash exposures and shots taken under continuous lighting, can be determined by a handheld light meter, flash meter, or combo meter that measures both kinds of illumination. With an external meter, you can measure highlights, shadows, backgrounds, or additional subjects separately, and use Manual exposure to make your settings.

- **When you want to outsmart the metering system.** Your 70D's metering system is "trained" to react to unusual lighting situations, such as backlighting, extra bright illumination, or low-key images with murky shadows. In many cases, it can counter these "problems" and produce a well-exposed image. But what if you don't *want* a well-exposed image? Manual exposure allows you to produce silhouettes in backlit situations, wash out all the middle tones to produce a luminous look, or underexpose to create a moody or ominous dark-toned photograph.

Adjusting Exposure with ISO Settings

Another way of adjusting exposures is by changing the ISO sensitivity setting. Sometimes photographers forget about this option, because the common practice is to set the ISO once for a particular shooting session (say, at ISO 100 or 200 for bright sunlight outdoors, or ISO 800 when shooting indoors) and then forget about ISO. ISOs higher than ISO 100 or 200 are seen as "bad" or "necessary evils." However, changing the ISO is a valid way of adjusting exposure settings, particularly with the Canon EOS 70D, which produces good results at ISO settings that create grainy, unusable pictures with some other camera models.

Indeed, I find myself using ISO adjustment as a convenient alternate way of adding or subtracting EV when shooting in Manual mode, and as a quick way of choosing equivalent exposures when in Auto or semi-automatic modes. For example, I've selected a Manual exposure with both f/stop and shutter speed suitable for my image using, say, ISO 200. I can change the exposure in full-stop increments by pressing the ISO button on top of the camera, and spinning the Main Dial one click at a time. The difference in image quality/noise at the base setting of ISO 200 is negligible if I dial in ISO 100 to reduce exposure a little, or change to ISO 400 to increase exposure. I keep my preferred f/stop and shutter speed, but still adjust the exposure.

Or, perhaps, I am using Tv mode and the metered exposure at ISO 200 is 1/500th second at f/11. If I decide on the spur of the moment I'd rather use 1/500th second at f/8, I can press the ISO button and spin the Main Dial to switch to ISO 100. Of course, it's a good idea to monitor your ISO changes, so you don't end up at ISO 1600 accidentally. ISO settings can, of course, also be used to boost or reduce sensitivity in particular shooting situations. The 70D can use ISO settings from ISO 100 up to 12800. You can also activate ISO expansion in the Shooting 3 menu (as described in Chapter 8) to enable settings up to H (ISO 25600 equivalent).

The camera can adjust the ISO automatically as appropriate for various lighting conditions. In Basic Zone modes, ISO is normally set between ISO 100 and ISO 6400, except in Landscape scene mode, where only ISO 100-1600 is used, and Handheld Night Scene mode, which uses ISO 100-12800.

When using flash, Auto ISO produces a setting of ISO 400 automatically, except when overexposure would occur (as when shooting subjects very close to the camera), in which case a lower setting (down to ISO 100) will be used. If you have an external dedicated flash attached, the 70D can set ISO in the range of 400 to 1600 automatically when using Creative Auto, Portrait, Landscape, Close-Up, Sports, or P exposure modes. That capability can be useful when shooting outdoor field sports at night and other "long distance" flash pictures, particularly with a telephoto lens, because you want to extend the "reach" of your external flash as far as possible (to dozens of feet or more), and boosting the ISO does that. Remember that if the Auto ISO ranges aren't suitable for you, individual ISO values can also be selected in any of the Creative Zone modes.

Tip

Find yourself locked out of ISO settings lower than 200 or higher than 12800? You've probably set Highlight Tone Priority to Enable in the Shooting 4 menu, as described in Chapter 8.

Dealing with Visual Noise

Visual image noise is that random grainy effect that some like to use as a special effect, but which, most of the time, is objectionable because it robs your image of detail even as it adds that "interesting" texture. Noise is caused by two different phenomena: high ISO settings and long exposures.

High ISO noise commonly first appears when you raise your camera's sensitivity setting above ISO 800. With Canon cameras, which are renown for their good ISO noise characteristics, noise may become visible at ISO 1600, and is usually fairly noticeable at ISO 3200. At the H setting (ISO 25600 equivalent), noise is usually quite bothersome, which is why that lofty sensitivity rating is disabled by default and must be activated using an option in the ISO Speed Settings entry of the Shooting 3 menu (discussed in Chapter 8). This kind of noise appears as a result of the amplification needed to increase the sensitivity of the sensor. While higher ISOs do pull details out of dark areas, they also amplify non-signal information randomly, creating noise.

A similar noisy phenomenon occurs during long time exposures, which allow more photons to reach the sensor, increasing your ability to capture a picture under low-light conditions. However, the longer exposures also increase the likelihood that some pixels will register random phantom photons, often because the longer an imager is "hot," the warmer it gets, and that heat can be mistaken for photons. There's also a special kind of noise that CMOS sensors like the one used in the 70D are potentially susceptible to. With a CCD, the entire signal is conveyed off the chip and funneled through a single amplifier and analog-to-digital conversion circuit. Any noise introduced there is, at least, consistent. CMOS imagers, on the other hand, contain millions of individual amplifiers and A/D converters, all working in unison. Because all these circuits don't necessarily process in precisely the same way all the time, they can introduce something called fixed-pattern noise into the image data.

Fortunately, Canon's electronics geniuses have done an exceptional job minimizing noise from all causes in the 70D. Even so, you might still want to apply the optional long exposure noise reduction. This type of noise reduction involves the 70D taking a second, blank exposure, and comparing the random pixels in that image with the photograph you just took. Pixels that coincide in the two represent noise and can safely be suppressed. This noise reduction system, called *dark frame subtraction,* effectively doubles the amount of time required to take a picture, and is used only for exposures longer than one second. Noise reduction can reduce the amount of detail in your picture, as some image information may be removed along with the noise. So, you might want to use this feature with moderation. Some types of images don't require noise reduction, because the grainy pattern tends to blend into the overall scene.

To activate your 70D's long exposure noise reduction features, go to the Shooting 4 menu, as explained further in Chapter 8.

You can also apply noise reduction to a lesser extent using Photoshop, and when converting RAW files to some other format, using your favorite RAW converter, or an industrial-strength product like Noise Ninja (www.picturecode.com) to wipe out noise after you've already taken the picture.

Making EV Changes

Sometimes you'll want more or less exposure than indicated by the 70D's metering system. Perhaps you want to underexpose to create a silhouette effect, or overexpose to produce a high-key look. It's easy to use the 70D's Exposure Compensation system to override the exposure recommendations, available in any Creative Zone mode except Manual. There are two ways to make exposure value (EV) changes with the 70D. One method is fast, but limited to display plus/minus three stops of compensation. The second method is slower, but allows setting up to 5 stops of compensation in either 1/3 or full stop increments.

Fast EV Changes

Activate the exposure meters by tapping the shutter release button. Then, rotate the QCD while looking through the viewfinder or at the back panel LCD monitor. Spin to the right to make the image brighter (add exposure), and to the left to make the image darker (subtract exposure). The exposure scale in the viewfinder and on the LCD indicates the EV change you've made. The EV change you've made remains for the exposures that follow, until you manually zero out the EV setting with the AV button + Main Dial. EV changes are ignored when using M or any of the Basic Zone modes. (If you're unable to make an adjustment, you may have set the Lock switch to the locked position. Rotate it downward to reactivate the Quick Control Dial.)

Slower EV Changes

You can also use the second method for making EV changes with the 70D. It can be a little slower, but allows you to set up to plus/minus five stops of adjustment. You also have the option of setting exposure bracketing at the same time:

1. Press the MENU button and navigate to the Expo. Comp./AEB entry on the Shooting 3 menu.

2. When the screen appears, use the touch screen, rotate the Quick Control Dial, or press the left/right multi-controller buttons to add or subtract EV adjustment. The screen has helpful labels (Darker on the left and Brighter on the right) to make sure you're adding/subtracting when you really want to. (See Figure 4.19.) Note that you can also set exposure bracketing, as discussed in Chapter 8, by rotating the Main Dial while viewing this screen. (See Figure 4.20.)

3. Choose SET to confirm your choice.

Figure 4.19
EV changes are displayed on the scale in the LCD when using the Shooting 3 menu.

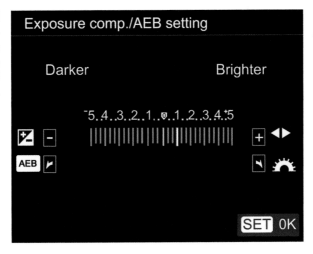

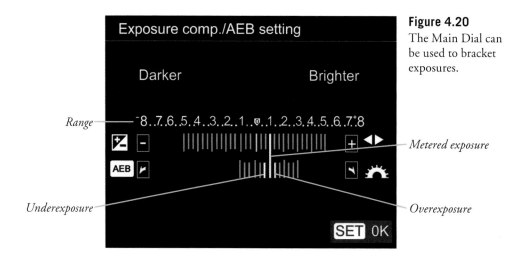

Figure 4.20
The Main Dial can be used to bracket exposures.

Bracketing Parameters

Bracketing is a method for shooting several consecutive exposures using different settings, as a way of improving the odds that one will be exactly right. Before digital cameras took over the universe, it was common to bracket exposures, shooting, say, a series of three photos at 1/125th second, but varying the f/stop from f/8 to f/11 to f/16. In practice, smaller than whole-stop increments were used for greater precision. Plus, it was just as common to keep the same aperture and vary the shutter speed, although in the days before electronic shutters, film cameras often had only whole increment shutter speeds available. Figure 4.21 shows a typical bracketed series.

Today, cameras like the 70D can bracket exposures much more precisely, and bracket white balance as well (using the WB Shift/Bkt entry found in the Shooting 3 menu and described in Chapter 8). While WB bracketing is sometimes used when getting color absolutely correct in the camera is important, autoexposure bracketing (AEB) is used much more often. When this feature is activated,

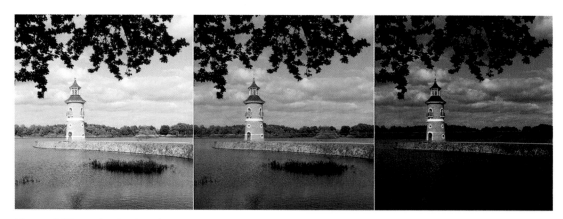

Figure 4.21 In this bracketed series you can see overexposure (left), metered exposure (center), and underexposure (right).

the 70D takes three (and only three) consecutive photos: one at the metered "correct" exposure, one with less exposure, and one with more exposure, using an increment of your choice up to plus 2/minus 2 stops. (Choose between increments by setting Custom Function I-01 to 0 [1/3 stop] or 1 [1/2 stop].) In Av mode, the shutter speed will change, while in Tv mode, the aperture speed will change.

Bracketing Auto Cancel

The final relevant entry in the Custom Function I: Exposure menu is 03: Bracketing Auto Cancel. When you activate bracketing (in the Shooting 3 menu, described shortly), the 70D continues to shoot bracketed exposures until you manually turn the bracket feature off, assuming you have this setting disabled. That's a good thing. If you're out shooting a series of bracketed exposures (especially for HDR), it's convenient to have your bracket setting be "sticky" and still be active even if you turn your camera off. Some shooters like to bracket virtually *everything* and like to leave bracketing on routinely.

However, much of the time you'll want to turn bracketing off, and may not want to visit the Shooting 3 menu to deactivate it manually. Set Bracketing Auto Cancel to On, and bracketing is cancelled when you turn the 70D off, change lenses, use the flash, or change memory cards. When this setting is set to Off, bracketing remains in effect until you manually turn it off *or use the flash*. The flash still cancels bracketing, but your settings are retained.

Bracketing Sequence

Also in the Custom Function I: Exposure menu, you'll find a 04: Bracketing Sequence entry, which allows you to specify the order in which the autoexposure bracketing series are exposed. Your choice will depend both on personal preference, and what you intend to do with the bracketed shots. The options include:

- **0 - + :** The exposure sequence is standard exposure, decreased exposure, increased exposure. With this default value, your base exposure will be captured and saved first on your memory card, followed by the progressively reduced exposure images, then the shots with increased exposure. You might prefer this order if you expect your standard exposure will be the preferred image and arranged first in the queue of each bracket set, and want the alternate exposures to follow.

- **- 0 +:** The sequence is decreased exposure, standard exposure, increased exposure. This order is the most logical to use if you're shooting with the intention to combine images using HDR (high dynamic range) techniques in your image editor or HDR utility. The final bracketed array is stored on your memory card starting with the most underexposed shot, and progressing to the best exposed, and then on to the overexposures. That makes it easy to use all of your bracketed shots in the HDR sequence, or to select only some of them to combine.

- **+ 0 -:** This sequence is the inverse of the last one, progressing from increased exposure to standard exposure and decreased exposure. You might prefer this order if you expect to see your best exposures on the plus side of the exposure sequence, and want them to be displayed first.

Number of Exposures

In the Custom Function I: Exposure menu, under the 05: Number of Bracketed Shots entry, you can elect to bracket 2, 3, 5, or 7 shots:

- **2 shots.** The 70D will capture one image at the *base* or standard exposure (which can be the metered exposure, or one that's more or less than the metered exposure, as I'll explain shortly). It then takes one additional shot that provides either *more* or *less* exposure relative to that "base" image. Rotate the QCD to the right to specify more exposure for the second shot, or to the left to specify less exposure. The *amount* of additional/less exposure is determined by the increment you select. (Read on! I'll tie all the parameters together in an upcoming section.)

- **3, 5, 7 shots.** The camera captures one image at the base exposure, and then two, four, or six shots bracketed around that exposure, respectively. That translates to one over/one under at the 3-shot setting, two over/two under at the 5-shot setting, and three over/three under when using the 7-shot option.

Increment Between Exposures

You can choose the size of the jump between each of the bracketed exposures. To do that, you'll need to visit the Expo. Comp/AEB entry in the Shooting 3 menu. There, you can select from plus/minus 1/3 to 3 full stops in 1/3 stop increments, by rotating the Main Dial. The next section provides instructions for producing a bracketed set.

Using AEB is trickier than it needs to be, but has been made more flexible than with some earlier models. With the 70D you can now choose to bracket only overexposures or underexposures—a very useful improvement! Just follow these steps:

1. **Activate the Expo. Comp./AEB screen.** Press the MENU button and navigate to the Shooting 3 menu, where you'll find the Expo. Comp./AEB option. Choose SET to select this choice.

2. **Set the bracket range.** Rotate the Main Dial to spread out or contract the three bars to include the desired range you want to cover. For example, in Figure 4.22 (top), the red highlighted bars are separated from the center bar by a full f/stop, so the bracketing will produce one image at one stop *less* than the zero point (the large center bar), one at the zero point, and one at one stop more than that. Figure 4.22 (bottom) shows the bars more widely separated, for a bracketed set two stops under and two stops over the midpoint.

3. **Adjust zero point.** By default, the bracketing is zeroed around the center of the scale, which represents the correct exposure as metered by the 70D. But you might want to have your three bracketed shots all biased toward overexposure or underexposure. Perhaps you feel that the metered exposure will be too dark or too light, and you want the bracketed shots to lean in the other direction. Rotate the QCD or use the left/right multi-controller buttons to move the bracket spread toward one end of the scale or the other. Figure 4.22 (top) shows the bracketing biased toward overexposure, while in 4.22 (bottom), the zero point is clustered around underexposure. (Actually, the exposure bar at left will be four stops under the metered exposure, the center bar two stops under, and the right bar at the metered value.)

Figure 4.22

Use the left/right multi-controller buttons to bias the bracketing toward more or less exposure, and the Main Dial to set the bracket range.

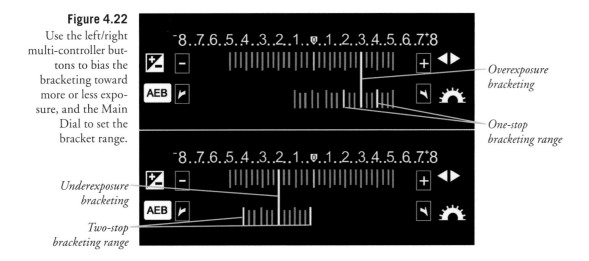

Overexposure bracketing

One-stop bracketing range

Underexposure bracketing

Two-stop bracketing range

NON-BRACKETING IS EXPOSURE COMPENSATION

When the three bracket indicators aren't separated, using the left/right multi-controller buttons simply, in effect, adds or subtracts exposure compensation. You'll be shooting a "bracketed" set of one picture, with the zero point placed at the portion of the scale you indicated. Until you rotate the Main Dial to separate the three bracket indicators by at least one indicator, this screen just supplies EV adjustment. Also keep in mind that the increments shown will be either 1/3 stop or 1/2 stop, depending on how you've set C.Fn I-01.

4. **Confirm your choice.** Choose SET to enter the settings.

5. **Take your three photos.** You can use Single shooting mode to take the trio of pictures yourself, use the self-timer (which will expose all three pictures after the delay), or switch to Continuous shooting mode to take the three pictures in a burst.

6. **Monitor your shots.** As the images are captured, three indicators will appear on the exposure scale in the viewfinder, with one of them flashing for each bracketed photo, showing when the base exposure, underexposure, and overexposure are taken.

7. **Turn bracketing off when done.** Bracketing remains in effect when the set is taken so you can continue shooting bracketed exposures until you use the electronic flash, turn off the camera, or return to the menu to cancel bracketing.

NOTE

AEB is disabled when you're using Multi Shot Noise Reduction, taking long time exposures with the Bulb setting, or have enabled the Auto Lighting Optimizer in the Shooting 3 menu (in which case the optimizer will probably override and nullify bracketing).

Working with HDR

High dynamic range (HDR) photography is quite the rage these days, and entire books have been written on the subject. It's not really a new technique—film photographers have been combining multiple exposures for ages to produce a single image of, say, an interior room while maintaining detail in the scene visible through the windows.

Suppose you wanted to photograph a dimly lit room that had a bright window showing an outdoors scene. Proper exposure for the room might be on the order of 1/60th second at f/2.8 at ISO 200, while the outdoors scene probably would require f/11 at 1/400th second. That's almost a 7 EV step difference (approximately 7 f/stops) and well beyond the dynamic range of any digital camera, including the Canon 70D.

Until camera sensors gain much higher dynamic ranges (which may not be as far into the distant future as we think), special tricks like Active D-Lighting and HDR photography will remain basic tools. With the Canon 70D, you can create in-camera HDR exposures, or shoot HDR the old-fashioned way—with separate bracketed exposures that are later combined in a tool like Photomatix or Adobe's Merge to HDR Pro image editing feature. I'm going to show you how to use both.

Using HDR Mode

Here are some tips for using this built-in feature:

- **Use a tripod if possible.** Because there may be some camera movement between the continuous shots, you'll get better results if you mount the 6D on a tripod.

- **Moving objects may produce ghosts.** In this case, there may be some *subject* motion between shots, producing "ghost" effects.

- **Misalignment.** If you *don't* use a tripod, when Auto Image Align is activated, this mode does a good job of realigning your multiple images when they are merged. However, it can't do a perfect job, particularly with repetitive patterns that are difficult for the camera's "brains" to sort out. Some misalignment is possible.

- **Shutter speeds vary.** The camera brackets by adjusting the shutter speed within the increment range selected, *even if you're using Tv or M modes and have specified a shutter speed.*

- **Unwanted cropping.** Because the processor needs to be able to shift each individual image slightly in any (or all) of four directions in Auto Align mode (described next), it needs to crop the image slightly to trim out any non-image areas that result. Your final image will be slightly smaller than one shot in other modes.

- **Weird colors.** Some types of lighting, including fluorescent and LED illumination, "cycle" many times a second, and colors can vary between shots. You may not even notice this when single shooting, but it becomes more obvious when using any continuous shooting mode, including HDR mode. The combined images may have strange color effects.

- **Can't use any RAW mode, or ISOs higher than 25600.** Your image will be recorded as a Large JPEG only, and HDR is disabled when you're using ISO expansion to enable sensitivity settings higher than 25600. While you can use HDR mode if Auto Lighting Optimizer has been enabled, the camera will disable it while shooting your HDR images, then re-enable it when you turn HDR mode off.

- **The process takes time.** Forget about firing off a large number of HDR shots in a row. After the 6D captures its three images, it takes a few seconds to process them and save your final image. Be patient.

Access HDR mode from the Shooting 4 menu, and you'll be taken to a menu with three entries:

- **Adjust Dynamic Range.** There are five choices in this entry. Select Disable HDR to turn HDR completely off. The others select the number of stops of dynamic range improvement the HDR feature will provide. Choose Auto to allow the 6D to examine your scene and select an appropriate EV range. As you gain experience you might want to select the range yourself, in order to achieve a particular look. You can choose plus/minus 1, 2, or 3 EV.

- **Continuous HDR.** Choose 1 Shot Only if you plan to take just a single HDR exposure and want the feature disabled automatically thereafter, or Every Shot to continue using HDR mode for all subsequent exposures until you turn it off.

- **Auto Image Align.** HDR images are ideally produced with the camera on a tripod, in order to reduce the ghosting effects from a series of pictures that each aren't perfectly aligned with the other. You can choose Enable to have the camera attempt to align all three HDR exposures, or select Disable when using a tripod. The success of the automatic alignment will vary, depending on the shutter speed used (higher is better), and the amount of camera movement (less is better!).

HDR Backlight Control

The 70D's in-camera HDR feature, available as a Special Scene option when the Mode Dial is in the SCN position, is simple, not particularly flexible, but still surprisingly effective in creating high dynamic range images. It's also remarkably easy to use. Although it combines only three images to create a single HDR photograph, and while it's not as good as the manual HDR method I'll describe in the section after this one, it's a *lot* faster.

Figure 4.23 (left) shows you a typical situation in which you might want to use this setting. When the exposure is set for the interior of the cathedral, the beautiful backlit stained glass windows are washed out and have no detail. When the exposure is adjusted to produce detail in the glass panes, the rest of the cathedral goes dark. The quickie solution is to use the 70D's HDR Backlight Control. It captures three consecutive images and then merges them to preserve both highlight and shadow detail, as you can see in Figure 4.24, which has a much fuller range of tones.

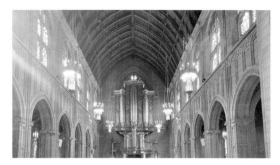
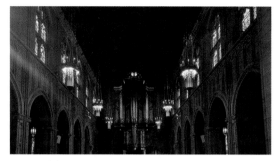

Figure 4.23 Exposing for the cathedral interior produces overexposed backlit stained glass windows (left), while exposing for the windows captures a murky cathedral interior.

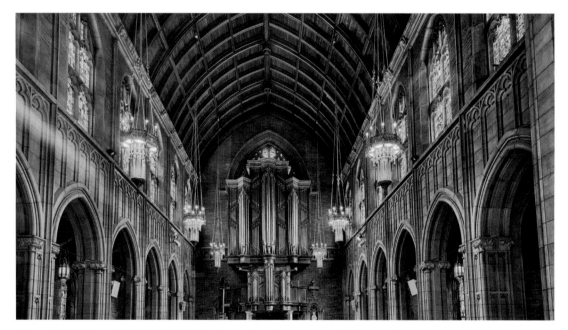

Figure 4.24 The 70D's HDR Backlight Control mode captures a full range of tones.

Here are some tips for using this feature (these also apply to the Handheld Night Scene mode, which also merges multiple shots to create a single improved image):

- **Use a tripod if possible.** Because there may be some camera movement between the continuous shots, you'll get better results if you mount the 70D on a tripod.

- **Moving objects may produce ghosts.** In this case, there may be some *subject* motion between shots, producing "ghost" effects.

- **Misalignment.** If you *don't* use a tripod, this scene mode does a good job of realigning your multiple images when they are merged. However, it can't do a perfect job, particularly with repetitive patterns that are difficult for the camera's "brains" to sort out. Some misalignment is possible.

- **Unwanted cropping.** Because the processor needs to be able to shift each individual image slightly in any (or all) of four directions, it needs to crop the image slightly to trim out any non-image areas that result. Your final image will be slightly smaller than one shot in other modes.
- **Can't use RAW or RAW+L.** Your image will be recorded as a Large JPEG only.
- **The process takes time.** Forget about firing off a large number of HDR Backlight Control shots in a row. After the 70D captures its three images, it takes a few seconds to process them and save your final image. Be patient.

Bracketing and Merge to HDR

As I mentioned, HDR photography involves shooting two or three or more images at different bracketed exposures, giving you an "underexposed" version with lots of detail in highlights that would otherwise be washed out; an "overexposed" rendition that preserves detail in the shadows; and several intermediate shots. These are combined to produce a single image that has an amazing amount of detail throughout the scene's entire tonal range.

I call this technique a fad because the reason it exists in the first place is due to a (temporary, I hope) defect in current digital camera sensors. It's presently impossible to capture the full range of brightness that we perceive; digital cameras, including the EOS 70D, can't even grab the full range of brightness that *film* can see, as I showed you in Figures 4.2 and 4.3 at the beginning of this chapter.

But as the megapixel race slows down, sensor designers have already begun designing capture electronics that have larger density (dynamic) ranges, and cameras like the 70D with its HDR Backlight Control feature, will eventually produce images similar to what we're getting now with HDR manipulation in image editors.

When you're using Merge to HDR Pro, a feature found in Adobe Photoshop (similar functions are available in other programs, including the Mac/PC utility Photomatix [www.hdrsoft.com; free to try, $99 to buy]), you'd take several pictures. As I mentioned earlier, one would be exposed for the shadows, one for the highlights, and perhaps one for the midtones. Then, you'd use the Merge to HDR command (or the equivalent in other software) to combine all of the images into one HDR image that integrates the well-exposed sections of each version. You can use the EOS 70D's bracketing feature to produce those images.

The next steps show you how to combine the separate exposures into one merged high dynamic range image. The sample images in Figure 4.25 show the results you can get from a four-shot (manually) bracketed sequence.

The images should be as identical as possible, except for exposure. So, it's a good idea to mount the 70D on a tripod, use a remote release, and take all the exposures at once.

Just follow these steps:

1. **Set up the camera.** Mount the 70D on a tripod.

2. **Choose an f/stop.** Set the camera for Manual exposure and select an aperture that will provide a correct exposure at your initial settings for the series of manually bracketed shots. *And then leave this adjustment alone!* You don't want the aperture to change for your series, as that would change the depth-of-field. You want the 70D to adjust exposure *only* using the shutter speed.

3. **Choose manual focus.** You don't want the focus to change between shots, so set the 70D to manual focus, and carefully focus your shot.

4. **Choose RAW exposures.** Set the camera to take RAW files, which will give you the widest range of tones in your images.

5. **Take your bracketed set.** Press the button on the remote (or carefully press the shutter release or use the self-timer) and take the set of bracketed exposures, adjusting the shutter speed manually. Try spacing your four shots one f/stop apart.

6. **Continue with the Merge to HDR Pro steps listed next.** You can also use a different program, such as Photomatix, if you know how to use it.

The next steps show you how to combine the separate exposures into one merged high dynamic range image.

1. **Copy your images to your computer.** If you use an application to transfer the files to your computer, make sure it does not make any adjustments to brightness, contrast, or exposure. You want the real raw information for Merge to HDR Pro to work with.

2. **Activate Merge to HDR Pro.** Choose File > Automate > Merge to HDR Pro.

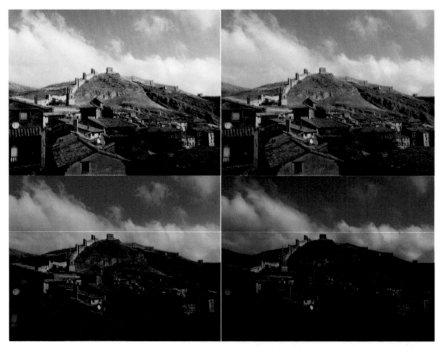

Figure 4.25
Four bracketed photos should look like this.

3. **Select the photos to be merged.** Use the Browse feature to locate and select your photos to be merged. You'll note a checkbox that can be used to automatically align the images if they were not taken with the camera mounted on a rock-steady support. This will adjust for any slight movement of the camera that might have occurred when you changed exposure settings.

4. **Choose parameters (optional).** The first time you use Merge to HDR Pro, you can let the program work with its default parameters. Once you've played with the feature a few times, you can read the Adobe help files and learn more about the options than I can present in this non-software-oriented camera guide.

5. **Click OK.** The merger begins.

6. **Save.** Once HDR merge has done its thing, save the file to your computer.

If you do everything correctly, you'll end up with a photo like the one shown in Figure 4.26.

What if you don't have the opportunity, inclination, or skills to create several images at different exposures, as described? If you shoot in RAW format, you can still use Merge to HDR, working with a *single* original image file. What you do is import the image into Photoshop several times, using Adobe Camera Raw to create multiple copies of the file at different exposure levels.

For example, you'd create one copy that's too dark, so the shadows lose detail, but the highlights are preserved. Create another copy with the shadows intact and allow the highlights to wash out. Then, you can use Merge to HDR to combine the two and end up with a finished image that has the extended dynamic range you're looking for. (This concludes the image-editing portion of the chapter. We now return you to our alternate sponsor: photography.)

Figure 4.26
You'll end up with an extended dynamic range photo like this one.

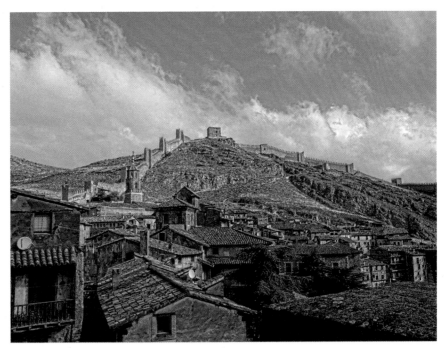

Fixing Exposures with Histograms

Your 70D's histograms are a simplified display of the numbers of pixels at each of 256 brightness levels, producing an interesting mountain range effect. Although separate charts may be provided for brightness and the red, green, and blue channels, when you first start using histograms, you'll want to concentrate on the brightness histogram.

Each vertical line in the graph represents the number of pixels in the image for each brightness value, from 0 (black) on the left to 255 (white) on the right. The vertical axis measures that number of pixels at each level. The 70D provides a "live" histogram on the screen when using Live View mode, and offers two different histogram views in Playback mode when using the shooting information display (Figure 4.27, left) and histogram display (Figure 4.28, right). The former shows a simple brightness/luminance histogram, while the histogram display allows you to see brightness as well as separate red, green, and blue channel histograms.

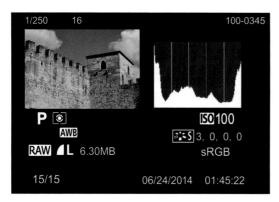
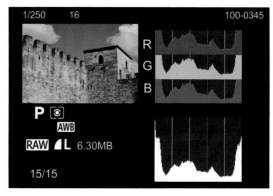

Figure 4.27   **Figure 4.28**

Shooting information display, with luminance histogram (left); Histogram display with luminance, red, green, and blue histograms (right).

Histograms and Contrast

Although histograms are most often used to fine-tune exposure, you can glean other information from them, such as the relative contrast of the image. Figure 4.29 shows a histogram representing an image having normal contrast. In such an image, most of the pixels are spread across the image, with a healthy distribution of tones throughout the midtone section of the graph. That large peak at the right side of the graph represents all those light tones in the sky. A normal-contrast image you shoot may have less sky area, and less of a peak at the right side, but notice that very few pixels hug the right edge of the histogram, indicating that the lightest tones are not being clipped because they are off the chart.

With a lower-contrast image, like the one shown in Figure 4.30, the basic shape of the previous histogram will remain recognizable, but gradually will be compressed together to cover a smaller area of the gray spectrum. The squished shape of the histogram is caused by all the grays in the original image being represented by a limited number of gray tones in a smaller range of the scale.

Instead of the darkest tones of the image reaching into the black end of the spectrum and the whitest tones extending to the lightest end, there is a small gap at either end. Consequently, the blackest areas of the scene are now represented by a light gray, and the whites by a somewhat lighter gray. The overall contrast of the image is reduced. Because all the darker tones are actually a middle gray or lighter, the scene in this version of the photo appears lighter as well.

Going in the other direction, increasing the contrast of an image produces a histogram like the one shown in Figure 4.31. In this case, the tonal range is now spread over the entire width of the chart, but, except for the bright sky (which you can see peaks at right), there is not much variation in the

Figure 4.29
This image has fairly normal contrast, even though there is a peak of light tones at the right side representing the sky.

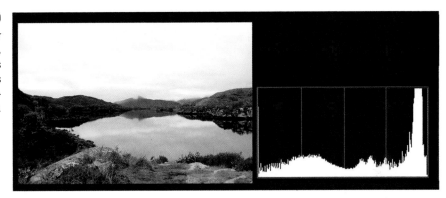

Figure 4.30
This low-contrast image has all the tones squished into one section of the grayscale.

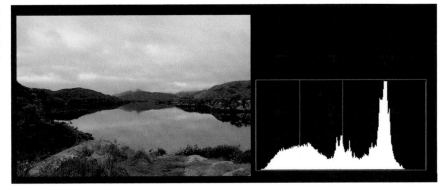

Figure 4.31
A high-contrast image produces a histogram in which the tones are spread out.

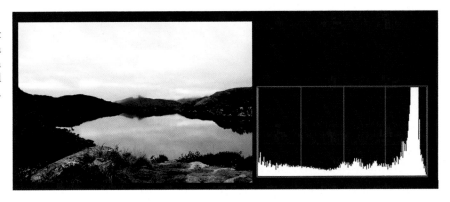

middle tones; the mountain "peaks" are not very high. When you stretch the grayscale in both directions like this, the darkest tones become darker (that may not be possible) and the lightest tones become lighter (ditto). In fact, shades that might have been gray before can change to black or white as they are moved toward either end of the scale.

The effect of increasing contrast may be to move some tones off either end of the scale altogether, while spreading the remaining grays over a smaller number of locations on the spectrum. That's exactly the case in the example shown. The number of possible tones is smaller and the image appears harsher.

Understanding Histograms

The important thing to remember when working with the histogram display in your 70D is that changing the exposure does *not* change the contrast of an image. The curves illustrated in the previous three examples remain exactly the same shape when you increase or decrease exposure. I repeat: The proportional distribution of grays shown in the histogram doesn't change when exposure changes; it is neither stretched nor compressed. However, the tones as a whole are moved toward one end of the scale or the other, depending on whether you're increasing or decreasing exposure. You'll be able to see that in some illustrations that follow.

So, as you reduce exposure, tones gradually move to the black end (and off the scale), while the reverse is true when you increase exposure. The contrast within the image is changed only to the extent that some of the tones can no longer be represented when they are moved off the scale.

To change the *contrast* of an image, you must do one of three things:

- **Change the 70D's contrast setting** using the menu system. You'll find these adjustments in your camera's Picture Styles, as explained in Chapter 8.

- **Use your camera's tone "booster."** The Highlight Tone Priority and Auto Lighting Optimizer features, described in Chapter 8, can also adjust contrast.

- **Alter the contrast of the scene itself,** for example by using a fill light or reflectors to add illumination to shadows that are too dark.

- **Attempt to adjust contrast in post-processing** using your image editor or RAW file converter. You may use features such as Levels or Curves (in Photoshop, Photoshop Elements, and many other image editors), or work with HDR software to cherry-pick the best values in shadows and highlights from multiple images.

Of the four of these, the third—changing the contrast of the scene—is the most desirable, because attempting to fix contrast by fiddling with the tonal values is unlikely to be a perfect remedy. However, adding a little contrast can be successful because you can discard some tones to make the image more contrasty. However, the opposite is much more difficult. An overly contrasty image rarely can be fixed, because you can't add information that isn't there in the first place.

What you *can* do is adjust the exposure so that the tones *that are already present in the scene* are captured correctly. Figure 4.32 shows the histogram for an image that is badly underexposed. You can guess from the shape of the histogram that many of the dark tones to the left of the graph have been clipped off. There's plenty of room on the right side for additional pixels to reside without having them become overexposed. So, you can increase the exposure (either by changing the f/stop or shutter speed, or by adding an EV value) to produce the corrected histogram shown in Figure 4.33.

Conversely, if your histogram looks like the one shown in Figure 4.34, with bright tones pushed off the right edge of the chart, you have an overexposed image, and you can correct it by reducing exposure. In addition to the histogram, the 70D has its Highlights feature, which shows areas that

Figure 4.32
A histogram of an underexposed image may look like this.

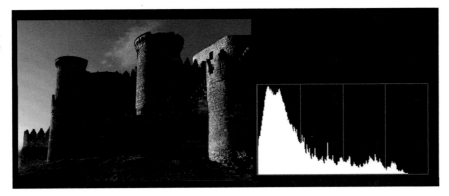

Figure 4.33
Adding exposure will produce a histogram like this one.

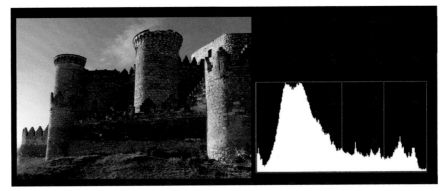

Figure 4.34
A histogram of an overexposed image will show clipping at the right side.

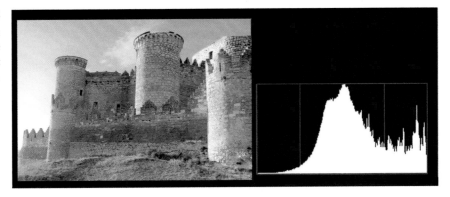

are overexposed with flashing tones (often called "blinkies") in the review screen. Depending on the importance of this "clipped" detail, you can adjust exposure or leave it alone. For example, if all the dark-coded areas in the review are in a background that you care little about, you can forget about them and not change the exposure, but if such areas appear in facial details of your subject, you may want to make some adjustments.

In working with histograms, your goal should be to have all the tones in an image spread out between the edges, with none clipped off at the left and right sides. Underexposing (to preserve highlights) should be done only as a last resort, because retrieving the underexposed shadows in your image editor will frequently increase the noise, even if you're working with RAW files. A better course of action is to expose for the highlights, but, when the subject matter makes it practical, fill in the shadows with additional light, using reflectors, fill flash, or other techniques rather than allowing them to be seriously underexposed.

The more you work with histograms, the more useful they become. One of the first things that histogram veterans notice is that it's possible to overexpose one channel even if the overall exposure appears to be correct. For example, flower photographers soon discover that it's really, really difficult to get a good picture of a rose. The exposure and luminance histogram may look okay—but there's no detail in the rose's petals. Looking at the RGB histograms can show why: the red channel is probably blown out. If you look at the red histogram, you'll probably see a peak at the right edge that indicates that highlight information has been lost. In fact, the green channel may be blown, too, and so the green parts of the flower also lack detail. Only the blue channel's histogram would typically be entirely contained within the boundaries of the chart, and, on first glance, the white luminance histogram at top of the column of graphs seems fairly normal.

Any of the primary channels, red, green, or blue, can blow out all by themselves, although bright reds seem to be the most common problem area. More difficult to diagnose are overexposed tones in one of the "in-between" hues on the color wheel. Overexposed yellows (which are very common) will be shown by blowouts in *both* the red and green channels. Too-bright cyans will manifest as excessive blue and green highlights, while overexposure in the red and blue channels reduces detail in magenta colors. As you gain experience, you'll be able to see exactly how anomalies in the RGB channels translate into poor highlights and murky shadows.

The only way to correct for color channel blowouts is to reduce exposure. As I mentioned earlier, you might want to consider filling in the shadows with additional light to keep them from becoming too dark when you decrease exposure. In practice, you'll want to monitor the red channel most closely, followed by the blue channel, and slightly decrease exposure to see if that helps. Because of the way our eyes perceive color, we are more sensitive to variations in green, so green channel blowouts are less of a problem, unless your main subject is heavily colored in that hue. If you plan on photographing a frog hopping around on your front lawn, you'll want to be extra careful to preserve detail in the green channel, using bracketing or other exposure techniques outlined in this chapter.

While you can often recover poorly exposed photos in your image editor, your best bet is to arrive at the correct exposure in the camera, minimizing the tweaks that you have to make in post-processing.

Basic Zone Modes

The final factor in the exposure equation is one that your 70D offers little control over: Basic Zone modes. Your Canon 70D includes Basic Zone shooting modes that can automatically make all the basic settings needed for certain types of shooting situations, such as Portraits, Landscapes, Close-ups, Sports, Night Portraits, and "No-Flash zone" pictures. They are especially useful when you suddenly encounter a picture-taking opportunity and don't have time to decide exactly which Creative Zone mode you want to use. Instead, you can spin the Mode Dial to the appropriate Basic Zone mode and fire away, knowing that, at least, you have a fighting chance of getting a good or usable photo.

Basic Zone modes are also helpful when you're just learning to use your 70D. Once you've learned how to operate your camera, you'll probably prefer one of the Creative Zone modes that provide more control over shooting options. The Basic Zone scene modes may give you few options or none at all. The AF mode, drive mode, and metering mode are all set for you. Here are the modes available directly from the Mode Dial:

- **Scene Intelligent Auto.** All the photographer has to do in this mode is press the shutter release button. Every other decision is made by the camera's electronics.
- **Flash Off.** Absolutely prevents the flash from flipping up and firing, which you might want in some situations, such as religious ceremonies, museums, classical music concerts, and your double-naught spy activities.
- **Creative Auto.** Similar to Scene Intelligent Auto, Creative Auto, like the scene modes described next, allows you to change some parameters.
- **Portrait.** This mode tends to use wider f/stops and faster shutter speeds, providing blurred backgrounds and images with no camera shake. If you hold down the shutter release, the 70D will take a continuous sequence of photos, which can be useful in capturing fleeting expressions in portrait situations.
- **Landscape.** The 70D tries to use smaller f/stops for more depth-of-field, and boosts saturation slightly for richer colors.
- **Close-Up.** This mode is similar to the Portrait setting, with wider f/stops to isolate your close-up subjects, and high shutter speeds to eliminate the camera shake that's accentuated at close focusing distances. However, if you have your camera mounted on a tripod or are using an image-stabilized (IS) lens, you might want to use the Creative Zone Aperture-priority (Av) mode instead, so you can specify a smaller f/stop with additional depth-of-field.

- **Sports.** In this mode, the 70D tries to use high shutter speeds to freeze action, switches to continuous shooting to allow taking a quick sequence of pictures with one press of the shutter release, and uses AI Servo AF to continually refocus as your subject moves around in the frame. You can find more information on autofocus options in Chapter 5.

With the Mode Dial in the SCN position, you can also choose:

- **Night Portrait.** Combines flash with ambient light to produce an image that is mainly illuminated by the flash, but the background is exposed by the available light. This mode uses longer exposures, so a tripod, monopod, or IS lens is a must.
- **Handheld Night Scene.** This mode, like HDR Backlight Control, takes multiple shots and combines them into one improved image.
- **HDR Backlight Control.** This mode combines three shots to improve both highlight and shadow detail, as described earlier in this chapter.

That Quick Control Screen Again

I've previously described how to use the Quick Control screen when working with Creative Zone modes, to change many settings, such as ISO, shutter speed, aperture, and other parameters. When using Basic Zone modes, your options are different. In each case, you can activate the Quick Control screen by pressing the Quick Control button. Then, one of several different screens will appear on your LCD.

Scene Intelligent Auto/ Auto (No Flash)

In either of these modes, your only choices are Single shooting and Self-timer/10-second remote control. Press the INFO. button to exit.

Creative Auto Mode

When the Mode Dial is set to Creative Auto, a screen like the one shown in Figure 4.35 appears. You can then do one of three things:

- **Change shooting parameters by Ambience.** Press the Quick Control button and then the up multi-controller button to select the ambience box. When the top box on the screen is highlighted, it will display the most recent "ambience" setting you've selected (Standard, unless you've made a change). Ambience is a type of picture style that adjusts parameters like sharpness or color richness to produce a particular look.
    - Press the left/right multi-controller buttons or rotate the Main Dial and select from among: Vivid, Soft, Warm, Intense, Cool, Brighter, Darker, or Monochrome.
    - Once you've selected your ambience, if you want to change its intensity, press the down cross key to highlight Effect.
    - You can then rotate the Main Dial to change the Effect to Low, Standard, or Strong. Press the Quick Control button to exit.

Figure 4.35
Quick Control
screen in Creative
Auto mode.

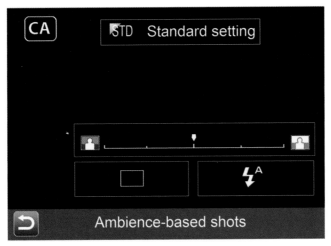

- **Press the multi-controller down button to highlight Background: Blurredfl> Sharp.** Then, rotate the Main Dial to adjust the amount of background blurring. The 70D will try to use a larger f/stop to reduce depth-of-field and blur the background, or a smaller f/stop and increased depth-of-field to sharpen the background.

- **Press the multi-controller down button to highlight Drive mode/Flash firing.** Then press the SET button to pop up the Drive mode/Flash firing screen. In this screen, you can rotate the Main Dial to change among the various drive modes, or use the multi-controller buttons to switch among flash modes.

Other Basic Zone Modes

When you select one of the other Basic Zone modes, your options are similar to those in Creative Auto mode:

- **Change shooting parameters by Ambience.** After you've pressed the Q button, when the top box on the screen is highlighted, it will display the most recent "ambience" setting you've selected.

  - Press the left/right multi-controller buttons or rotate the Main Dial and select from among: Vivid, Soft, Warm, Intense, Cool, Brighter, Darker, or Monochrome, the same choices available in Creative Auto mode.

  - Once you've selected your Ambience, if you want to change its intensity, press the down multi-controller button to highlight Effect.

  - You can then rotate the Main Dial to change the Effect to Low, Standard, or Strong. Press the Quick Control button to exit.

- **Press the multi-controller directional button down to highlight Default Settings.** This option is available only if you're using Portrait, Landscape, Close-up, and Sports modes. The prompt in the blue box at the bottom of the screen will change to Shoot by Lighting or Scene Type. You can then rotate the Main Dial to cycle through Default setting, Daylight, Shade, Cloudy, Tungsten Light, Fluorescent Light, or Sunset. You can also press the SET button and see a menu listing each of these options simultaneously.

- **Press the multi-controller directional button down to highlight Drive mode/Self-timer.** In this screen, you can press the left/right multi-controller buttons or rotate the Main Dial to switch between the available drive mode (either Single shot, or Continuous shooting, depending on the Basic Zone mode selected) and 10-second Self-timer/Remote.

Find your desired ambience in Table 4.2.

Table 4.2 Selecting Ambience

Ambience Setting	Effect
Standard	This is the customized set of parameters for each Basic Zone mode, each tailored specifically for Portrait, Landscape, Close-Up, Sports, or other mode.
Vivid	Produces a look that is slightly sharper and with richer colors for the relevant Basic Zone mode.
Soft	Reduced sharpness for adult portraits, flowers, children, and pets.
Warm	Warmer, soft tones. An alternative setting for portraits and other subjects that you want to appear both soft and warm.
Intense	Darker tones with increased contrast to emphasize your subject. This setting is great for portraits of men.
Cool	Darker, cooler tones. Use with care on human subjects, which aren't always flattered by the icier look this setting can produce.
Brighter	Overall lighter image with less contrast.
Darker	Produces a darker image.
Monochrome	Choose from black-and-white, sepia, or blue (cyanotype) toning.

PREVIEW AMBIENCE

If you set ambience in Live View mode, the 70D will provide a preview image that simulates the effect your ambience setting will have on the finished image. Examples of each ambience setting can be seen in Figure 4.36.

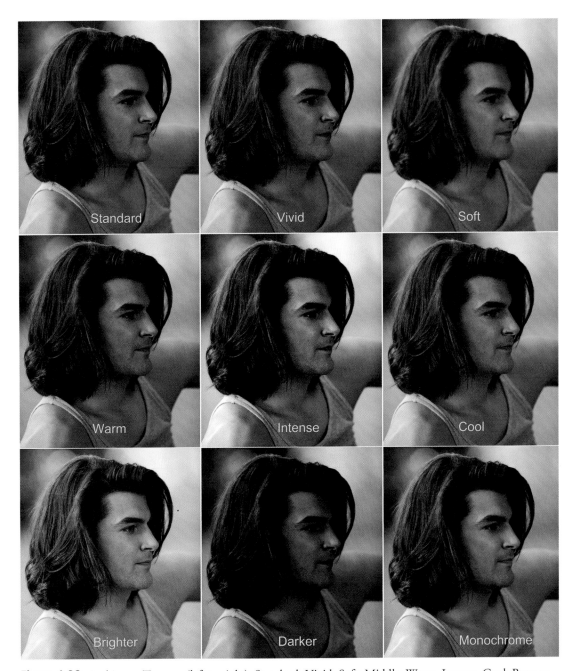

Figure 4.36 Ambience: Top row (left to right): Standard, Vivid, Soft; Middle: Warm, Intense, Cool; Bottom: Brighter, Darker, Monochrome.

5

Mastering the Mysteries of Autofocus

Capturing a compelling photograph involves a lot more than just correct exposure. The right tonal range, proper white balance, good color, and other factors all can help elevate your image from good to exceptional. But one of the most important and, sometimes, the most frustrating aspects of shooting with a highly automated—yet fully adjustable—camera like the EOS 70D is achieving sharp focus. Your camera has lots of AF controls and options and new users and veterans alike can quickly become confused. In this chapter, I'm going to clear up the mysteries of autofocus and show you exactly how to use your 70D's AF features to their fullest. I'll even tell you when to abandon the autofocus system and turn to the ancient art of manual focus, too.

How Focus Works

This section describes the differences between contrast detection and phase detection autofocus, and details how linear and cross-type AF sensors work in the 70D's advanced focusing system. Even those who are familiar with these concepts should still read this section carefully, because Canon has made some revolutionary changes in AF with the introduction of its Dual Pixel CMOS AF sensor design in which every single pixel is split into two photodiodes that can be used to provide advanced autofocus features in Live View and Movie modes. You'll find the nitty-gritty of selecting AF modes and AF areas starting with the section headed "Working with the AF System."

Although Canon added autofocus capabilities in the 1980s, back in the day of film cameras, prior to that focusing was always done manually. Honest. Even though viewfinders were bigger and brighter than they are today, special focusing screens, magnifiers, and other gadgets were often used to help the photographer achieve correct focus. Imagine what it must have been like to focus manually under demanding, fast-moving conditions such as sports photography.

I don't have to imagine it. I did it for many years. I started my career as a sports photographer, and then traveled the country as a roving photojournalist for more years than I like to admit. (Okay, eighteen years. You forced it out of me.) Indeed, I was a holdout for manual focus right through the film era, even as AF lenses became the norm and autofocus systems in cameras were (gradually) perfected. I purchased my first autofocus lens back in 2004, at the same time I switched from non-SLR digital cameras and my film cameras to digital SLR models.

Manual focusing was problematic because our eyes and brains have poor memory for correct focus, which is why your eye doctor must shift back and forth between sets of lenses and ask "Does that look sharper—or was it sharper before?" in determining your correct prescription. Similarly, manual focusing involves jogging the focus ring back and forth as you go from almost in focus, to sharp focus, to almost focused again. The little clockwise and counterclockwise arcs decrease in size until you've zeroed in on the point of correct focus. What you're looking for is the image with the most contrast between the edges of elements in the image.

The camera also looks for these contrast differences among pixels to determine relative sharpness. There are two ways that sharp focus is determined: phase detection and contrast detection. The camera also looks for these contrast differences among pixels to determine relative sharpness. To get the most from your camera, you really need to understand both. We'll start with the easier of the two: contrast detection.

Contrast Detection

Contrast detection is a slower mode and was used exclusively by Canon dSLRs in Live View and Movie modes until very recently, when Canon added a small number of special pixels to the sensor of cameras like the Rebel T4i and T5i that allowed a limited type of phase detection autofocus. The new Dual Pixel CMOS AF used by the Canon 70D goes much further, as I'll explain later in this chapter. To appreciate the innovation, you need to understand traditional contrast detection first.

The relatively slow contrast detection method was necessary because, to allow live viewing of the sensor image, the camera's mirror has to be flipped up out of the way so that the illumination from the lens can continue through the open shutter to the sensor. Your view through the viewfinder is obstructed, of course, and there is no partially silvered mirror to reflect some light down to the autofocus sensors. So, an alternate means of autofocus must be used in Live View, and that method is *contrast detection*. The 70D does have a Live View Quick Mode feature that temporarily flips the mirror back down to allow traditional phase detection autofocus, but Quick Mode is not available when shooting movies. And, unless you use Quick Mode, which I'll discuss later, focus must be achieved either manually (with the Live View on the color LCD monitor as a focusing screen), or by contrast detection. That is, until Dual Pixel CMOS AF was introduced, a new feature enabled by enhanced sensor technology which allows on-sensor phase detection.

Contrast detection is a bit easier to understand and is illustrated by Figure 5.1, which uses an extreme enlargement of a shot of some wood siding (actually a 19th century outhouse). At top in the figure, the transitions between pixels are soft and blurred. When the image is brought into focus

Figure 5.1
Focus in contrast detection mode evaluates the increase in contrast in the edges of subjects, starting with a blurry image (top) and producing a sharp, contrasty image (bottom).

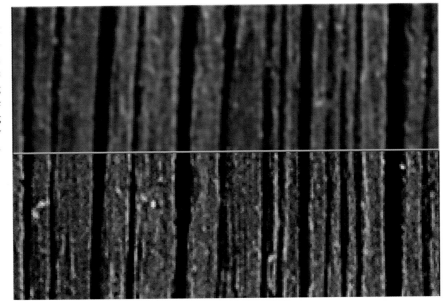

(bottom), the transitions are sharp and clear. Although this example is a bit exaggerated so you can see the results on the printed page, it's easy to understand that when maximum contrast in a subject is achieved, it can be deemed to be in sharp focus.

As I noted, contrast detection is used in Live View modes (other than Quick Mode) and Movie mode, even when Dual Pixel CMOS AF is also active. (In effect, you get two AF systems from one sensor.) Contrast detection works best with static subjects, because it is inherently slower and not well suited for tracking moving objects. Contrast detection works less well than phase detection in dim light, because its accuracy is determined by its ability to detect variations in brightness and contrast. You'll find that contrast detection works better with faster lenses, too, because larger lens openings admit more light that can be used by the sensor to measure contrast.

Phase Detection

Like all digital SLRs that use an optical viewfinder and mirror system to preview an image (that is, when not in Live View mode), the Canon EOS 70D calculates focus using what is called a *passive phase detection* system. It's passive in the sense that the ambient illumination in a scene (or that illumination augmented with a focus-assist beam) is used to determine correct focus. (An *active* phase detection system might use a laser, sonar, or other special signal. In the photographic realm only a few rare models—including one ancient system from Polaroid—resorted to such tactics.)

Parts of the image from two opposite sides of the lens are directed down to the floor of the camera's mirror box, where an autofocus sensor array resides; the rest of the illumination from the lens bounces upward toward the optical viewfinder system and the autoexposure sensors. Figure 5.2 is a wildly over-simplified illustration that may help you visualize what is happening.

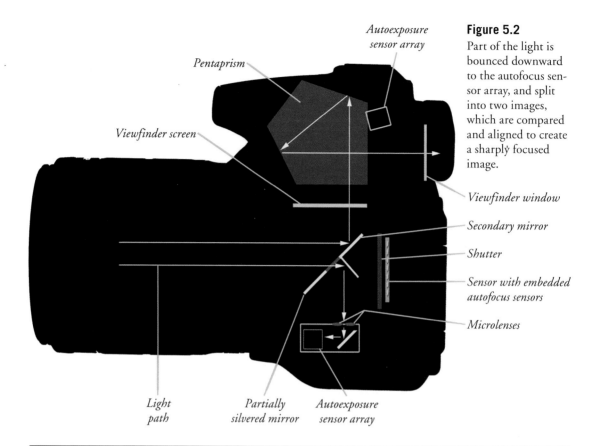

Autoexposure
sensor array

Pentaprism

Viewfinder screen

Light
path

Partially
silvered mirror

Autoexposure
sensor array

Figure 5.2
Part of the light is bounced downward to the autofocus sensor array, and split into two images, which are compared and aligned to create a sharply focused image.

Viewfinder window

Secondary mirror

Shutter

Sensor with embedded autofocus sensors

Microlenses

SIMPLIFICATION MADE OVERLY SIMPLE

To reduce the complexity of the diagram, it doesn't show the actual path of the light passing through the lens, as it converges to the point of focus. That point is either the viewfinder screen when the mirror is down or the sensor plane when the mirror is flipped up and the shutter has opened. Nor does it show the path of the light directed to the autoexposure sensor. Only two of the pairs of autofocus microlenses are shown, and greatly enlarged so you can see their approximate position. All we're concerned about here is how light reaches the autofocus sensor.

As light emerges from the rear element of the lens, most of it is reflected upward toward the focusing screen, where the relative sharp focus (or lack of it) is displayed (and which can be used to evaluate manual focus). It then bounces off two more reflective surfaces in the pentaprism (in the 70D; other cameras may use a less expensive and less bright *pentamirror* system instead) emerging at the optical viewfinder correctly oriented left/right and up/down. (The image emerges from the lens reversed.) Some of the illumination is directed to the autoexposure sensor at the top of the pentaprism housing.

A small portion of the illumination passes through the partially silvered center of the main mirror, and is directed downward to the autofocus sensor array, which includes 19 separate autofocus "detectors." Conceptually, these function as shown in Figure 5.3, another simplified illustration. The illumination arrives from opposite sides of the lens surface and is directed through separate microlenses, producing two half images. These images are compared with each other, much like (actually, *exactly* like) a two-window rangefinder used in surveying, weaponry, and non-SLR cameras like the venerable Leica M film models.

When the image is out of focus—or out of phase—as in Figure 5.4 (top), the two halves, each representing a slightly different view from opposite sides of the lens, don't line up. Sharp focus is achieved when the images are "in phase," and aligned, as in Figure 5.4 (bottom).

As with any rangefinder-like function, accuracy is better when the "base length" between the two images is larger. (Think back to your high school trigonometry; you could calculate a distance more accurately when the separation between the two points where the angles were measured was greater.) For that reason, phase detection autofocus is more accurate with larger (wider) lens openings than with smaller lens openings, and may not work at all when the f/stop is smaller than f/5.6 or f/8. Obviously, the "opposite" edges of the lens opening are farther apart with a lens having an f/2.8 maximum aperture than with one that has a smaller, f/5.6 maximum f/stop, and the base line is much longer. The 70D is able to perform these comparisons and then move the lens elements directly to the point of correct focus very quickly, in milliseconds.

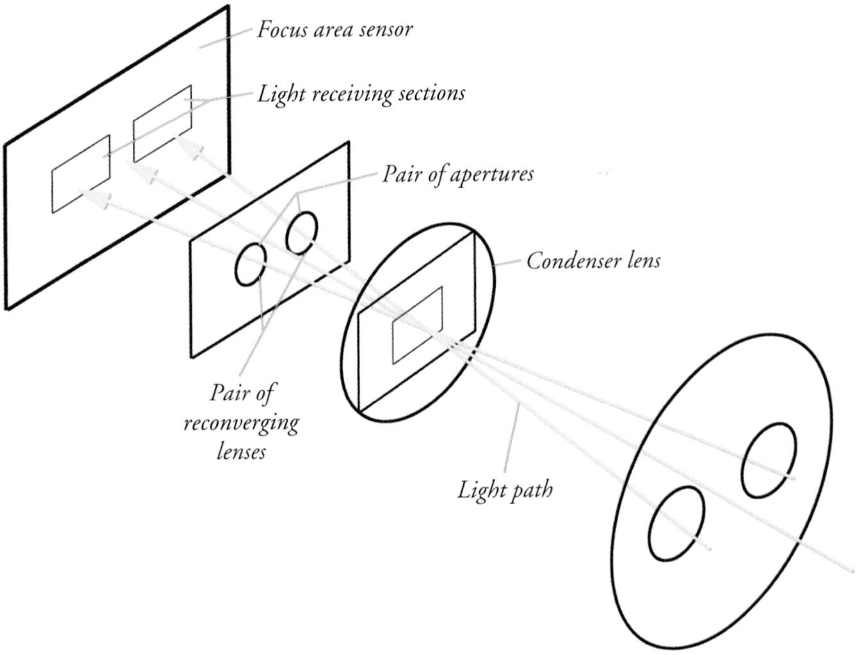

Figure 5.3
In phase detection, parts of an image are split in two and compared.

Focus area sensor

Light receiving sections

Pair of apertures

Condenser lens

Pair of reconverging lenses

Light path

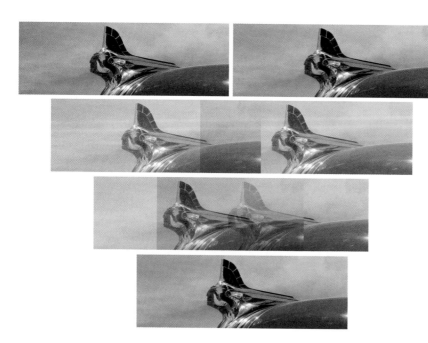

Figure 5.4
When the image is in focus, the two halves of the image align, as with a rangefinder.

Unfortunately, while the 70D's focus system finds it easy to measure degrees of apparent focus at each of the focus points in the viewfinder, it doesn't really know with any certainty *which* object should be in sharpest focus. Is it the closest object? The subject in the center? Something lurking *behind* the closest subject? A person standing over at the side of the picture? Many of the techniques for using autofocus effectively involve telling the EOS 70D exactly what it should be focusing on, by choosing a focus zone or by allowing the camera to choose a focus zone for you. I'll address that topic shortly.

Dual Pixel CMOS AF

Now that you understand contrast and phase detection, you can appreciate the miracle that is Canon's Dual Pixel CMOS AF system. Used in Live View mode while shooting stills and movies, it works much more quickly than the camera's more traditional contrast detection system.

However, an array of special pixels, which cover 80 percent of the frame horizontally and vertically, provide the same type of split-image rangefinder phase detection AF that is available when using the optical viewfinder. The most important aspect of the system is that it doesn't rob the camera of any imaging resolution. It would have been possible to place AF sensors *between* the pixels used to capture the image, but that would leave the sensor with less area with which to capture light. Keep in mind that CMOS sensors, unlike earlier CCD sensors, have more on-board circuitry which already consumes some of the light-gathering area. Microlenses are placed above each photosensitive site to focus incoming illumination on the sensor and to correct for the oblique angles from which some photons may approach the imager. (Older lenses, designed for film, are the worst offenders in terms of emitting light at severely oblique angles; newer "digital" lenses do a better job of directing photons onto the sensor plane with a less "slanted" approach.)

With the Dual Pixel CMOS AF system, the same photosites capture both image and autofocus information. Each pixel is divided into two photodiodes, facing left and right when the camera is held in horizontal orientation (or above and below each other in vertical orientation; either works fine for autofocus purposes). Each pair functions as a separate AF sensor, allowing a special integrated circuit to process the raw autofocus information before sending it on to the 70D's digital image processor, which handles both AF and image capture. For the latter, the information grabbed by *both* photodiodes is combined, so that the full photosensitive area of the sensor pixel is used to capture the image.

While traditional contrast detection frequently involves frustrating "hunting" as the camera continually readjusts the focus plane trying to find the position of maximum contrast, adding Dual Pixel CMOS AF phase detection allows the 70D to focus smoothly, which is important for speed, and essential when shooting movies (where all that hunting is unfortunately captured for posterity). Movie Servo AF tracking is improved, allowing shooting movies of subjects in motion. The system works with (at this writing) 103 different lenses, both current and previously available optics, and works especially well with lenses that have speedy USM or STM motors.

Cross-Type Focus Point

We're going to explore one special aspect of the optical viewfinder's AF system next. So far, we've only looked at focus sensors that calculate focus in a single direction. Figure 5.5 illustrates a horizontally oriented linear focus sensor evaluating a subject that is made up, predominantly, of vertical lines. But what does such a sensor do when it encounters a subject that isn't conveniently aligned at right angles to the sensor array? You can see the problem in Figure 5.6 (left), which pictures the same weathered wood siding rotated 90 degrees. The horizontal grain of the wood isn't divided as neatly by the split image, so focusing using phase detection is more difficult. The lines in the grain don't cross the AF sensor at right angles any more.

Figure 5.5
A horizontal sensor handles vertical lines easily.

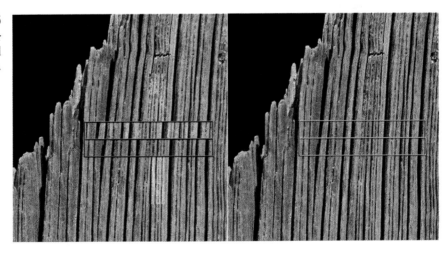

You can see the "solution" at right in Figure 5.6, in the form of a vertical linear sensor, which does a better job of interpreting horizontal lines. By mixing both types in a focusing system, the vertical sensors could detect differences in horizontal lines, while the horizontal sensors took care of the vertical lines. Both varieties are equally adept at handling *diagonal* lines, which crossed each type at a 45-degree angle.

However, a better solution is the use of a *cross-type* sensor, shown in a simplified version in Figure 5.7. Such sensors are a merger of vertical and horizontal linear sensors, thus including sensitivity to horizontal, vertical, and diagonal lines. In lower light levels, with subjects that are moving, or with subjects that have no pattern and less contrast to begin with, the cross-type sensor not only works faster but can focus subjects that a horizontal- or vertical-only sensor can't handle at all.

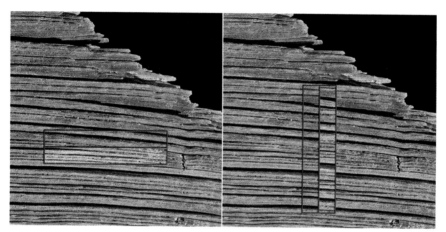

Figure 5.6

However, a horizontal sensor has problems with subjects that have parallel horizontal lines (left). A vertically oriented sensor is really needed for that type of subject (right).

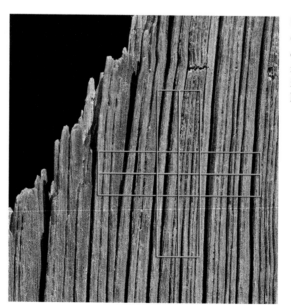

Figure 5.7

Cross-type sensors can achieve sharp focus with both horizontal and vertical lines.

In the EOS 70D all 19 of the available AF sensors are of the cross-type when used with lenses having a maximum aperture of f/3.2 to f/5.6. Further, lenses with a maximum aperture of f/1.0 to f/2.8 provide cross-type sensing *plus* simultaneous ultra-high precision vertical-line sensitive autofocus at the center focus position. The system does not provide 19-point cross-type focusing with a limited number of older lenses, specifically the EF 35-80mm f/4-5.6, EF 35-80mm f/4-5.6 II, EF 35-80mm f/4-5.6 III, EF 35-80mm f/4-5.6 USM, EF 35-105mm f/4.5-5.6, EF 35-105mm f/4.5-5.6 USM, EF 80-200mm f/4.5-5.6 II, and EF 80-200mm f/4.5-5.6 USM. With these lenses, only seven cross-type sensors are available—the center point and the points in the columns immediately to the left and right of the center point (which forms an "H" pattern). (See Figure 5.8.)

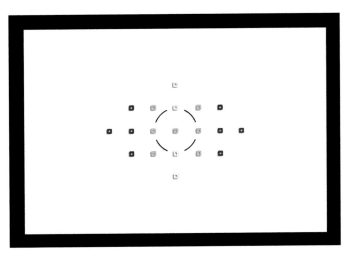

Figure 5.8
With the older lenses listed above, only the green-coded points operate as cross-type sensors. The yellow-coded points are vertical line-sensitive sensors, and the magenta-coded points function as horizontal line-sensitive sensors. (The colors pictured do not appear in your viewfinder.)

Focus Modes

Focus modes tell the camera *when* to evaluate and lock in focus. They don't determine *where* focus should be checked; that's the function of other autofocus features. Focus modes tell the camera whether to lock in focus once, say, when you press the shutter release halfway (or use some other control, such as the AF-ON button), or whether, once activated, the camera should continue tracking your subject and, if it's moving, adjust focus to follow it.

The 70D has three AF modes: One-Shot AF (also known as single autofocus), AI Servo (continuous autofocus), and AI Focus AF (which switches between the two as appropriate). I'll explain all of these in more detail later in this section. But first, some confusion…

MANUAL FOCUS

With manual focus activated by sliding the AF/MF switch on the lens, your 70D lets you set the focus yourself. There are some advantages and disadvantages to this approach. While your batteries will last longer in manual focus mode, it will take you longer to focus the camera for each photo, a process that can be difficult. Modern digital cameras, even dSLRs, depend so much on autofocus that the viewfinders are no longer designed for optimum manual focus. Pick up any film camera and you'll see a bigger, brighter viewfinder with a focusing screen that's a joy to focus on manually.

Adding Circles of Confusion

You know that increased depth-of-field brings more of your subject into focus. But more depth-of-field also makes autofocusing (or manual focusing) more difficult because the contrast is lower between objects at different distances. This is an added factor *beyond* the rangefinder aspects of lens opening size in phase detection. An image that's dimmer is more difficult to focus with any type of focus system, phase detection, contrast detection, or manual focus.

So, focus with a 200mm lens (or zoom setting) may be easier in some respects than at a 28mm focal length (or zoom setting) because the longer lens has less apparent depth-of-field. By the same token, a lens with a maximum aperture of f/1.8 will be easier to autofocus (or manually focus) than one of the same focal length with an f/4 maximum aperture, because the f/4 lens has more depth-of-field *and* a dimmer view. That's yet another reason why lenses with a maximum aperture smaller than f/5.6 can give your 70D's autofocus system fits—increased depth-of-field joins forces with a dimmer image that's more difficult to focus using phase detection.

To make things even more complicated, many subjects aren't polite enough to remain still. They move around in the frame, so that even if the 70D is sharply focused on your main subject, it may change position and require refocusing. An intervening subject may pop into the frame and pass between you and the subject you meant to photograph. You (or the 70D) have to decide whether to lock focus on this new subject, or remain focused on the original subject. Finally, there are some kinds of subjects that are difficult to bring into sharp focus because they lack enough contrast to allow the 70D's AF system (or our eyes) to lock in. Blank walls, a clear blue sky, or other subject matter may make focusing difficult.

If you find all these focus factors confusing, you're on the right track. Focus is, in fact, measured using something called a *circle of confusion*. An ideal image consists of zillions of tiny little points, which, like all points, theoretically have no height or width. There is perfect contrast between the point and its surroundings. You can think of each point as a pinpoint of light in a darkened room. When a given point is out of focus, its edges decrease in contrast and it changes from a perfect point to a tiny disc with blurry edges (remember, blur is the lack of contrast between boundaries in an image). (See Figure 5.9.)

If this blurry disc—the circle of confusion—is small enough, our eye still perceives it as a point. It's only when the disc grows large enough that we can see it as a blur rather than a sharp point that a

Figure 5.9

When a pinpoint of light (left) goes out of focus, its blurry edges form a circle of confusion (center and right).

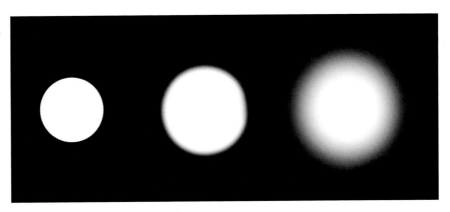

given point is viewed as out of focus. You can see, then, that enlarging an image, either by displaying it larger on your computer monitor or by making a large print, also enlarges the size of each circle of confusion. Moving closer to the image does the same thing. So, parts of an image that may look perfectly sharp in a 5 × 7-inch print viewed at arm's length, might appear blurry when blown up to 11 × 14 and examined at the same distance. Take a few steps back, however, and it may look sharp again.

To a lesser extent, the viewer also affects the apparent size of these circles of confusion. Some people see details better at a given distance and may perceive smaller circles of confusion than someone standing next to them. For the most part, however, such differences are small. Truly blurry images will look blurry to just about everyone under the same conditions.

Technically, there is just one plane within your picture area, parallel to the back of the camera (or sensor, in the case of a digital camera), that is in sharp focus. That's the plane in which the points of the image are rendered as precise points. At every other plane in front of or behind the focus plane, the points show up as discs that range from slightly blurry to extremely blurry until the out-of-focus areas become one large blur that de-emphasizes the background.

In practice, the discs in many of these planes will still be so small that we see them as points, and that's where we get depth-of-field. Depth-of-field is just the range of planes that include discs that we perceive as points rather than blurred splotches. The size of this range increases as the aperture is reduced in size and is allocated roughly one-third in front of the plane of sharpest focus, and two-thirds behind it. The range of sharp focus is always greater behind your subject than in front of it.

Your Autofocus Mode Options

Choosing the right autofocus mode and the way in which focus points are selected is your key to success. Using the wrong mode for a particular type of photography can lead to a series of pictures that are all sharply focused—on the wrong subject. When I first started shooting sports with an autofocus SLR (back in the film camera days), I covered one game alternating between shots of base runners and outfielders with pictures of a promising young pitcher, all from a position next to the third-base dugout. The base runner and outfielder photos were great, because their backgrounds didn't distract the autofocus mechanism. But all my photos of the pitcher had the focus tightly zeroed in on the fans in the stands behind him. Because I was shooting film instead of a digital camera, I didn't know about my gaffe until the film was developed. A simple change, such as locking in focus or focus zone manually, or even manually focusing, would have done the trick.

To save battery power, unless Continuous Autofocus is activated, your 70D doesn't start to focus the lens until you partially depress the shutter release or AF-ON button. But, autofocus isn't some mindless beast out there snapping your pictures in and out of focus with no feedback from you after you press that button. There are several settings you can modify that return at least a modicum of control to you. Your first decision should be whether you set the 70D to One-Shot, AI Servo AF, or AI Focus AF. With the camera set for one of the Creative Zone modes, press the AF button on the top panel and use the Main Dial or QCD to select the focus mode you want (see Figure 5.10). Press SET to confirm your choice. (The AF/M switch on the lens must be set to AF before you can change autofocus mode.)

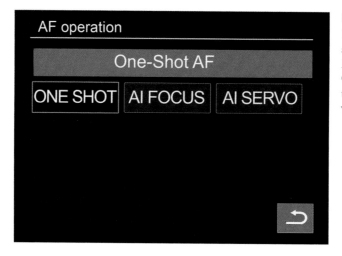

Figure 5.10
Press the AF button and then rotate the Main Dial or Quick Control Dial until the AF choice you want is selected.

One-Shot AF

In this mode, also called *single autofocus*, focus is set once and remains at that setting until the button is fully depressed, taking the picture, or until you release the shutter button without taking a shot. For non-action photography, this setting is usually your best choice, as it minimizes out-of-focus pictures (at the expense of spontaneity). The drawback here is that you might not be able to take a picture at all while the camera is seeking focus; you're locked out until the autofocus mechanism is happy with the current setting. One-Shot AF/Single Autofocus is sometimes referred to as *focus priority* for that reason. Because of the small delay while the camera zeroes in on correct focus, you might experience slightly more shutter lag. This mode uses less battery power.

When sharp focus is achieved, the selected focus point will flash red in the viewfinder, and the focus confirmation light at the lower right will illuminate and remain lit as long as focus is maintained and you continue to hold down the shutter release. The exposure will be locked at the same time. By keeping the shutter button depressed halfway, you'll find you can reframe the image while retaining the focus (and exposure) that's been set. You can also use the AE Lock/FE Lock button to retain the exposure calculated from the center AF point while reframing.

AI Servo AF

This mode, also known as *continuous autofocus* is the mode to use for sports and other fast-moving subjects. In this mode, once the shutter release is partially depressed, the camera sets the focus but continues to monitor the subject, so that if it moves or you move, the lens will be refocused to suit. Focus and exposure aren't really locked until you press the shutter release down all the way to take the picture. You'll often see continuous autofocus referred to as *release priority.* If you press the shutter release down all the way while the system is refining focus, the camera will go ahead and take a picture, even if the image is slightly out of focus. You'll find that AI Servo AF produces the least amount of shutter lag of any autofocus mode: press the button and the camera fires. It also uses the most battery power, because the autofocus system operates as long as the shutter release button is partially depressed.

AI Servo AF uses a technology called *predictive AF*, which allows the 70D to calculate the correct focus if the subject is moving toward or away from the camera at a constant rate. It uses either the automatically selected AF point or the point you select manually to set focus.

AI Focus AF

This setting is actually a combination of the first two. When selected, the camera focuses using One-Shot AF and locks in the focus setting. But, if the subject begins moving, it will switch automatically to AI Servo AF and change the focus to keep the subject sharp. AI Focus AF is a good choice when you're shooting a mixture of action pictures and less dynamic shots and want to use One-Shot AF when possible. The camera will default to that mode, yet switch automatically to AI Servo AF when it would be useful for subjects that might begin moving unexpectedly, such as children or pets.

Manual Focus

With manual focus activated by sliding the AF/MF switch on the lens, your 70D lets you set the focus yourself, both using the eyelevel optical viewfinder and on the LCD monitor in Live View mode. There are some advantages and disadvantages to this approach. While your batteries will last longer in manual focus mode through the optical viewfinder, it will take you longer to focus the camera for each photo, a process that can be difficult. Modern digital cameras, even dSLRs, depend so much on autofocus that the viewfinders of models that have less than full-frame-sized sensors are no longer designed for optimum manual focus. Pick up any film camera and you'll see a bigger, brighter viewfinder with a focusing screen that's a joy to focus on manually. You really needed to use a full-frame digital camera, like the Canon EOS 6D, to get such a bright view and easy manual focus.

Selecting an AF Area Selection Mode

The Canon EOS 70D uses nineteen different focus points to calculate correct focus. In any of the Basic Zone shooting modes, the focus point is selected automatically by the camera. In the Creative Zone modes, you can allow the camera to select the focus point automatically, or you can specify which focus point should be used. There are three AF Area Selection modes. They are shown in Figure 5.11, left to right:

- **Single-point AF (Manual Selection).** You can choose one AF point for focus.

- **Zone AF (Manual Zone Selection).** Select any of five different focus zones, each with multiple focus points. The specific zones are shown in Figure 5.12.

- **19-point Automatic Selection AF.** The camera will choose the focus point for you. This mode is always used in Basic Zone exposure modes.

To choose the AF Area, just follow these steps:

1. Make sure the lens AF/MF switch is set to AF.

2. Tap the shutter release to activate the focus system.

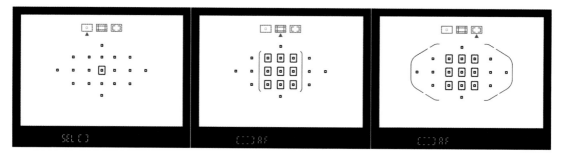

Figure 5.11 The three AF Area Selection modes are Single-point AF (Manual Selection), left; Zone AF (Manual Zone Selection), middle; 19-point Automatic Selection AF, right.

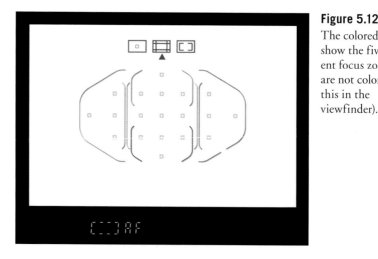

Figure 5.12
The colored outlines show the five different focus zones (they are not colored like this in the viewfinder).

3. Press the AF Area Selection Mode button located northeast of the Main Dial. The current focus selection indicators will be highlighted in red.

4. Continue pressing, if necessary, until the method has an up-pointing triangle underneath it in the viewfinder (or is highlighted on the LCD monitor). Figure 5.11 shows the viewfinder view.

As explained in Chapter 9, you can use C.Fn II-07 to limit the AF area selection modes available, and C.Fn II-08 to adjust the controls used to choose the selection mode. When choosing a focus point manually, the viewfinder indicator will display **SEL AF** (for Single-point selection) or [ ] AF (for the other two modes) at the bottom of the frame.

In the single point manual selection mode, press the focus point selection button (in the upper-right corner of the back of the camera) or the focus point selection mode button. Then, use the multi-controller to move the active focus point around the frame. If you press SET, the AF center point will be selected. You can also rotate the Main Dial to move the focus point to the left or right in the middle row of sensors, and rotate the QCD to move up and down rows. In zone AF mode, rotating either the Main Dial or Quick Control Dial will switch from zone to zone in a loop.

While automatic point selection works well and is often best for moving subjects, manual point selection can be quite useful when you have time to zero in on a particular subject. This mode is certainly your best choice when you want to focus precisely on a subject that is surrounded by fine detail, as shown in Figure 5.13. The heron was not moving and my camera and 400mm lens were

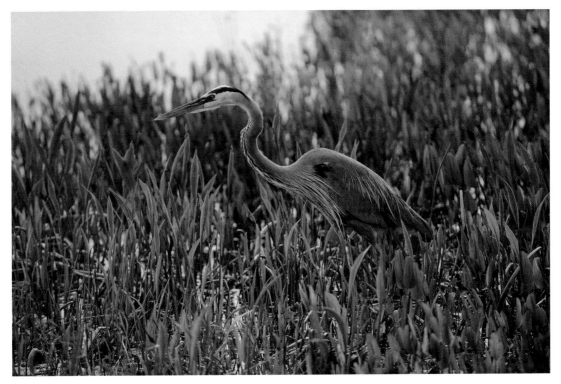

Figure 5.13 Manual point selection allowed focusing precisely on the heron, despite the surrounding detail.

mounted on a sturdy tripod, so it was easy to place the focus spot exactly where I wanted it. Keep in mind that the portion of the sensor used to autofocus is not precisely represented by the rectangle shown in the viewfinder, so if you're focusing on, say, the near eye of a portrait subject turned at a 45-degree angle with a wide aperture, you might end up focusing on the bridge of their nose instead. You'll want to keep the actual focus area in mind in situations where focus is that critical.

Focus Stacking

If you are doing macro (close-up) photography of flowers, or other small objects at short distances, the depth-of-field often will be extremely narrow. In some cases, it will be so narrow that it will be impossible to keep the entire subject in focus in one photograph. Although having part of the image out of focus can be a pleasing effect for a portrait of a person, it is likely to be a hindrance when you are trying to make an accurate photographic record of a flower, or small piece of precision equipment. One solution to this problem is focus stacking, a procedure that can be considered like HDR translated for the world of focus—taking multiple shots with different settings, and, using software as explained below, combining the best parts from each image in order to make a whole that is better than the sum of the parts. Focus stacking requires a non-moving object, so some subjects, such as flowers, are best photographed in a breezeless environment, such as indoors.

For example, see Figures 5.14 through 5.16, in which I took photographs of three colorful crayons. As you can see from these images, the depth-of-field was extremely narrow, and only a small part of the subject was in focus for each shot.

Now look at Figure 5.17, in which the entire subject is in reasonably sharp focus. This image is a composite, made up of the three shots above, as well as 10 others, each one focused on the same scene, but at very gradually increasing distances from the camera's lens. All 13 images were then combined in Adobe Photoshop using the focus stacking procedure. Here are the steps you can take to combine shots for the purpose of achieving sharp focus in this sort of situation:

1. **Set the camera firmly on a solid tripod.** A tripod or other equally firm support is absolutely essential for this procedure.

2. **Attach a remote release.** You want to be able to trigger the camera without moving it.

3. **Set the camera to manual focus mode.** Use the procedure described in the previous section to activate manual focus.

4. **Set the exposure, ISO, and white balance manually.** Use test shots if necessary to determine the best values. This step in the Shooting menu will help prevent visible variations from arising among the multiple shots that you'll be taking. You don't want the camera to change the ISO setting or white balance between shots.

5. **Set the quality of the images to RAW.** Use the Shooting 1 menu to make this adjustment. Having RAW images will give you flexibility when combining the images.

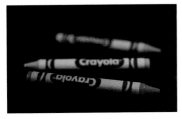 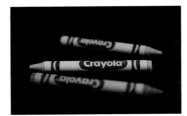 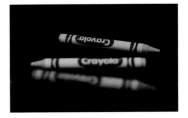

Figure 5.14   **Figure 5.15**   **Figure 5.16**

These three shots were all focused on different distances within the same scene. No single shot could bring the entire subject into sharp focus.

Figure 5.17

Three partially out-of-focus shots have been merged, along with ten others, through a focus stacking procedure in Adobe Photoshop, to produce a single image with the entire subject in focus.

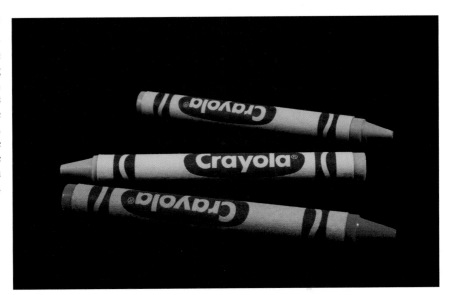

6. **Turn off image stabilization.** If your lens has IS, turn it off. You don't need it when the camera is securely mounted on a tripod, and disabling image stabilization will keep the 70D from making any sort of image adjustment between exposures.

7. **Focus manually on the very closest point of the subject to the lens.** Use the focus ring on the lens.

8. **Trip the shutter.** Use the remote.

9. **Carefully refocus.** Gently rotate the focus ring on the lens to focus on a point slightly farther away from the lens and trip the shutter again.

10. **Continue taking photographs** in this way until you have covered the entire subject with in-focus shots.

The next step is to process the images you've taken in Photoshop. Transfer the images to your computer, and then follow these steps:

1. In Photoshop, select File > Scripts > Load Files into Stack. In the dialog box that then appears, navigate on your computer to find the files for the photographs you have taken, and highlight them all.

2. At the bottom of the next dialog box that appears, check the box that says, "Attempt to Automatically Align Source Images," then click OK. The images will load; it may take several minutes for the program to load the images and attempt to arrange them into layers that are aligned based on their content.

3. Once the program has finished processing the images, go to the Layers panel and select all of the layers. You can do this by clicking on the top layer and then Shift-clicking on the bottom one.

4. While the layers are all selected, in Photoshop go to Edit > Auto-Blend Layers. In the dialog box that appears, select the two options, Stack Images and Seamless Tones and Colors, then click OK. The program will process the images, possibly for a considerable length of time.

5. If the procedure worked well, the result will be a single image made up of numerous layers that have been processed to produce a sharply focused rendering of your subject. If it did not work well, you may have to take additional images the next time, focusing very carefully on small slices of the subject as you move progressively farther away from the lens.

Although this procedure can work very well in Photoshop, you also may want to try it with programs that were developed more specifically for focus stacking and related procedures, such as Helicon Focus (www.heliconsoft.com), PhotoAcute (www.photoacute.com), or CombineZM (www.hadleyweb.pwp.blueyonder.co.uk).

Fine-Tuning the Autofocus of Your Lenses

The Canon EOS 70D has a feature called AF Microadjustment, which I hope you never need to use, because it is applied only when you find that a particular lens is not focusing properly. If the lens happens to focus a bit ahead or a bit behind the actual point of sharp focus, and it does that consistently, you can use the microadjustment feature to "calibrate" the lens's focus.

Caution! Use this control, which allows you to tweak the point of focus of individual lenses, with care. Well intentioned, but inaccurate adjustments can turn slight focus problems into major ones. I'll cover this drastic correctional step in detail next.

Why is the focus "off" for some lenses in the first place? There are lots of factors, including the age of the lens (an older lens may focus slightly differently), temperature effects on certain types of glass, humidity, and tolerances built into a lens's design that all add up to a slight misadjustment, even though the components themselves are, strictly speaking, within specs. A very slight variation in your lens's mount can cause focus to vary slightly. With any luck (if you can call it that), a lens that doesn't focus exactly right will at least be consistent. If a lens always focuses a bit behind the subject, the symptom is *back focus*. If it focuses in front of the subject, it's called *front focus*.

You're almost always better off sending such a lens in to Canon to have them make it right. But that's not always possible. Perhaps you need your lens recalibrated right now, or you purchased a used lens that is long out of warranty. If you want to do it yourself, the first thing to do is determine whether your lens has a back focus or front focus problem.

For a quick-and-dirty diagnosis (*not* a calibration; you'll use a different target for that), lay down a piece of graph paper on a flat surface, and place an object on the line at the middle, which will represent the point of focus (we hope). Then, shoot the target at an angle using your lens's widest aperture and the autofocus mode you want to test. Mount the camera on a tripod so you can get accurate, repeatable results.

If your camera/lens combination doesn't suffer from front or back focus, the point of sharpest focus will be the center line of the chart, as you can see in Figure 5.18. If you do have a problem, one of the other lines will be sharply focused instead. Should you discover that your lens consistently front or back focuses, it needs to be recalibrated. Unfortunately, it's only possible to calibrate a lens for a single focusing distance. So, if you use a particular lens (such as a macro lens) for close focusing, calibrate for that. If you use a lens primarily for middle distances, calibrate for that. Close-to-middle distances are most likely to cause focus problems, anyway, because as you get closer to infinity, small changes in focus are less likely to have an effect.

Lens Tune-Up

The key tool you can use to fine-tune your lens is the AF Microadjustment entry, C.Fn II-13. You'll find the process easier to understand if you first run through this quick overview of the menu options:

- **Disable.** Deactivates autofocus microadjustment. You might want to use this if you've mounted a different copy of a lens you've registered for adjustment. For example, a photojournalist might make an adjustment for his or her personal lens, and then need to borrow a different copy of the exact same lens from a friend or a department's equipment pool. The 70D can't tell the two lenses apart, so it's probably best to disable the microadjustment feature while using that "foreign" lens.

- **Adjust all by same amount.** The same adjustment is applied to all your lenses. You'd use this if your camera, rather than just a lens or two, requires calibration. (In this case, I particularly recommend sending the camera back to Canon for repair.)

- **Adjust by lens.** You can set an adjustment individually for up to 40 different lens combinations (lens+teleconverter combinations are registered separately). If you discover you don't care for the calibrations you make in certain situations (say, it works better for the lens you have mounted at middle distances, but is less successful at correcting close-up focus errors), or, as described above, are using a different copy of the exact same lens, you can deactivate the feature as you require. Adjustment values range from −20 to +20.

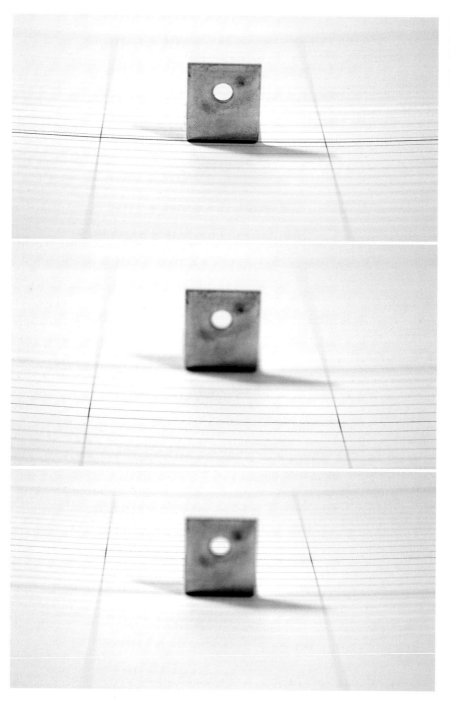

Figure 5.18
Correct focus (top),
front focus (middle),
and back focus
(bottom).

Evaluate Current Focus

The first step is to capture a baseline image that represents how the lens you want to fine-tune autofocuses at a particular distance. You'll often see advice for photographing a test chart with millimeter markings from an angle, and the suggestion that you autofocus on a particular point on the chart. Supposedly, the markings that actually *are* in focus will help you recalibrate your lens. The problem with this approach is that the information you get from photographing a test chart at an angle doesn't actually tell you what to do to make a precise correction. So, your lens back focuses three millimeters behind the target area on the chart. So what? Does that mean you change the value –3 increments? Or –15 increments? Angled targets are a "shortcut" that don't save you time.

Instead, you'll want to photograph a target that represents what you're actually trying to achieve: a plane of focus locked in by your lens that represents the actual plane of focus of your subject. For that, you'll need a flat target, mounted precisely perpendicular to the sensor plane of the camera. Then, you can take a photo, see if the plane of focus is correct, and if not, dial in a bit of fine-tuning in the AF Microadjustment menu, and shoot again. Lather, rinse, and repeat until the target is sharply focused.

You can use the focus target shown in Figure 5.19, or you can use a chart of your own, as long as it has contrasty areas that will be easily seen by the autofocus system, and without very small details that are likely to confuse the AF. Download your own copy of my chart from www.dslrguides.com/FocusChart.pdf. (The URL is case sensitive.) Then print out a copy on the largest paper your printer can handle. (I don't recommend just displaying the file on your monitor and focusing on that; it's unlikely you'll have the monitor screen lined up perfectly perpendicular to the camera sensor.) Then, follow these steps:

1. **Position the camera.** Place your camera on a sturdy tripod with a remote release attached, positioned at roughly eye-level at a distance from a wall that represents the distance you want to test for. Keep in mind that autofocus problems can be different at varying distances and lens focal lengths, and that you can enter only *one* correction value for a particular lens. So, choose a distance (close-up or mid range) and zoom setting with your shooting habits in mind.

2. **Set the autofocus mode.** Choose the autofocus mode (One-Shot AF or AI Servo AF) you want to test. (Because AI Auto mode just alternates between the two, you don't need to test that mode.)

3. **Level the camera (in an ideal world).** If the wall happens to be perfectly perpendicular, you can use a bubble level, plumb bob, or other device of your choice to ensure that the camera is level to match. Many tripods and tripod heads have bubble levels built in. Avoid using the center column, if you can. When the camera is properly oriented, lock the legs and tripod head tightly.

4. **Level the camera (in the real world).** If your wall is not perfectly perpendicular, use this old trick. Tape a mirror to the wall, and then adjust the camera on the tripod so that when you look through the viewfinder at the mirror, you see directly into the reflection of the lens. Then, lock the tripod and remove the mirror.

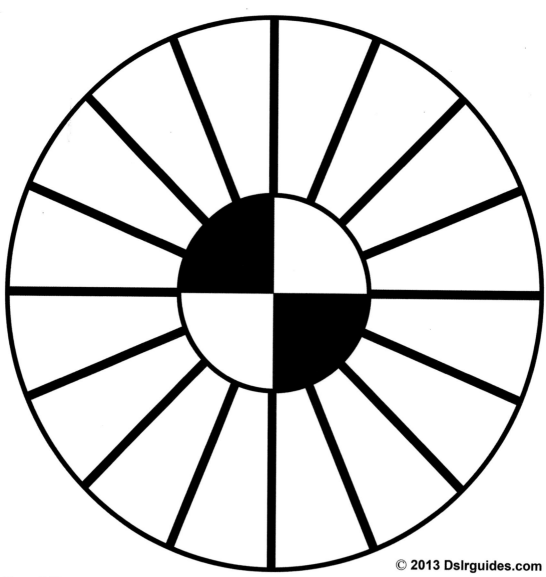

Figure 5.19 Use this focus test chart, or create one of your own.

5. **Mount the test chart.** Tape the test chart on the wall so it is centered in your camera's viewfinder.

6. **Photograph the test chart using AF.** Allow the camera to autofocus, and take a test photo, using the remote release to avoid shaking or moving the camera.

7. **Make an adjustment and rephotograph.** Make a fine-tuning adjustment (described next) and photograph the target again.

8. **Evaluate the image.** If you have the camera connected to your computer with a USB cable or through a Wi-Fi connection, so much the better. You can view the image after it's transferred to your computer. Otherwise, *carefully* open the camera card door and slip the memory card out and copy the images to your computer.

9. **Evaluate focus.** Which image is sharpest? That's the setting you need to use for this lens. If your initial range doesn't provide the correction you need, repeat the steps between –20 and +20 until you find the best fine-tuning.

Make Adjustments

Making the adjustments is simple. From the AF Microadjustment entry, C.Fn II-13, select AF Microadjustment, and choose from Adjust All By Same Amount, Adjust By Lens, or Disable.

■ **Adjust All By Same Amount.** Use this if all your lenses appear to front focus or back focus all the time, and consistently. Highlight the entry and press the SET button. You can clear current adjustment settings by pressing the Trash button. Or, press the Q button to produce a screen with a scale from –20 to +20. (See Figure 5.20.) Use the Quick Control Dial to choose a value, and press SET to confirm.

■ **Adjust By Lens.** Follow these steps:

1. Highlight Adjust By Lens and press the Q button. A screen similar to the one shown in Figure 5.21 will appear. For a prime lens, there will be only a single adjustment scale; for a zoom lens, there will be one scale for W (wide angle) and one for T (telephoto) focal lengths.

2. Press the INFO. button. The Review/Edit lens information screen appears. It shows the name of the currently mounted lens and a 10-digit serial number (or 0000000000 if the number cannot be obtained). Note that while the 70D can differentiate among various lenses, it "sees" all copies of the exact same lens as identical. If you own two copies of the same 50mm f/1.4 lens, the identical adjustment will be applied to both of them.

3. If the serial number is obtained, you can select OK to move on to the next step. If you need to edit the serial number, you can use the QCD to highlight any digit, then press SET to edit that digit. Rotate the QCD to increase or decrease the value of the digit. Select OK when finished.

4. Select the scale and then rotate the QCD to adjust between –20 and +20 (no letters required). Moving the indicator to the right moves the focus point to the rear of the standard point of focus. Adjusting to the left moves the focus point to a position in front of the default focus point.

5. Press SET to confirm your changes. The 70D has enough memory to store values for 40 different lenses or lens+tele-extender combinations (handy!). If you want to register more than 40 lenses, select a lens with an adjustment that can be deleted, mount it on the camera, and reset its adjustment to 0. That will free up a slot for a different lens.

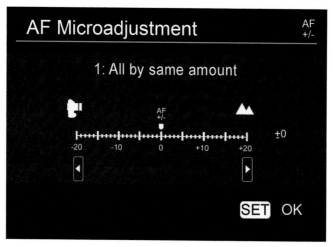

Figure 5.20
Adjustments toward the left move the focus plane closer to the camera; adjustments to the right move it farther away.

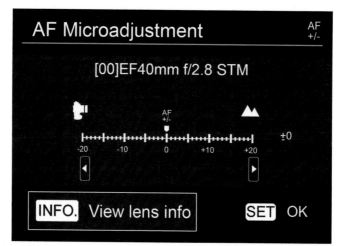

Figure 5.21
Press the INFO. button to view information about the lens mounted on the camera.

NOTE

The –20/+20 increments are not fixed values: they are based on the amount of depth-of-field available with the lens at its widest aperture. Canon states that each increment represents one-eighth of the available depth-of-field at the focal length being adjusted. That means that the increments are not only very fine, but produce different amounts of adjustment based on whether you are tweaking a wide angle or telephoto focal length.

6

Live View and Movies

Cameras like the Canon EOS 70D are loaded with killer features. And, by killer, I mean that new capabilities found in digital SLRs have virtually killed off whole categories of cameras, such as high-end, point-and-shoot cameras that lack interchangeable lenses or superzoom optics, and, in the future, camcorders. Who needs a camcorder when your digital SLR can shoot full HD 1080p video *and* stills?

Live view has been around long enough that it's becoming old hat for some, but, we have learned, it was really just a precursor to one of the 70D's deadliest killer features—full HD video shooting. Indeed, the opening montages of *Saturday Night Live* were all shot using Canon cameras, so you can see that movie shooting with your camera has a lot of potential. You can now buy fancy harnesses, rigs, and Steadycam setups for Canon digital cameras, turning the more ambitious among us into one-person motion picture studios, ready and able to shoot everything from family vacation movies suitable for broadcasting on PBS during pledge week to full-length feature films. It's mind-boggling to see how far movie-shooting dSLRs have progressed in the past several years.

Although this is a fairly hefty chapter that emphasizes a broad range of video techniques, movie shooting is an entirely separate discipline from still photography, and the things you can do with the 70D deserve an entire book of their own. I've expanded the number of pages devoted to movie shooting, but this is, after all, my *Guide to Digital SLR Photography*, not *Digital SLR Photography and Movie Shooting*, and an extra 100 or so pages stuffed into this tome is not in the offing. What I hope to accomplish in the next pages is to spark your interest in learning more about the 70D's video capabilities and give you enough information to get you started.

Working with Live View

Of course, live view is tightly integrated with movie shooting, so we'll start with that. Live view (and to a lesser extent movie shooting) is one of those features that, despite increasing evidence to the contrary, experienced SLR users (especially those dating from the film era) sometimes think they don't need—until they try it. But live view and movie shooting have become a permanent fixture, even for latecomers to the party. Indeed, many point-and-shoot models don't even *have* optical viewfinders, and my favorite compact camera, the Canon PowerShot G16, has only a marginally useful vestigial optical finder. So, we have an entire generation of amateur photographers who think the only way to frame and compose an image is to hold the camera out at arm's length so the back-panel LCD can be viewed more easily.

While dSLR veterans are finally warming up to live view, many still underuse the video capture capabilities of cameras like the 70D. After all, who needs to shoot home movies, and why would you eschew a big, bright, magnified through-the-lens optical view that showed depth-of-field fairly well, and which was easily visible under virtually all ambient light conditions? LCD displays, after all, were small, tended to wash out in bright light, and didn't really provide you with an accurate view of what your picture was going to look like.

Today, however, the Canon EOS 70D has a gorgeous 3-inch LCD that can be viewed under a variety of lighting conditions and from wide-ranging angles, so you don't have to be exactly behind the display to see it clearly. It offers a 98-percent view of the sensor's capture area. It's large enough to allow manual focusing. If you want to use automatic focus, you have several options. You can opt for Quick mode, described in Chapter 5, which briefly flips the mirror back down for autofocusing, interrupting live view, and then restoring the sensor preview image after focus is achieved. Or, you can use the 70D's combination contrast detection/phase detection hybrid mode for automatic focus (also described in detail in the last chapter).

Live View Essentials

You may not have considered just what you can do with live view, because the capability is so novel. But once you've played with it, you'll discover dozens of applications for this feature. Here's a list of things to think about.

- **Preview your images on a TV.** Connect your EOS 70D to an HDTV with the optional HDMI cable, and you can preview your image on a large screen.

- **Preview remotely.** Extend the cable between the camera and TV screen, and you can preview your images some distance away from the camera.

- **Shoot from your computer.** Canon gives you the software you need to control your camera from your computer, so you can preview images and take pictures or movies without physically touching the EOS 70D.

■ **Shoot from tripod or handheld.** Of course, holding the camera out at arm's length to preview an image is poor technique, and will introduce a lot of camera shake. If you want to use live view for handheld images, use an image-stabilized lens and/or a high shutter speed. A tripod is a better choice if you can use one.

■ **Watch your power.** Live view uses a lot of juice and will deplete your battery rapidly. Canon estimates that you can get 210 to 230 shots per battery when using live view, depending on the temperature. Expect slightly fewer exposures when using flash. The optional AC adapter is a useful accessory.

Enabling Live View

You need to take some steps before using live view. This workflow prevents you from accidentally using live view when you don't mean to, thus potentially losing a shot, and it also helps ensure that you've made all the settings necessary to successfully use the feature efficiently. Here are the steps to follow:

1. **Choose a shooting mode.** Live view works with any exposure mode, including Scene Intelligent Auto and Creative Auto. You can even switch from one Basic Zone mode to another or from one Creative Zone mode to another while live view is activated. (If you change from Basic to Creative, or vice versa while live view is on, it will be deactivated and must be restarted.)

2. **Enable live view.** You'll need to activate live view by choosing Live View Shoot. setting from the Live View Shooting menu (when the Mode Dial is set to a Creative Zone mode; if you're using a Basic Zone mode, an abbreviated list of live view options is found in the Live View Shooting menu). Press SET and use the QCD or multi-controller pad to select Enable and press the SET button again to exit.

3. **Choose other live view functions.** Select from the other live view functions in the Live View Shooting menu (described next), then press the MENU button to exit from the Live View Function Settings menu. Make sure you're using a Creative Zone mode if you want to view the full array of live view function options.

4. **Select live view or movie shooting.** Press the Live View button on the right side of the viewfinder to begin or end live view. Rotate the Stills/Movie switch located to the right of the viewfinder to the Movie position if you want to shoot video instead of stills.

Here are the options available from the two Live View Shooting menus. Figure 6.1 shows the Live View Shooting 1 menu; the second Live View Shooting menu (not shown) has only two entries, Silent LV Shoot. and Metering Timer.

■ **Live View Shooting.** Enables/disables live view shooting. Disabling live view does not affect movie shooting.

■ **AF Method.** Select Face Detection + Tracking mode, FlexiZone Multi mode, FlexiZone Single mode, and Quick mode autofocus options.

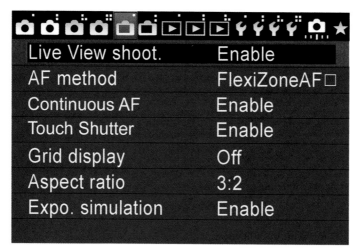

Figure 6.1
Live view function settings can be found in the Live View Shooting menu.

- **Continuous AF.** Enable or disable continuous autofocus. The camera will refocus continually even while the shutter release button is not partially depressed, and then more quickly lock in on your subject when you do activate autofocus. This "prefocus" mode speeds up the AF process, but depletes your battery more quickly. If you switch AF to Quick Mode, Continuous AF is disabled and must be reactivated when you change to a non-Quick Mode method. You should turn this feature off before sliding the lens switch to the Manual focus position.

- **Touch Shutter.** Enable or Disable the Touch Shutter feature, which allows you to specify a point of focus, activate AF, and take a picture with a tap on the touch screen.

- **Grid Display.** Overlays Grid 1 on the screen to help you compose your image and align vertical and horizontal lines; Grid 2, which consists of four rows of six boxes; or Grid 3, which adds diagonal lines.

- **Aspect Ratio.** Allows you to choose an aspect ratio, or proportions of your image, from 3:2, 4:3, 16:9, or 1:1. JPEG images will be stored using the selected ratio; RAW images will be saved using the default 3:2 proportions, but the desired cropping can be restored in your image-editing software. (See Figure 6.2.)

- **Exposure Simulation.** This option determines whether the live view image mimics the exposure level of the final image, or whether a bright image is shown that may be easier to view under high ambient lighting conditions.

  - **Enable.** The live view image corresponds to the brightness level of the actual image using the current exposure/exposure compensation settings.

  - **During DOF Preview.** The live view image is adjusted to simulate your exposure settings only when you press the depth-of-field preview button. This is a handy mode to use if you want the LCD monitor to remain as bright as possible, but retain the ability to preview exposure effects by pressing a button.

  - **Disable.** The live view image is always shown at standard brightness.

Figure 6.2
Aspect ratios of (clockwise from upper left) 3:2, 4:3, 16:9, and 1:1 can be specified.

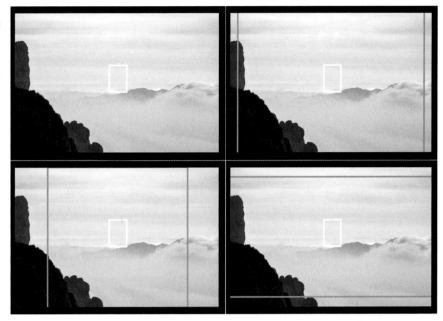

- **Silent LV Shooting.** This choice, and Metering Timer, are found on the Live View Shooting 2 menu (not shown). Reduces the noise level, using either of two modes. Mode 1 produces a quieter shooting sound level in Live View mode, and enables continuous shooting at up to 4.1 fps. Mode 2 separates the *ker* from the *clunk* sounds. Press the shutter release all the way, and the camera emits a small click as the picture is taken. When you release the button at least halfway, a discreet second click is heard. The camera ignores this setting if you're using a remote control, and defaults to Mode 1. Disable turns off silent shooting.

- **Metering Timer.** Specify how long the metering system remains active before switching off. You can select 4, 16, or 30 seconds, plus 1, 10, or 30 minutes. Tap the shutter release to restart the timer.

Activating Live View

Once you've enabled live view for later use, you can continue taking pictures normally through the 70D's viewfinder. When you're ready to activate live view, press the Live View button on the back of the camera, to the immediate right of the viewfinder window. The mirror will flip up, and the sensor image will appear on the LCD. Press the INFO. button to cycle among a display that is blank (except for the image and focus zone), one that contains basic shooting information, a full display with settings, one that adds a live histogram (see Figure 6.3.), and a full information screen that includes the electronic level display.

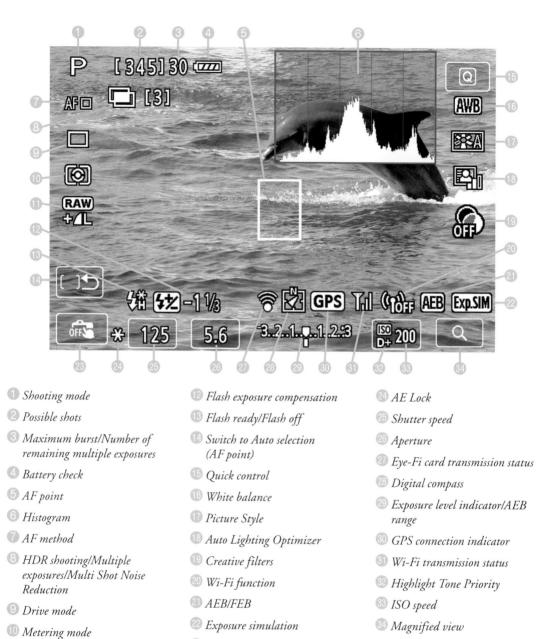

1 Shooting mode

2 Possible shots

3 Maximum burst/Number of remaining multiple exposures

4 Battery check

5 AF point

6 Histogram

7 AF method

8 HDR shooting/Multiple exposures/Multi Shot Noise Reduction

9 Drive mode

10 Metering mode

11 Image recording quality

12 Flash exposure compensation

13 Flash ready/Flash off

14 Switch to Auto selection (AF point)

15 Quick control

16 White balance

17 Picture Style

18 Auto Lighting Optimizer

19 Creative filters

20 Wi-Fi function

21 AEB/FEB

22 Exposure simulation

23 Touch shutter

24 AE Lock

25 Shutter speed

26 Aperture

27 Eye-Fi card transmission status

28 Digital compass

29 Exposure level indicator/AEB range

30 GPS connection indicator

31 Wi-Fi transmission status

32 Highlight Tone Priority

33 ISO speed

34 Magnified view

Figure 6.3 Press the INFO. button to increase or decrease the amount of information shown on the LCD in Live View mode.

Everything is not shown at one time; additional information may appear on the screen, depending on what focus or other mode you are working with, or optional accessories you are using:

- **Focus points.** If you've set focus to Quick mode, the same 19 focus points visible in the viewfinder will be shown on the LCD for reference. You can select any of these points with the multi-controller pad, and when the 70D activates autofocus by flipping down the mirror, the selected point in the optical system will be used to focus. In focus modes other than Quick mode, the active focus point will be shown.

- **Switch to Auto Selection.** In Quick mode, an icon will appear at the lower-left side of the touch screen that can be tapped to change to autofocus point selection.

- **AEB/FEB.** These icons will appear next to the Exp. Sim indicator when you're using autoexposure bracketing or flash exposure bracketing with an external flash unit.

- **Highlight Tone Priority.** If activated, a D+ will be shown next to the ISO indicator.

Final Image Simulation

When Exp. Sim. is displayed in white on the live view screen, it indicates that the LCD screen image brightness is an approximation of the brightness of the image that will be captured. If the Exp. Sim. display is blinking, it shows that the screen image does *not* represent the appearance of the final image because the light level is too dim or too bright. When using flash or bulb exposure, or night scene modes, the Exp. Sim. indicator is dimmed out to show you that the LCD image is not being adjusted to account for the actual exposure.

The 70D applies any active Picture Style settings to the LCD image, so you can have a rough representation of the image as it will appear when modified. Sharpness, contrast, color saturation, and color tone will all be applied. In addition, the camera applies the following parameters to the live view image shown:

- White balance/white balance correction
- Creative filters
- Shoot by ambience/lighting/scene choices
- Metering mode/Exposure
- Auto lighting optimization
- Peripheral illumination correction
- Chromatic aberration correction
- Highlight Tone Priority
- Aspect ratio
- Depth-of-field when DOF button is pressed

Silent Shooting

Although Silent Shooting is far from a stealth photography mode, it does produce a quieter shutter noise than what you get when not in Live View mode. That's because the mirror has already been flipped out of the way, so the sound produced primarily comes from the opening and closing of the shutter. You can activate silent shooting from the Live View function settings in the Live View Shooting 2 menu. You have three choices:

- **Mode 1.** This mode reduces the noise level of the shutter, but allows taking several shots in succession, including continuous shooting (at roughly 7.0 fps).

- **Mode 2.** This mode reduces the noise even further by delaying the action when you press the shutter release down (only a slight click is heard). When you let up slightly on the shutter release, the shot is taken, producing another soft click. Continuous shooting is not possible in Mode 2.

- **Disable.** Turns off the feature, producing the normal shutter noise sounds. This mode should be used if you're working with a tilt/shift lens, or an extension tube. Although you'll hear two clicks when using this mode, only one picture will be exposed. If you use flash, Mode 1 and Mode 2 are automatically disabled.

Quick Control

Press the Q button or tap the Q icon at the upper right of the touch screen while using a Creative Zone in live view, and you can adjust any of the values shown in the left and right hand columns. These include AF mode, Drive mode, White Balance, Picture Style, Auto Lighting Optimizer settings, Image quality settings, and Built-in flash functions. Figure 6.4 shows the focus mode adjustment screen that appears. If you're using a Basic Zone mode, you can change AF mode, self-timer settings, and several other settings, depending on the Basic Zone mode you are using:

- **Shoot by ambience.** Can be changed when using Creative Auto, Portrait, Landscape, Close-Up, Sports, and Night Portrait modes.

- **Shoot by lighting or scene type.** Can be changed in Portrait, Landscape, Close-Up, and Sports modes.

- **Blurring/Sharpening the background.** Can be changed in Creative Auto mode.

- **Automatic Flash Firing.** Can be changed in Creative Auto mode; it is set automatically in Scene Intelligent Auto, Auto (Flash Off), Portrait, Close-Up, and Night Portrait modes.

- **Flash on at all times (Fill flash).** Can be set in Creative Auto mode.

- **Flash Off.** Can be set in Creative Auto mode; it is set automatically in Auto (Flash Off), Landscape, and Sports modes.

- **Drive mode, continuous shooting.** Can be set in Creative Auto, Portrait, and Sports modes.

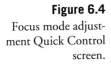

Figure 6.4

Focus mode adjustment Quick Control screen.

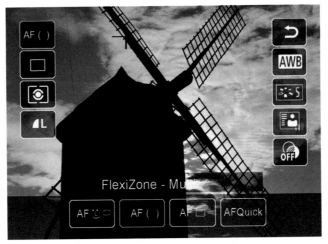

CREATIVE FILTERS LIVE

Canon has added the ability to apply Creative Filters (described in Chapter 8) as you shoot images—and preview their looks before snapping a photo—when using live view. You'll find the Creative Filters options in the lower-right corner of the live Quick Control screen, as seen in Figure 6.2.

Focusing in Live View

Press the AF-ON button or press the shutter button halfway to activate autofocus using the currently set live view autofocus mode. Those modes are Live mode, Live "Face Detection" mode, and Quick mode. You can also use manual focus. To change the focus mode while using live view, you can press the AF button and rotate the Main Dial to choose the mode you want, highlighted on the live view screen. I'll describe each of these separately.

Face Detection+Tracking Mode

This mode also uses contrast detection, using the relative sharpness of the image as it appears on the sensor to determine focus. The 70D will search the frame for a human face and attempt to focus on the face. Like Live mode, this method is less precise, and usually takes longer than Quick mode. To autofocus using Live (Face Detection) mode, follow these steps:

1. **Set lens to autofocus.** Make sure the focus switch on the lens is set to AF.

2. **Activate live view.** Press the Start/Stop button. Select Face Detection.

3. **(Live) Face detection.** A frame will appear around a face found in the image. If only one face is detected, the frame will be green; if more than one face is found, the frame will be white and have left/right triangles flanking it. (See Figure 6.5, left.) In that case, use the multi-controller to move the frame to the face you want to use for focus. If no face is detected, the AF focus frame will be displayed and focus will be locked into the center.

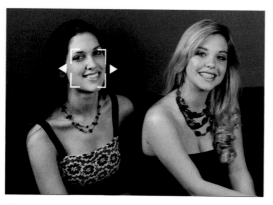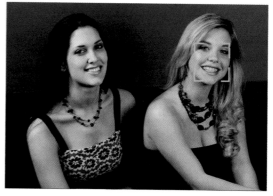

Figure 6.5 If multiple faces are found (left), the bracket can be moved among them. When focus is achieved (right), the bracket turns green.

4. **Focus.** Press the AF-ON button to focus the camera on the face within the positioned Face Detection frame. When focus is locked in, the AF frame will turn green and the beeper, if activated, will chime. (See Figure 6.5, right.) If focus cannot be achieved, the AF frame will turn orange.

5. **Press and hold the shutter release to take the picture.** Press the shutter release all the way down to take the picture.

FlexiZone (Multi) Mode

This mode allows focusing over a wide area. It's very similar to the FlexiZone (Multi) mode available when not using live view, as described in Chapter 5. In automatic selection mode, the camera selects one of 31 AF points. The 70D can automatically select the focus *area* from up to 31 different AF positions in the frame, or any of nine different *zones* you select. Review Chapter 5 if you need to refresh your knowledge of this mode.

FlexiZone - Single AF Mode

To autofocus using FlexiZone mode, follow these steps:

1. **Set lens to autofocus.** Make sure the focus switch on the lens is set to AF.

2. **Activate live view.** Press the Start/Stop button.

3. **Choose AF point.** Use the Quick Control Dial's center multi-controller pad to move the AF point anywhere you like on the screen, except for the edges. Press the SET or Trash button to return the AF point to the center of the screen.

4. **Select subject.** Compose the image on the LCD so the selected focus point is on the subject.

5. **Press and hold the AF-ON button.** When focus is achieved, the AF frame turns green, and you'll hear a beep if the sound has been turned on in the Shooting 1 menu. If the 70D is unable to focus, the AF point turns orange instead.

6. **Take picture.** Press the shutter release all the way down to take the picture.

Quick Mode

This mode uses phase detection, as described in Chapter 5. It temporarily interrupts Live View mode to allow the EOS 70D to focus the same AF sensor used when you focus through the viewfinder. Because the step takes a second or so, you may get better results using this autofocus mode when the camera is mounted on a tripod. If you handhold the 70D, you may displace the point of focus achieved by the autofocus system. It also simplifies the operation if you use One-Shot focus and center the focus point. You can use AI Servo and Automatic or Manual focus point selection, but if the focus point doesn't coincide with the subject you want to focus on, you'll end up with an out-of-focus image. Just follow these steps.

1. **Set lens to autofocus.** Make sure the focus switch on the lens is set to AF.

2. **Activate live view.** Press the Start/Stop button. Small boxes representing the optical AF system's 19 focus points will be shown. Select One-Shot AF mode.

3. **Choose AF area selection mode.** Press the AF area selection button (upper-right corner of the back of the camera).

4. **Choose AF point.** Use the QCD's center multi-controller pad to select the specific AF point from those available. You can also use the Main Dial to move the AF point horizontally, or the QCD to move it vertically. You can press SET to toggle back and forth between the center AF point and automatic point selection.

5. **Select subject.** Compose the image on the LCD so the selected focus point is on the subject.

6. **Press the shutter release halfway.** The LCD will blank as the mirror flips down, reflecting the view of the subject to the phase detection AF sensor.

7. **Wait for focus.** When the 70D is able to lock in focus using phase detection, a beep (if activated) will sound. If you are handholding the 70D, you may hear several beeps as the AF system focuses and refocuses with each camera movement. Then, the mirror will flip back up, and the live view image reappears. The AF focus point will be highlighted in green on the LCD. If focus was impossible, the AF point will blink in orange.

8. **Take picture.** Press the shutter release all the way down to take the picture. (You can't take a photo while Quick mode AF is in process, until the mirror flips back up.)

Manual Mode

Focusing manually on an LCD screen isn't as difficult as you might think, but Canon has made the process even easier by providing a magnified view. Just follow these steps to focus manually.

1. **Set lens to manual focus.** Make sure the focus switch on the lens is set to MF.

2. **Move magnifying frame.** Use the multi-controller to move the focus frame that's superimposed on the screen to the location where you want to focus. You can press the SET or Trash button to center the focus frame in the middle of the screen.

3. **Press the Magnify button.** The area of the image inside the focus frame will be magnified 5X. (See Figure 6.6.) Press the Magnify button again to increase the magnification to 10X. A third press will return you to the full-frame view. The enlarged area is artificially sharpened to make it easier for you to see the contrast changes, and simplify focusing. When zoomed in, press the shutter release halfway and the current shutter speed and aperture are shown in orange. If no information at all appears, press the INFO. button.

4. **Focus manually.** Use the focus ring on the lens to focus the image. When you're satisfied, you can zoom back out by pressing the Magnify button.

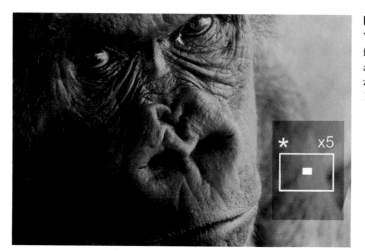

Figure 6.6

You can manually focus the center area, which can be zoomed in 5X or 10X.

Shooting Movies

The Canon EOS 70D can shoot full HD movies with stereo sound at 1920 × 1080 resolution, or Standard HD video at 1280 × 720 resolution. VGA movies can also be shot at 640 × 480 resolution.

In some ways, the camera's Movie mode is closely related to the 70D's Live View still mode. In fact, the 70D uses live view type imaging to show you the video clip on the LCD as it is captured. Many of the functions and setting options are the same, so the information in the previous sections will serve you well as you branch out into shooting movies with your camera. This section will concentrate on the differences between live view and movie shooting.

To shoot in Movie mode, just rotate the Stills/Movie switch to the Movie position. The live view screen shown in Figure 6.7 appears. Press the Start/Stop button to begin/end capture. That's quite simple, but there are some additional things you need to keep in mind before you start:

■ **Turn off Wi-Fi.** Disable Wi-Fi in the Set-up 3 menu, as movie shooting is not available when it is active.

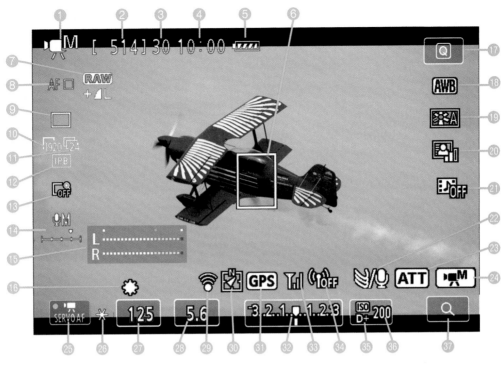

Figure 6.7 The live view screen in Movie mode.

1. *Movie shooting mode*
2. *Possible shots*
3. *Maximum burst*
4. *Movie shooting remaining time/ Elapsed time*
5. *Battery check*
6. *AF point*
7. *Image-recording quality*
8. *AF method*
9. *Drive mode*
10. *Movie recording size*
11. *Frame rate*
12. *Compression method*
13. *Digital zoom*
14. *Recording level: Manual*
15. *Level meter*
16. *LED light*
17. *Quick control*
18. *White balance*
19. *Picture Style*
20. *Auto Lighting Optimizer*
21. *Video snapshot*
22. *Wind filter*
23. *Attenuator*
24. *Exposure mode*
25. *Movie Servo AF*
26. *AE lock*
27. *Shutter speed*
28. *Aperture*
29. *Eye-Fi card transmission status*
30. *Digital compass*
31. *GPS connection indicator*
32. *Exposure level indicator*
33. *Wi-Fi transmission status*
34. *Wi-Fi function*
35. *Highlight tone priority*
36. *ISO speed*
37. *Magnify/Digital zoom*

- **Choose your resolution.** The 70D can capture movies in Full High Definition (1920 × 1080 pixel) resolution at 30, 25, or 24 fps; Standard High Definition (1280 × 720 at 60/50 fps); and 640 × 480 resolution at 30 or 25 fps. I'll show you how to specify resolution in the next section.

- **You can still shoot stills.** Press the shutter release all the way down at any time while filming movies in order to capture a still photo. Movie capture will stop for about one second while a still image is captured, leaving a gap in your clip, but will resume automatically after the picture is taken. The 70D will use the Image Quality settings you specify in the Shooting 1 menu, and will operate only in Single shooting drive mode (Continuous shooting or Self-timer delays are not possible). The flash is disabled. You can also extract a 2MP, 1MP, or .3MP image from your movie clips using ZoomBrowser. Still photos are stored as separate files.

- **Use the right card.** You'll want to use a fast memory card, at least a Class 6 SDHC card; a Class 10 card is even better. Slower cards may not work properly. Choose a memory card with at least 4GB capacity (8GB or 16GB are preferable). If the card you are working with is too slow, a five-level thermometer-like "buffer" indicator may appear at the right side of the LCD, showing the status of your camera's internal memory. If the indicator reaches the top level because the buffer is full, movie shooting will stop automatically.

- **Use a fully charged battery.** Canon says that a fresh battery will allow about one hour of filming at normal (non-Winter) temperatures.

- **Image stabilizer uses extra power.** If your lens has an image stabilizer, it will operate at all times (not just when the shutter button is pressed halfway, which is the case with still photography) and use a considerable amount of power, reducing battery life. You can switch the IS feature off to conserve power. Mount your camera on a tripod, and you don't need IS anyway.

- **Silent running.** You can connect your 70D to a television or video monitor while shooting movies, and see the video portion on the bigger screen as you shoot. However, the sound will not play—that's a good idea, because, otherwise, you could likely get a feedback loop of sound going. The sound will be recorded properly and will magically appear during playback once shooting has concluded.

Movie Shooting Menus

The two Movie shooting menus appear when the Stills/Movie switch is rotated counter clockwise to the Movie position, highlighted with a red movie camera icon. Note that the full roster of choices in the Movie 1 menu are available only when using Creative Zone modes; in Basic Zone modes only the AF Method and Movie Servo AF entries appear.

Movie 1 Menu

Here is an introduction to the options available in the Movie 1 menu (see Figure 6.8).

- **AF Method.** Three of the four AF modes available in live view, as described earlier in this chapter are options. Select Face Detection+Tracking mode, FlexiZone Multi mode, or FlexiZone Single mode. Quick mode autofocus is not available when capturing video.

Figure 6.8
The Movie 1 menu.

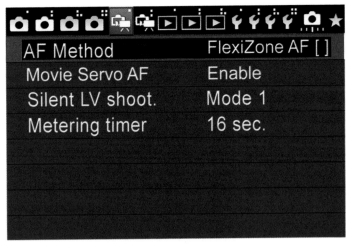

- **Movie Servo AF.** This is roughly the equivalent of live view's Continuous AF mode, which you can enable or disable. The camera will refocus continually even while the shutter release button is not partially depressed, and then more quickly lock in on your subject when you do activate autofocus. This "prefocus" mode speeds up the AF process, but depletes your battery more quickly. Turn Movie Servo AF off before sliding the lens switch to the Manual focus position.

Keep in mind that this continual refocusing process can produce motor noise that will be picked up by the 70D's microphones. You should use an extra-quiet STM lens (described in Chapter 10), or connect an external microphone positioned farther away from the lens to minimize lens operation noise. You can temporarily halt continual focusing (for example, when the correct focus point has been achieved and you don't expect it to change during the shot) by tapping the Servo AF icon in the lower left of the LCD screen. Pressing the Flash button has the same effect. You can also use C.Fn III-04 Custom Controls to assign the AF Stop function to a button, as described in Chapter 9.

- **Silent LV Shooting.** Reduces the noise level *when shooting still photos while in Movie mode.* You can specify Mode 1, which produces a quieter shooting sound level in Live View mode. Mode 2 separates the *ker* from the *clunk* sounds. Press the shutter release all the way, and the camera emits a small click as the picture is taken. When you release the button at least halfway, a discreet second click is heard. The camera ignores this setting if you're using a remote control, and defaults to Mode 1. Disable turns off silent shooting.

- **Metering Timer.** Specify how long the metering system remains active before switching off. You can select 4, 16, or 30 seconds, plus 1, 10, or 30 minutes. Tap the shutter release to restart the timer.

Movie 2 Menu

In the Movie 2 menu (see Figure 6.9), you'll see these options:

- **Grid Display.** Overlays Grid 1 on the screen to help you compose your image and align vertical and horizontal lines; Grid 2, which consists of four rows of six boxes; or Grid 3, which adds diagonal lines.

- **Movie Rec. Size.** Choose either 1920 × 1080 (full HD) or 1280 × 720 pixels (standard HD). Full HD is available in either 30 or 24 fps variations, and Standard HD can be shot at 60 fps—all using progressive scan (1080p or 720p) with your choice of All-I or IPB compression schemes. You can also select VGA resolution shooting at 30 fps with IPB compression. I'll explain these variations later in the chapter. (Substitute 25 fps and 50 fps for 24/60 fps, respectively if you live in a country that does not use the US-standard NTSC video system, as outlined later in this chapter.)

- **Digital Zoom.** This feature allows you to digitally zoom in during capture to produce a 3X to 10X telephoto effect when shooting in full HD mode. You should use a tripod to minimize camera shake from the high magnifications used.

  When activated, pressing the multi-controller pad's up/down buttons produces a zoom bar, with the up key zooming in and the down key zooming out. Movie Servo AF is disabled in this mode, and FlexiZone - Single AF, fixed at the center point, is always used. Autofocus may be slower, because contrast detect AF is always used in this mode. ISO speed is limited to ISO 6400 or less.

- **Sound Recording.** Choose Auto, Manual, or Disable; plus enable or disable wind filter and/or attenuator. In Basic Zone modes, your choices are On and Off (for automatic levels), and the wind filter will automatically be activated.

  - **Auto.** The 70D sets the audio level for you.

  - **Manual.** Choose from 64 different sound levels. Select Rec Level and rotate the QCD while viewing the decibel meter at the bottom of the screen to choose a level that averages –12 dB for the loudest sounds.

  - **Disable.** Shoot silently, and add voice over, narration, music, or other sound later in your movie-editing software.

    You can use your 70D's built-in microphone or plug in a stereo microphone into the 3.5mm jack on the side of the camera. An external microphone is a good idea because the built-in microphone can easily pick up camera operation, such as the autofocus motor in a lens.

  - **Wind filter.** Choose between Enable and Disable. Enable to reduce the effects of wind noise on the microphone. This also reduces low (bass) tones in the sound recording. If wind is not a problem, you'll get better quality audio with this option disabled. Even better is to use an external microphone with a wind shield.

  - **Attenutator.** Even if you are using Auto audio levels, or setting an appropriate level manually, a sudden loud sound can cause distortion. If you find that these disruptive noises are occurring, set the Attenuator to Enable. Otherwise, you'll get better sound quality with the Attenuator disabled.

- **Time code.** This is a reference used during editing to match up video clips and audio precisely during editing. I'll explain the Time Code options in the next section.

- **Video snapshot.** Video snapshots are movie clips, all the same length, assembled into video "albums" as a single continuous movie. You can choose a fixed length of 2, 4, or 8 seconds for all clips in a particular album. You can select Enable or Disable; when the feature is enabled you can also specify Album Settings, Snapshot Length, Create a New Album, or Add to an Existing Album. I'll explain how to use video snapshots shortly.

Figure 6.9
The Movie 2 menu.

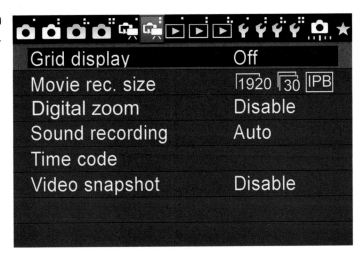

USEFUL DIGITAL ZOOM

Your EOS 70D's digital zoom feature is an exception to the rule (in still photography) that digital zooming is usually a bad thing. For movie shooting, it is a quite useful feature. Still cameras, mostly point-and-shoot models, with a digital zoom have justifiably received a bad rap. That's because, when shooting stills, digital zoom does nothing but crop the image, enlarging fewer pixels to fill the original frame. An image that starts out as 4800 × 3200 pixels and 15MP might end up "zoomed" to a 2400 × 1600 pixel (3.8MP) final image. You can usually crop in your image editor more effectively.

However, when shooting movies, the 70D's 5472 × 3648 pixel (20MP) sensor view is *already* cropped to 1920 × 1080 pixels (2MP). A center strip of the sensor's image is resampled *downward* to condense the information into an HD movie frame. Reducing available pixel data generally results in better image quality than blowing an image up by producing new pixels out of thin air with interpolation. So, the 70D's movie digital zoom will always be downsampling, because there is plenty of information in its APS-C frame to produce a decent 1920 × 1080-pixel frame even at 3X to 10X zooms. You'll still see noise and other artifacts at higher magnifications, but the results are quite usable.

Time Code

Advanced video shooters find SMPTE (Society of Motion Picture and Television Engineers)-compatible time codes embedded in the video files to be an invaluable reference during editing. To oversimplify a bit, the time system provides precise *hour:minute:second:frame* markers that allow identifying and synchronizing frames and audio. The time code system includes a provision for "dropping" frames to ensure that the fractional frame rate of captured video (remember that a 24 fps setting actually yields 23.976 frames per second while a 30 fps capture gives you 29.97 actual "frames" per second) can be matched up with actual time spans.

As I noted in the introductions to this book and this part, I won't be covering the most technical aspects of movie shooting. If you're at the stage where you're using time codes, you don't need a primer, anyway. However, the Time Code submenu does include five options:

- **Count up.** Choose Rec Run, in which the time code counts up only when you are actually capturing video; or Free Run (also known as Time of Day), which allows the time code to run up even between shooting clips. The latter is useful when you want to synchronize clips between multiple cameras that are shooting the same event. When using Free Run, even if the cameras record at different times, you'll be able to match the video that was captured at the exact same moment during editing.

- **Start Time Setting.** Normally, the 70D uses the camera's internal clock to specify the hours:minutes:seconds, with frames set to :00 when you begin shooting. This entry allows you to manually enter any hour:minute:second:frame of your choice, or to Reset the start time to 00:00:00:00.

- **Movie Rec. Count.** Here you can decide whether to display the elapsed time for the current clip on the LCD, or the Time Code while capturing video.

- **Movie Play Count.** This gives you the same choices during playback, allowing you to choose elapsed time or Time Code.

- **Drop Frame.** As I mentioned, the 30 fps setting yields 29.97 actual frames per second, and 60 fps gives you 59.95 frames per second, causing a discrepancy between the actual time and the time code that's recorded. Choose enable and the camera will skip some time code numbers at intervals to eliminate the discrepancy. Note that only the index *numbers* are skipped so they will match the frames; the camera does not delete any actual frames. When disabled, you may notice a difference of several seconds per hour.

Compression, Resolution, and Frame Rates

Even intermediate movie shooters can be confused by the number of different choices for resolution and frame rates. This section will help clarify things for you. First, compression.

Compression

Compression is easiest to understand, so I'll get it out of the way first. The 70D stores files using the standard H.264/MPEG-4 codec ("coder-decoder"), but for all resolution settings except 640 × 480, you can select either ALL-I or IPB compression methods.

- **ALL-I (All Intraframe).** In this mode, the camera takes each individual frame that you shoot and attempts to compress it before writing the frame to your memory card. You can think of All-I compression as a series of still images, each squeezed down by discarding (hopefully) redundant information. While this compression method is not the most efficient way to reduce file size, because individual frames are stored in their entirety, the resulting files are easier to edit.

- **IPB (I-frame/P-frame/B-frame).** This is a newer compression method that uses *interframe* compression; that is, only certain "key" frames are saved, with other frames "simulated" or interpolated from information contained in the frames that precede and succeed them. I-frames are the complete or *intraframes* (the only kind used by All-I compression); P-frames are "predicted picture" frames, which record *only the pixel changes* from the previous frame (say, a runner traveling across a fixed background); B-frames are "bi-predictive picture" frames, created by using the differences from the preceding *and* following frames. This interpolation produces image quality that is a bit lower and which requires more of your camera's DIGIC+ processing power, but file sizes are smaller.

  Video encoded using IPB must be converted, or transcoded to a format compatible with your video-editing software. The compression scheme can produce more artifacts, particularly in frames with lots of motion throughout the frame. I use this method only when the ability to shoot longer is very important.

In normal output mode, you can record up to 16 minutes at 235MB/minute using IPB compression before the 70D reaches its 4GB per file limit (more on that shortly). In contrast, the larger ALL-I files will reach the 4GB limit in about five minutes at 685MB/minute. So, if you really need to capture a continuous shot in *one* file (say, a performance) you might want to use IPB.

But wait, there's more! The 4GB limitation is not as noxious as you might think, and you can continue capture without, in practice, an interruption. Roughly 30 seconds before the 4GB file size is reached, the elapsed shooting time/time code displayed on the LCD will begin blinking. If you continue past 4GB, a new movie file will be created automatically. This process continues until you've reached the maximum shooting time of 29 minutes, 59 seconds (established because some jurisdictions classify equipment that can capture more than 30 minutes as "camcorders" at higher tax rates). You can patch two or more clips together in editing. Note that the 70D will not switch to your second memory card during capture even if Auto Switch Card is activated.

Resolution

Next up, resolution:

- **1920 × 1080.** This resolution is so-called "full HD" and is the maximum resolution displayed when using the HDTV format. Many monitors and most HD televisions can display this resolution, and you'll have the best image quality when you use it. Use this resolution for your "professional" productions, especially those you'll be editing and converting to nifty-looking DVDs. However, the top-of-the line resolution requires the most storage space, approximately 330 megabytes per minute, yielding about 44 minutes of "shooting time" on a 16GB memory card. (Of course the maximum length of a single continuous clip is nearly 30 minutes.)

- **1280 × 720.** "Standard HD" provides less resolution, and can be displayed on any monitor or television that claims HDTV compatibility. If your production will appear only on computer monitors with 1280 × 720 resolution, or on HDTVs that max out at 720p, this resolution will be fine.

- **640 × 480.** This is so-called VGA resolution, suitable for display on computer monitors and, possibly, old standard definition televisions. (Remember the ones with CRT tubes instead of LCD, LED, or plasma displays?) This lower-resolution format is less demanding of your storage, too, requiring about 82 megabytes per minute capture, and providing more than three hours of video clips on a single 16GB card. You'll use this resolution for productions destined for display on the internet, and other similar uses.

Frame Rates

Frame rates are a trickier proposition. Fortunately, one seemingly confusing set of alternatives can be dispensed with quickly: The 50 fps/25 fps and 60/30 fps options can be considered as pairs of *video* oriented frame rates. The 60/30 fps rates are used only where the NTSC television standard is in place, such as North America, Japan, Korea, and a few other places. The 50/25 frame rates are used where the PAL standard reigns, such as Europe, Russia, China, Africa, Australia, and other places. For simplicity, I'll refer just to the 60/30 frame rates in this section; if you're reading this in India, just convert to 50/25.

The third possibility is 24 fps, which is a standard frame rate used for motion pictures. Keep in mind that the rates are *nominal*. A 24 fps setting actually yields 23.976 frames per second; 30 fps gives you 29.97 actual "frames" per second.

The difference lies in the two "worlds" of motion images: film and video. The standard frame rate for motion picture film is 24 fps, while the video rate, at least in the United States, Japan, and those other places using the NTSC standard is 30 fps (actually 60 interlaced *fields* per second, which is why we can choose either 30 frames/fields per second or 60 frames/fields per second). Computer-editing software can handle either type, and convert between them. The choice between 24 fps and 30 fps is determined by what you plan to do with your video.

The short explanation is that, for technical reasons I won't go into here, shooting at 24 fps gives your movie a "film" look, excellent for showing fine detail. However, if your clip has moving subjects, or you pan the camera, 24 fps can produce a jerky effect called "judder." A 30 or 60 fps rate produces a home-video look that some feel is less desirable, but which is smoother and less jittery when displayed on an electronic monitor. I suggest you try both and use the frame rate that best suits your tastes and video-editing software.

Capturing Video

To shoot movies with your camera, just follow these steps:

1. **Change to Movie mode.** Rotate the Stills/Movie switch to the Movie setting.

2. **Focus.** Use the autofocus or manual focus techniques described in the preceding sections to achieve focus on your subject.

3. **Begin filming.** Press the Start/Stop button to begin shooting. A red dot appears in the upper-right corner of the screen to show that video/sound are being captured. The access lamp also flashes during shooting.

4. **Changing shooting functions.** As with live view, you can change settings or review images normally when shooting video.

5. **Lock exposure.** You can lock in exposure by pressing the Index/Reduce button on the back of the 70D, located just aft of the Main Dial. Unlock exposure again by pressing the button once more.

6. **Stop filming.** Press the Start/Stop button again to stop filming.

7. **View your clip.** Press the Playback button (located to the right of the LCD). You will see a still frame with the clip timing and a symbol telling you to press the SET button to see the clip. A series of video controls appear at the bottom of the frame. Press SET again and the clip begins. A blue thermometer bar progresses in the upper-left corner as the timing counts down. Press SET to stop at any time.

Video Snapshots

Video snapshots are movie clips, all the same length, assembled into video albums as a single movie. You can choose a fixed length of 2, 4, or 8 seconds for all clips in a particular album. I use the 2-second length to compile mini-movies of fast-moving events, such as parades, giving me a lively album of clips that show all the things going on without lingering too long on a single scene. The 8-second length is ideal for landscapes and many travel clips, because the longer scenes give you time to absorb all the interesting things to see in such environments. The 4-second clips are an excellent way to show details of a single subject, such as a cathedral or monument when traveling, or an overview of the action at a sports event.

Activate the video snapshot feature in the Movie 2 menu, as described above. Then, follow these steps:

1. **Begin an album.** In Movie mode, press the Start/Stop button. The 70D will begin shooting a clip, and a set of blue bars will appear at the bottom of the frame showing you how much time remains before shooting stops automatically. (See Figure 6.10.)

2. **Save your clip as a video snapshot album.** A confirmation appears at the bottom of the LCD. Press the left/right QCD or multi-controller pad to choose the left-most icon, Save as Album.

3. **Press SET.** Your first clip will be saved as the start of a new album.

4. **Shoot additional clips.** Press the Movie button to shoot more clips of the length you have chosen, and indicated by the blue bars at the bottom of the frame. At the end of the specified time, the confirmation screen will appear again. (See Figure 6.11.)

5. **Add to album or create new album.** Select the left-most icon again if you want to add the most recent clip to the album you just started. Alternatively, you can press the left/right QCD or multi-controller pad to choose the second icon from the left, Save as a New Album. That will complete your previous album, and start a new one with the most recent clip.

   Or, if you'd like to review the most recent clip first to make sure it's worth adding to an album, select the Playback Video Snapshot icon (second from the right) and review the clip you just shot. You can then Add to Album, Create New Album, or Delete the Clip.

6. **Delete most recent clip.** If you decide the most recent clip is not one you'd like to add to your current album, you can select Do Not Save to Album/Delete without Saving to Album (the right-most icon).

7. **Switch from Video Snapshots to conventional movie clips.** If you want to stop shooting video snapshots and resume shooting regular movie clips (of a variable length), navigate to the Movie 2 menu again, and disable Video Snapshot.

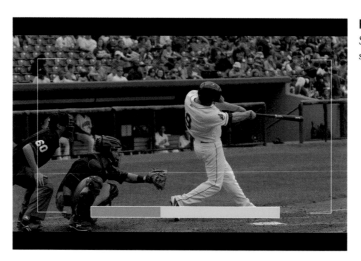

Figure 6.10
Shooting a video snapshot.

Figure 6.11
Save your clip as a
video snapshot
album.

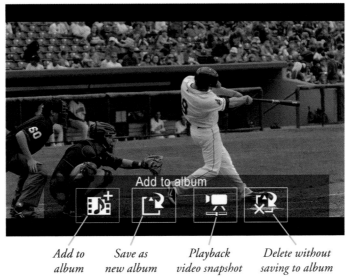

Add to   Save as   Playback   Delete without
album   new album   video snapshot   saving to album

You can play back your snapshots that have been combined into an album using the same Playback screen used to review stills and movies. In single image display, an icon in the upper left of the review image indicates that the snapshot can be played back by pressing the SET button.

The clips in a video album can be edited, either by deleting a particular snapshot from the collection or moving it to a new location within the album. Video album editing is much like editing conventional video clips, as described next.

Playback and Editing

You can play back your video snapshots from the confirmation screen. Or, you can exit Movie mode and review your stills and images and play any of them back by pressing the playback button located just below the Q button. A movie or album will be marked with an icon in the upper-left corner. If you're viewing thumbnails, the movies will be identified by a sprocket hole marking. Press the SET button to play back a movie or album when you see this icon.

As a movie or album is being played back, a screen of options appears at the bottom of the screen, as shown in Figure 6.12. When the icons are shown, use the left/right QCD or multi-controller pad to highlight one, and then press the SET button to activate that function:

- **MENU.** Exits playback mode.
- **Playback.** Begins playback of the movie or album. To pause playback, press the SET button again. That restores the row of icons so you can choose a function.
- **Slow motion.** Displays the video in slow motion.
- **First frame.** Jumps to the first frame of the video, or the first scene of an album's first video snapshot.

■ **Previous frame.** Press SET to view previous frame; hold down SET to rewind movie.

■ **Next frame.** Press SET to view next frame; hold down SET to fast forward movie.

■ **Last frame.** Jumps to last frame of the video, or the last scene of the album's last video snapshot.

■ **Edit.** Summons an editing screen (see Figure 6.13).

■ **Background music/volume.** Select to turn background music on/off. Rotate the Main Dial to adjust the volume of the background music.

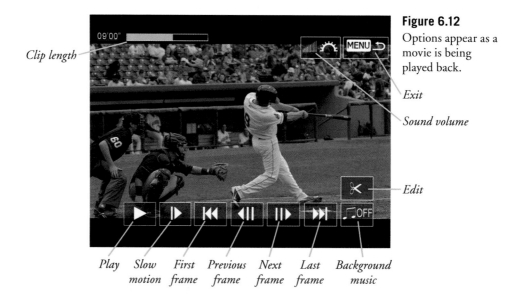

Figure 6.12
Options appear as a movie is being played back.

Clip length

Exit

Sound volume

Edit

Play   *Slow*   *First*   *Previous*   *Next*   *Last*   *Background*
          motion   *frame*   *frame*   *frame*   *frame*   *music*

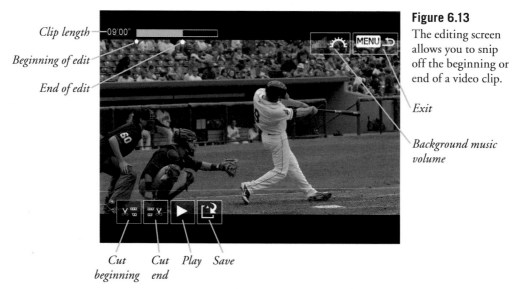

Figure 6.13
The editing screen allows you to snip off the beginning or end of a video clip.

Clip length

Beginning of edit

End of edit

Exit

Background music volume

Cut   *Cut*   *Play*   *Save*
beginning   *end*

While reviewing your video, you can trim from the beginning or end of your video clip by selecting the scissors symbol. The icons that appear have the following functions:

- **Cut beginning.** Trims off all video prior to the current point.
- **Cut end.** Removes video after the current point.
- **Play video.** Play back your video to reach the point where you want to trim the beginning or end.
- **Save.** Saves your video to the memory card. A screen appears offering to save the clip as a New File, or to Overwrite the existing movie with your edited clip.
- **Exit.** Exits editing mode.
- **Adjust volume.** Modifies the volume of the background music.

Tips for Shooting Better Movies

Producing high-quality movies can be a real challenge for amateur photographers. After all, by comparison we're used to watching the best productions that television, video, and motion pictures can offer. Whether it's fair or not, our efforts are compared to what we're used to seeing produced by experts. While this chapter can't make you into a pro videographer, it can help you improve your efforts.

There are a number of different things to consider when planning a video shoot, and when possible, a shooting script and storyboard can help you produce a higher quality video.

Lens Craft

I cover the use of lenses with the 70D in more detail in Chapter 10, but a discussion of lens selection when shooting movies may be useful at this point. In the video world, not all lenses are created equal. The two most important considerations are depth-of-field, or the beneficial lack thereof, and zooming. I'll address each of these separately.

Depth-of-Field and Video

Have you wondered why professional videographers have gone nuts over still cameras that can also shoot video? As I mentioned, the producers of *Saturday Night Live* could afford to have Alex Buono, their director of photography, use the niftiest, most expensive high-resolution video cameras to shoot the opening sequences of the program. Instead, Buono opted for a pair of digital SLR cameras. One thing that makes digital still cameras so attractive for video is that they have relatively large sensors, which provides improved low-light performance and results in the oddly attractive reduced depth-of-field, compared with most professional video cameras.

But wait! you say. No matter what size sensor is used to capture a full HD video frame, isn't the number of pixels in that frame exactly the same—1920 × 1080 pixels? That's true—the final resolution of the video image is exactly 1920 × 1080 pixels, whether you're capturing that frame with a point-and-shoot camera, a professional video camera, or a digital SLR like the 70D. But that's only the *final* resolution. The number of pixels used to capture each video frame varies by sensor size.

For example, your 70D does *not* use only its central 1920 × 1080 pixels to capture a full HD video frame. Instead, the 70D captures a video frame using the proportions of a 16:9 area of its sensor. Your wide-angle and telephoto lenses retain their same fields of view, and you can frame and compose your video through the viewfinder normally, with only the top and bottom of the frame cropped off to account for the wider video aspect ratio.

The roughly 15 million pixels used to *capture* the image are processed to create the 2,073,600 pixels of the final video frame. That's why the 70D gives you such great video quality, and why your video images retain roughly the same field of view and exact same depth-of-field you get with full-frame still images.

Figure 6.14 provides a comparison of the relative size of sensors. The typical size of a professional video camera sensor is shown at lower right. The sensor of the typical point-and-shoot camera like the PowerShot G16 is shown just northeast of it, and the proportions of the PowerShot G1 X are shown at the lower-left corner. In comparison, the 70D's image-grabber at upper left is *much* larger when compared with the sensors used in many pro video cameras and the even smaller sensors found in the typical consumer camcorder.

A larger sensor calls for the use of longer focal lengths to produce the same field of view, so, in effect, a larger sensor has reduced depth-of-field. And *that's* what makes cameras like the 70D attractive from a creative standpoint. Less depth-of-field means greater control over the range of what's in

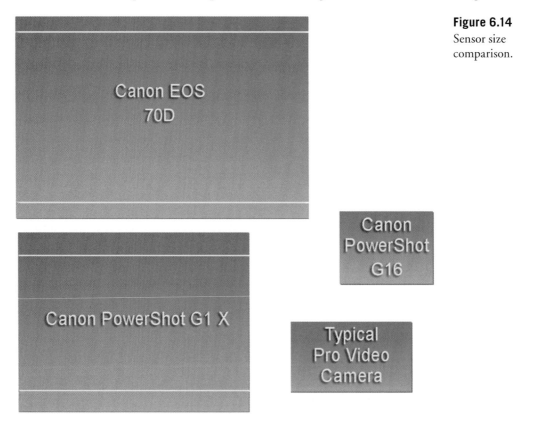

Figure 6.14
Sensor size comparison.

focus. Your 70D, with its larger sensor, has a distinct advantage over consumer camcorders in this regard, and even does a better job than many professional video cameras.

Zooming and Video

When shooting still photos, a zoom is a zoom is a zoom. The key considerations for a zoom lens used only for still photography are the maximum aperture available at each focal length ("How *fast* is this lens?"), the zoom range ("How far can I zoom in or out?"), and its sharpness at any given f/ stop ("Do I lose sharpness when I shoot wide open?").

When shooting video, the priorities may change, and there are two additional parameters to consider. The first two I listed, lens speed and zoom range, have roughly the same importance in both still and video photography. Zoom range gains a bit of importance in videography, because you can always/usually move closer to shoot a still photograph, but when you're zooming during a shot most of us don't have that option (or the funds to buy/rent a dolly to smoothly move the camera during capture). But, oddly enough, overall sharpness may have slightly less importance under certain conditions when shooting video. That's because the image changes in some way many times per second, so any given frame doesn't hang around long enough for our eyes to pick out every single detail. You want a sharp image, of course, but your standards don't need to be quite as high when shooting video.

Here are the remaining considerations:

- **Zoom lens maximum aperture.** The speed of the lens matters in several ways. A zoom with a relatively large maximum aperture lets you shoot in lower light levels, and a big f/stop allows you to minimize depth-of-field for selective focus. Keep in mind that the maximum aperture may change during zooming. A lens that offers an f/3.5 maximum aperture at its widest focal length may provide only f/5.6 worth of light at the telephoto position.

- **Zoom range.** Use of zoom during actual capture should not be an everyday thing, unless you're shooting a kung-fu movie. However, there are effective uses for a zoom shot, particularly if it's a "long" one from extreme wide angle to extreme close-up (or vice versa). Most of the time, you'll use the zoom range to adjust the perspective of the camera *between* shots, and a longer zoom range can mean less trotting back and forth to adjust the field of view. Zoom range also comes into play when you're working with selective focus (longer focal lengths have less depth-of-field), or want to expand or compress the apparent distance between foreground and background subjects. A longer range gives you more flexibility.

- **Linearity.** Interchangeable lenses may have some drawbacks, as many photographers who have been using the video features of their digital SLRs have discovered. That's because, unless a lens is optimized for video shooting, zooming with a particular lens may not necessarily be linear. Rotating the zoom collar manually at a constant speed doesn't always produce a smooth zoom. There may be "jumps" as the elements of the lens shift around during the zoom. Keep that in mind if you plan to zoom during a shot, and are using a lens that has proved, from experience, to provide a non-linear zoom. (Unfortunately, there's no easy way to tell ahead of time whether you own a lens that is well suited for zooming during a shot.)

Keeping Things Stable and on the Level

Camera shake's enough of a problem with still photography, but it becomes even more of a nuisance when you're shooting video. The image-stabilization feature found in many lenses (and some third-party optics) can help minimize this. That's why these lenses make an excellent choice for video shooting if you're planning on going for the handheld cinema verité look.

Just realize that while handheld camera shots—even image stabilized—may be perfect if you're shooting a documentary or video that intentionally mimics traditional home movie-making, in other contexts it can be disconcerting or annoying. And even IS can't work miracles. As I'll point out in the next section, it's the camera movement itself that is distracting—not necessarily any blur in our subject matter.

If you want your video to look professional, putting the 70D on a tripod will give you smoother, steadier video clips to work with. It will be easier to intercut shots taken from different angles (or even at different times) if everything was shot on a tripod. Cutting from a tripod shot to a handheld shot, or even from one handheld shot to another one that has noticeably more (or less) camera movement can call attention to what otherwise might have been a smooth cut or transition.

Remember that telephoto lenses and telephoto zoom focal lengths magnify any camera shake, even with IS, so when you're using a longer focal length, that tripod becomes an even better idea. Tripods are essential if you want to pan from side to side during a shot, dolly in and out, or track from side to side (say, you want to shoot with the camera in your kid's coaster wagon). A tripod and (for panning) a fluid head built especially for smooth video movements can add a lot of production value to your movies.

Shooting Script

A shooting script is nothing more than a coordinated plan that covers both audio and video and provides order and structure for your video when you're in planned, storytelling mode. A detailed script will cover what types of shots you're going after, what dialogue you're going to use, audio effects, transitions, and graphics. A good script needn't constrain you: as the director you are free to make changes on the spot during actual capture. But, before you change the route to your final destination, it's good to know where you were headed, and how you originally planned to get there.

When putting together your shooting script, plan for lots and lots of different shots, even if you don't think you'll need them. Only amateurish videos consist of a bunch of long, tedious shots. You'll want to vary the pace of your production by cutting among lots of different views, angles, and perspectives, so jot down your ideas for these variations when you put together your script.

If you're shooting a documentary rather than telling a story that's already been completely mapped out, the idea of using a shooting script needs to be applied more flexibly. Documentary filmmakers often have no shooting script at all. They go out, do their interviews, capture video of people, places, and events as they find them, and allow the structure of the story to take shape as they learn more about the subject of their documentary. In such cases, the movie is typically "created" during editing, as bits and pieces are assembled into the finished piece.

Storyboards

A storyboard makes a great adjunct to a detailed shooting script. It is a series of panels providing visuals of what each scene should look like. While the ones produced by Hollywood are generally of very high quality, there's nothing that says drawing skills are important for this step. Stick figures work just fine if that's the best you can do. The storyboard just helps you visualize locations, placement of actors/actresses, props and furniture, and also helps everyone involved get an idea of what you're trying to show. It also helps show how you want to frame or compose a shot. You can even shoot a series of still photos and transform them into a "storyboard" if you want, such as in Figure 6.15.

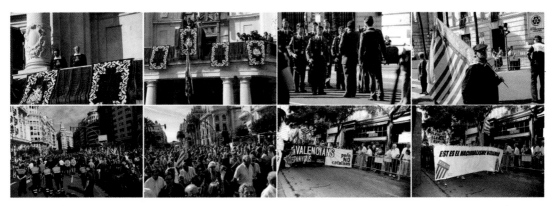

Figure 6.15 A storyboard is a series of simple sketches or photos to help visualize a segment of video.

Storytelling in Video

Today's audience is used to fast-paced, short-scene storytelling. In order to produce interesting video for such viewers, it's important to view video storytelling as a kind of shorthand code for the more leisurely efforts print media offers. Audio and video should always be advancing the story. While it's okay to let the camera linger from time to time, it should only be for a compelling reason and only briefly.

Above all, look for movement in your scene as you shoot. You're not taking still photographs! Perhaps your ideal still picture of an old castle in Segovia, Spain might be to show the edifice in its modern-day surroundings, but a movie needs to show something *moving,* like the hang glider who soared overhead when I captured the image shown in Figure 6.16.

It only takes a second or two for an establishing shot to impart the necessary information. For example, many of the scenes for a video documenting a model being photographed in a Rock 'n' Roll music setting might be close-ups and talking heads, but an establishing shot showing the studio where the video was captured helps set the scene.

Provide variety too. If you put your shooting script together correctly, you'll be changing camera angles and perspectives often and never leave a static scene on the screen for a long period of time.

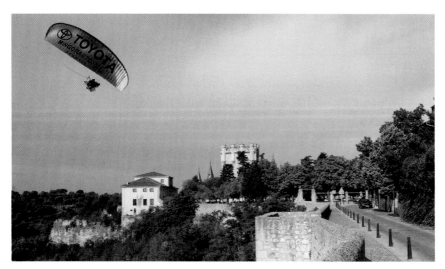

Figure 6.16
Movies need motion to come alive.

(You can record a static scene for a reasonably long period and then edit in other shots that cut away and back to the longer scene with close-ups that show each person talking.)

When editing, keep transitions basic! I can't stress this one enough. Watch a television program or movie. The action "jumps" from one scene or person to the next. Fancy transitions that involve exotic "wipes," dissolves, or cross fades take too long for the average viewer and make your video ponderous.

Composition

In movie shooting, several factors restrict your composition, and impose requirements you just don't always have in still photography (although other rules of good composition do apply). Here are some of the key differences to keep in mind when composing movie frames:

- **Horizontal compositions only.** Some subjects, such as basketball players and tall buildings, just lend themselves to vertical compositions. But movies are shown in horizontal format only. So if you're interviewing a local basketball star, you can end up with a worst-case situation like the one shown in Figure 6.17. If you want to show how tall your subject is, it's often impractical to move back far enough to show him full-length. You really can't capture a vertical composition. Tricks like getting down on the floor and shooting up at your subject can exaggerate the perspective, but aren't a perfect solution.

- **Wasted space at the sides.** Moving in to frame the basketball player as outlined by the yellow box in Figure 6.17 means that you're still forced to leave a lot of empty space on either side. (Of course, you can fill that space with other people and/or interesting stuff, but that defeats your intent of concentrating on your main subject.) So when faced with some types of subjects in a horizontal frame, you can be creative, or move in *really* tight. For example, if I was willing to give up the "height" aspect of my composition, I could have framed the shot as shown by the green box in the figure, and wasted less of the image area at either side.

Figure 6.17
Movie shooting
requires you to fit all
your subjects into a
horizontally oriented
frame.

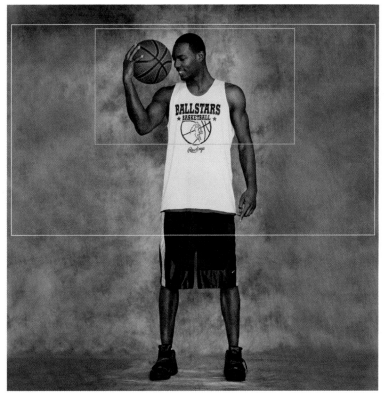

■ **Seamless (or seamed) transitions.** Unless you're telling a picture story with a photo essay, still pictures often stand alone. But with movies, each of your compositions must relate to the shot that preceded it, and the one that follows. It can be jarring to jump from a long shot to a tight close-up unless the director—you—is very creative. Another common error is the "jump cut" in which successive shots vary only slightly in camera angle, making it appear that the main subject has "jumped" from one place to another. (Although everyone from French New Wave director Jean-Luc Goddard to Guy Ritchie—Madonna's ex—have used jump cuts effectively in their films.) The rule of thumb is to vary the camera angle by at least 30 degrees between shots to make it appear to be seamless. Unless you prefer that your images flaunt convention and appear to be "seamy."

■ **The time dimension.** Unlike still photography, with motion pictures there's a lot more emphasis on using a series of images to build on each other to tell a story. Static shots where the camera is mounted on a tripod and everything is shot from the same distance are a recipe for dull videos. Watch a television program sometime and notice how often camera shots change distances and directions. Viewers are used to this variety and have come to expect it. Professional video productions are often done with multiple cameras shooting from different angles and positions. But many professional productions are shot with just one camera and careful planning, and you can do just fine with your 70D.

Here's a look at the different types of commonly used compositional tools:

- **Establishing shot.** Much like it sounds, this type of composition, as shown in Figure 6.18, left, establishes the scene and tells the viewer where the action is taking place. Let's say you're shooting a video of your offspring's move to college; the establishing shot could be a wide shot of the campus with a sign welcoming you to the school in the foreground. Another example would be for a child's birthday party; the establishing shot could be the front of the house decorated with birthday signs and streamers or a shot of the dining room table decked out with party favors and a candle-covered birthday cake. Or, in Figure 6.18, left, I wanted to show the studio where the video was shot.

- **Medium shot.** This shot is composed from about waist to head room (some space above the subject's head). It's useful for providing variety from a series of close-ups and also makes for a useful first look at a speaker. (See Figure 6.18, right.)

- **Close-up.** The close-up, usually described as "from shirt pocket to head room," provides a good composition for someone talking directly to the camera. Although it's common to have your talking head centered in the shot, that's not a requirement. In Figure 6.19, left, the subject was offset to the right. This would allow other images, especially graphics or titles, to be superimposed in the frame in a "real" (professional) production. But the compositional technique can be used with 70D videos, too, even if special effects are not going to be added.

- **Extreme close-up.** When I went through broadcast training back in the '70s, this shot was described as the "big talking face" shot and we were actively discouraged from employing it. Styles and tastes change over the years and now the big talking face is much more commonly used (maybe people are better looking these days?) and so this view may be appropriate. Just remember, the 70D is capable of shooting in high-definition video and you may be playing the video on a high-def TV; be careful that you use this composition on a face that can stand up to high definition. (See Figure 6.19, right.)

- **"Two" shot.** A two shot shows a pair of subjects in one frame. They can be side by side or one in the foreground and one in the background. (See Figure 6.20, left.) This does not have to be a head to ground composition. Subjects can be standing or seated. A "three shot" is the same principle except that three people are in the frame.

- **Over-the-shoulder shot.** Long a composition of interview programs, the "over-the-shoulder shot" uses the rear of one person's head and shoulder to serve as a frame for the other person. This puts the viewer's perspective as that of the person facing away from the camera. (See Figure 6.20, right.)

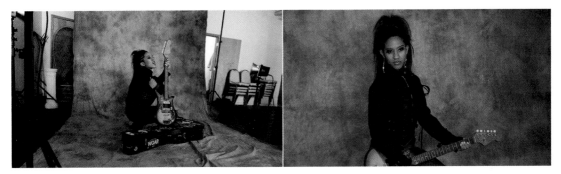

Figure 6.18 An establishing shot sets the stage for your video scene (left). A medium shot is used to introduce a character and provide context via their surroundings (right).

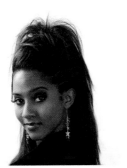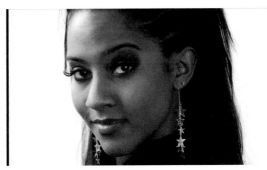

Figure 6.19 A close up generally shows the full face with a little head room at the top and down to the shoulders at the bottom of the frame (left). An extreme close-up is a very tight shot that cuts off everything above the top of the head and below the chin (or even closer!)(right).

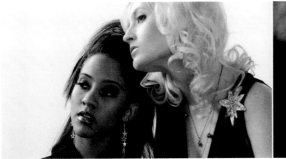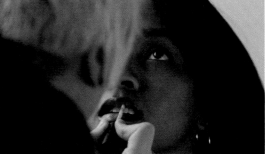

Figure 6.20 A "two shot" features two people in the frame. This version can be framed at various distances such as medium or close up (left). An "over-the-shoulder" shot is a popular shot for interview programs, making viewers feel like they're asking the questions (right).

Lighting for Video

Much like in still photography, how you handle light pretty much can make or break your videography. Lighting for video can be more complicated than lighting for still photography, since both subject and camera movement is often part of the process.

Lighting for video presents several concerns. First off, you want enough illumination to create a useable video. Beyond that, you want to use light to help tell your story or increase drama. Let's take a better look at both.

Illumination

You can significantly improve the quality of your video by increasing the light falling in the scene. This is true indoors or out, by the way. While it may seem like sunlight is more than enough, it depends on how much contrast you're dealing with. If your subject is in shadow (which can help them from squinting) or wearing a ball cap, a video light can help make them look a lot better.

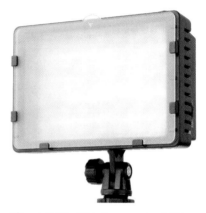

Figure 6.21 This inexpensive LED video light cost $35.

Lighting choices for amateur videographers are a lot better these days than they were a decade or two ago. An inexpensive incandescent video light, which will easily fit in a camera bag, can be found for $15 or $20. You can even get a good-quality LED video light for less than $100. (See Figure 6.21.) Work lights sold at many home improvement stores can also serve as video lights since you can set the camera's white balance to correct for any color casts. You'll need to mount these lights on a tripod or other support, or, perhaps, to a bracket that fastens to the tripod socket on the bottom of the camera.

Much of the challenge depends upon whether you're just trying to add some fill light on your subject versus trying to boost the light on an entire scene. A small video light will do just fine for the former. It won't handle the latter.

Another option 70D owners should consider is the LED video light built right into the Canon 320EX flash unit. It provides enough light for fill and illuminating subjects not too far from the camera.

Creative Lighting

While ramping up the light intensity will produce better technical quality in your video, it won't necessarily improve the artistic quality of it. Whether we're outdoors or indoors, we're used to seeing light come from above. Videographers need to consider how they position their lights to provide even illumination while up high enough to angle shadows down low and out of sight of the camera.

When considering lighting for video, there are several factors. One is the quality of the light. It can either be hard (direct) or soft (diffused). Hard light is good for showing detail, but can also be very harsh and unforgiving. "Softening" the light, but diffusing it somehow, can reduce the intensity of the light but make for a kinder, gentler light as well.

While mixing light sources isn't always a good idea, one approach is to combine window light with supplemental lighting. Position your subject with the window to one side and bring in either a supplemental light or a reflector to the other side for reasonably even lighting.

Lighting Styles

Some lighting styles are more heavily used than others. Some forms are used for special effects, while others are designed to be invisible. At its most basic, lighting just illuminates the scene, but when used properly it can also create drama. Let's look at some types of lighting styles:

- **Three-point lighting.** This is a basic lighting setup for one person. A main light illuminates the strong side of a person's face, while a fill light lights up the other side. A third light is then positioned above and behind the subject to light the back of the head and shoulders. (See Figure 6.22.)

- **Flat lighting.** Use this type of lighting to provide illumination and nothing more. It calls for a variety of lights and diffusers set to raise the light level in a space enough for good video reproduction, but not to create a particular mood or emphasize a particular scene or individual. With flat lighting, you're trying to create even lighting levels throughout the video space and minimize any shadows. Generally, the lights are placed up high and angled downward (or possibly pointed straight up to bounce off of a white ceiling). (See Figure 6.23.)

- **"Ghoul lighting."** This is the style of lighting used for old horror movies. The idea is to position the light down low, pointed upward. It's such an unnatural style of lighting that it makes its targets seem weird and "ghoulish."

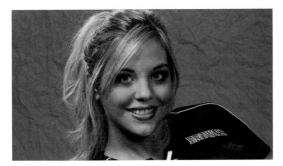

Figure 6.22 With three-point lighting, two lights are placed in front and to the side of the subject (45-degree angles are ideal) and positioned about a foot higher than the subject's head. Another light is directed on the background in order to separate the subject and the background.

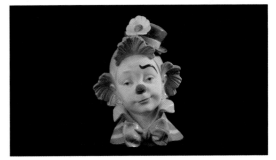

Figure 6.23 Flat lighting is another approach for creating even illumination. Here the lights can be bounced off of a white ceiling and walls to fill in shadows as much as possible. It is a flexible lighting approach since the subject can change positions without needing a change in light direction.

■ **Outdoor lighting.** While shooting outdoors may seem easier because the sun provides more light, it also presents its own problems. As a general rule of thumb, keep the sun behind you when you're shooting video outdoors, except when shooting faces (anything from a medium shot and closer) since the viewer won't want to see a squinting subject. When shooting another human this way, put the sun behind her and use a video light to balance light levels between the foreground and background. If the sun is simply too bright, position the subject in the shade and use the video light for your main illumination. Using reflectors (white board panels or aluminum foil covered cardboard panels are cheap options) can also help balance light effectively.

Audio

When it comes to making a successful video, audio quality is one of those things that separates the professionals from the amateurs. We're used to watching top-quality productions on television and in the movies, yet the average person has no idea how much effort goes in to producing what seems to be "natural" sound. Much of the sound you hear in such productions is actually recorded on carefully controlled sound stages and "sweetened" with a variety of sound effects and other recordings of "natural" sound.

Tips for Better Audio

Since recording high-quality audio is such a challenge, it's a good idea to do everything possible to maximize recording quality. Here are some ideas for improving the quality of the audio your camera records:

■ **Get the camera and its microphone close to the speaker.** The farther the microphone is from the audio source, the less effective it will be in picking up that sound. While having to position the camera and its built-in microphone closer to the subject affects your lens choices and lens perspective options, it will make the most of your audio source. Of course, if you're using a very wide-angle lens, getting too close to your subject can have unflattering results, so don't take this advice too far. It's important to think carefully about what sounds you want to capture. If you're shooting video of an acoustic combo that's not using a PA system, you'll want the microphone close to them, but not so close that, say, only the lead singer or instrumentalist is picked up, while the players at either side fade off into the background.

■ **Use an external microphone.** You'll recall the description of the camera's external microphone port in Chapter 3. As noted, this port accepts a stereo mini-plug from a standard external microphone, allowing you to achieve considerably higher audio quality for your movies than is possible with the camera's built-in microphones (which are disabled when an external mic is plugged in). An external microphone reduces the amount of camera-induced noise that is picked up and recorded on your audio track. (The action of the lens as it focuses can be audible when the built-in microphones are active.)

The external microphone port can provide plug-in power for microphones that can take their power from this sort of outlet rather than from a battery in the microphone. You may find suitable microphones from companies such as Shure and Audio-Technica. If you are on a quest for really superior audio quality, you can even obtain a portable mixer that can plug into this jack, such as the affordable Rolls MX124 (around $150) (www.rolls.com), letting you use multiple high-quality microphones (up to four) to record your soundtrack.

An exciting new option designed specifically for still cameras like the 70D is the Beachtek DXA-SLR PRO HDSLR Audio Adapter. It's more expensive, at around $450, but has even more professional sound options and clips right onto the bottom of your camera using the tripod mounting socket. (See Figure 6.24.)

One advantage that a sound mixing device like the DSX-SLR PRO offers over the stock 70D is that it adds a quality headphone output jack to your camera, so you can monitor the sound being recorded (you can also listen to your soundtrack through the headphones during playback, which is *way* better than using the 70D's built-in speaker). The adapter has two balanced XLR microphone inputs and can also accept line input (from another audio source), and provides cool features like AGC (automatic gain control), built-in limiting, and VU meters you can use to monitor sound input.

■ **Hide the microphone.** Combine the first few tips by using an external mic, and getting it as close to your subject as possible. If you're capturing a single person, you can always use a lapel microphone (described in the next section). But if you want a single mic to capture sound from multiple sources, your best bet may be to hide it somewhere in the shot. Put it behind a vase, using duct tape to fasten the microphone and fix the mic cable out of sight (if you're not using a wireless microphone).

■ **Turn off any sound makers you can.** Little things like fans and air handling units aren't obvious to the human ear, but will be picked up by the microphone. Turn off any machinery or devices that you can plus make sure cell phones are set to silent mode. Also, do what you can to minimize sounds such as wind, radio, television, or people talking in the background.

Figure 6.24
The Beachtek DXA-SLR PRO HDSLR Audio Adapter offers professional sound mixing options.

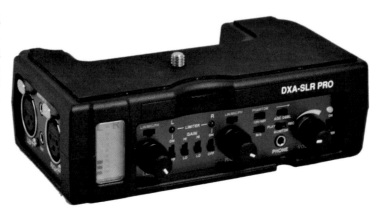

- **Make sure to record some "natural" sound.** If you're shooting video at an event of some kind, make sure you get some background sound that you can add to your audio as desired in postproduction.

- **Consider recording audio separately.** Lip-syncing is probably beyond most of the people you're going to be shooting, but there's nothing that says you can't record narration separately and add it later. It's relatively easy if you learn how to use simple software video-editing programs like iMovie (for the Macintosh) or Windows Movie Maker (for Windows PCs). Any time the speaker is off-camera, you can work with separately recorded narration rather than recording the speaker on-camera. This can produce much cleaner sound.

External Microphones

The single most important thing you can do to improve your audio quality is to use an external microphone. The 70D's internal stereo microphones mounted on the front of the camera will do a decent job, but have some significant drawbacks, partially spelled out in the previous section:

- **Camera noise.** There are plenty of noise sources emanating from the camera, including your own breathing and rustling around as the camera shifts in your hand. Manual zooming is bound to affect your sound, and your fingers will fall directly in front of the built-in mics as you change focal lengths. An external microphone isolates the sound recording from camera noise.

- **Distance.** Anytime your 70D is located more than 6 to 8 feet from your subjects or sound source, the audio will suffer. An external unit allows you to place the mic right next to your subject.

- **Improved quality.** Obviously, Canon wasn't able to install a super-expensive, super high-quality microphone. Not all owners of the 70D would be willing to pay the premium, especially if they didn't plan to shoot much video themselves. An external microphone will almost always be of better quality.

- **Directionality.** The 70D's internal microphones generally record only sounds directly in front of them. An external microphone can be either of the directional type or omnidirectional, depending on whether you want to "shotgun" your sound or record more ambient sound.

You can choose from several different types of microphones, each of which has its own advantages and disadvantages. If you're serious about movie making with your 70D, you might want to own more than one. Common configurations include:

- **Shotgun microphones.** These can be mounted directly on your 70D. I prefer to use a bracket, which further isolates the microphone from any camera noise. One thing to keep in mind is that while the shotgun mic will generally ignore any sound coming from *behind* it, it will pick up any sound it is pointed at, even *behind* your subject. You may be capturing video and audio of someone you're interviewing in a restaurant, and not realize you're picking up the lunchtime conversation of the diners seated in the table behind your subject. Outdoors, you may record your speaker, as well as the traffic on a busy street or freeway in the background.

- **Lapel microphones.** Also called *lavalieres*, these microphones attach to the subject's clothing and pick up their voice with the best quality. You'll need a long enough cord or a wireless mic (described later). These are especially good for video interviews, so whether you're producing a documentary or grilling relatives for a family history, you'll want one of these.

- **Handheld microphones.** If you're capturing a singer crooning a tune, or want your subject to mimic famed faux newscaster Wally Ballou, a handheld mic may be your best choice. They serve much the same purpose as a lapel microphone, and they're more intrusive—but that may be the point. A handheld microphone can make a great prop for your fake newscast! The speaker can talk right into the microphone, point it at another person, or use it to record ambient sound. If your narrator is not going to appear on-camera, one of these can be an inexpensive way to improve sound.

- **Wired and wireless external microphones.** This option is the most expensive, but you get a receiver and a transmitter (both battery-powered, so you'll need to make sure you have enough batteries). The transmitter is connected to the microphone, and the receiver is connected to your 70D. In addition to being less klutzy and enabling you to avoid having wires on view in your scene, wireless mics let you record sounds that are physically located some distance from your camera. Of course, you need to keep in mind the range of your device, and be aware of possible signal interference from other electronic components in the vicinity.

WIND NOISE REDUCTION

Always use the windscreen provided with an external microphone to reduce the effect of noise produced by even light breezes blowing over the microphone. Many mics include a low-cut filter to further reduce wind noise. However, these can also affect other sounds. External mics often have their own low-cut filter switch. Your 70D has its own wind filter, discussed earlier in this chapter.

7

Advanced Shooting

You can happily spend your entire shooting career using the techniques and features already explained in this book. Great exposures, sharp pictures, and creative compositions are all you really need to produce great shot after great shot. But, those with enough interest in getting the most out of their Canon EOS 70D who buy this book probably will be interested in going beyond those basics to explore some of the more advanced techniques and capabilities of the camera. Capturing the briefest instant of time, transforming common scenes into the unusual with lengthy time exposures, and working with new tools like Wi-Fi are all tempting avenues for exploration. So, in this chapter, I'm going to offer longer discussions of some of the more advanced techniques and capabilities that I like to put to work.

Continuous Shooting

The Canon EOS 70D's Continuous shooting mode reminds me how far digital photography has brought us. The first accessory I purchased when I worked as a sports photographer some years ago was a motor drive for my film SLR. It enabled me to snap off a series of shots in rapid succession, which came in very handy when a fullback broke through the line and headed for the end zone. Even a seasoned action photographer can miss the decisive instant when a crucial block is made, or a baseball superstar's bat shatters and pieces of cork fly out. Continuous shooting simplifies taking a series of pictures, either to ensure that one has more or less the exact moment you want to capture or to capture a sequence that is interesting as a collection of successive images.

The 70D's "motor drive" capabilities are, in many ways, much superior to what you got with a film camera. For one thing, a motor-driven film camera ate up film at an incredible pace, which is why many of them were used with cassettes that hold hundreds of feet of film stock. At three frames per second (typical of film cameras), a short burst of a few seconds burned up as much as half of an ordinary 36 exposure roll of film. Digital cameras, in contrast, have reusable "film," so if you waste a few dozen shots on non-decisive moments, you can erase them and shoot more. Save only the best shots, like the series shown in Figure 7.1.

To use the 70D's Continuous shooting mode, press the Drive button on top of the camera and use the touch screen, Quick Control Dial, or multi-controller to select one of three Continuous shooting icons (Continuous High, Continuous Low, and Silent Continuous). Alternatively, you can press the Q button to pop up the Quick Control screen and use the touch screen or physical controls to specify the drive mode. When you partially depress the shutter button, the viewfinder will display a number representing the maximum number of shots you can take at the current quality settings. (If your battery is low, this figure will be lower.)

Continuous shooting can be affected by the speed with which your 70D is able to focus. So, in AI Servo AF mode, the frames-per-second rate may be lower. Lenses that inherently focus more slowly (see Chapter 10 for information on the various types of autofocus motors built into Canon lenses), and scenes that are poorly lit can also affect the frame rate. The buffer in the 70D will generally allow you to take as many as 40 JPEG Large/Fine frames at 7 fps, 15 RAW images, and 8 RAW+JPEG Large Fine pictures in a single burst (when using a UHS-I, or Ultra High Speed I compatible memory card). To increase this number, reduce the image quality setting by switching to JPEG only (from JPEG+RAW), to a lower JPEG quality setting, or by reducing the 70D's resolution from L to M or S.

The reason the size of your bursts is limited by the buffer is that continuous images are first shuttled into the 70D's internal memory, then doled out to the memory card as quickly as they can be written to the card. Technically, the 70D takes the RAW data received from the digital image processor and converts it to the output format you've selected—either JPG or CR2 (RAW) or both—and deposits it in the buffer ready to store on the card.

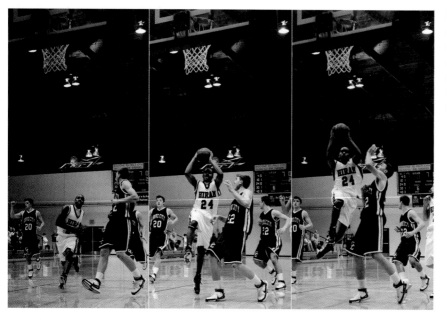

Figure 7.1
Continuous shooting allows you to capture an entire sequence of exciting moments as they unfold.

BURSTS NOT JUST FOR ACTION

I often use Continuous shooting mode even when I'm not busy shooting action. As I've mentioned before, bursts make sense when you're shooting HDR or bracketing. But here's a technique you might not have thought of—continuous shooting can give you sharper images!

When I'm photographing concerts, I most frequently use my 70-200mm f/2.8 IS zoom, handheld, with image stabilization turned on, and using the highest continuous frame rate at my disposal. I enjoy greater mobility by not using a monopod (and a tripod would be even more of a ball-and-chain, even if not forbidden by the venue). I'm generally shooting at around 1/180th second, which is usually fast enough to eliminate blur from the performers' motion. IS has no effect on stopping *their* movement, of course, and it does a fairly good job of eliminating camera/photographer shake. However, I invariably find that if I shoot in Continuous, one of the middle frames in a sequence will be sharpest. Even the most seasoned photographer will add a little bump to the camera when they squeeze (not stab) the shutter release.

This internal "smart" buffer can suck up photos much more quickly than the memory card and, indeed, some memory cards are significantly faster or slower than others. You'll get the fastest frame rate when using a shutter speed of 1/500th second, the widest lens opening of the lens, One-Shot autofocus, and when image stabilization is turned off. When One-Shot AF is active, the 70D will focus only once at the beginning of the continuous sequence, and then use that focus setting for the rest of the shots in the burst. If your subject is moving, you can use AI Servo AF instead, at a slightly slower continuous frame rate.

Setting ISO Speed Noise Reduction to High or Multi Shot Noise Reduction in the Shooting 4 menu also limits the length of your continuous burst. You'll also see a decrease if Chromatic Aberration is enabled in the Shooting 2 menu's Lens Aberration Correction entry, or you have the camera set to do white balance bracketing. (In such cases, the 70D stores three copies of each image snapped, slowing down the burst rate.) While you can use flash in Continuous mode, the camera will wait for the flash to recycle between shots, slowing down the continuous shooting rate.

When the buffer fills, you can't take any more continuous shots (a buSY indicator appears in the viewfinder) until the 70D has written some of them to the card, making more room in the buffer. (You should keep in mind that faster memory cards write images more quickly, freeing up buffer space faster.)

More Exposure Options

In Chapter 4, you learned techniques for getting the *right* exposure, but I haven't explained all your exposure options just yet. You'll want to know about the *kind* of exposure settings that are available to you with the Canon EOS 70D. There are options that let you control when the exposure is made, or even how to make an exposure that's out of the ordinary in terms of length (time or bulb exposures). The sections that follow explain your camera's special exposure features, and even discuss a few it does not have (and why it doesn't).

A Tiny Slice of Time

Exposures that seem impossibly brief can reveal a world we didn't know existed. In the 1930s, Dr. Harold Edgerton, a professor of electrical engineering at MIT, pioneered high-speed photography using a repeating electronic flash unit he patented called the *stroboscope*. As the inventor of the electronic flash, he popularized its use to freeze objects in motion, and you've probably seen his photographs of bullets piercing balloons and drops of milk forming a coronet-shaped splash.

Electronic flash freezes action by virtue of its extremely short duration—as brief as 1/50,000th second or less. Although the EOS 70D's built-in flash unit can give you these ultra-quick glimpses of moving subjects, an external flash, such as one of the Canon Speedlites, offers even more versatility. You can read more about using electronic flash to stop action in Chapter 11.

Of course, the 70D is fully capable of immobilizing all but the fastest movement using only its shutter speeds, which range all the way up to 1/8,000th second. Indeed, you'll rarely have need for such a brief shutter speed in ordinary shooting. If you wanted to use an aperture of f/2.8 at ISO 100 outdoors in bright sunlight, for some reason, a shutter speed of 1/4,000th second would more than do the job. You'd need a faster shutter speed only if you moved the ISO setting to a higher sensitivity (but why would you do that?). Under less than full sunlight, 1/4,000th second is more than fast enough for any conditions you're likely to encounter, so you're unlikely to ever need the top shutter speed built into your camera.

Most sports action can be frozen at 1/2,000th second or slower, and for many sports a slower shutter speed is actually preferable—for example, to allow the wheels of a racing automobile or motorcycle, or the propeller on a classic aircraft to blur realistically.

But if you want to do some exotic action-freezing photography without resorting to electronic flash, the 70D's top shutter speed is at your disposal. Here are some things to think about when exploring this type of high-speed photography:

- **You'll need a lot of light.** High shutter speeds cut very fine slices of time and sharply reduce the amount of illumination that reaches your sensor. To use 1/8,000th second at an aperture of f/6.3, you'd need an ISO setting of 1600—even in full daylight. To use an f/stop smaller than f/6.3 or an ISO setting lower than 1600, you'd need *more* light than full daylight provides. (That's why electronic flash units work so well for high-speed photography when used as the sole illumination; they provide both the effect of a brief shutter speed and the high levels of illumination needed.)

- **Forget about reciprocity failure.** If you're an old-time film shooter, you might recall that very brief shutter speeds (as well as very high light levels and very *long* exposures) produced an effect called *reciprocity failure,* in which given exposures ended up providing less than the calculated value because of the way film responded to very short, very intense, or very long exposures of light. Solid-state sensors don't suffer from this defect, so you don't need to make an adjustment when using high shutter speeds (or brief flash bursts).

- **Don't combine high shutter speeds with electronic flash.** You might be tempted to use an electronic flash with a high shutter speed. Perhaps you want to stop some action in daylight with a brief shutter speed and use electronic flash only as supplemental illumination to fill in the shadows. Unfortunately, under most conditions you can't use flash in subdued illumination with your 70D at any shutter speed faster than 1/250th second. That's the fastest speed at which the camera's focal plane shutter is fully open: at shorter speeds, the "slit" described above comes into play, so that the flash will expose only the small portion of the sensor exposed by the slit during its duration. (Check out "Avoiding Sync Speed Problems" in Chapter 11 if you want to see how you *can* use shutter speeds shorter than 1/250th second with certain Canon Speedlites, albeit at much reduced effective power levels.)

Working with Short Exposures

You can have a lot of fun exploring the kinds of pictures you can take using very brief exposure times, whether you decide to take advantage of the action-stopping capabilities of your built-in or external electronic flash or work with the Canon EOS 70D's faster shutter speeds. Here are a few ideas to get you started:

- **Take revealing images.** Fast shutter speeds can help you reveal the real subject behind the façade, by freezing constant motion to capture an enlightening moment in time. Legendary fashion/portrait photographer Philippe Halsman used leaping photos of famous people, such as the Duke and Duchess of Windsor, Richard Nixon, and Salvador Dali to illuminate their real selves. Halsman said, "*When you ask a person to jump, his attention is mostly directed toward the act of jumping and the mask falls so that the real person appears.*" Try some high-speed portraits of people you know in motion to see how they appear when concentrating on something other than the portrait. (See Figure 7.2.)

- **Create unreal images.** High-speed photography can also produce photographs that show your subjects in ways that are quite unreal. A helicopter in mid-air with its rotors frozen makes for an unusual picture. Figure 7.3 shows a pair of pictures. At top, a shutter speed of 1/1000th second virtually stopped the rotation of the chopper's rotors, while the bottom image, shot at 1/250th second, provides a more realistic view of the blurry blades as they appeared to the eye.

- **Capture unseen perspectives.** Some things are *never* seen in real life, except when viewed in a stop-action photograph. Edgerton's balloon bursts were only a starting point. Freeze a hummingbird in flight for a view of wings that never seem to stop. Or, capture the splashes as liquid falls into a bowl, as shown in Figure 7.4. No electronic flash was required for this image (and wouldn't have illuminated the water in the bowl as evenly). Instead, a clutch of high-intensity lamps and an ISO setting of 1600 allowed the EOS 70D to capture this image at 1/2,000th second.

■ **Vanquish camera shake and gain new angles.** Here's an idea that's so obvious it isn't always explored to its fullest extent. A high enough shutter speed can free you from the tyranny of a tripod, making it easier to capture new angles, or to shoot quickly while moving around, especially with longer lenses. I tend to use a monopod or tripod for almost everything when I'm not using an image-stabilized lens, and I end up missing some shots because of a reluctance to adjust my camera support to get a higher, lower, or different angle. If you have enough light and can use an f/stop wide enough to permit a high shutter speed, you'll find a new freedom to choose your shots. I have a favored 170mm-500mm lens that I use for sports and wildlife photography, almost invariably with a tripod, as I don't find the "reciprocal of the focal length" rule particularly helpful in most cases. (I would *not* handhold this hefty lens at its 500mm setting with a 1/500th second shutter speed under most circumstances.) However, at 1/2,000th second or faster, and with a sufficiently high ISO setting (I recommend ISO 800-1600) to allow such a speed, it's entirely possible for a steady hand to use this lens without a tripod or monopod's extra support, and I've found that my whole approach to shooting animals and other elusive subjects changes in high-speed mode. Selective focus allows dramatically isolating my prey wide open at f/6.3, too.

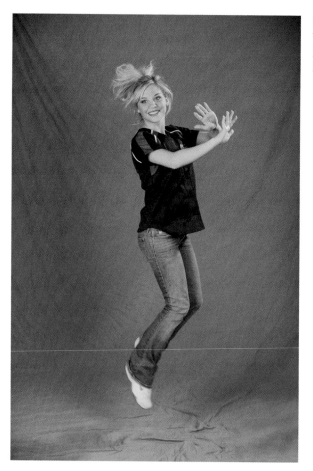

Figure 7.2
When your subjects leap, the real person inside emerges.

Figure 7.3

Top: the chopper's blades are frozen at 1/1,000th second; bottom: a more realistic blurry rendition at 1/250th second shutter speed.

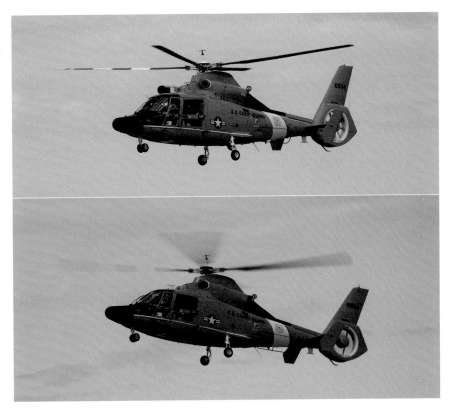

Figure 7.4

A large amount of artificial illumination and an ISO 1600 sensitivity setting allowed capturing this shot at 1/2,000th second without use of an electronic flash.

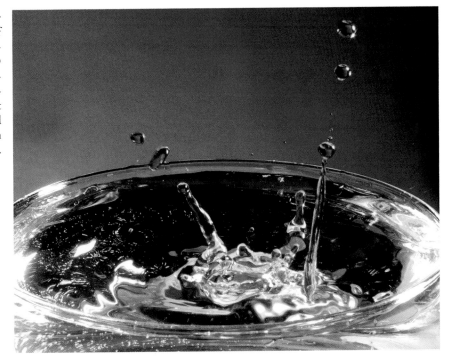

Long Exposures

Longer exposures are a doorway into another world, showing us how even familiar scenes can look much different when photographed over periods measured in seconds. At night, long exposures produce streaks of light from moving, illuminated subjects like automobiles or amusement park rides. Extra-long exposures of seemingly pitch-dark subjects can reveal interesting views using light levels barely bright enough to see by. At any time of day, including daytime (in which case you'll often need the help of neutral-density filters, which reduce the amount of light passing through the lens, to make the long exposure practical), long exposures can cause moving objects to vanish entirely, because they don't remain stationary long enough to register in a photograph.

Three Ways to Take Long Exposures

There are actually three common types of lengthy exposures: *timed exposures, bulb exposures*, and *time exposures*. The EOS 70D offers only the first two, but once you understand all three, you'll see why Canon made the choices it did. Because of the length of the exposure, all of the following techniques should be used with a tripod to hold the camera steady.

- **Timed exposures.** These are long exposures from 1 second to 30 seconds, measured by the camera itself. To take a picture in this range, simply use Manual or Tv modes and use the Main Dial to set the shutter speed to the length of time you want, choosing from preset speeds of 1.0, 1.5, 2.0, 3.0, 4.0, 6.0, 8.0, 10.0, 15.0, 20.0, or 30.0 seconds (if you've specified 1/2 stop increments for exposure adjustments), or 1.0, 1.3, 1.6, 2.0, 2.5, 3.2, 4.0, 5.0, 6.0, 8.0, 10.0, 13.0, 15.0, 20.0, 25.0, and 30.0 seconds (if you're using 1/3 stop increments). The advantage of timed exposures is that the camera does all the calculating for you. There's no need for a stop-watch. If you review your image on the LCD and decide to try again with the exposure doubled or halved, you can dial in the correct exposure with precision. The disadvantage of timed exposures is that you can't take a photo for longer than 30 seconds.

WATCH OUT FOR AMP NOISE

When exposures extend past 30 seconds into the realm of several minutes—or more—all digital cameras are theoretically susceptible to a phenomenon called *amp noise*, which manifests itself as a purplish glow, often around the edges of an image, creating an aurora borealis-style ghost effect. Amp noise happens when the sensor heats up during a long exposure, and some cameras fall victim more readily than others. The EOS 70D resists this phenomenon better than most dSLRs, but you should be aware it exists, even if you'd need to use an uncommon exposure (on the order of 30 minutes or so) to create the effect with your camera.

- **Bulb exposures.** This type of exposure is so-called because in the olden days the photographer squeezed and held an air bulb attached to a tube that provided the force necessary to keep the shutter open. Traditionally, a bulb exposure is one that lasts as long as the shutter release button is pressed; when you release the button, the exposure ends. To make a bulb exposure with the 70D, set the camera on M using the Mode Dial, then rotate the Main Dial all the way past the longest available shutter speeds to the Bulb position. Then, press the shutter to start the exposure, and press it again to close the shutter.

- **Time exposures.** This is a setting found on some cameras to produce longer exposures. With cameras that implement this option, the shutter opens when you press the shutter release button, and remains open until you press the button again. Usually, you'll be able to close the shutter using a mechanical cable release (now virtually extinct) or, more commonly, an electronic release cable. The advantage of this approach is that you can take an exposure of virtually any duration without the need for special equipment (the tethered release is optional). You can press the shutter release button, go off for a few minutes, and come back to close the shutter (assuming your camera is still there). The disadvantages of this mode are exposures must be timed manually, and with shorter exposures, it's possible for the vibration of manually opening and closing the shutter to register in the photo. For longer exposures, the period of vibration is relatively brief and not usually a problem—and there is always the release cable option to eliminate photographer-caused camera shake entirely. While the 70D does not have a built-in time exposure capability, you can simulate it with the bulb exposure technique, described previously, or use a remote control with the facility.

Working with Long Exposures

Because the EOS 70D produces such good images at longer exposures, and there are so many creative things you can do with long-exposure techniques, you'll want to do some experimenting. Get yourself a tripod or another firm support and take some test shots with long exposure noise reduction both enabled and disabled using the entry in the Shooting 4 menu, as explained in Chapter 8 (to see whether you prefer low noise or high detail) and get started. Here are some things to try:

- **Make people invisible.** One very cool thing about long exposures is that objects that move rapidly enough won't register at all in a photograph, while the subjects that remain stationary are portrayed in the normal way. That makes it easy to produce people-free landscape photos and architectural photos at night or, even, in full daylight if you use a neutral-density filter (or two or three) to allow an exposure of at least a few seconds. At ISO 100, f/22, and a pair of 8X (three-stop) neutral-density filters, you can use exposures of nearly two seconds; overcast days and/or more neutral-density filtration would work even better if daylight people-vanishing is your goal. They'll have to be walking *very* briskly and across the field of view (rather than directly toward the camera) for this to work. At night, it's much easier to achieve this effect with the 20- to 30-second exposures that are possible, as you can see in Figures 7.5 and 7.6.

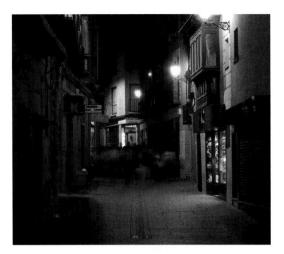

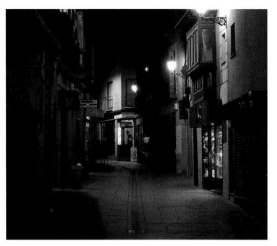

Figure 7.5 This alleyway is thronged with people, as you can see in this two-second exposure using only the available illumination.

Figure 7.6 With the camera still on a tripod, a 30-second exposure rendered the passersby almost invisible.

- **Create streaks.** If you aren't shooting for total invisibility, long exposures with the camera on a tripod or monopod can produce some interesting streaky effects, as you can see in Figure 7.7. You don't need to limit yourself to indoor photography, however. Even a single 8X ND filter will let you shoot at f/22 and 1/6th second in full daylight at ISO 100.

- **Produce light trails.** At night, car headlights and taillights and other moving sources of illumination can generate interesting light trails. Your camera doesn't even need to be mounted on a tripod; handholding the 70D for longer exposures adds movement and patterns to your trails. If you're shooting fireworks, a longer exposure of several seconds may allow you to combine several bursts into one picture, as shown in Figure 7.8, which was shot with a tripod-mounted camera.

- **Blur waterfalls, etc.** You'll find that waterfalls and other sources of moving liquid produce a special type of long exposure blur, because the water merges into a fantasy-like veil that looks different at different exposure times, and with different waterfalls. Cascades with turbulent flow produce a rougher look at a given longer exposure than falls that flow smoothly. Although blurred waterfalls have become almost a cliché, there are still plenty of variations for a creative photographer to explore, as you can see in Figure 7.9.

- **Show total darkness in new ways.** Even on the darkest nights, there is enough starlight or glow from distant illumination sources to see by, and, if you use a long exposure, there is enough light to take a picture, too. Figure 7.10 shows San Juan, Puerto Rico late at night.

Figure 7.7
These dancers pro-
duced a swirl of
movement during
the 1/8th second
exposure.

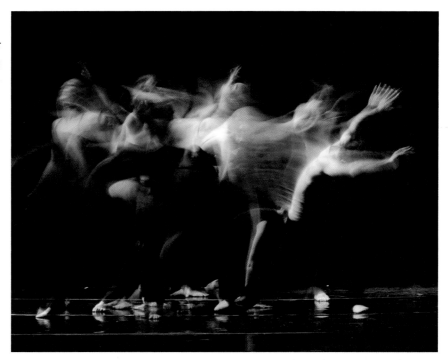

Figure 7.8
A long exposure and
a tripod allows cap-
turing several bursts
of fireworks in one
image.

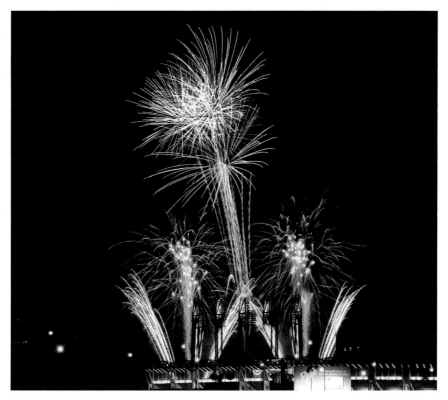

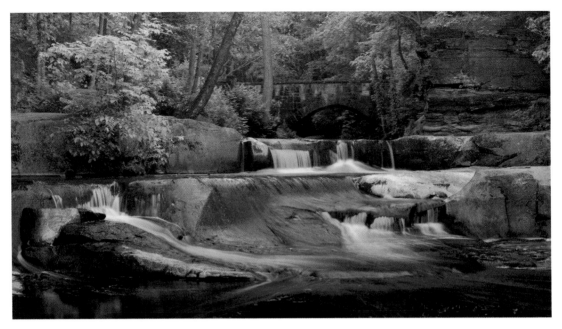

Figure 7.9 A 1/4-second exposure blurred the falling water.

Figure 7.10 A 20-second exposure revealed this view of San Juan, Puerto Rico.

Delayed Exposures

Sometimes it's desirable to have a delay of some sort before a picture is actually taken. Perhaps you'd like to get in the picture yourself, and would appreciate it if the camera waited 10 seconds after you press the shutter release to actually take the picture. Maybe you want to give a tripod-mounted camera time to settle down and damp any residual vibration after the release is pressed to improve sharpness for an exposure with a relatively slow shutter speed. It's possible you want to explore the world of time-lapse photography. The next sections present your delayed exposure options.

Self-Timer

The EOS 70D has a built-in self-timer with 10-second and 2-second delays. Activate the timer by pressing the DRIVE button and press the multi-controller buttons or rotate the QCD until the drive modes appear on the LCD status panel and LCD monitor. Press the shutter release button halfway to lock in focus on your subjects (if you're taking a self-portrait, focus on an object at a similar distance and use focus lock). When you're ready to take the photo, continue pressing the shutter release the rest of the way. The lamp on the front of the camera will blink slowly for eight seconds (when using the 10-second timer) and the beeper will chirp (if you haven't disabled it in the Shooting menu, as described in Chapter 8). During the final two seconds, the beeper sounds more rapidly and the lamp remains on until the picture is taken. The top-panel LCD displays a countdown while all this is going on.

Another way to use the self-timer is with the mirror lockup feature (which can be enabled using the Shooting 2 menu, as explained in Chapter 8). This is something you might want to do if you're shooting close-ups, landscapes, or other types of pictures using the self-timer, to trip the shutter in the most vibration-free way possible. Forget to bring along your tripod, but still want to take a close-up picture with a precise focus setting? Set your digital camera to the self-timer function, then put the camera on any reasonably steady support, such as a fence post or a rock. When you're ready to take the picture, press the shutter release. The camera might teeter back and forth for a second or two, but it will settle back to its original position before the self-timer activates the shutter. The self-timer remains active until you turn it off—even if you power down the 70D, so remember to turn it off when finished.

Time-Lapse/Interval Photography

Who hasn't marveled at a time-lapse photograph of a flower opening, a series of shots of the moon marching across the sky, or one of those extreme time-lapse picture sets showing something that takes a very, very long time, such as a building under construction.

You probably won't be shooting such construction shots, unless you have a spare 70D you don't need for a few months (or are willing to go through the rigmarole of figuring out how to set up your camera in precisely the same position using the same lens settings to shoot a series of pictures at intervals). However, other kinds of time-lapse photography are entirely within reach.

Although the EOS 70D can't take time-lapse/interval photographs all by itself, if you're willing to tether the camera to a computer (a laptop will do) using the USB cable, you can take time-lapse photos using EOS Utility software furnished with your camera.

Here are some tips for effective time-lapse photography:

- **Use AC power.** If you're shooting a long sequence, consider connecting your camera to an AC adapter, as leaving the 70D on for long periods of time will rapidly deplete the battery.

- **Make sure you have enough storage space.** Unless your memory card has enough capacity to hold all the images you'll be taking, you might want to change to a higher compression rate or reduced resolution to maximize the image count.

- **Make a movie.** While time-lapse stills are interesting, you can increase your fun factor by compiling all your shots into a motion picture using your favorite desktop movie-making software.

- **Protect your camera.** If your camera will be set up for an extended period of time (longer than an hour or two), make sure it's protected from weather, earthquakes, animals, young children, innocent bystanders, and theft.

- **Vary intervals.** Experiment with different time intervals. You don't want to take pictures too often or less often than necessary to capture the changes you hope to image.

Geotagging and Wi-Fi

These days, Wi-Fi (built into your 70D) and GPS capabilities (available using an accessory Canon GP-E2 receiver) work together with your EOS 70D in interesting new ways. Wireless capabilities allow you to upload photos directly from your 70D to your computer at home or in your studio, or, through a hotspot at your hotel or coffee shop back to your home computer or to a photo-sharing service like Facebook or Flickr. A special Wi-Fi-enabled memory card that you slip in the SD slot of your camera can also be used to perform this magic. GPS capabilities—built right into some of those Wi-Fi cards using positioning information obtained over the network—allow you to mark your photographs with location information, so you don't have to guess where a picture was taken.

Both capabilities are very cool. Wi-Fi uploads can provide instant backup of important shots and sharing. Geotagging is most important as a way to associate the geographical location where the photographer was when a picture was taken, with the actual photograph itself. It can be done with location-mapping capabilities, or through add-on devices that third parties make available for your 70D.

Geotagging

Geotagging can also be done by attaching geographic information to the photo after it's already been taken. This is often done with online sharing services, such as Flickr, which allow you to associate your uploaded photographs with a map, city, street address, or postal code. When properly geotagged and uploaded to sites like Flickr, users can browse through your photos using a map, finding pictures you've taken in a given area, or even searching through photos taken at the same location by other users.

Canon offers a GP-E2 GPS receiver that can be purchased for less than $400, and connects through the 70D's hot shoe. It records locational data such as latitude, longitude, and altitude, and saves it to the EXIF metadata in your image files, where it can be retrieved by compatible software to plot to maps or insert into your uploads to Flickr or other sites. You can even track your trajectory of movement with the receiver's logging function, and there is a built-in electric compass that logs the camera's orientation for each shot.

If you're looking for an even less expensive GPS solution, with supplementary Wi-Fi capabilities to boot, try one of the memory cards offered by Transcend or Eye-Fi (www.eye.fi). Eye-Fi cards have been around longer and offer a wider choice of models. Each Eye-Fi card is an SDHC memory card with a wireless transmitter built in. You insert it in your camera just as with any ordinary card (see Figure 7.11), and then specify which networks to use. You can add as many as 32 different networks. The next time your camera is on within range of a specified network, your photos and videos can be uploaded to your computer and/or to your favorite sharing site. During setup, you can customize where you want your images uploaded. The Eye-Fi card will only send them to the computer and to the sharing site you choose.

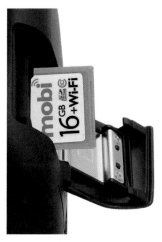

Uploads over these networks can go to your own destinations or to any of 25 popular sharing websites, including Flickr, Facebook, Costco, Adorama, Smugmug, YouTube, Shutterfly, or Walmart. Online Sharing is included as a lifetime, unlimited service with all

Figure 7.11 The Eye-Fi card is a memory card with built-in Wi-Fi and GPS capabilities.

X2 cards. Although the Eye-Fi card does not have a GPS receiver, it uses information from connected Wi-Fi networks to determine the current location, and embeds that in the image files stored on the card. Your EOS 70D has an Eye-Fi Settings entry with two entries at the bottom of the Set-up 1 menu that appear when you have an Eye-Fi card inserted:

- **Eye-Fi trans.** This setting has two options: Enable and Disable. Because the Eye-Fi card draws its power from the 70D, you might want to disable the capability when you don't want it, in order to save some juice. I tend to leave it on all the time, and allow the card to upload information to the networks I've specified. When enabled, the card can also draw location information from the hotspots it accesses, associating geographical information with each shot, too.

- **Connection info.** This displays current information about your Eye-Fi card's link to your network or hotspot, and other data, such as the firmware version. (See Figure 7.12.)

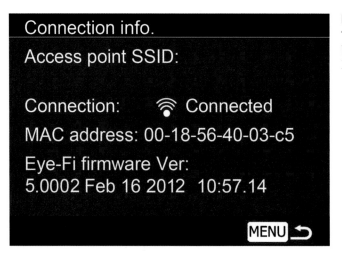

Figure 7.12
The EOS 70D has built-in support for Eye-Fi cards.

You'll want to turn off Eye-Fi when traveling on an airplane (just as you disable your cell phone, tablet, or laptop's wireless capabilities when required to do so). In addition, use of Wi-Fi cards may be restricted or banned outside the United States, because the telecommunications laws differ in other countries.

When uploading to online sites, you can specify not just where your images are sent, but how they are organized, by specifying preset album names, tags, descriptions, and even privacy preferences on certain sharing sites. (You should be cautious about sharing your location when using social media sites.) Some Eye-Fi cards also include geotagging service, which help you view uploaded photos on a map, and sort them by location. Eye-Fi's geotagging uses Wi-Fi Positioning System (WPS) technology. Using built-in Wi-Fi, the Eye-Fi card senses surrounding Wi-Fi networks as you take pictures. When photos are uploaded, the Eye-Fi service then adds the geotags to your photos. You don't need to have the password or a subscription for the Wi-Fi networks the card accesses; it can grab the location information directly without the need to "log in." You don't need to set up or control the Eye-Fi card from your camera. Software on your computer manages all the parameters.

If you frequently travel outside the range of your home (or business) Wi-Fi network, an optional service called Hotspot Access is available, allowing you to connect to any AT&T Wi-Fi hotspot in the USA. In addition, you can use your own Wi-Fi accounts from commercial network providers, your city, even organizations you belong to such as your university.

The card has another interesting feature called Endless Memory. When pictures have been safely uploaded to an external site, the card can be set to automatically erase the oldest images to free up space for new pictures. You choose the threshold where the card starts zapping your old pictures to make room.

Eye-Fi currently offers several models, from about $50 to $100. The most sophisticated options are found in the Eye-Fi X2 cards, available in capacities up to 16GB, and which can add geographic location labels to your photo (so you'll know where you took it), and frees you from your own computer network by allowing uploads from more than 10,000 Wi-Fi hotspots around the USA. Very cool, and the ultimate in picture backup. Eye-Fi has added the ability to upload from your camera to your smartphone, too, using an Android or iOS application.

In June, 2013, the company introduced the latest wrinkle in its lineup, the Mobi, available in 8GB, 16GB, and 32GB Class 10 forms for $49, $79, and $99, respectively. The Mobi was shown in Figure 7.11, earlier. The other Eye-Fi cards can be used to upload only when you're located near a Wi-Fi connection, either a local area network (say, at work or your home) or a nearby Wi-Fi hotspot. The Mobi has its own specialized "hot spot" built right into the tiny card. That is, you can go to your phone or tablet's settings screen and, if your camera is powered up and has the Mobi card in the slot, you'll be able to select the memory card's network just as you would any Wi-Fi hotspot.

However, the Mobi's network can be used only to communicate between the memory card and your phone/tablet. All you need to do is download the free Eye-Fi app from the Apple or Android app store, and "pair" the card with your device using a unique access code supplied with the card itself. You can use the same code with any device that needs to communicate with the Mobi card, so you can pair it with any number of smart phones or tablets that you use.

My biggest beef with any of the Eye-Fi cards is slow uploads, whether to my network, to online destinations, to a smartphone, or to an iPad. You can't really shoot "tethered" with them because you'll invariably shoot faster than the uploads can take place. And, for sure, avoid instant upload of *everything* to social networking sites (specify automatic upload of images marked with Protect only) if you're using public settings and don't want everyone to see and comment on every picture you take. Let's keep the clunkers to ourselves!

Using Built-in Wi-Fi

While the Eye-Fi cards' wireless capabilities are interesting, your Canon EOS 70D's built-in Wi-Fi features are much more impressive. As detailed in Chapter 9, the camera has two entries in the Set-up 3 menu:

■ **Wi-Fi.** Use this entry to enable or disable the EOS 70D's built-in Wi-Fi capabilities. Turning Wi-Fi off will save power if you don't need the feature. You'll also need to turn off Wi-Fi if you want to shoot movies, or need to connect your camera to a computer using the USB/Digital terminal, as those features are not possible when Wi-Fi is turned on.

■ **Wi-Fi Function.** This entry allows you to activate Wi-Fi features, described next.

General Wi-Fi Guidelines

Here are some general tips for using the EOS 70D's built-in Wi-Fi functions:

■ **Conserve processing power.** Wi-Fi uses some of your camera's internal CPU's processing muscle, so when the 70D is busy communicating with another device, give Wi-Fi top priority. Don't press the shutter release, rotate the Mode Dial, or review images with the Playback button. If you do, Wi-Fi functions may be interrupted.

- **Some functions are disabled.** When Wi-Fi is enabled, movie shooting is disabled. In addition, the 70D cannot communicate with a computer, printer, GPS, or other device with a direct connection or USB cable link. Finally, you can't use an Eye-Fi card and the internal Wi-Fi functions simultaneously; if you've set the 70D's Wi-Fi functions to Enable, any Eye-Fi card is automatically disabled.

- **Avoid auto shutoff.** You'll want to disable the 70D's automatic power-saving shutdown feature when actively using the Wi-Fi feature. In the Set-up 2 menu, set Auto Power Off to Disable, or to an increment that you feel will be sufficiently long, such as 30 minutes.

- **Monitor connection status.** Wi-Fi status can be seen within the information displays on both the camera's LCD monitor and LCD panel. When Wi-Fi is disabled, or enabled but no connection is available, an OFF indicator is shown in both places. When a connection is available, the indicators are animated when data is being transmitted, and blink if the camera is waiting for a reconnection or there is a connection error.

To activate and begin using the 70D's Wi-Fi capabilities, just follow these steps:

1. **Enable Wi-Fi.** Navigate to the Set-up 3 menu and select Wi-Fi. Highlight Enable in the screen that appears and press SET.

2. **Access Functions.** Scroll down and select the Wi-Fi Function entry. The first time you use Wi-Fi Functions, a screen will pop up prompting you to enter a nickname for your camera. The sidebar that follows explains how to enter the nickname.

3. **Select function.** When your camera has acquired a nickname, the screen shown in Figure 7.13 appears. Use the Quick Control Dial to navigate to the Wi-Fi function you want to activate and press SET. Choose from:

   - Transfer images between the camera and a computer.
   - Connect to a smart phone.
   - Link to your computer using the EOS Utility.
   - Print directly from a Wi-Fi-compatible printer.
   - Upload images to web pages on the Internet.
   - View images on a DLNA (Digital Living Network Alliance) device, such as your smart TV, home media server, or even a smart phone that can connect through your home network.
   - Press INFO. to adjust general settings, including editing a previously entered nickname, viewing error details, and clearing all Wi-Fi settings. Your camera's MAC (Media Access Control) address is also displayed. That's the "label" the network uses to identify individual wireless devices that are connected. You probably won't need it unless you need to block a particular MAC address from access to a network for some reason, or simply want to use your router's screens to see what devices are connected.

4. **Enter parameters.** Each of the modes has its own set of parameters, described in the sections that follow.

Figure 7.13
Wi-Fi Function
screen.

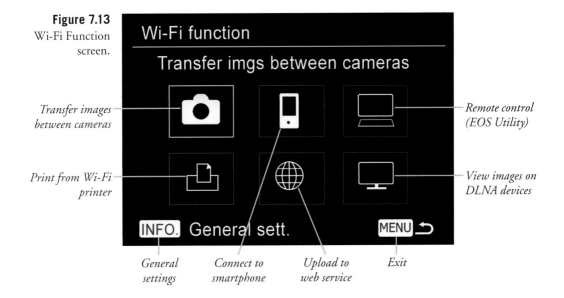

Transfer images
between cameras

Print from Wi-Fi
printer

Remote control
(EOS Utility)

View images on
DLNA devices

General
settings

Connect to
smartphone

Upload to
web service

Exit

ENTERING TEXT

The entry screen has two sections, the entered text area, and an alphabetical character selection area. Press the Q button to toggle between the two. In the selection area, navigate to the character you want to add and press SET. You can enter up to 16 characters in your nickname (such as "Canon 70D"). Press the Trash button to erase a character, the INFO. button to cancel text entry, and MENU to finish and confirm your nickname by selecting OK on the screen that pops up. If you later want to change the nickname, press the INFO. button when the Wi-Fi Function screen is displayed.

Transferring Images Between Cameras

You can easily transfer JPEG images and movie files between Canon cameras introduced in 2012 or later that have *built-in* wireless functions (your 70D cannot communicate with cameras that have Wi-Fi capabilities solely through an Eye-Fi card). Note that the destination camera must support a transmitted video file's movie format to display it. Your 70D can connect to only one other Canon camera at a time. To exchange images with another camera, one at a time, just follow these steps:

1. **Choose image transfer.** Navigate to the Wi-Fi Function menu in the Set-up 3 menu and select the Transfer Imgs Between Cameras icon, located at upper left in Figure 7.13.

2. **Make connection.** A screen appears that says "Start connection on target camera." Switch to the other camera and activate the connection there. (Refer to the instructions for the destination camera if necessary to carry out this step.) The process may take a few seconds.

3. **Connection established.** If a connection cannot be established, a warning "Could not establish connection" (Err 101) appears. Otherwise, as soon as the connection is made, the 70D registers the nickname of the target camera and connection information for re-use to pair the two cameras in the future.

4. **Files displayed.** The image files on your camera are displayed so you can select which images to transmit. (See Figure 7.14.) Note that the "EOS Camera" notation in the upper-right corner is for illustration purposes; it will be replaced by the name of the actual camera you have connected to. In my case, I used my EOS 6D, and "6D" appeared in the corner display.

5. **Specify image file.** Scroll among the available images, and press the SET button to select one. You can press the Index/Reduce button and rotate the Main Dial to the left to switch to an index/thumbnail display, or to the right to return to single-image display.

6. **Resize (optional).** You can transmit the image shown on the screen (see Figure 7.15), but you don't need to transmit the full resolution image. You can choose Resize Image.

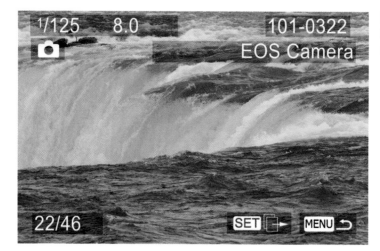

Figure 7.14
Select image to transmit.

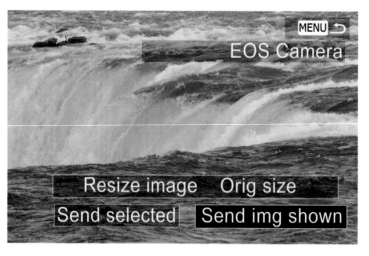

Figure 7.15
Resize image, or send in its original size.

7. **Start transfer.** When the size of the image to be sent is shown, select Send Img Shown and press SET to start the transfer. A progress screen is displayed during the transmission.

8. **Send additional images.** Repeat Steps 5-7 to send additional images.

9. **Terminate connection.** Press the MENU button to display the transfer confirmation screen, select OK, and press SET to end the transfer connection.

You can also select a batch of up to 50 individual files and send them in one group. (Don't worry: automatic power off is disabled during transmission.) The steps are similar to those listed above, except when you reach Step 7, choose Resize Image, followed by Send Selected. Then choose additional images, which are marked with a check mark in the upper-left corner of the display. When finished choosing images to transmit, press the Q button. You can then resize the selected images in a batch and choose Send to transmit all the selected images. (See Figure 7.16.)

Figure 7.16
Sending batches of images.

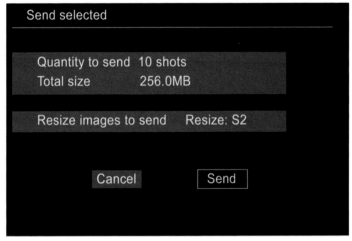

Connecting to a Smartphone

Your 70D can use its Wi-Fi connection to interface with a smartphone using an app that's available for both iOS and Android operating systems. Navigate to your phone's App store or Google Play and download the free Canon EOS Remote application, which should look something like Figure 7.17.

The camera and phone connect through a wireless LAN, either an external network (such as your home network, or one at a hotel or other site), or using the camera as an access point (so that no separate network is required). The latter mode is especially convenient, because you can use it anywhere if the camera and phone are located within range of the 70D's network capabilities. Using an external LAN might be your choice if you wanted to communicate between your camera and the phone over a greater distance.

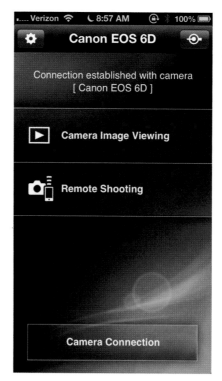

Figure 7.17
Link your camera to your smartphone through an app.

To link up through your camera's internal access point, just follow these steps:

1. Enable Wi-Fi in the Set-up 3 menu, then navigate to Wi-Fi Function entry.

2. Choose the Connect to Smartphone option, the center icon in the top row of the Wi-Fi Function screen shown earlier in Figure 7.13.

3. Select Camera Access Point Mode from the Connection Method screen that appears next (see Figure 7.18).

4. The Network Settings screen pops up. In virtually all cases, you can select Easy Connection. Choose Manual Connection only if you are knowledgeable about setting up LANs and have some special reason for wanting to make all the settings yourself.

5. A message appears displaying the name of the 70D's internal access point (the SSID, or *service set identifier* and an encryption key). This will be the nickname you chose for the camera earlier.

6. Switch to your smartphone and use its settings utility to connect to the camera's access point. You'll be asked for a password, which will be the encryption key displayed on the camera.

7. A screen will appear on the camera's LCD with the message "Start the EOS app on the smartphone." The 70D's SSID (nickname), the encryption key (password), IP address, and Mac address will also be displayed. For most of us, that data is just informational, and needed only by networking gurus with special applications for it.

8. Launch the EOS Remote app. It will automatically search for camera access points and display the name of your detected camera. Tap the name of the camera on the screen of the smartphone.

9. When pairing is complete, a message appears on the 70D's LCD monitor offering to connect to the smartphone (see Figure 7.19). Choose OK and press SET.

10. The current settings needed to link the 70D and your smartphone are stored in the camera, and given the name SET1. You can change this name to something else, such as "David's iPhone" by highlighting the current settings label and pressing SET. The 70D's text entry screen, described earlier, appears. Once settings are stored, reconnecting the camera to that smartphone is as simple as choosing the settings name from the camera, and activating the camera's access point on the phone.

Figure 7.18
Choose Camera Access Point Mode.

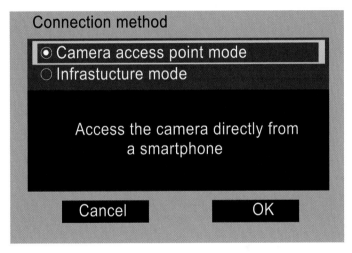

Figure 7.19
Connect to the smartphone.

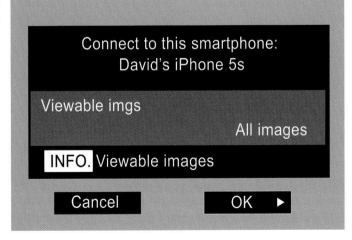

11. Once the camera and smartphone are linked, you can use the phone to view images or control the camera remotely.

12. Terminate the connection by highlighting Exit on the screen displayed on the camera and pressing SET, then confirming by choosing OK and pressing SET once again.

When accessing the 70D through the EOS Remote utility on the smartphone, you can carry out the following functions:

- **Camera Image Viewing.** View the images stored on the 70D's memory card on the smartphone. You can also save any of those images (except movies) on the smartphone; both JPEG and RAW images on the camera are stored on your camera in S2 JPEG format. Movies cannot be saved. You can also delete images stored on the camera's memory card remotely from the smartphone.

- **Remote Shooting.** You can view the 70D's Live View image on the smartphone, make various camera settings, and take pictures remotely.

- **Remote Settings.** You can change the settings of the EOS Remote app using the settings (gear-shaped) icon. Options include name of the device (the smartphone), changing image display thumbnail size, automatic live view, display of AF button, and setting of the 70D's clock.

OTHER Wi-Fi CONNECTIONS

If you prefer to link your EOS 70D to another device (including smartphones, printers, or computers) using a Wi-Fi connection other than the camera's built-in access point, you can set up a standard link, either semi-automatically using Easy Connection or Find Network functions, or manually by entering the information about the external network. It would be impossible to cover all the options for connecting to a network/access point, and choosing among WPS (Wi-Fi Protected Setup) variations for the various Windows and Mac operating systems in this book. I recommend using the 70D's internal access point to everyone who isn't intimately familiar with wireless networking. Canon does provide a PDF file (EOS70D_WIFI_EN_000.PDF) with all the parameters a LAN-savvy photographer needs to connect to a favorite network. As this is a photography book rather than computer manual, I'm not going to go into depth on any advanced options.

Remote Control with EOS Utility

The third way to connect your EOS 70D to an external device wirelessly is through the EOS Utility installed on your computer. The EOS Utility allows remote operation of your camera over a wireless connection, including image capture and other operations. Wireless movie shooting is disabled. Note that the bundled EOS Utility also allows controlling the camera over a wired connection by linking it to a computer with the digital/USB cable furnished with the 70D. Wireless control is usually more convenient, but you can opt to skip a wireless connection and drive your 70D from a wired connection to your computer instead.

Before you can operate your 70D wirelessly from a computer, the two devices must be paired, a step you might have performed before to, say, link your smartphone to your auto's Bluetooth receiver for hands-free operation. You'll need the WTFPairing application installed from your Canon Digital Solutions CD at the same time you installed the EOS Utility using the Easy Installation option. (If you used Custom installation, you must select the pairing utility separately, or install it now.) Then, just follow these steps (which will use the most automatic way; as mentioned above, you LAN gurus are free to enter your own parameters for network, authentication, and other settings):

1. With Wi-Fi enabled, access the Wi-Fi Function entry in the Set-up 3 menu and choose Remote Control (EOS Utility), which is the third icon from the left on the top row, as shown in Figure 7.13.

2. The Wireless LAN Setup Method screen, shown in Figure 7.20, appears. Choose Find Network and press SET twice.

3. The 70D will search for available networks while a Busy... notice is displayed, then produce a screen like the one shown in Figure 7.21.

4. Press SET and use the QCD to scroll down among available networks (if you have more than one), and press SET to select it. If your networks aren't found, you can choose Search Again, or, if you're one of those LAN gurus, you can select Enter Connection and work your way through a maze of choices (Infrastructure or Ad Hoc network; Open System, Shared Key, WPA-PSK, WPA2-PSK authentication; and none or WEP encryption). If you don't understand that alphabet soup, you probably shouldn't be messing with it.

5. Press SET to OK your selection, then choose the key (password) format of the target network (if it's not an open system). You'll probably just choose the default 8 to 63 ASCII characters, which are most commonly used for LAN passwords.

6. Press SET once more and you'll be whisked to the 70D's text entry screen, where you can enter the password for your network. When finished, press the MENU button to confirm.

7. The Busy... notice will appear again, and you'll be asked to set your IP address, either using a Manual Setting or, in most cases selecting the Auto Setting and allowing your network to specify the IP address.

Figure 7.20

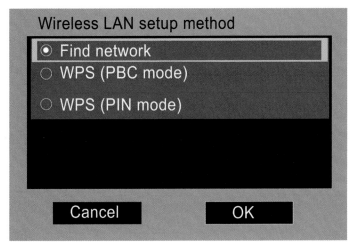

8. Press SET twice more and a Start Pairing Devices screen appears on the LCD monitor. That's your cue to begin working with the pairing application on your computer. Select OK and press SET, and a screen similar to the one seen in Figure 7.22 appears (the numerals in the EOS name will vary, as they represent the last six digits of the MAC address of the camera).

9. A dialog box will pop up on your computer when the WTFPair software detects your camera. Its name, MAC address, and IP address will be displayed. Highlight the camera name, and click Connect.

10. When the computer is paired, a screen like the one shown in Figure 7.23 appears. Press SET to confirm.

11. You'll be given the opportunity to save the settings for this linkup in the screen shown in Figure 7.24; highlight Settings Name, press SET, and you'll get another visit to the 70D's text entry screen to choose a name. Exit that screen, as always, by pressing MENU, then use OK to work your way out of the wireless LAN function screens. You can now control your camera wirelessly using your computer's EOS Utility.

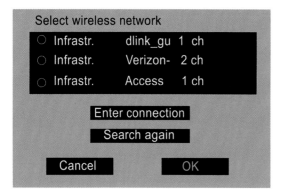

Figure 7.21

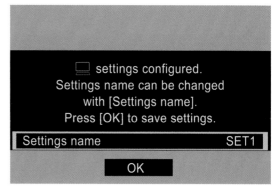

Figure 7.22

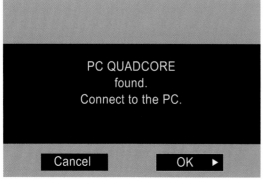

Figure 7.23

Figure 7.24

When the EOS Utility is active, the same controls available when the 70D and your computer are linked over the digital/USB cable are available. You can choose from an Accessories pane, which offers access features including the WFT Utility (for making advanced communications changes), and the Picture Style Editor (used to create and modify Picture Styles using the parameters described later in Chapter 8). The other pane, Control Camera, has five options labeled:

- **Starts to download images.** Transfers images from your camera to the computer, loading them into Digital Photo Professional.

- **Lets you select and download images.** Provides a preview of the images on your memory card and lets you select and download only those you choose.

- **Camera settings/Remote shooting.** This choice produces a panel on your computer with complete controls for operating the camera wirelessly using the mode selected on the Mode Dial, including adjusting shutter speed and/or aperture (if the mode allows it), setting white balance and ISO, exposure mode and compensation, image quality, and other parameters. Three menu tabs allow making changes for the Shooting menu, Flash Control menu, and Set-up menu. The Remote Live View window even allows you to view what the camera's sensor is seeing. All the most important camera features for remote shooting are available over the wireless link.

- **Register background music.** Shows a list of .wav music files stored on your camera, and allows you to add and register additional clips, edit the track name, and play the clips.

- **Set up web services.** You can create and/or log into a Canon Image Gateway account, described later.

Printing from Wi-Fi Printer

Many (perhaps most) printers today have built-in wireless capabilities, allowing you to print out directly from your computer without a physical link between the computer and printer. The EOS 70D adds the same function to your camera/printer setup, so you can make hard copies of your images from files in your camera without the bother of transferring them to a computer first. All you need is your 70D and a PictBridge-compatible printer that conforms to the DPS over IP standard. (More alphabet soup: *Digital Photo Solutions* and *Internet Protocol*.) To use this feature, you must:

- **Configure your printer for wireless printing.** The instructions vary from printer to printer, so you should consult your printer manual for the procedures. Once you've done this, you'll be able to print photos from your camera, plus files from your computer and other compatible devices, such as smartphones. Wireless printing is *not* limited to camera-to-printer communications.

- **Link your camera to the printer.** The procedures are the same as those mentioned earlier. You can use your camera's built-in access point. A list of detected printers is displayed, and, as before, you can save the camera-printer connection to a setting for re-use later. Multiple printer connections can be registered.

■ **Printing images.** Once linked, you can print by pressing the Playback button and scrolling to the image you want to output. Select printing parameters, number of prints, and other settings just as you would for printing over a wired connection to a PictBridge printer.

Uploading to a Web Service

This wireless option allows you to select images and upload them to the Canon Image Gateway, which is a free of charge service. You can register online through your computer and through this entry. Once you've become a member, you can upload photos, create photo albums, and use other Canon Image Gateway services. The site also can interface with other web services you have an account with, including e-mail, Twitter, YouTube, and Facebook.

All you need is your EOS 70D and a computer with the EOS Utility installed. Before you can interface with the Canon gateway wirelessly, you must connect your camera and computer using the conventional digital/USB connection, log onto the Gateway through the "globe" icon, and configure the camera's settings to allow access to the Web services. (Remember that Wireless capabilities must be set to Disable any time you want to use a wired connection between your camera and computer.)

Then, you can remove the direct link, turn wireless features back on, and connect to your computer through the wireless access methods described earlier in this chapter. Still images can be uploaded to the Gateway, and movies to YouTube. Images can be uploaded directly to Facebook, or shared with Facebook and Twitter users by posting a link back to the Canon Image Gateway location of the files. As with the image transfer features described earlier, you can resize images before uploading, and send photos one by one or in batches.

Viewing Images on DLNA Devices

If you have a DLNA (Digital Living Network Alliance) compatible TV, game machine (such as PlayStation or xBox), smartphone, or other device labeled as a "media player," you can view the images in your camera on that display. Consult your destination device's instructions for setting the media display component to receive information from your camera. You can then connect the 70D and the DLNA device using connection controls similar to those described earlier in this chapter.

Part III

Configuring Your Canon EOS 70D

The next two chapters are devoted to helping you dig deeper into the customization capabilities of your EOS 70D, so you can exploit all those cool features that your previous camera might have lacked. Chapters 8 and 9 list every setting and option found in the Shooting, Playback, Set-up, and My Menu tabs. I explained your options with the single Live View and two Movie menus in Chapter 6.

- **Chapter 8, "Customizing with the Shooting and Playback Menus":** In this chapter, you'll learn some easy stuff—like how to turn your 70D's Beep on or off, along with some very important capabilities, like using the camera's lens aberration correction facility to banish vignetted corners and color fringes. I explain Picture Styles, recap the most important Live View/Movie options originally discussed in Chapter 6, and show you how to apply creative filters and assemble your own photo books.

- **Chapter 9, "Customizing with the Set-up Menu, Custom Menu, and My Menu":** A broad array of setup and customization options are here. You'll learn how to format memory cards, adjust LCD brightness and screen colors, and enter time zones and dates. You'll even discover how to set up your own listings of menu commands with the My Menus option.

8

Customizing with the Shooting and Playback Menus

The Canon 70D is undoubtedly the most customizable, tweakable, fine-tunable camera Canon has offered non-professional users. In fact, this versatility has made the 70D surprisingly popular among professional photographers as well. If your camera doesn't behave in exactly the way you'd like, chances are you can make a small change in the Shooting, Playback, and Set-up menus that will tailor the 70D to your needs. In fact, if you don't like the *menus*, you can create your own using the clever My Menu system.

This chapter and the next will help you sort out the settings you can make to customize how your Canon 70D uses its features, shoots photos, displays images, and processes the pictures after they've been taken. As I've mentioned before, this book isn't intended to replace the manual you received with your 70D, nor have I any interest in rehashing its contents. You'll still find the original manual useful as a standby reference that lists every possible option in exhaustive (if mind-numbing) detail—without really telling you how to use those options to take better pictures. There is, how-ever, some unavoidable duplication between the Canon manual and this chapter, because I'm going to explain the key menu choices and the options you may have in using them. You should find, though, that this chapter gives you the information you need in a much more helpful format, with plenty of detail on why you should make some settings that are particularly cryptic.

I'm not going to waste a lot of space on some of the more obvious menu choices. For example, you can probably figure out that the Beep option in the Shooting 1 menu deals with the solid-state beeper in your camera that sounds off during various activities (such as the self-timer countdown). You can certainly decipher the import of the two options available in the Shooting 2 menu for the

Red-Eye Reduc. entry (Enable, Disable), assuming you know what red-eye reduction is. (I'll explain it if you don't.) So, in this chapter, I'll devote no more than a sentence or two to the blatantly obvious settings and concentrate on the more confusing aspects of 70D setup, such as Automatic Exposure Bracketing. I'll cover the Shooting menus (including live view shooting) and Playback menus in this chapter, and turn to the Set-up, Custom Functions, and My Menu options in Chapter 9. Movie options were explained in Chapter 6.

Let's start off with an overview of the 70D's menus themselves.

Anatomy of the 70D's Menus

If you have jumped directly to the Canon 70D from an ancient model like the EOS 30D, you're in for a pleasant surprise from a menu perspective. Like all recent EOS cameras, this model abandons the time-consuming scrolling through one endless menu in favor of multiple individually tabbed menus, each with a single screen of options (so you won't need to scroll within a menu to see all the entries). The menus are much cleaner, too.

If you've used another EOS model, you'll find the 70D's menu system familiar, but with a more attractive look that includes "shaded" menu tabs (see Figure 8.1). Some menu items have been moved around and/or renamed. With the current system, just press the MENU button, spin the Main Dial to highlight the menu tab you want to access, and then scroll up and down within a menu with the multi-controller. If you have small enough fingers, you can use the touch screen, too. What could be easier?

Tapping the MENU button brings up a typical menu like the one shown in the figure. (If the camera goes to "sleep" while you're reviewing a menu, you may need to wake it up again by tapping the shutter release button.) Different menu tabs are provided, depending on the shooting mode:

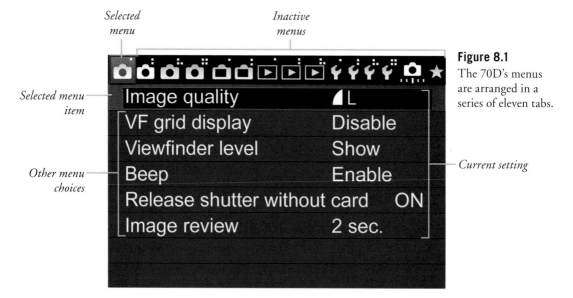

Selected menu

Inactive menus

Selected menu item

Other menu choices

Figure 8.1
The 70D's menus are arranged in a series of eleven tabs.

Current setting

In this chapter, I'm going to explain all the tabs and all the menu entries, and not take the time to mention which of those are not available when using scene and other modes. The automatic modes are intended for situations when you don't want full control over your 70D's operation, anyway, and menu limitations go with the territory. The Movie menus were previously discussed in Chapter 6 and won't be repeated here.

The 70D's tabs are color-coded: red for Shooting, Live View Shooting, and Movie menus; blue for Playback menus; amber for Set-up menus; brown for the Custom menu; and green for the My Menu tab. The currently selected menu's icon is white within a background corresponding to its color code. All the inactive menus are dimmed.

MENU NAVIGATION

Remember: you can use the touch screen to move from menu to menu, or, alternatively, you can work with the Main Dial and the multi-controller or Quick Control Dial to highlight a particular menu entry. Press SET to select a menu item.

You can jump from tab to tab even if you've highlighted a particular menu setting on another tab—and the 70D will remember which menu entry you've highlighted when you return to that menu. The memorization works even if you leave the menu system or turn off your camera. The 70D always remembers the last menu entry you used with a particular tab. So, if you generally use the Format Card command each time you access the Set-up 1 menu, that's the entry that will be highlighted when you choose that tab. The camera remembers which tab was last used, too, so, potentially, formatting your memory card might take just a couple presses (the MENU button, SET to select the highlighted Format command, then a tap, or a click of the multi-controller to choose OK, and another SET to start the format process).

Here are the things to watch for as you navigate the menus:

■ **Menu tabs.** In the top row of the menu screen, the menu that is currently active will be highlighted as described earlier. One, two, three, or four dots in the tab lets you know if you are in, say Set-up 1, Set-up 2, Set-up 3, or Set-up 4. Just remember that the red camera icons stand for still, live view, and movie shooting options; the two blue right-pointing triangles represent playback options; the four yellow wrench icons stand for set-up options; and the green star stands for personalized menus defined for the star of the show—you.

■ **Selected menu item.** The currently selected menu entry within a given tab will have a black background and will be surrounded by a box the same hue as its color code.

■ **Other menu choices.** The other menu items visible on the screen will have a dark gray background.

■ **Current setting.** The current settings for visible menu items are shown in the right-hand column, until one menu item is selected (by choosing SET). At that point all the settings vanish from the screen except for those dealing with the active menu choice.

When you've moved the menu highlighting to the menu item you want to work with, choose the SET button to select it. The current settings for the other menu items in the list will be hidden, and a list of options for the selected menu item (or a submenu screen) will appear. Within the menu choices, you can scroll up or down with the touch screen or multi-controller; choose SET to select the choice you've made; and choose MENU again to exit.

Shooting Menu Options

You'll find that the Shooting menu options are those that you access second most frequently when you're using your 70D. You might make such adjustments as you begin a shooting session, or when you move from one type of subject to another. Canon makes accessing these changes very easy.

This section explains the options of the four Shooting menus and how to use them. The options you'll find in these red-coded menus include:

- Image Quality
- VF Grid Display
- Viewfinder level
- Beep
- Release Shutter without Card
- Image Review
- Lens Aberration Correction
- Flash Control
- Red-Eye Reduction
- Mirror Lockup
- Exposure Compensation/ AEB (Automatic Exposure Bracketing)
- ISO Speed Settings
- Auto Lighting Optimizer
- White Balance
- Custom White Balance
- WB Shift/BKT
- Color Space
- Picture Style
- Long Exposure Noise Reduction
- High ISO Speed Noise Reduction
- Highlight Tone Priority
- Dust Delete Data
- Multiple Exposure
- HDR Mode

Image Quality

You can choose the image quality settings used by the 70D to store its files. You have four choices to make when selecting a quality setting:

- **Resolution.** The number of pixels captured determines the absolute resolution of the photos you shoot with your 70D. Your choices range from 20 megapixels (Large or L), measuring 5472 × 3648; 8.9 megapixels (Medium or M), measuring 3648 × 2432 pixels; 5 megapixels (Small 1 or S1), 2736 × 1824 pixels; 2.5 megapixels (Small 2 or S2), 1920 × 1280; and 350,000 pixels (Small 3 or S3), 720 × 480. You can also choose RAW-only sizes of RAW (5472 × 3648 pixels; 20MP); M-RAW (4104 × 2736; 11 MP); or S-RAW (2736 × 1824; 5 MP).

- **JPEG compression.** To reduce the size of your image files and allow more photos to be stored on a given memory card, the 70D uses JPEG compression to squeeze the images down to a smaller size. This compacting reduces the image quality a little, so you're offered your choice of Fine compression and Normal compression. The symbols help you remember that Fine compression (represented by a quarter-circle) provides the smoothest results, while Normal compression (signified by a stair-step icon) provides "jaggier" images.

■ **JPEG, RAW, or both.** You can elect to store only JPEG versions of the images you shoot or you can save your photos as uncompressed, loss-free RAW files, which consume about four times as much space on your memory card (up to 20MB per file). Or, you can store both at once as you shoot. Many photographers elect to save *both* a JPEG and a RAW file, so they'll have a JPEG version that might be usable as-is, as well as the original "digital negative" RAW file in case they want to do some processing of the image later. You'll end up with two different versions of the same file: one with a JPG extension, and one with the CR2 extension that signifies a Canon RAW file.

To choose the combination you want, access the menus, scroll to Image Quality, and press the SET button. A screen similar to the one shown in Figure 8.2 will appear with two rows of choices. Spin the Main Dial to choose from: -- (no RAW), RAW, M RAW, or S RAW. Rotate the QCD to select one of the JPEG choices: -- (no JPEG), Large, Medium, or Small in Fine or Normal compression (represented by smooth and stepped icons, respectively), plus Small 2 or Small 3 JPEG, at the resolutions listed above. A red box appears around the currently selected choice. If you choose -- for both RAW and JPEG, then JPEG Fine will be used.

Why so many choices? There are some limited advantages to using the Medium and Small resolution settings, Normal JPEG compression setting, and the two lower resolution RAW formats. They all allow stretching the capacity of your memory card so you can shoehorn quite a few more pictures onto a single memory card. That can come in useful when on vacation and you're running out of storage, or when you're shooting non-critical work that doesn't require full resolution. The Small 2 and Small 3 settings can be useful for photos taken for real estate listings, web page display, photo ID cards, or similar non-critical applications.

For most work, using lower resolution and extra compression is often false economy. You never know when you might actually need that extra bit of picture detail. Your best bet is to have enough memory cards to handle all the shooting you want to do until you have the chance to transfer your photos to your computer or a personal storage device.

Figure 8.2
Choose your resolution, JPEG compression, and file format from this screen.

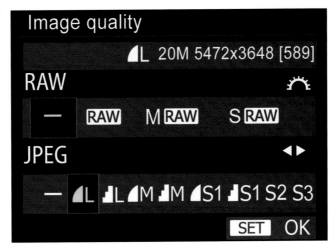

However, reduced image quality can sometimes be beneficial if you're shooting sequences of photos rapidly, as the 70D is able to hold more of them in its internal memory buffer before transferring to the memory card. Still, for most sports and other applications, you'd probably rather have better, sharper pictures than longer periods of continuous shooting.

JPEG vs. RAW

You'll sometimes be told that RAW files are the "unprocessed" image information your camera produces, before it's been modified. That's nonsense. RAW files are no more unprocessed than camera film was after it had been through the chemicals to produce a negative or transparency. Back in the film days, a lot could happen in the developer that affected the quality of a film image—positively and negatively—and, similarly, your digital image undergoes a significant amount of processing before it is saved as a RAW file. Canon even applies a name (DIGIC 5) to the digital image processing (DIP) chip used to perform this magic.

A RAW file is more similar to a film camera's processed negative. It contains all the information, captured in 14-bit channels per color (and stored in a 16-bit space), with no compression, no sharpening, no application of any special filters or other settings you might have specified when you took the picture. Those settings are *stored* with the RAW file so they can be applied when the image is converted to a form compatible with your favorite image editor. However, using RAW conversion software such as Adobe Camera Raw or Canon's Digital Photo Professional, you can override those settings and apply settings of your own. You can select essentially the same changes there that you might have specified in your camera's picture-taking options.

RAW exists because sometimes we want to have access to all the information captured by the camera, before the camera's internal logic has processed it and converted the image to a standard file format. RAW doesn't save as much space as JPEG. What it does do is preserve all the information captured by your camera after it's been converted from analog to digital form. Of course, the 70D's RAW format preserves the *settings* information.

So, why don't we always use RAW? Although some photographers do save only in RAW format, it's more common to use either RAW plus one of the JPEG options or just shoot JPEG and avoid RAW altogether. That's because having only RAW files to work with can significantly slow down your workflow. While RAW is overwhelmingly helpful when an image needs to be fine-tuned, in other situations working with a RAW file, when all you really need is a good quality, un-tweaked JPEG image, consumes time that you may not want to waste. For example, RAW images take longer to store on the memory card, and require more post-processing effort, whether you elect to go with the default settings in force when the picture was taken, or just make minor adjustments.

As a result, those who depend on speedy access to images or who shoot large numbers of photos at once may prefer JPEG over RAW. Wedding photographers, for example, might expose several thousand photos during a bridal affair and offer hundreds to clients as electronic proofs for possible inclusion in an album or transfer to a CD or DVD. These wedding shooters, who want JPEG images as their final product, take the time to make sure that their in-camera settings are correct, minimizing the need to post-process photos after the event. Given that their JPEGs are so good (in most cases thanks, in large part, to the pro photographer's extensive experience), there is little need to get bogged down shooting RAW.

Sports photographers also eschew RAW files. I visited a local Division III college one sunny September afternoon and managed to cover a football game, trot down a hill to shoot a women's soccer match later that afternoon, and ended up in the adjacent field house shooting a volleyball invitational tournament an hour later. I managed to shoot 1,920 photos, most of them at a 3.7 fps clip, in about four hours. I certainly didn't have any plans to do post-processing on very many of those shots, and firing the 70D at its maximum frame rate didn't allow RAW shooting, so carefully exposed and precisely focused JPEG images were my file format of choice that day.

JPEG was invented as a more compact file format that can store most of the information in a digital image, but in a much smaller size. JPEG predates most digital SLRs, and was initially used to squeeze down files for transmission over slow dialup connections. Even if you were using an early dSLR with 1.3 megapixel files for news photography, you didn't want to send them back to the office over a modem (Google it) at 1,200 bps.

But, as I noted, JPEG provides smaller files by compressing the information in a way that loses some image data. JPEG remains a viable alternative because it offers several different quality levels. At the highest quality Fine level, you might not be able to tell the difference between the original RAW file and the JPEG version. You've squeezed the image significantly without losing much visual information at all.

In my case, I shoot virtually everything at RAW+JPEG Fine. Most of the time, I'm not concerned about filling up my memory cards, as I usually have a minimum of five fast 16GB memory cards with me. I also have some 32GB SD cards that are a little slower (so I don't use them for sports), but with even more capacity. If I think I may fill up all those cards, I have Apple's Camera Connection Kit for my iPad, and can transfer photos to that device. As I mentioned earlier, when shooting sports I'll shift to JPEG Fine (with no RAW file) to squeeze a little extra speed out of my 70D's Continuous shooting mode, and to reduce the need to wade through eight-photo bursts taken in RAW format. On the other hand, on my last trip to Europe, I took only RAW (instead of my customary RAW+JPEG) photos to fit more images onto my iPad, as I planned on doing at least some post-processing on many of the images for a travel book I was working on.

VF Grid Display

This menu item allows you to enable or disable a grid of three horizontal and four vertical lines (the two center lines are interrupted by the focus area brackets) in the optical viewfinder that give you finer control over the placement of images in your frame. You can keep horizons and architectural features level using this optional viewfinder display.

Viewfinder Level

In addition to the electronic level that can be activated on the LCD monitor, the 70D has two levels accessible in the viewfinder. One is a simple icon display you can review while shooting (see Figure 3.13 earlier in this book), and best suited for handheld shooting, as it is available all the time when activated. A second electronic level, which uses the autofocus points in the viewfinder, can be activated momentarily by pressing a button assigned to activate that function using the C.Fn III-04 (Custom Controls) entry in the Custom menu. Select Operation/Others, Custom Controls, highlight DOF Preview Button, and assign VF Electronic Level to that button. Then, each time you press the DOF button, the advanced viewfinder level will appear. (See Figure 8.3.) You'd want to use this version when the camera is mounted on a tripod, because the more precise positioning is not needed all the time when the camera is relatively fixed. Although the figure shows the viewfinder level when the camera is held in the horizontal position, it also operates in vertical orientation, using AF points that run across the short dimension of the viewfinder.

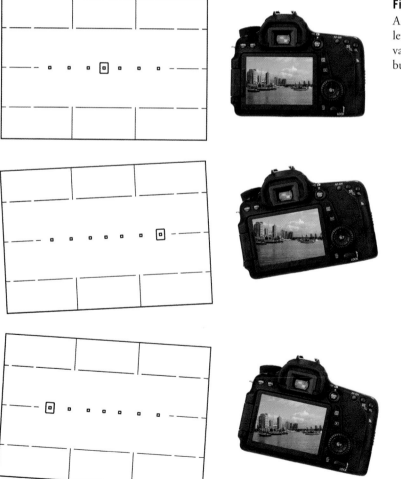

Figure 8.3
A second viewfinder level can be activated by pressing a button.

Beep

The 70D's internal beeper provides a helpful chirp to signify various functions, such as the countdown of your camera's self-timer. You can switch it off if you want to avoid the beep because it's annoying, impolite, or distracting (at a concert or museum), or undesired for any other reason. It's one of the few ways to make the 70D a bit quieter, other than Live View's "silent shoot" mode. (I've actually had new dSLR owners ask me how to turn off the "shutter sound" the camera makes; such an option was available in the point-and-shoot camera they'd used previously.) Select Beep from the menu, choose SET, and use the touch screen or multi-controller to choose Enable or Disable, or Touch To Silence (which silences the beep only during touch screen operations), as you prefer, as shown in Figure 8.4. Use SET again to activate your choice.

Figure 8.4

Silence your camera's beep when it might prove distracting.

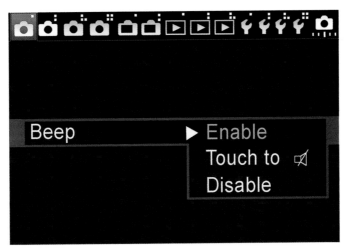

Release Shutter without Card

This entry in the Set-up 1 menu gives you the ability to snap off "pictures" without a memory card installed—or to lock the camera shutter release if that is the case. It is sometimes called Play mode, because you can experiment with your camera's features or even hand your 70D to a friend to let him fool around, without any danger of pictures actually being taken. Back in our film days, we'd sometimes finish a roll, rewind the film back into its cassette surreptitiously, and then hand the camera to a child to take a few pictures—without actually wasting any film. It's hard to waste digital film, but Release Shutter without Card mode is still appreciated by some, especially camera vendors who want to be able to demo a camera at a store or trade show, but don't want to have to equip each and every demonstrator model with a memory card. Choose this menu item, invoke SET, select Enable or Disable, and SET again to turn this capability on or off.

Image Review

You can adjust the amount of time an image is displayed for review on the LCD after each shot is taken. You can elect to disable this review entirely (Off), or choose display times of 2, 4, or 8 seconds. You can also select Hold, an indefinite display, which will keep your image on the screen until you use one of the other controls, such as the shutter button, Main Dial, or multi-controller. Turning the review display off or choosing a brief duration can help preserve battery power. However, the 70D will always override the review display when the shutter button is partially or fully depressed, so you'll never miss a shot because a previous image was on the screen. Choose Image Review from the Shooting 1 menu, and select Off, 2 sec., 4 sec., 8 sec., or Hold, as shown in Figure 8.5. If you want to retain an image on the screen for a longer period, but don't want to use Hold as your default, press the Erase button under the LCD monitor. The image will display until you choose Cancel or Erase from the menu that pops up at the bottom of the screen. A longer review time gives you an opportunity to delete a non-keeper without a visit to the menu system.

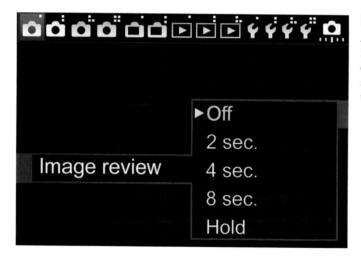

Figure 8.5
Adjust the time an image is displayed on the LCD for review after a picture is taken.

Lens Aberration Correction

With certain lenses, under certain conditions, your images might suffer from one of two aberrations, both of which can be partially corrected by activating the correction items offered in this menu entry. This is the first entry in the Shooting 2 menu. (See Figure 8.6.)

Peripheral Illumination Correction

One defect is caused by a phenomenon called *vignetting*, which is a darkening of the four corners of the frame because of a slight amount of fall-off in illumination at those nether regions. This menu option allows you to activate Peripheral Illumination Correction, a clever feature built in to the 70D that partially (or fully) compensates for this effect. Depending on the f/stop you use, the lens mounted on the camera, and the focal length setting, vignetting can be non-existent, slight, or may be so strong that it appears you've used a too-small hood on your camera. (Indeed, the wrong lens hood can produce a vignette effect of its own.) Vignetting can be affected by the use of a telephoto converter (more on those in Chapter 10). Select this entry from the Lens Aberration Correction screen (see Figure 8.7).

Peripheral illumination drop-off, even if pronounced, may not be much of a problem. I actually *add* vignetting, sometimes, when shooting portraits and some other subjects. Slightly dark corners tend to focus attention on a subject in the middle of the frame. On the other hand, vignetting with subjects that are supposed to be evenly illuminated, such as landscapes, is seldom a benefit.

To minimize the effects of corner light fall-off, you can process RAW files using Digital Photo Professional, or, if you want your JPEG files fixed as you shoot them, by using this menu option.

Figure 8.6
The Shooting 2 menu.

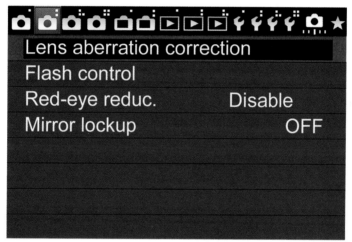

Figure 8.7
The Lens Aberration Correction screen.

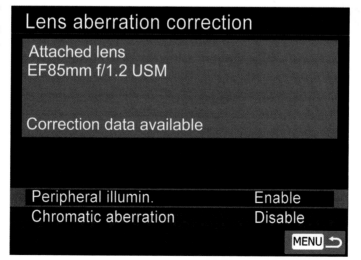

Figure 8.8 shows an image without peripheral illumination correction at top, and a corrected image at the bottom. I've exaggerated the vignetting a little to make it more evident on the printed page. Keep in mind that the amount of correction available with Digital Photo Pro can be a little more intense than that applied in the camera. In addition, the higher the ISO speed, the less correction is applied. If you see severe vignetting with a particular lens, focal length, or ISO setting, you might want to turn off this feature, shoot RAW, and apply correction using DPP instead.

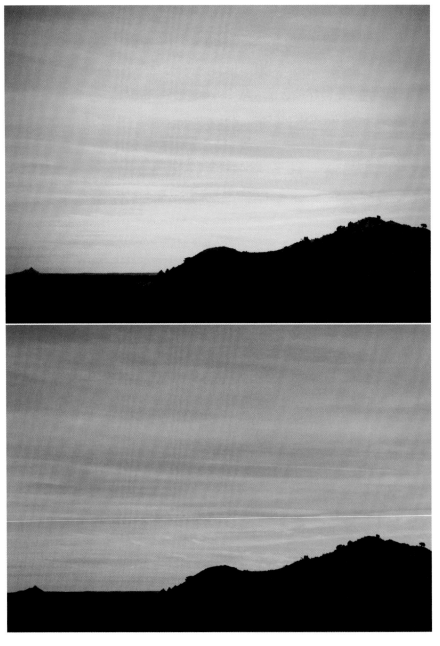

Figure 8.8
Vignetting (top) is undesirable in a landscape photo. You can correct this defect in the camera or by using Digital Photo Pro software.

When you select this menu option from the Shooting 1 menu, the screen shown in Figure 8.9 appears. The lens currently attached to the camera is shown, along with a notation whether correction data needed to brighten the corners is already registered in the camera. (Information about 25 of the most popular lenses is included in the 70D's firmware.) If so, you can use the touch screen or multi-controller to choose Enable to activate the feature, or Disable to turn it off. Select SET to confirm your choice. Note that in-camera correction must be specified *before* you take the photo, so that the magical DIGIC 5 processing engine can lighten the corners of your photo before it is saved to the memory card.

Chromatic Aberration Correction

The second defect involves fringes of color around backlit objects, produced by *chromatic aberration*, which comes in two forms: *longitudinal/axial*, in which all the colors of light don't focus in the same plane; and *lateral/transverse*, in which the colors are shifted to one side. (See Figure 8.9.) Your 70D has a database of information about certain lenses, similar to the one provided for peripheral illumination correction.

When this feature is enabled, the 70D will automatically correct images taken with one of the supported lenses to reduce or eliminate the amount of color fringing seen in the final photograph. (See Figure 8.10.)

If lens aberration correction information for your lens is not registered in the camera, you can remedy that deficit using the EOS Utility (also described in Chapter 13). Just follow these steps:

1. **Link up your camera.** Connect your 70D to your computer using the USB cable supplied with the camera.

2. **Launch the EOS Utility.** Load the utility and click on Camera Settings/Remote Shooting from the splash screen that appears.

3. **Select the Shooting menu.** It's located on the menu bar about midway in the control panel that appears on your computer display. The Shooting menu icon is the white camera on a red background.

4. **Click on the Lens Aberration Correction choice.** The selection screen will appear.

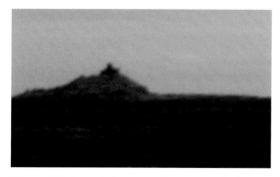

Figure 8.9 Lateral chromatic aberration, which shows as color fringes, can be corrected using the lens aberration correction feature.

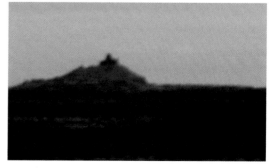

Figure 8.10 The corrected image displays much less fringing.

5. **Choose your lens.** Select the category containing the lens you want to register from the panels at the top of the new screen; then place a check mark next to all the lenses you'd like to register in the camera.

6. **Confirm your choice.** Click OK to send the data from your computer to the 70D and register your lenses.

7. **Activate correction.** When a newly registered lens is mounted on the camera, you will be able to activate the anti-vignetting feature for that lens from the Set-up 1 menu.

The Lens Aberration Correction feature is a more versatile fixer-upper than the Peripheral Illumination Correction feature found in earlier cameras. Once you've registered a lens as described above, you can use the RAW Image Processing entry in the Playback 1 menu to enable or disable peripheral illumination correction, chromatic aberration correction, general lens distortion correction, and make other changes to the RAW file—after it's been shot—right in the camera. I'll describe this capability later in this chapter.

Flash Control

This multi-level menu entry includes six settings for controlling the Canon 70D's built-in, pop-up electronic flash unit, as well as accessory flash units you can attach to the camera (see Figure 8.11). I'll provide in-depth coverage of how you can use these options in Chapter 11, but will list the main options here for reference.

Flash Firing

Use this option to enable or disable the built-in electronic flash. You might want to totally disable the 70D's flash (both built-in and accessory flash) when shooting in sensitive environments, such as concerts, in museums, or during religious ceremonies. When disabled, the flash cannot fire even if you accidentally elevate it, or have an accessory flash attached and turned on. If you turn off the flash here, it is disabled in any exposure mode. You can also select Flash Off from the Mode Dial.

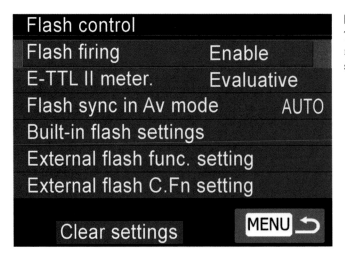

Figure 8.11
The Flash Control menu entry has six setting submenus.

E-TTL II Metering

You can choose Evaluative (Matrix) or Average metering modes for the electronic flash exposure meter. Evaluative looks at selected areas in the scene to calculate exposure, and is the best choice for most images because it attempts to interpret the type of scene being shot; Average calculates flash exposure by reading the entire scene, and it is possibly a good option if you want exposure to be calculated for the overall scene.

Flash Sync in AV mode

You can select the flash synchronization speed that will be used when working in Aperture-priority mode; choose from Auto (the 70D selects the shutter speed from 30 seconds to 1/250th second), to a range embracing only the speeds from 1/250th to 1/60th second, or fixed at 1/250th second.

Normally, in Aperture-priority mode when using flash, you specify the f/stop to be locked in. The exposure is then adjusted by varying the output of the electronic flash. Because the primary exposure comes from the flash, the main effect of the shutter speed selected is on the secondary exposure from the ambient light on the scene.

Auto is your best choice under most conditions. The 70D will choose a shutter speed that balances the flash exposure and available, ambient light. The 1/250th to 1/60th second setting locks out slower shutter speeds, preventing blur from camera/subject movement in the secondary ("ghost") exposure. However, the background may be rendered dark, if the flash is not strong enough to illuminate it. The 1/250th second (fixed) setting further reduces the chance of getting those blurry ghosts, but there is more of a chance the background will be dark. You'll find a more detailed explanation of these options in Chapter 11.

Built-in Flash Setting

There are a total of five possible choices for this menu screen, plus Clear Settings. The additional options are grayed out unless you're working in wireless flash mode. All these are explained in Chapters 11 and 12.

- **Flash mode.** This entry is available only if you've selected Custom Wireless, and allows you to choose from automatic exposure calculation (E-TTL II) or manual flash exposure.

- **Shutter sync.** Available only in Normal Firing mode, you can choose 1st curtain sync, which fires the pre-flash used to calculate the exposure before the shutter opens, followed by the main flash as soon as the shutter is completely open. This is the default mode, and you'll generally perceive the pre-flash and main flash as a single burst. Alternatively, you can select 2nd curtain sync, which fires the pre-flash as soon as the shutter opens, and then triggers the main flash in a second burst at the end of the exposure, just before the shutter starts to close. (If the shutter speed is slow enough, you may clearly see both the pre-flash and main flash as separate bursts of light.) This action allows photographing a blurred trail of light of moving objects with sharp flash exposures at the beginning and the end of the exposure. This type of flash exposure is slightly different from what some other cameras produce using 2nd curtain sync. I'll explain how it works in Chapter 11.

If you have an external compatible Speedlite attached, you can also choose High-speed sync, which allows you to use shutter speeds faster than 1/250th second, using the External Flash Function Setting menu, described next and explained in Chapter 11.

■ **Flash exposure compensation.** If you'd rather adjust flash exposure using a menu than with the ISO/Flash exposure compensation button, you can do that here. Select this option with the SET button, then dial in the amount of flash EV compensation you want using the multi-controller. The EV that was in place before you started to make your adjustment is shown as a blue indicator, so you can return to that value quickly. Use SET again to confirm your change, then tap MENU or press the MENU button twice to exit.

■ **Wireless functions.** These choices appear when you've enabled Wireless operation. I'm going to leave the explanation of these options for Chapter 12, which is an entire chapter dedicated to using the 70D's wireless shooting capabilities, first introduced in the EOS 7D.

External Flash Function Setting

You can access this menu only when you have a compatible electronic flash attached and switched on. If you press the INFO. button while adjusting flash settings, both the changes made to the settings of an attached external flash and to the built-in flash will be cleared. These options are quite complex, so I'm going to save the description of them for Chapters 11 and 12.

External Flash Custom Function Setting

Many external Speedlites from Canon include their own list of Custom Functions, which can be used to specify things like flash metering mode and flash bracketing sequences, as well as more sophisticated features, such as modeling light/flash (if available), use of external power sources (if attached), and functions of any slave unit attached to the external flash. This menu entry allows you to set an external flash unit's Custom Functions from your 70D's menu.

Clear Settings

This entry allows you to zero-out any changes you've made to your flash's settings, and return them to their factory default settings. You can individually clear built-in flash settings, external flash settings, and external flash's Custom Function settings.

Red-Eye Reduction

Your 70D has a Red-Eye Reduction flash mode. Unfortunately, your camera is unable, on its own, to always *eliminate* the red-eye effects that occur when an electronic flash (or, rarely, illumination from other sources) bounces off the retinas of the eye and into the camera lens. Animals seem to suffer from yellow or green glowing pupils, instead; the effect is equally undesirable. The effect is worst under low-light conditions (exactly when you might be using a flash) as the pupils expand to allow more light to reach the retinas. The most you can hope for is to *reduce* or minimize the red-eye effect.

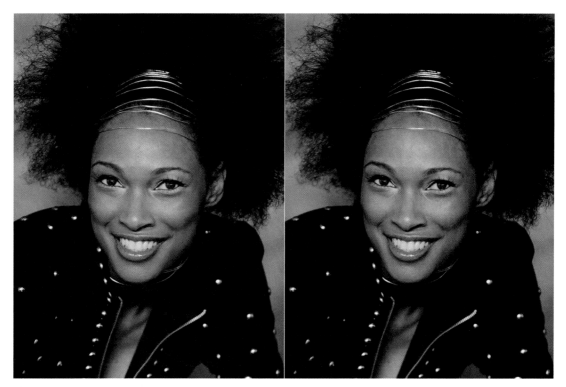

Figure 8.12 Red-eye (left) is tamed (right), thanks to the 70D's red-eye reduction lamp.

The best way to truly eliminate red-eye is to raise the flash up off the camera so its illumination approaches the eye from an angle that won't reflect directly back to the retina and into the lens. The extra height of the built-in flash may not be sufficient, however. That alone is a good reason for using an external flash. If you're working with your 70D's built-in flash, your only recourse may be to switch on the Red-Eye Reduction feature. It causes a lamp on the front of the camera to illuminate with a half-press of the shutter release button, which may cause your subjects' pupils to contract, decreasing the amount of the red-eye effect. (You may have to ask your subject to look at the lamp to gain maximum effect.) Figure 8.12 shows the effects of wider pupils (left) and those that have been contracted using the 70D's Red-Eye Reduction feature.

Mirror Lockup

This option allows you to flip up the 70D's mirror prior to exposure. Note that the camera has a second mirror lockup option available under Sensor Cleaning in the Set-up 4 menu. You should be extra careful not to confuse the two.

Here is the difference:

- **Mirror Lockup.** This option is used while shooting. When enabled from this menu entry, the camera flips the mirror up out of the way when you press the shutter button down all the way. At that point, the viewfinder image will vanish (the mirror is no longer reflecting the image toward the focus screen), and a blinking mirror-up icon appears on the LCD panel. Shooting function settings and menu adjustments are disabled at this point. You must press the shutter release fully a *second* time to actually take the photo. The net result is that the (minor) vibration caused by the action of the mirror is eliminated, which can be important when shooting with a very long telephoto lens, or taking close-ups.

- **Clean Manually.** Select Clean Manually from the Sensor Cleaning entry in the Set-up 4 menu. The mirror will flip up immediately and the shutter will open, exposing the sensor. You can then safely clean your sensor using your favorite method (as described in Chapter 14). The shutter won't close and the mirror won't flip down until you power off the camera. The function can't be activated unless your battery or external source has enough power to maintain this configuration.

In general, only advanced dSLRs like the 70D offer the Mirror Lockup option in Shooting mode, so you might not even be familiar with its advantages. In recent years, only the cleaning mode mirror flip-up feature has been common. When using Mirror Lockup, keep the following in mind:

- **Avoid excessive lockup times.** Unlike cleaning mode, the shutter remains closed while the mirror is locked up, and, in virtually all cases, a lens will be attached to the camera and focusing light on the sensor plane (or shutter curtains, before exposure). This bright light can actually damage the shutter, particularly if the camera is accidentally pointed toward the sun. So, a good rule of thumb is to lock up the mirror only just before you want to take the picture (the mirror's vibration will be damped within about one second), and never shoot directly toward the sun. Fortunately, if you lock the mirror up and *don't* take a picture, the mirror will flip back down after 30 seconds automatically.

- **Use a tripod.** Obviously, if you're using mirror lockup to avoid vibration, you're almost certainly working with the camera on a tripod, too. Even with image stabilization, a handheld camera will produce more vibration than any mirror action.

- **Self-timer or remote release recommended.** Even though you've delayed the exposure until mirror vibration has damped, pressing the shutter release (even gently) can introduce a bit of motion to a camera mounted on the sturdiest tripod. The 70D's self-timer can be used, but that option doesn't allow you to select the precise moment of exposure. Instead, use a remote release. Perhaps you've framed a shot of some distant wildlife with a super-telephoto. Your first press flips the mirror up to ready the camera for the shot; then, a second or two later your quarry looks toward the camera and you press again to take the picture. With a self-timer, you don't have that flexibility.

- **Self-timer with Bulb exposures.** This combination can be problematic. You'll need to hold the shutter button down during the self-timer countdown when using a Bulb exposure. Releasing the button before the countdown has elapsed eliminates the actual exposure. You'll hear a shutter click, but no picture will be taken. You're better off using a remote release for mirror-up Bulb exposures.

- **No continuous shooting.** Sorry, but you can't lock up the mirror and take a series of shots. Continuous shooting is disabled when Mirror Lockup is active.

Exposure Compensation/Automatic Exposure Bracketing

The first entry on the Shooting 3 menu is Expo. Comp./AEB, or exposure compensation and automatic exposure bracketing. (See Figure 8.13.) As you learned in Chapter 4, exposure compensation (added/subtracted by pressing the multi-controller while this menu screen is visible) increases or decreases exposure from the metered value.

Exposure bracketing using the 70D's AEB feature is a way to shoot several consecutive exposures using different settings, to improve the odds that one will be exactly right. Automatic exposure bracketing is also an excellent way of creating the base exposures you'll need when you want to combine several shots to create a high dynamic range (HDR) image. (You'll find a discussion of HDR photography—one of the latest rages—in Chapter 4, too.)

To activate automatic exposure bracketing, select this menu choice, then rotate the Main Dial to spread or contract the three dots beneath the scale until you've defined the range you want the bracket to cover, shown as full-stop jumps in Figure 8.14. Then, use the touch screen, QCD, or multi-controller to move the brackets right or left, biasing the bracketing toward underexposure (move left) or overexposure (move right).

When AEB is activated, the three bracketed shots will be exposed in this sequence: metered exposure, decreased exposure, increased exposure. You'll find more information about exposure bracketing in Chapter 4.

Figure 8.13
Exposure compensation/exposure bracketing is the first entry in the Shooting 3 menu.

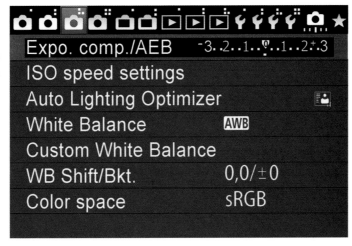

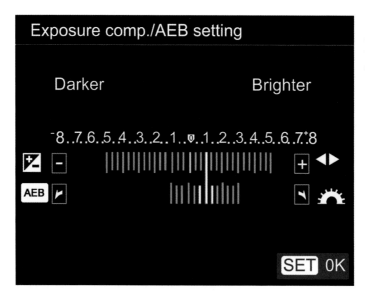

Figure 8.14
Set the range of the three bracketed exposures.

ISO Speed Settings

Use this entry to select a specific ISO speed using a menu instead of the top-panel ISO button/ menus, or to limit the range of ISO settings and shutter speeds that the camera selects automatically. The four subentries include:

- **ISO Speed.** You can choose Auto (the 70D will choose an ISO sensitivity appropriate for the light levels/exposure settings you've specified) or a fixed sensitivity from ISO 100 to ISO 12800, in one-third stop increments (for example, ISO 100, 125, or 160). If ISO expansion has been enabled using the ISO Speed Range choice (next), you can also choose H (25600 equivalent).

- **ISO Speed Range.** This option lets you specify both a minimum and maximum ISO sensitivity that can be selected manually using the ISO Speed option (above). Perhaps you have a preferred range and don't want to accidentally use any ISO setting below ISO 100 or higher than ISO 3200. You can specify those limits here. Available ranges are ISO 100-12800 for the minimum and ISO 200-H for the maximum, if you expand the ISO range to H (equivalent of ISO 25600).

- **Auto ISO Range.** Ordinarily, the 70D will select only ISO sensitivities between ISO 100 and ISO 12800. In Auto ISO mode, you can use the QCD to set the minimum to ISO 100 to ISO 6400 and the maximum up to H (ISO 25600 equivalent), using whole stop limits (for example ISO 100, 200, or 400, but not ISO 125 or 160). Note that you can't set a minimum that's higher than the maximum, or vice versa. This option allows advanced shooters to enable auto- mated ISO selection within limits they can tightly control. If you were shooting indoor sports in Shutter-priority (Tv) mode, you might want to specify a 1/500th second shutter speed, and allow the camera to adjust the ISO between, say, ISO 400 and ISO 3200. Limits you set here will also be applied to the ISO Speed Safety Shift feature.

■ **Minimum Shutter Speed.** Use this when working with Program (P) or Aperture-priority (Av) modes to specify the slowest shutter speed that will be used when Auto ISO is enabled. (In Shutter-priority [Tv] mode, you always choose the shutter speed.) This option ensures that the Auto ISO changes will kick in before the camera reduces the shutter speed below a value you select. You can choose speeds from 1 second to 1/250th second. For example, perhaps you are shooting indoor sports and elect to choose Aperture-priority instead of Shutter-priority (say, your lens works better at f/4 than its maximum aperture of f/2.8, and you want to work with f/4 all the time). Set 1/250th second as a minimum shutter speed, and if a correct exposure calls for a shutter speed slower than that at f/4, Auto ISO will be used to boost the sensitivity instead.

However, if you've handicapped the 70D by selecting an Auto ISO range that doesn't include a sensitivity high enough, the camera will *override this setting* and use a shutter speed lower than the minimum you specify anyway. The camera assumes (rightly or wrongly) that your upper ISO boundary is more important than your lower shutter speed limit. The lesson here is that if you really, really want to enforce a minimum shutter speed when using Auto ISO, make sure your upper limit is high enough. Note that the Minimum Shutter Speed setting is ignored when using flash.

Auto Lighting Optimizer

The Auto Lighting Optimizer provides a partial fix for images that are too dark or flat. Such photos typically have low contrast, and the Auto Lighting Optimizer improves them—as you shoot—by increasing both the brightness and contrast as required. The feature can be activated in Program, Aperture-priority, and Shutter-priority modes. You can select from four settings: Standard (the default value, which is always selected when using Scene Intelligent Auto and Creative Auto modes, and used for Figure 8.15), plus Low, High, and Disable. Press the INFO. button to add/remove a check mark icon that indicates the Auto Lighting Optimizer is disabled during manual exposure. Since you're likely to be specifying a particular exposure in Manual mode, you probably don't want the optimizer to interfere with your settings, so disabling the feature is the default.

White Balance

If automatic white balance or one of the six preset settings available (Daylight, Shade, Cloudy, Tungsten, White Fluorescent, or Flash) aren't suitable, you can set a custom white balance using this menu option or a specific color temperature value. The screen shown in Figure 8.16 is identical to the one that pops up when you select White Balance from the Quick Control screen (except for the color of the highlighting). If you choose the "K" entry, you can select an exact color temperature from 2,500K to 10,000K using the Main Dial.

Of course, unless you own a specialized tool called a color temperature meter, you probably won't know the exact color temperature of your scene. However, knowing the color temperatures of the six preset options can help you if you decide to tweak them by choosing a different color temperature setting.

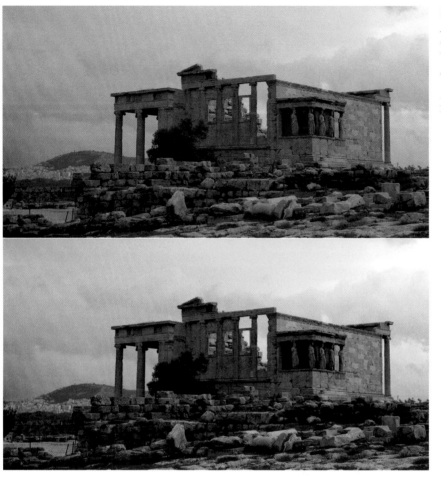

Figure 8.15
Auto Lighting
Optimizer can
brighten dark, low-
contrast images
(top), giving them a
little extra snap and
brightness (bottom).

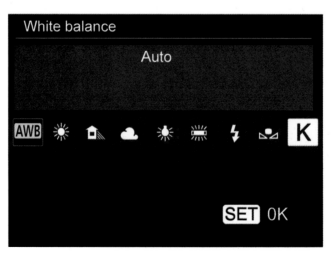

Figure 8.16
White balance pre-
sets can be chosen
here.

The values used by the 70D are as follows:

- **Auto (AWB).** 3000-7000K
- **Daylight.** 5200K
- **Shade.** 7000K
- **Cloudy.** 6000K
- **Tungsten.** 3200K

- **White fluorescent.** 4000K
- **Flash.** 6000K
- **Custom.** 2000-10000K
- **Color temperature.** 2500-10000K
  (Settable in 100K increments)

The problem with the available presets (Daylight, Shade, etc.) is that you have only six of them, and in any given situation, all of them are likely to be wrong—strictly speaking. The good news is that they are likely to be only a *little bit* wrong. The human eye is very adaptable, so in most cases you'll be perfectly happy with the results you get if you use Auto, or choose a preset that's in the white balance ballpark.

But if you absolutely must have the correct color balance, or are frequently dissatisfied with the color balance the 70D produces when using Auto or one of the presets, you can always shoot RAW, and adjust the final color balance in your image editor when converting the .cr2 file. Or, you can use a custom white balance procedure, described next.

Custom White Balance

If automatic white balance or one of the six preset settings available (Daylight, Shade, Cloudy, Tungsten, White Fluorescent, or Flash) aren't suitable, you can set a custom white balance using this menu option. The custom setting you establish will then be applied whenever you select Custom using the White Balance menu.

To set the white balance to an appropriate color temperature under the current ambient lighting conditions, focus manually (with the lens set on MF) on a plain white or gray object, such as a card or wall, making sure the object fills the spot metering circle in the center of the viewfinder. Then, take a photo. Next press the MENU button and select Custom WB from the Shooting 3 menu. Use the multi-controller until the reference image you just took appears and choose SET to store the white balance of the image as your Custom setting. Only compatible images that can be used to specify a custom white balance will be shown on the screen. Custom white balance images are marked with a custom icon, and cannot be removed (although they can be replaced with a new custom white balance image).

A WHITE BALANCE LIBRARY

Shoot a selection of blank-card images under a variety of lighting conditions on a spare memory card. If you want to "recycle" one of the color temperatures you've stored, insert the card and set the Custom white balance to that of one of the images in your white balance library, as described above.

White Balance Shift and Bracketing

White balance shift allows you to dial in a white balance color bias along the blue-yellow/amber dimensions, and/or magenta/green scale. In other words, you can set your color balance so that it is a little bluer or yellower (only), a little more magenta or green (only), or a combination of the two bias dimensions. You can also bracket exposures, taking several consecutive pictures each with a slightly different color balance biased in the directions you specify.

The process is a little easier to visualize if you look at Figure 8.17. The center intersection of lines BA and GM (remember high school geometry!) is the point of zero bias. Move the point at that intersection using the multi-controller to locate it at any point on the graph using the blue-yellow/amber and green-magenta coordinates. The amount of shift will be displayed in the SHIFT box to the right of the graph.

White balance bracketing is like white balance shifting, only the bracketed changes occur along the bias axis you specify. The three squares in Figure 8.17 show that the white balance bracketing will occur in two-stop steps along the blue-yellow/amber axis. The amount of the bracketing is shown in the lower box to the right of the graph.

This form of bracketing is similar to exposure bracketing, but with the added dimension of hue. Bias bracketing can be performed in any JPEG-only mode. You can't use any RAW format or RAW+JPEG format because the RAW files already contain the information needed to fine-tune the white balance and white balance bias.

When you select WB SHIFT/BKT, the adjustment screen appears. First, you press the Quick Control Dial to set the range of the shift in either the green/magenta dimension (rotate clockwise to change the vertical separation of the three dots representing the separate exposures) or in the blue-yellow/amber dimension by rotating the QCD counter clockwise. Use the multi-controller to move the bracket set around within the color space, and outside the green-magenta or blue-yellow/amber axes.

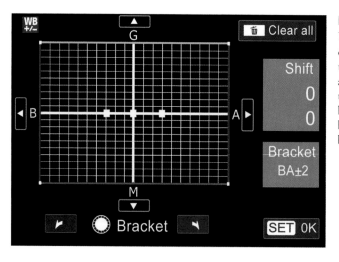

Figure 8.17
Use the touch screen or multi-controller to specify color balance bracketing using green-magenta bias or to specify blue-yellow/amber bias.

In most cases, it's fairly easy to determine if you want your image to be more green, more magenta, more blue, or more yellow, although judging your current shots on the LCD screen can be tricky unless you view the screen in a darkened location so it will be bright and easy to see. Bracketing is covered in Chapter 4.

Color Space

When you are using one of the Creative Zone modes, you can select one of two different color spaces (also called *color gamuts*) using this menu entry, shown previously among the other menu choices in Figure 8.13. One color space is named *Adobe RGB* (because it was developed by Adobe Systems in 1998), while the other is called *sRGB* (supposedly because it is the *standard* RGB color space). These two color gamuts define a specific set of colors that can be applied to the images your 70D captures.

The Color Space menu choice applies directly to JPEG images shot using P, Tv, Av, and M exposure modes. When you're using Scene Intelligent Auto or Creative Auto modes, the 70D uses the sRGB color space for all the JPEG images you take. RAW images are a special case. They have the information for *both* sRGB and Adobe RGB, but when you load such photos into your image editor, it will default to sRGB (with Scene Intelligent Auto or Creative Auto shots) or the color space specified here unless you change that setting while importing the photos. (See the "Best of Both Worlds" sidebar that follows for more information.)

You may be surprised to learn that the 70D doesn't automatically capture *all* the colors we see. Unfortunately, that's impossible because of the limitations of the sensor and the filters used to capture the fundamental red, green, and blue colors, as well as that of the elements used to display those colors on your camera and computer monitors. Nor is it possible to *print* every color our eyes detect, because the inks or pigments used don't absorb and reflect colors perfectly. In short, your sensor doesn't capture all the colors that we can see, your monitor can't display all the colors that the sensor captures, and your printer outputs yet another version.

On the other hand, the 70D does capture quite a few more colors than we need. The original 14-bit RAW image contains a possible 4.4 *trillion* different hues, which are condensed down to a mere 16.8 million possible colors when converted to a 24-bit (eight bits per channel) image. While 16.8 million colors may seem like a lot, it's a small subset of 4.4 trillion captured, and an even smaller subset of all the possible colors we can see. The set of colors, or gamut, that can be reproduced or captured by a given device (scanner, digital camera, monitor, printer, or some other piece of equipment) is represented as a color space that exists within the larger full range of colors.

That full range is represented by the odd-shaped splotch of color shown in Figure 8.18, as defined by scientists at an international organization called the International Commission on Illumination (usually known as the CIE for its French name *Commission internationale de l'éclairage*) back in 1931. The colors possible with Adobe RGB are represented by the larger, black triangle in the figure, while the sRGB gamut is represented by the smaller white triangle.

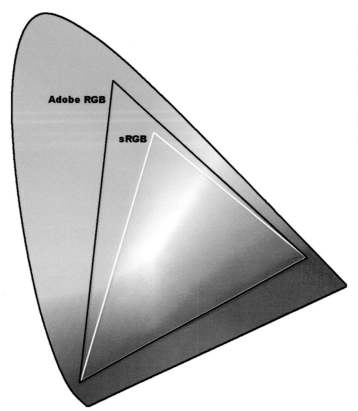

Figure 8.18
The outer figure shows all the colors we can see; the two inner outlines show the boundaries of Adobe RGB (black triangle) and sRGB (white triangle).

Regardless of which triangle—or color space—is used by the 70D, you end up with some combination of 16.8 million different colors that can be used in your photograph. (No one image will contain all 16.8 million! If each and every pixel in a 20-megapixel photo were a different color—which is extremely unlikely—you'd need only 20 million different colors.) But, as you can see from the figure, the colors available will be *different*.

Adobe RGB is what is often called an *expanded* color space, because it can reproduce a range of colors that is spread over a wider range of the visual spectrum. Adobe RGB is useful for commercial and professional printing. You don't need this range of colors if your images will be displayed primarily on your computer screen or output by your personal printer.

The other color space, sRGB, is recommended for images that will be output locally on the user's own printer, as this color space matches that of the typical inkjet printer fairly closely. While both Adobe RGB and sRGB can reproduce the exact same 16.8 million absolute colors, Adobe RGB spreads those colors over a larger portion of the visible spectrum, as you can see in the figure. Think of a box of crayons (the jumbo 16.8 million crayon variety). Some of the basic crayons from the original sRGB set have been removed and replaced with new hues not contained in the original box. Your "new" box contains colors that can't be reproduced by your computer monitor, but which work just fine with a commercial printing press.

BEST OF BOTH WORLDS

As I mentioned, if you're using a Basic Zone mode, the 70D selects the sRGB color space automatically. In addition, you may choose to set the sRGB color space with this menu entry to apply that gamut to all your other photos as well. But, in either case, you can still easily obtain Adobe RGB versions of your photos if you need them. Just shoot using RAW+JPEG. You'll end up with sRGB JPEGs suitable for output on your own printer, but you can still extract an Adobe RGB version from the RAW file at any time. It's like capturing two different color spaces at once—sRGB and Adobe RGB—and getting the best of both worlds.

Of course, choosing the right color space doesn't solve the problems that result from having each device in the image chain manipulating or producing a slightly different set of colors. To that end, you'll need to investigate the wonderful world of *color management*, which uses hardware and software tools to match or *calibrate* all your devices, as closely as possible, so that what you see more closely resembles what you capture, what you see on your computer display, and what ends up on a printed hardcopy. Entire books have been devoted to color management, and most of what you need to know doesn't directly involve your Canon 70D, so I won't detail the nuts and bolts here.

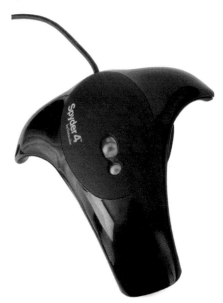

To manage your color, you'll need, at the bare minimum, some sort of calibration system for your computer display, so that your monitor can be adjusted to show a standardized set of colors that is repeatable over time. (What you see on the screen can vary as the monitor ages, or even when the room light changes.) I use the Spyder4 monitor color correction system from Datacolor (www.datacolor.com) for my computer's dual 26-inch wide screen LCD displays. The unit checks room light levels every five minutes, and reminded me to recalibrate every week or two using the small sensor device shown in Figure 8.19, which attaches temporarily to the front of the screen and interprets test patches that the software displays during calibration. The rest of the time, the sensor sits in its stand, measuring the room illumination, and adjusting my monitors for higher or lower ambient light levels.

Figure 8.19 Datacolor's Spyder4 monitor color correction system is an inexpensive device for calibrating your display.

If you're willing to make a serious investment in equipment to help you produce the most accurate color and make prints, you'll want a more advanced system (up to $500) like the various other Spyder products from Datacolor or Colormunki from X-Rite (www.colormunki.com).

Picture Style

The Picture Styles feature, the first entry in the Shooting 4 menu (see Figure 8.20), is one of the most important tools for customizing the way your Canon 70D renders its photos. It carries the "ambience" idea of tweaking images as they are shot to a new level. Picture Styles are a type of fine-tuning you can apply to your photos to change certain characteristics of each image taken using a particular Picture Style setting. The parameters you can specify for full-color images include the amount of sharpness, degree of contrast, the richness of the color, and the hue of skin tones. For black-and-white images, you can tweak the sharpness and contrast, but the two color adjustments (meaningless in a monochrome image) are replaced by controls for filter effects (which I'll explain shortly), and sepia, blue, purple, or green tone overlays.

The Canon 70D has five preset color Picture Styles, for Standard, Portrait, Landscape, Neutral, and Faithful pictures, plus Auto, and three user-definable settings called User Def. 1, User Def. 2, and User Def. 3, which you can define to apply to any sort of shooting situation you want, such as sports, architecture, or baby pictures. There is also a sixth, Monochrome, Picture Style that allows you to adjust filter effects or add color toning to your black-and-white images. See Figure 8.21 for the main Picture Style menu.

Picture Styles are extremely flexible. Canon has set the parameters for the five predefined color Picture Styles and the single monochrome Picture Style to suit the needs of most photographers. But you can adjust any of those "canned" Picture Styles to settings you prefer. Better yet, you can use those three User Definition files to create brand-new styles that are all your own. If you want rich, bright colors to emulate Velvia film or the work of legendary photographer Pete Turner, you can build your own color-soaked style. If you want soft, muted colors and less sharpness to create a romantic look, you can do that, too. Perhaps you'd like a setting with extra contrast for shooting outdoors on hazy or cloudy days.

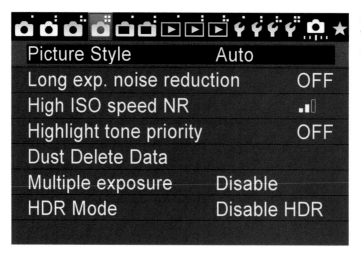

Figure 8.20
The Shooting 4 menu.

Figure 8.21
Ten different Picture Styles are available from this scrolling menu; these six plus Monochrome and three User Def. styles not shown.

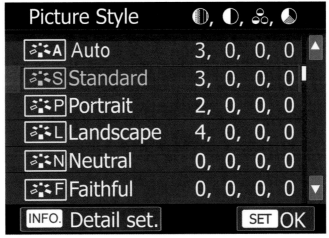

The parameters applied when using Picture Styles follow. Figure 8.22 shows exaggerated examples of the first four (color photo) attributes, as applied by Picture Styles (your real-world tweaks may not be quite this drastic, but are more difficult to represent on the printed page):

- **Sharpness.** This parameter determines the apparent contrast between the outlines or edges in an image, which we perceive as image sharpness. You can adjust the sharpness of the image between values of 0 (no sharpening added) to 7 (dramatic additional sharpness). When adjusting sharpness, remember that more is not always a good thing. A little softness is necessary (and is introduced by a blurring "anti-alias" filter in front of the sensor) to reduce or eliminate the moiré effects that can result when details in your image form a pattern that is too close to the pattern, or frequency, of the sensor itself. The default levels of sharpening (which are, for most Picture Styles, not 0) were chosen by Canon to allow most moiré interference to be safely blurred to invisibility, at the cost of a little sharpness. As you boost sharpness (either using a Picture Style or in your image editor), moiré can become a problem, plus, you may end up with those noxious "halos" that appear around the edges of images that have been oversharpened. Use this adjustment with care.

- **Contrast.** Use this control, with values from –4 (low contrast) to +4 (higher contrast), to change the number of middle tones between the deepest blacks and brightest whites. Low contrast settings produce a flatter-looking photo, while high contrast adjustments may improve the tonal rendition while possibly losing detail in the shadows or highlights.

- **Saturation.** This parameter, adjustable from –4 (low saturation) to +4 (high saturation) controls the richness of the color, making, say, a red tone appear to be deeper and fuller when you increase saturation, and tend more toward lighter, pinkish hues when you decrease saturation of the reds. Boosting the saturation too much can mean that detail may be lost in one or more of the color channels, producing what is called "clipping." You can detect this phenomenon when using the RGB histograms, as described in Chapter 4.

- **Color tone.** This adjustment has the most effect on skin tones, making them either redder (0 to −4) or yellower (0 to +4).

- **Filter effect (Monochrome only).** Filter effects do not add any color to a black-and-white image. Instead, they change the rendition of gray tones as if the picture were taken through a color filter. I'll explain this distinction more completely in the sidebar "Filters vs. Toning" later in this section.

- **Toning effect (Monochrome only).** Using toning effects preserves the monochrome tonal values in your image, but adds a color overlay that gives the photo a sepia, blue, purple, or green cast.

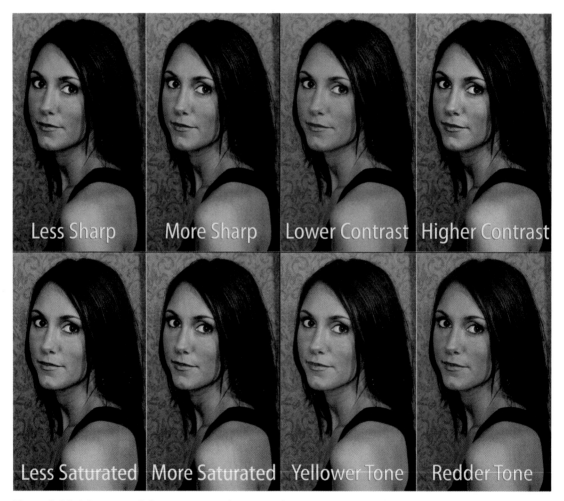

Figure 8.22 These sets of photos represent the main color image Picture Styles parameters: sharpness (upper-left pair); contrast (upper-right pair); saturation (lower-left pair); and color tone (lower-right pair).

The predefined Picture Styles are as follows:

- **Auto.** Adjusts the color to make outdoor scenes look more vivid, with richer colors.

- **Standard.** This Picture Style applies a set of parameters, including boosted sharpness, that are useful for most picture taking, and which are applied automatically when using Basic Zone modes other than Portrait or Landscape.

- **Portrait.** This style boosts saturation for richer colors when shooting portraits, which is particularly beneficial for women and children, while reducing sharpness slightly to provide more flattering skin texture. The Basic Mode Portrait setting uses this Picture Style. You might prefer the Faithful style for portraits of men when you want a more rugged or masculine look, or when you want to emphasize character lines in the faces of older subjects of either gender.

- **Landscape.** This style increases the saturation of blues and greens, and increases both color saturation and sharpness for more vivid landscape images. The Basic Zone Landscape mode uses this setting.

- **Neutral.** This Picture Style is a less saturated and lower-contrast version of the Standard style. Use it when you want a more muted look to your images, or when the photos you are taking seem too bright and contrasty (say, at the beach on a sunny day).

- **Faithful.** The goal of this style is to render the colors of your image as accurately as possible, roughly in the same relationships as seen by the eye.

- **Monochrome.** Use this Picture Style to create black-and-white photos in the camera. If you're shooting JPEG only, the colors are gone forever. But if you're shooting JPEG+RAW you can convert the RAW files to color as you import them into your image editor, even if you've shot using the Monochrome Picture Style. Your 70D displays the images in black-and-white on the screen during playback, but the colors are there in the RAW file for later retrieval.

Tip

You can use the Monochrome Picture Style even if you are using one of the RAW formats alone, without a JPEG version. The 70D displays your images on the screen in black-and-white, and marks the RAW image as monochrome so it will default to that style when you import it into your image editor. However, the color information is still present in the RAW file and can be retrieved, at your option, when importing the image.

Selecting Picture Styles

Canon makes selecting a Picture Style for use very easy, and, to prevent you from accidentally changing an existing style when you don't mean to, divides *selection* and *modification* functions into two separate tasks. There are actually two different ways to choose from among your existing Picture Styles.

One way is to choose Picture Styles from the Shooting 4 menu and press SET to produce the main Picture Style menu screen. Use the multi-controller to rotate among the choices. (Neutral, Faithful, Monochrome, and User Def. 1, User Def. 2, and User Def. 3 are shown in Figure 8.23; the rest appear when you scroll using the multi-controller.) The current settings for each Picture Style are shown on the right half of the screen. Choose SET to activate your choice. Then select MENU to exit the menu system. You can see that even with this method, switching among Picture Styles is fast and easy enough to allow you to shift gears as often as you like during a shooting session.

But your 70D offers an even simpler way to activate a Picture Style. Press the Q button and navigate to the Picture Styles section, and choose SET. Then use the multi-controller to scroll through the list of available styles on the screen that appears, shown in Figure 8.24. When you use this method, the current settings for a particular style are shown *only* when you've highlighted that style. Select SET to activate the style of your choice.

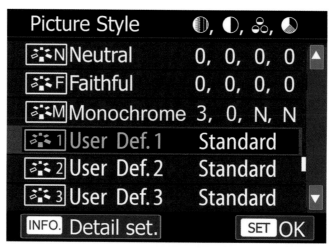

Figure 8.23
You can select a style from the Picture Style menu in Shooting 4 menu.

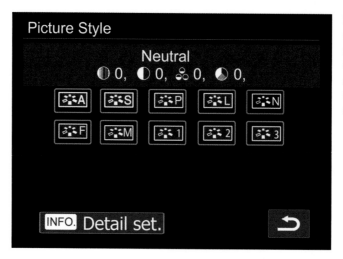

Figure 8.24
Choose Picture Style from the Quick Control menu to choose a style from this fast-access screen.

Defining Picture Styles

Canon makes interpreting current Picture Style settings and applying changes very easy. As you saw in Figures 8.22 and 8.23, the current settings of the visible Picture Style options are shown as numeric values on the menu screen. Some camera vendors use word descriptions, like Sharp, Extra Sharp, or Vivid, More Vivid that are difficult to relate to. The 70D's settings, on the other hand, are values on uniform scales, with seven steps (from 1 to 7) for sharpness, and plus/minus four steps clustered around a zero (no change) value for contrast and saturation (so you can change from low contrast/low saturation, –4, to high contrast/high saturation, +4), as well as color tone (–4/reddish to +4/yellowish). The individual icons at the top of Figure 8.23 represent (left to right) Sharpness, Contrast, Saturation, and Color Tone.

You can change one of the existing Picture Styles or define your own whenever the Shooting 4 menu version of the Picture Styles menu, or the pop-up selection screen shown in Figure 8.24, is visible. Just press the INFO. button when either screen is on the LCD. Follow these steps:

1. **Choose a style to modify.** Use the touch screen or multi-controller to scroll to the style you'd like to adjust.

2. **Activate adjustment mode.** Press the INFO. button to choose Detail Set. If you're coming from the Shooting 4 menu, the screen that appears next will look like the one shown in Figure 8.20 for the five color styles or three User Def. styles. If you've accessed the adjustment screen by pressing the Picture Styles button first, the screen looks much the same, but has blue highlighting instead of red.

3. **Choose a parameter to change.** Use the touch screen or multi-controller to scroll among the four parameters, plus Default Set. at the bottom of the screen, which restores the values to the preset numbers.

4. **Activate changes.** Choose SET to change the values of one of the four parameters. If you're redefining one of the default presets, the menu screen will look like Figure 8.25, which represents the Landscape Picture Style.

Figure 8.25
Each parameter can be changed separately.

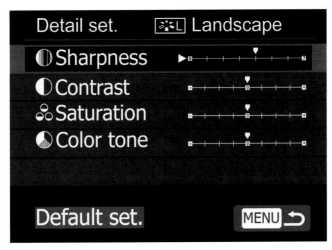

5. **Adjust values.** Use the touch screen or multi-controller to move the triangle to the value you want to use. Note that the previous value remains on the scale, represented by a gray triangle. This makes it easy to return to the original setting if you want.

6. **Confirm changes.** Choose SET to lock in that value, then press the MENU button three times to back out of the menu system.

Any Picture Style that has been changed from its defaults will be shown in the Picture Style menu with blue highlighting the altered parameter. You don't have to worry about changing a Picture Style and then forgetting that you've modified it. A quick glance at the Picture Style menu will show you which styles and parameters have been changed.

Making changes in the Monochrome Picture Style is slightly different, as the Saturation and Color Tone parameters are replaced with Filter Effect and Toning Effect options. (Keep in mind that once you've taken a photo using a Monochrome Picture Style, you can't convert the image back to full color.) You can choose from Yellow, Orange, Red, or Green filters, or None, and specify Sepia, Blue, Purple, or Green toning, or None. You can still set the Sharpness and Contrast parameters that are available with the other Picture Styles. Figure 8.26 shows filter effects being applied to the Monochrome Picture Style.

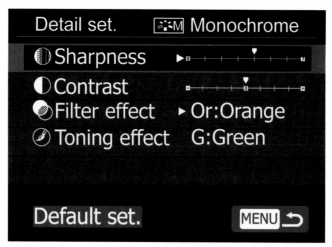

Figure 8.26
Apply changes to the Monochrome Picture Style.

FILTERS VS. TONING

Although some of the color choices overlap, you'll get very different looks when choosing between Filter Effects and Toning Effects. Filter Effects add no color to the monochrome image. Instead, they reproduce the look of black-and-white film that has been shot through a color filter. That is, Yellow will make the sky darker and the clouds will stand out more, whereas Orange makes the sky even darker and sunsets more full of detail. The Red filter produces the darkest sky of all and darkens green objects, such as leaves. Human skin may appear lighter than normal. The Green filter has the opposite effect on leaves, making them appear lighter in tone. Figure 8.27 shows the same scene shot with no filter, then Yellow, Green, and Red filters.

The Sepia, Blue, Purple, and Green Toning Effects, on the other hand, all add a color cast to your monochrome image. Use these when you want an old-time look or a special effect, without bothering to recolor your shots in an image editor. Figure 8.28 shows the various Toning Effects available.

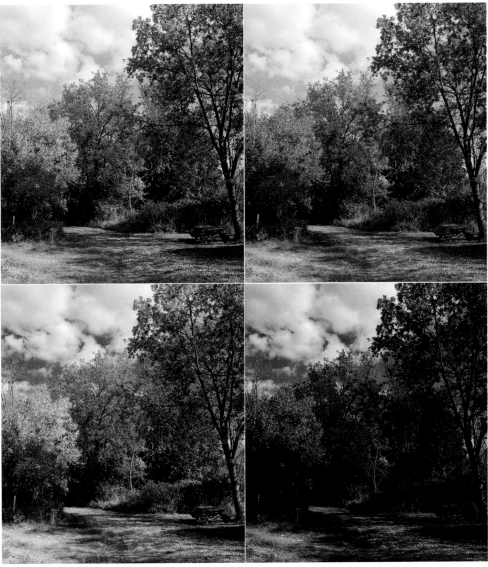

Figure 8.27 No filter (upper left); Yellow filter (upper right); Green filter (lower left); and Red filter (lower right).

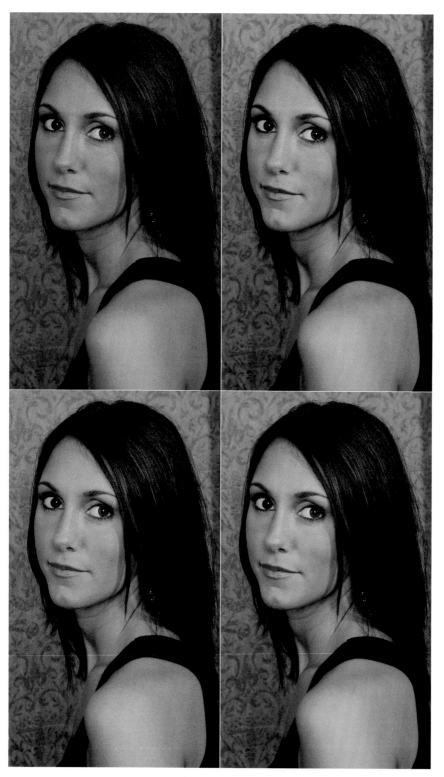

Figure 8.28
Select from among four color filters in the Monochrome Picture Style, including Sepia (top left); Blue (top right); Purple (lower left); and Green (lower right).

Adjusting Styles with the Picture Style Editor

If you'd rather edit Picture Styles in your computer, the Picture Style Editor supplied for your camera in versions for both Windows and Macs allows you to create your own custom Picture Styles, or edit existing styles, including the Standard, Landscape, Faithful, and other predefined settings already present in your 70D. You can change sharpness, contrast, color saturation, and color tone—and a lot more—and then save the modifications as a PF2 file that can be uploaded to the camera, or used by Digital Photo Professional (described in Chapter 13) to modify a RAW image as it is imported.

To create and load your own Picture Style, just follow these steps:

1. **Load the editor.** Launch the Picture Style Editor (PSE, not to be confused with the *other* PSE, Photoshop Elements).

2. **Access a RAW file.** Load a RAW CR2 image you'd like to use as a reference into PSE. You can drag a file from a folder into the editor's main window, or use the Open command in the File menu.

3. **Choose an existing style to base your new style on.** Select any of the base styles except for Standard. Your new style will begin with all the attributes of the base style you choose, so start with one that already is fairly close to the look you want to achieve ("tweaking" is easier than building a style from the ground up).

4. **Split the screen.** You can compare the appearance of your new style with the base style you are working from. Near the lower-left edge of the display pane are three buttons you can click to split the old/new styles vertically, horizontally, or return to a single image.

5. **Dial in basic changes.** Click the Advanced button in the Tool palette to pop up the Advanced Picture Style Settings dialog box that appears at left in the figure. These are the same parameters you can change in the camera. Click OK when you're finished.

6. **Make advanced changes.** The Tool palette has additional functions for adjusting hue, tonal range, and curves. Use of these tools is beyond the scope of a single chapter, let alone a notation in a list, but if you're familiar with the advanced tools in Photoshop, Photoshop Elements, Digital Photo Pro, or another image editor, you can experiment to your heart's content. Note that these modifications go way beyond what you can do with Picture Styles in the camera itself, so learning how to work with them is worth the effort. Figure 8.29 shows an image taken using the Standard Picture Style (left) and a custom User Def. style with enhanced saturation, sharpness, and contrast (right).

7. **Save your Picture Style.** When you're finished, choose Save Picture Style File from the File menu to store your new style as a PF2 file on your hard disk. Add a caption and copyright information to your style in the boxes provided. If you click Disable Subsequent Editing, your style will be "locked" and protected from further changes, and the modifications you did make will be hidden from view (just in case you dream up your own personal, "secret" style). But you'll be unable to edit that style later on. If you think you might want to change your custom Picture Style, save a second copy without marking the Disable Subsequent Editing box.

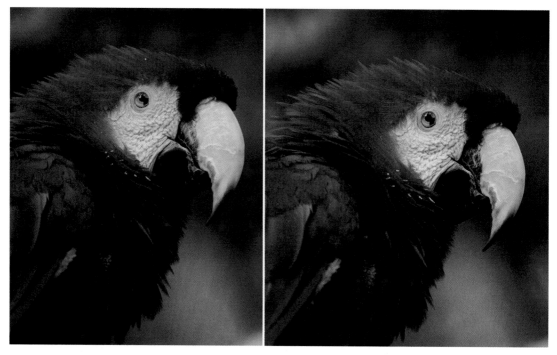

Figure 8.29 Image taken using Standard Picture Style (left) and custom User Def. Picture Style with enhanced saturation, sharpness, and contrast (right).

Uploading a Picture Style to the Camera

Now it's time to upload your new style to your Canon 70D into one of your three User Def. slots in the Picture Style array. Just follow these steps:

1. **Link your camera for upload.** Connect your camera to your computer using the USB cable, turn the 70D on, launch the EOS Utility, and click the Camera Settings/Remote Shooting choice in the splash screen.

2. **Choose the Shooting menu.** It's marked with an icon of a white camera on a red background, from the menu bar located about midway in the control panel that appears on your computer display.

3. **Select Register User Defined Style.** Click on the box, outlined in red in the figure, to produce the Register Picture Style dialog box.

4. **Choose a User Def. tab.** Click on one of the three tabs, labeled User Def. 1, User Def. 2, or User Def. 3. Each tab will include the name of the current Picture Style active in that tab.

5. **Click the Open File button and choose the Picture Style file to load.** The Picture Styles you've saved (or downloaded from another source) will appear with a PF2 extension. Click on the one you want to use, and then click the Open button in the Open dialog box.

6. **Upload Picture Style to the camera.** The Register Picture Style File dialog box will return. Click OK and the Picture Style will be uploaded to the camera in the User Def. "slot" represented by the tab you've chosen. The name of the Picture Style will appear in the 70D's menu in place of User Def. 1 (or User Def. 2/User Def. 3). (See Figure 8.30.)

Figure 8.30
The new style will appear in the menu.

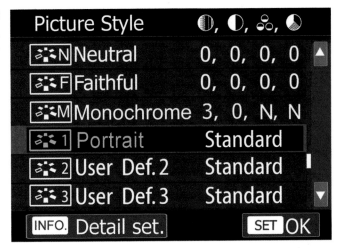

Changing a Picture Style's Settings from the EOS Utility

You can modify the settings of a Picture Style that's already loaded into your camera from the EOS Utility when your camera is linked to your computer. Just follow these steps:

1. **Link your camera to the computer.** Connect your camera to your computer using the USB cable, turn the 70D on, launch the EOS Utility, and click the Camera Settings/Remote Shooting choice in the splash screen.

2. **Choose the Shooting menu.** It's marked with an icon of a white camera on a red background, from the menu bar located about midway in the control panel that appears on your computer display.

3. **Access the Picture Style.** Click on the Picture Style choice to produce the screen shown at upper right in Figure 8.31. The currently active Picture Style in the camera will be shown, along with its detail settings.

4. **Choose a Picture Style to modify.** Click the Picture Style box (highlighted with a red box at upper left in Figure 8.31) to produce a listing of all the available Picture Styles, which you can see at right in Figure 8.31. For this illustration, I clicked on Landscape, which is highlighted with a red box.

5. **Click Detail Set.** At lower left Landscape is now highlighted. When you click on Detail Set., the dialog box shown at lower right in Figure 8.31 appears. You can move the sliders to change the settings, as described earlier. You can also click the Default Set. button to return the settings to their original values.

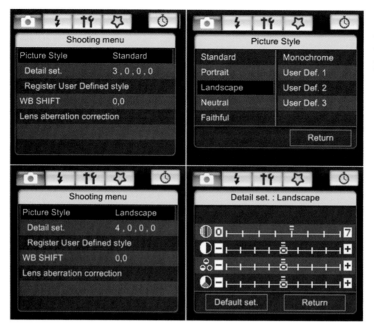

Figure 8.31
Adjust the settings of a Picture Style in your camera.

6. **Confirm choice.** Click Return when you've finished making changes, and the Picture Style you've modified will be changed in the camera.

7. **Exit EOS Utility.** Disconnect your camera from your computer, and your modified style is ready to use.

Getting More Picture Styles

I've found that careful Googling can unearth other Picture Styles that helpful fellow EOS owners have made available, and even a few from the helpful Canon company itself. My own search turned up this link: http://web.canon.jp/imaging/picturestyle/file/index.html, where Canon offers a half dozen or more useful PF2 files you can download and install on your own. Remember that Picture Style files are compatible between various Canon EOS camera models (that is, you can use a style created for the Canon 40D with your 70D), but you should be working with the latest software versions to work with the latest cameras and Picture Styles. If you installed your software from the CDs that came with your 70D, you're safe. If you owned an earlier EOS and haven't reinstalled the software since your camera upgrade, you might need to reinstall the software. It's available for download from the Canon website.

Try the additional styles Canon offers. They include:

■ **Studio Portrait.** Compared to the Portrait style built into the camera, this one, Canon says, expresses translucent skin in smooth tones, but with less contrast. (Similar to films in the pre-digital age that were intended for studio portraiture.)

■ **Snapshot Portrait.** This is another "translucent skin" style, but with increased contrast indoors or out.

- **Nostalgia.** This style adds an amber tone to your images, while reducing the saturation of blue and green tones.
- **Clear.** This style adds contrast for what Canon says is additional "depth and clarity."
- **Twilight.** Adds a purple tone to the sky just before and after sunset or sunrise.
- **Emerald.** Emphasizes blues and greens.
- **Autumn Hues.** Increases the richness of browns and red tones seen in Fall colors.

Long Exposure Noise Reduction

This entry allows you to enable or disable long exposure noise reduction, or allow the 70D to evaluate your scene and decide whether to use this noise-canceling adjustment. Visual noise is that graininess that shows up as multicolored specks in images, and this setting helps you manage it. In some ways, noise is like the excessive grain found in some high-speed photographic films. However, while photographic grain is sometimes used as a special effect, it's rarely desirable in a digital photograph.

The visual noise-producing process is something like listening to a CD in your car, and then rolling down all the windows. You're adding sonic noise to the audio signal, and while increasing the CD player's volume may help a bit, you're still contending with an unfavorable signal to noise ratio that probably mutes tones (especially higher treble notes) that you really want to hear.

The same thing happens when the analog signal is amplified: You're increasing the image information in the signal, but boosting the background fuzziness at the same time. Tune in a very faint or distant AM radio station on your car stereo. Then turn up the volume. After a certain point, turning up the volume further no longer helps you hear better. There's a similar point of diminishing returns for digital sensor ISO increases and signal amplification as well.

These processes create several different kinds of noise. Noise can be produced from high ISO settings. As the captured information is amplified to produce higher ISO sensitivities, some random noise in the signal is amplified along with the photon information. Increasing the ISO setting of your camera raises the threshold of sensitivity so that fewer and fewer photons are needed to register as an exposed pixel. Yet, that also increases the chances of one of those phantom photons being counted among the real-life light particles, too.

Fortunately, the 70D's sensor and its digital processing chip are optimized to produce the low noise levels, so ratings as high as ISO 800 can be used routinely (although there will be some noise, of course), and even ISO 3200 can generate good results.

A second way noise is created is through longer exposures. Extended exposure times allow more photons to reach the sensor, but increase the likelihood that some photosites will react randomly even though not struck by a particle of light. Moreover, as the sensor remains switched on for the longer exposure, it heats, and this heat can be mistakenly recorded as if it were a barrage of photons. This entry can be used to tailor the amount of noise-canceling performed by the digital signal processor.

- **Disable.** This setting disables long exposure noise reduction. Use this setting when you want the maximum amount of detail present in your photograph, even though higher noise levels will result. This setting also eliminates the extra time needed to take a picture caused by the noise reduction process. If you plan to use only lower ISO settings (thereby reducing the noise caused by ISO amplification), the noise levels produced by longer exposures may be acceptable. For example, you might be shooting a river spilling over rocks at ISO 100 with the camera mounted on a tripod, using a neutral-density filter and long exposure to cause the pounding water to blur slightly. To maximize detail in the non-moving portions of your photos, you can switch off long exposure noise reduction. Because the noise-reduction process used with Auto and Enable can effectively double the time required to take a picture, Disable is a good setting to use when you want to avoid this delay when possible.

- **Auto.** The 70D examines your photo taken with an exposure of one second or longer, and if long exposure noise is detected, a second, blank exposure is made and compared to the first image. Noise found in the "dark frame" image is subtracted from your original picture, and only the noise-corrected image is saved to your memory card.

- **Enable.** When this setting is activated, the 70D applies dark frame subtraction to all exposures longer than one second. You might want to use this option when you're working with high ISO settings (which will already have noise boosted a bit) and want to make sure that any additional noise from long exposures is eliminated, too. Noise reduction will be applied to some exposures that would not have caused it to kick in using the Auto setting.

> **Tip**
>
> While the "dark frame" is being exposed, the LCD screen will be blank during Live View mode, and the number of shots you can take in Continuous shooting mode will be reduced. White balance bracketing is disabled during this process.

High ISO Speed Noise Reduction

The other type of noise results from using higher ISO settings. This entry allows you to specify just how much or how little of this noise reduction to apply, which can be a valuable option because noise reduction does eliminate detail while blurring the amount of noise. The default is Standard noise reduction, but you can specify Low or High noise reduction, or disable noise reduction entirely. At lower ISO values, noise reduction improves the appearance of shadow areas without affecting highlights; at higher ISO settings, noise reduction is applied to the entire photo. Note that when the High option is selected, the maximum number of continuous shots that can be taken will decrease significantly, because of the additional processing time for the images.

- **Disable.** No additional noise reduction will be applied.
- **Low.** A smaller amount of noise reduction is used. This will increase the grainy appearance, but preserve more fine image detail.

- **Standard.** At lower ISO values, noise reduction is applied primarily to shadow areas; at higher ISO settings, noise reduction affects the entire image.

- **High.** More aggressive noise reduction is used, at the cost of some image detail, adding a "mushy" appearance that may be noticeable and objectionable. Because of the image processing applied by this setting, your continuous shooting maximum burst will decrease significantly.

- **Multi-Shot Noise Reduction.** The 70D takes four shots and combines them into a single JPEG image with reduced noise.

Highlight Tone Priority

This setting concentrates the available tones in an image from the middle grays up to the brightest highlights, in effect expanding the dynamic range of the image at the expense of shadow detail. You'd want to activate this option when shooting subjects in which there is lots of important detail in the highlights, and less detail in shadow areas. Highlight tones will be preserved, while shadows will be allowed to go dark more readily (and may exhibit an increase in noise levels). Bright beach or snow scenes, especially those with few shadows (think high noon, when the shadows are smaller) can benefit from using Highlight Tone Priority. Your choices:

- **Disable/OFF.** The 70D's normal dynamic range is applied. Note that when Highlight Tone Priority is switched off, the related Auto Lighting Optimizer setting (discussed earlier in this chapter) functions normally.

- **Enable/D+.** Highlight areas are given expanded tonal values, while the tones available for shadow areas are reduced. The ISO 100 sensitivity setting is disabled and only ISO 200 to ISO 25600 (or ISO 200-12800 for movies) are available. You can tell that this restriction is in effect by viewing the D+ icon shown in the viewfinder, on the ISO Selection screen, and in the shooting information display for a particular image. Image noise may slightly increase as the camera manipulates the image. Note that this setting disables the Auto Lighting Optimizer.

Dust Delete Data

This menu choice lets you "take a picture" of any dust or other particles that may be adhering to your sensor. The 70D will then append information about the location of this dust to your photos, so that the Digital Photo Professional software can use this reference information to identify dust in your images and remove it automatically. You should capture a Dust Delete Data photo from time to time as your final line of defense against sensor dust.

To use this feature, select Dust Delete Data to produce the screen shown in Figure 8.32. Select OK and choose SET. The camera will first perform a self-cleaning operation by applying ultrasonic vibration to the low-pass filter that resides on top of the sensor. Then, a screen will appear asking you to press the shutter button. Point the 70D at a solid-white card with the lens set on manual focus and rotate the focus ring to infinity. When you press the shutter release, the camera takes a photo of the card using Aperture-priority and f/22 (which provides enough depth-of-field [actually, in this case, *depth-of-focus*] to image the dust sharply). The "picture" is not saved to your memory

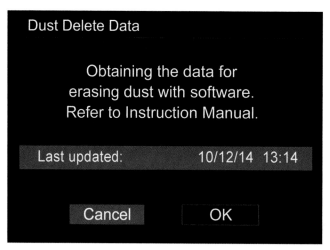

Figure 8.32
Capture updated dust data for your sensor to allow Digital Photo Professional to remove it automatically.

card but, rather, is stored in a special memory area in the camera. Finally, a "Data obtained" screen appears.

The Dust Delete Data information is retained in the camera until you update it by taking a new "picture." The 70D adds the information to each image file automatically.

Multiple Exposure

This option, shown in Figure 8.33, lets you combine two to nine separate images into one photo without the need for an image editor like Photoshop, and can be an entertaining way to return to those thrilling days of yesteryear, when complex photos were created in the camera itself. In truth, prior to the digital age, multiple exposures were a cool, groovy, far-out, hep/hip, phat, sick, fabulous way of producing composite images. Today, it's more common to take the lazy way out, snap two or more pictures, and then assemble them in an image editor like Photoshop.

However, if you're willing to spend the time planning a multiple exposure (or are open to some happy accidents), there is a lot to recommend the multiple exposure capability that Canon has bestowed on the 70D. For one thing, the camera is able to combine two or more images using the RAW data from the sensor, producing photos that are blended together more smoothly than is likely for anyone who's not a Photoshop guru. In addition, Canon has eliminated one annoying aspect of the feature found in some cameras: it's not necessary to return to the menu to activate multiple exposure for each and every set. If you want to take a series of pictures, you can set it once, and forget it. (But don't forget to turn it off when you're done!)

Multiple exposures cannot be captured if white balance bracketing, HDR shooting, or movie-making modes are in use. Before you begin snapping your own multiexposures, you'll need to set your parameters using the following options discussed below.

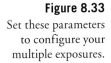

Figure 8.33
Set these parameters
to configure your
multiple exposures.

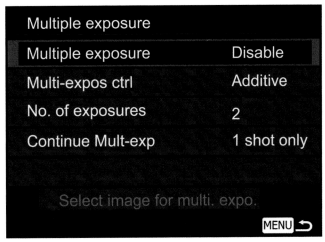

Multiple Exposure

The Disable option deactivates the multiexposure feature, but you can quickly choose either of the two On variations. This is the "master control" that allows you to turn multiple exposure on and off (leaving the other parameters you've set unchanged).

- **Disable.** Deactivates multiple exposure.
- **Enable.** Turns multiple exposure functions on.

Multi-Expos Ctrl

This essential parameter can determine how successful your multiple exposure is, by controlling how each individual exposure is merged with the overlapping portions of the other images in the series. Picture an image like the one shown in Figure 8.34. The dancer was photographed against a plain, dark background. He happened to be moving, too, so none of the three images overlapped with each other, or with any details of the featureless background. But in Figure 8.35, the dancer remained in place, so that each subsequent image overlapped the others slightly. The Multi-Exposure Control feature allows you to specify how the images are combined with these choices:

- **Additive.** Each individual shot in the series is by default given the full exposure, which is what I used for Figure 8.34. Because the background was totally black and the subject was moving and did not overlap, the effect was to combine three separate images into one image.

  However, you can manually adjust the amount of exposure each shot is given by dialing in exposure compensation, making this mode useful for overlapping images as well. The customary procedure is to specify –1 stop exposure compensation for two shots, –1.5 EV for three-shot multiple exposures, and –2 EV for four-shot multis. Manually calculating the amount of negative exposure compensation allows you to fine-tune the look of overlapping images.

■ **Average.** Choose this option and the 70D will apply appropriate negative exposure compensation for you, based on the number of exposures you're combining into a single image. If your multiple exposures happen to be of the same scene (rather than separate subjects), the camera will attempt to ensure that the background receives the equivalent of a full exposure. I used this option for Figure 8.35.

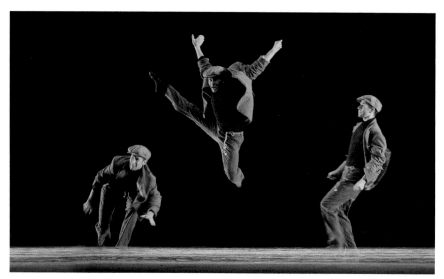

Figure 8.34
Multiple exposure using Additive exposure, and no exposure compensation.

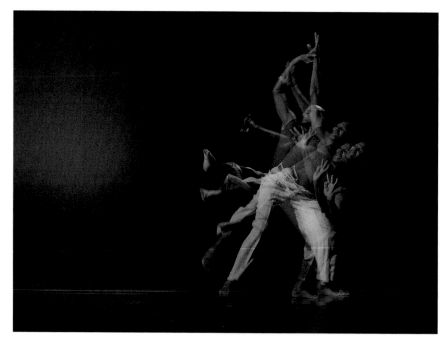

Figure 8.35
Multiple exposure using Average exposure.

No. of Exposures

You can choose from 2 to 9 exposures in each multiple exposure set. There is no selection screen for this option; highlight it and spin the QCD to choose the number of exposures. I recommend starting out with three multiple exposures when you begin exploring this tool; you'll quickly discover picture opportunities that call for more combined shots in a single image.

Continue Mult-exp

Choose 1 Shot Only or Continuously. Choose the former if you want to take a single multiple exposure series and then return to normal shooting with Multiple Exposure then disabled. Select Continuously if you plan to shoot a batch of different multiple exposures and don't want to return to the menu system to reactivate the feature after each shot.

MULTI NOTES

Some special conditions are required for your 70D to shoot multiple exposures. Some features are disabled, and others are locked in at particular values.

- Auto Lighting Optimizer, Highlight Tone Priority, and Peripheral Illumination/Chromatic Aberration Correction are disabled, and the Standard Picture Style will be used if you've chosen the Auto Picture Style setting. Multiple exposures are disabled if your camera is connected to a computer or printer via the USB cable.

- Most settings used for the first shot in a series are locked in for all subsequent images in that series, including image recording quality, ISO sensitivity, Picture Style, high ISO noise reduction, and color space.

- Other functions that cannot be changed while shooting multiple exposures will be dimmed in the camera menu.

HDR Mode

I described using the 70D's HDR Mode in detail in Chapter 4. To recap, this menu entry has three subentries you can adjust:

- **Adjust Dynamic Range.** Select Disable HDR, allow the camera to select a dynamic range automatically, or select the range yourself to achieve a particular look. You can choose plus/minus 1, 2, or 3 EV.

- **Continuous HDR.** Choose 1 Shot Only if you plan to take just a single HDR exposure and want the feature disabled automatically thereafter, or Every Shot to continue using HDR mode for all subsequent exposures until you turn it off. This is similar to the multiple exposure option described earlier.

■ **Auto Image Align.** You can choose Enable to have the camera attempt to align all three HDR exposures when shooting handheld, or select Disable when using a tripod. The success of the automatic alignment will vary, depending on the shutter speed used (higher is better), and the amount of camera movement (less is better!).

Live View and Movie Shooting Menus

The two Live View Shooting and two Movie menus were discussed in Chapter 6 and won't be duplicated here. You can find everything you need to know in the earlier chapter.

Playback Menu Options

The two blue-coded Playback menus are where you select options related to the display, review, and printing of the photos you've taken. The choices you'll find include:

- Protect Images
- Rotate Images
- Erase Images
- Print Order
- Photobook Set-up
- Creative Filters

- RAW Image Processing
- Resize
- Rating
- Slide Show
- Image Jump with Main Dial

- Highlight Alert
- AF Point Display
- Playback Grid
- Histogram Display
- Movie Play Count
- Ctrl over HDMI

Protect Images

This is the first of six entries in the Playback 1 menu (see Figure 8.36). If you want to keep an image from being accidentally erased (either with the Erase button or by using the Erase menu), you can mark that image for protection. There are two ways to protect one or more images.

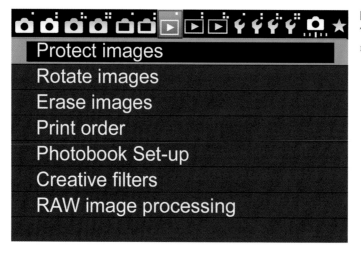

Figure 8.36
The Playback 1 menu.

- **Q button.** While viewing an image in playback mode, press the Q button. A Quick Control screen appears with a column of playback function choices in the left column. Protect is at the top, and when highlighted allows you to choose from Disable and Enable to mark an image as protected.

- **Playback menu.** Choose Protect Images and a screen appears with five options:
  - Select Images
  - All Images in Folder
  - Unprotect All Images in Folder
  - All Images on Card
  - Unprotect All Images on Card

If you choose Select Images, you can view and select individual images by pressing the SET button when they are displayed on the screen. A key icon will appear at the upper edge of the information display while still in the protection screen, and when reviewing that image later. To remove protection, repeat the process. You can scroll among the other images on your memory card using the QCD and protect/unprotect them in the same way. Image protection will not save your images from removal when the card is reformatted.

Rotate Images

While you can set the 70D to automatically rotate images taken in a vertical orientation using the Auto Rotate option in the Set-up 1 menu (as described in Chapter 9), you can manually rotate an image during playback using this menu selection. Select Rotate Image from the Playback 1 menu, use the touch screen or multi-controller to page through the available images on your memory card until the one you want to rotate appears, then choose SET. The image will appear on the screen rotated 90 degrees, as shown in Figure 8.37. Select SET again, and the image will be rotated 270 degrees.

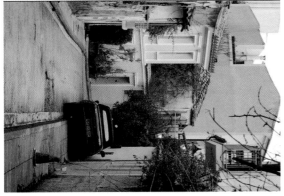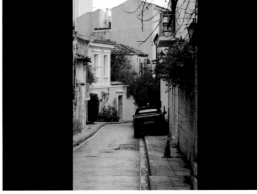

Figure 8.37 A vertically oriented image that isn't rotated appears larger on the LCD, but rotation allows viewing the photo without turning the camera.

Erase Images

Choose this menu entry and you'll be given three choices: Select and Erase Images, All Images in Folder, and All Images on Card. You can use the first two to selectively remove images, while the third option deletes all the pictures on a card. But, using the Format command is usually faster and more thorough.

- **Select and Erase Images.** View the images on your card by pressing the left/right multi-controller to scroll through them. To mark an image for deletion or to remove a checkmark, press the up/down multi-controller. When you're finished selecting, press the Trash button (to the left of the viewfinder window) and you'll be asked to confirm. Choose Cancel or OK and SET to finish.

- **All Images in Folder.** You'll be shown a list of the available folders on your memory card. Select SET, and a prompt will appear asking you to confirm, and reminding you that Protected images will not be removed.

- **All Images on Card.** A prompt will ask you to confirm this step. The All Images on Card choice removes all the pictures on the card, except for those you've marked with the Protect command, and does not reformat the memory card.

Print Order

The 70D supports the DPOF (Digital Print Order Format) that is now almost universally used by digital cameras to specify which images on your memory card should be printed, and the number of prints desired of each image. This information is recorded on the memory card, and can be interpreted by a compatible printer when the camera is linked to the printer using the USB cable, or when the memory card is inserted into a card reader slot on the printer itself. Photo labs are also equipped to read this data and make prints when you supply your memory card to them.

While marking images for printing is similar to the Erase procedure described earlier, you can read more about assembling print orders and printing photobooks in Chapter 13.

Photobook Set-up

You can select up to 998 images on your memory card, and then use the EOS Utility to copy them all to a specific folder on your computer. This is a handy way to transfer only specific images to a particular folder, and is especially useful when you're collecting photos to assemble in a photobook. Your choices include:

- **Select images.** You can mark individual images from any folder on your memory card.
- **All images in folder.** Mark all the images in a particular folder for transfer.
- **Clear all in folder.** Unmark all the images in a folder.
- **All images on card.** Mark all the images on the memory card for transfer to the specific folder.
- **Clear all on card.** Unmark all the images on the card.

Once you marked the images you want to transfer to the specified folder, use the EOS Utility to copy them, as described in Chapter 13.

Creative Filters

One new feature of the 70D is the ability to apply Creative Filters to images as you take the picture, and preview their effect before shooting during live view. However, the original method of applying interesting effects to images you've already taken remains available. You can process an image using one of these filters, and save a copy alongside the original. When you select this menu entry, you'll be taken to a screen that allows you to choose an image to modify. You can scroll through the available images with the touch screen or multi-controller or press the Index/Reduce button to view thumbnails and select from those. Only images that can be edited are shown. Then, select SET, and choose the filter you want to apply from a list at the bottom of the screen using the left/right multi-controller. Choose SET to activate the filter, then use the touch screen or left/right multi-controller again to adjust the amount of the effect (or select the area to be adjusted using the miniature effect). Choose SET once more to save your new image.

The seven effects include the following. Four of them (Grainy B/W, Soft Focus, Fish-Eye, Toy Camera Effect) are shown in Figure 8.38, and the Miniature Effect is shown in Figures 8.39 and 8.40.

- **Grainy B/W.** Creates a grainy monochrome image. You can adjust contrast among Low, Normal, and Strong settings.
- **Soft Focus.** Blur your image using Low, Normal, and Strong options.
- **Fish-eye Effect.** Creates a distorted, curved image.
- **Art Bold Effect.** Produces a three-dimensional oil painting effect. You can adjust contrast and saturation.

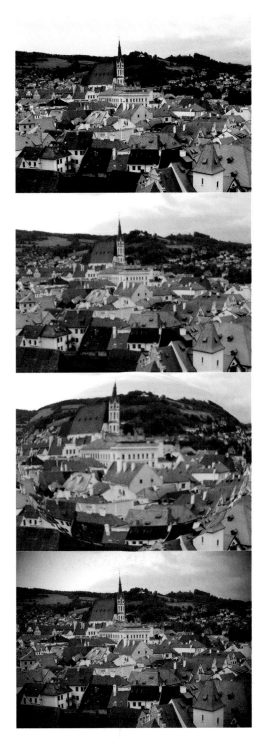

Figure 8.38 Top to bottom: Grainy B/W, Soft Focus, Fish-Eye, Toy Camera Effect.

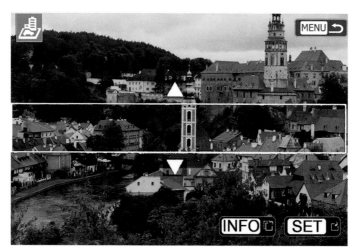

Figure 8.39
Choose the area for sharp focus by moving the white box within the frame.

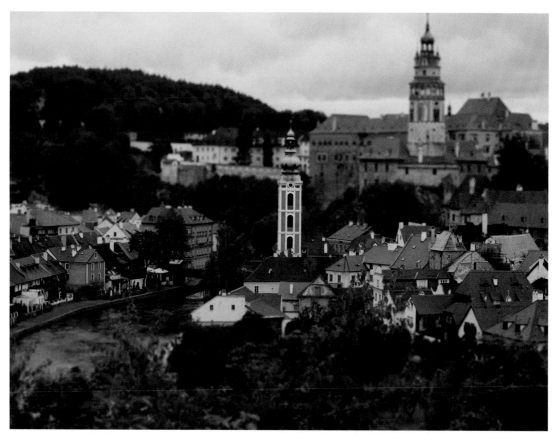

Figure 8.40 The resulting image looks like a miniature town, perhaps for a toy train layout.

■ **Water Painting Effect.** Gives you soft colors like a watercolor painting, and allows you to adjust color density.

■ **Toy Camera Effect.** Darkens the corners of an image, much as a toy camera does, and adds a warm or cool tone (or none), as you wish.

■ **Miniature Effect.** This is a clever effect, and it's hampered by a misleading name and the fact that its properties are hard to visualize (which is not a great attribute for a visual effect). This tool doesn't create a "miniature" picture, as you might expect. What it does is mimic tilt/shift lens effects that angle the lens off the axis of the sensor plane to drastically change the plane of focus, producing the sort of look you get when viewing some photographs of a diorama, or miniature scene. Confused yet? All you need to do is specify the area of the image that you want to remain sharp (see Figure 8.41) and you'll end up with a version like the one shown in Figure 8.42.

RAW Image Processing

You can produce JPEG versions of your full-size RAW images (but not M RAW or S RAW files) right in the camera. The original RAW shot is not modified. When you select this menu entry, only compatible RAW images are offered for your selection. Just follow these steps:

1. **View RAW images.** Rotate the QCD to scroll through compatible images. Press the Index/Reduce button and rotate the Main Dial counterclockwise to view a selection of index images instead.

2. **Select image to process.** Press SET to select an image for processing.

3. **Specify parameters.** A screen appears with a selection of parameters you can adjust. Navigate to the parameter you want to manipulate using the multi-selector. Your choices include:

   ■ Brightness   ■ Image Quality

   ■ White Balance   ■ Color Space

   ■ Picture Style   ■ Peripheral Illumination Correction

   ■ Auto Lighting Optimizer   ■ Distortion Correction

   ■ High ISO Noise Reduction   ■ Chromatic Aberration Correction

4. **Make adjustments.** When a parameter is highlighted you can rotate the QCD or press SET to change the settings; press INFO. to reset the settings to the original values of the RAW image; press the Magnify button to zoom in on the image.

5. **Save JPEG.** Navigate to the Save icon at the bottom left of the screen and press SET. Choose OK to save as a new file, or Cancel to abort the process. If the original was shot using live view and an aspect ratio other than 3:2, the image will be displayed in those proportions, and the JPEG will be saved in that aspect ratio.

Resize

If you've already taken an image and would like to create a smaller version (say, to send by e-mail), you can create one from this menu entry. Just follow these steps:

1. **Choose Resize.** Select this menu entry from the Playback 2 menu. (See Figure 8.41.)

2. **View images to resize.** You can scroll through the available images with the touch screen or multi-controller, or press the Index/Reduce button to view thumbnails and select from those. Only images that can be resized are shown. They include JPEG Large, Medium, Small 1, and Small 2 images. Small 3 and RAW images of any type cannot be resized.

3. **Select an image.** Choose SET to select an image to resize. A pop-up menu will appear on the screen offering the choice of reduced size images. These include M (Medium: 8MP, 3456 × 2304 pixels); S1 (Small 1: 4.5MP, 2592 × 1728 pixels); S2 (Small 2: 2.5MP, 1920 × 1280 pixels); or S3 (Small 3, .3MP, 720 × 480 pixels). You cannot resize an image to a size that is larger than its current size; that is, you cannot save a JPEG Medium image as JPEG Large.

4. **Resize and save.** Choose SET to save as a new file, and confirm your choice by selecting OK from the screen that pops up, or cancel to exit without saving a new version. The old version of the image is untouched.

Rating

If you want to apply a quality rating to images or movies you've shot (or use the rating system to represent some other criteria), you can use this entry to give particular images one, two, three, four, or five stars, or turn the rating system off. The Image Jump function can display only images with a given rating. Suppose you were photographing a track meet with multiple events. You could apply a one-star rating to jumping events, two stars to relays, three stars to throwing events, four stars to hurdles, and five stars to dashes. Then, using the Image Jump feature, you could review only images of one particular type.

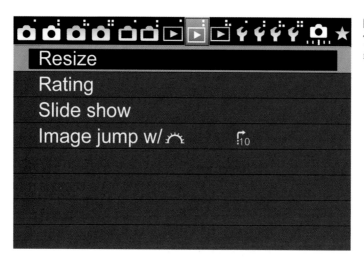

Figure 8.41
The Playback 2 menu.

With a little imagination you can apply the rating system to all sorts of categories. At a wedding, you could classify pictures of the bride, the groom, guests, attendants, and parents of the couple. If you were shooting school portraits, one rating could apply to First Grade, another to Second Grade, and so on. Given a little thought, this feature has many more applications than you might think. To use it, just follow these steps:

1. Choose the Rating menu item.

2. Use the touch screen or multi-controller to select an image or movie. Press the Index/Reduce button to display three images at once. Press the Magnify button to return to a single image.

3. When an image or movie is visible, press the up/down buttons to apply a one- to five-star rating. The display shows how many images have been assigned each rating so far.

4. When finished rating, choose MENU to exit.

Slide Show

Slide Show is a convenient way to review images one after another, without the need to manually switch between them. To activate, just choose Slide Show from the Playback 2 menu. During playback, you can press the SET button to pause the "slide show" (in case you want to examine an image more closely), or the INFO. button to change the amount of information displayed on the screen with each image. For example, you might want to review a set of images and their histograms to judge the exposure of the group of pictures. To set up your slide show, follow these steps:

1. **Begin setup.** Choose Slide Show from the Playback 2 menu, choosing SET to display the screen shown in Figure 8.42.

2. **Choose image selection method.** Navigate to All Images, and choose SET. Then use the touch screen or multi-controller to choose from All Images, Folder, or Date. Choose SET to activate that selection mode. If you selected All Images, skip to Step 4.

Figure 8.42
Set up your slide show using this screen.

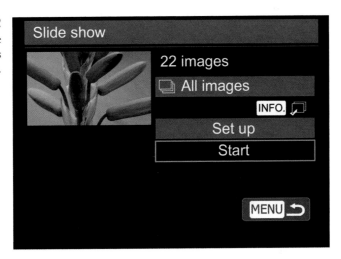

3. **Choose images.** If you've selected Folder or Date, press the INFO. button to produce a screen that allows you to select from the available folders, or the available image creation dates on your memory card. When you've chosen a folder or date, choose SET to confirm your choice.

4. **Choose Play Time and Repeat Options.** Highlight Setup and choose SET to produce a screen with playing time (1, 2, 3, or 5 seconds per image), and repeating options (On or Off). When you've specified either value, select MENU to confirm your choice, and then MENU once more to go back to the main Slide Show screen.

5. **Start the show.** Highlight Start and choose SET to begin your show. (If you'd rather cancel the show you've just set up, select MENU.)

6. **Use show options during display.** Press SET to pause/restart; INFO. to cycle among the four information displays described in the section before this one; MENU to stop the show.

Image Jump with Main Dial

As first described in Chapter 2, you can leap ahead or back during picture review by swiping across the touch screen with two fingers, or by rotating the Main Dial. You can select from a variety of increments that will be used with this menu entry. The Jump method is shown briefly on the screen as you leap ahead to the next image displayed, as shown in Figure 8.43. Your options are as follows:

- **1 image.** Rotating the Main Dial one click or swiping jumps forward or back 1 image.

- **10 images.** Rotating the Main Dial one click or swiping jumps forward or back 10 images.

- **100 images.** Rotating the Main Dial one click or swiping jumps forward or back 100 images.

- **Date.** Rotating the Main Dial one click or swiping jumps forward or back to the first image taken on the next or previous calendar date.

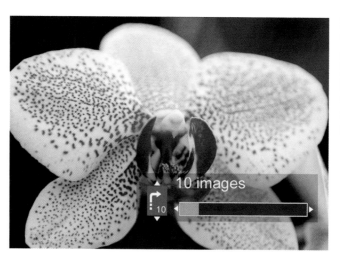

Figure 8.43
The Jump method is shown on the LCD briefly when you leap forward or back using the Main Dial or a two-fingered touch screen swipe.

- **Folder.** Rotating the Main Dial one click or swiping jumps forward or back to the first image in the next folder available on your memory card (if one exists).
- **Movies.** Rotating the Main Dial one click or swiping jumps forward or back, displaying movies you captured only.
- **Stills.** Rotating the Main Dial one click or swiping jumps forward or back, displaying still images only.
- **Rating.** Rotating the Main Dial one click or swiping jumps forward or back, displaying images by the ratings you've applied (as described next). Tap the touch screen or rotate the Main Dial to choose the rating parameter.

Highlight Alert

Choose Enable, and overexposed highlight areas will blink on the LCD screen during picture review. Set to Disable if you find this alert distracting. Many 70D users use the histogram displays during playback as a more precise indicator of over (and under) exposure. This is the first entry in the Playback 3 menu. (See Figure 8.44.)

AF Point Disp.

Select Enable, and the exact AF point(s) used to determine focus will be highlighted in red. If automatic AF point selection was used, you may find multiple points highlighted.

Playback Grid

You can superimpose a 3 × 3, 6 × 4, or 3 × 3 plus diagonal lines grid over your image during playback, or disable the grid display entirely.

Figure 8.44
The Playback 3 menu.

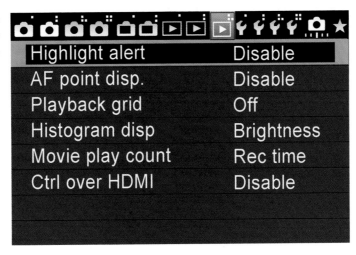

Highlight alert	Disable
AF point disp.	Disable
Playback grid	Off
Histogram disp	Brightness
Movie play count	Rec time
Ctrl over HDMI	Disable

Histogram Display

The 70D can show either a brightness histogram or set of three separate Red, Green, and Blue histograms in the full information display during picture review, or, it can show you both types of histogram in the partial information display. This entry gives you those options.

Brightness histograms give you information about the overall tonal values present in the image. The RGB histograms can show more advanced users valuable data about specific channels that might be "clipped" (details are lost in the shadows or highlights). This menu choice determines only how they are displayed during picture review. The amount of information displayed cycles through the following list as you repeatedly press the INFO. button in Playback mode:

- **Single image display.** Only the image itself is shown, with basic shooting information displayed in a band across the top of the image, as you can see at upper left in Figure 8.45.

- **Single image display+Image-recording quality.** Identical to Single image display, except that the image size, RAW format (if selected), and JPEG compression (if selected) are overlaid on the image in the lower-left corner of the frame.

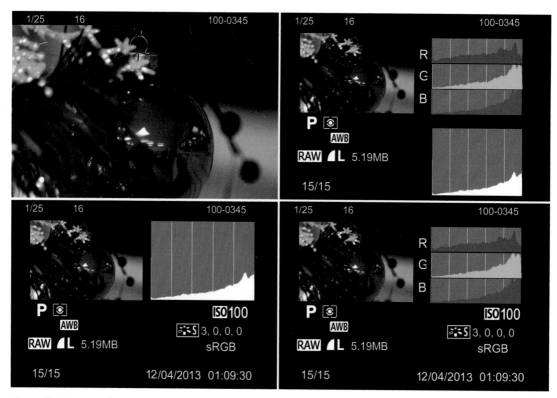

Figure 8.45 Press the INFO. button to cycle between Single image display (upper left); Single image display+Image-recording quality (not shown); Histogram display (upper right); Shooting information display with brightness histogram (bottom left); or RGB histogram (bottom right).

- **Histogram display.** Both RGB and brightness histograms are shown, along with partial shooting information. This menu choice has no effect on which histograms are shown in this display, which you can see at upper right in Figure 8.45.
- **Shooting information display.** Full shooting data is shown, along with either a brightness histogram (bottom left in Figure 8.45) or RGB histogram (bottom right in Figure 8.45). The type of histogram on view in this screen is determined by the setting you make in this menu choice. Select Histogram from the Playback 3 menu and choose Brightness or RGB. You can read more about *using* histograms in Chapter 4.

Movie Play Count

Determines whether the movie recording and playback time (Rec Time) is shown on the screen, or whether the Time Code (an absolute positional marker/index) is displayed instead. If you change the Movie Play Count setting as described in Chapter 6, or here, the other will be changed automatically. You'll find additional Time Code options in the Movie 2 menu, described in Chapter 6.

Ctrl over HDMI

When enabled, you can control playback operations over the HDMI cable and a television set's remote control when displaying your camera's output on an HDMI CEC-compatible television with a remote control. This option will allow you to access menus, choose a 9-image index, play movies and slide shows, change the amount of information displayed (similarly to the INFO. button), or rotate the image. Set to Disable if you do not have the correct TV hardware, or when testing has shown that your particular HDMI CEC television does not operate correctly in this mode.

9

Customizing with the Set-up Menu and My Menu

In the last chapter, I introduced you to the layout and general functions of the Canon EOS 70D's menu system, with specifics on how to customize your camera with the Shooting 1, Shooting 2, Shooting 3, and Shooting 4 menus, as well as the Playback 1 and Playback 2 menus. In this chapter, you'll learn how to work with the four Set-up menus, and how to assemble your own roster of favorite menu listings with the My Menu feature.

If you're jumping directly to this chapter and need some guidance in how to navigate the 70D's menu system, review the first few pages of Chapter 8. Otherwise, you're welcome to dive right in.

Set-up Menu Options

There are four amber-coded Set-up menus where you make adjustments on how your camera *behaves* during your shooting session, as differentiated from the Shooting menu, which adjusts how the pictures are actually taken. Your choices include:

- Select Folder
- File Numbering
- Auto Rotate
- Format Card
- Eye-Fi Settings
- Auto Power Off
- LCD Brightness
- LCD Off/On Button

- Date/Time/Zone
- Language
- GPS Device Settings
- Video System
- Feature Guide
- Touch Control
- INFO. Button Display Options
- Wi-Fi

- Wi-Fi Function
- Sensor Cleaning
- Battery Info
- Certification Logo Display
- Custom Shooting Mode
- Clear All Camera Settings
- Copyright Information
- Firmware Ver.

Select Folder

Choose this menu option, the first in the Set-up 1 menu (see Figure 9.1) to create a folder where the images you capture will be stored on your memory card, or to switch between existing folders. Just follow these steps:

1. **Choose Select Folder.** Access the option from the Set-up 1 menu.

2. **View list of available folders.** The Select Folder screen pops up with a list of the available folders on your memory card, with names like 100CANON, 101CANON, etc.

3. **Choose a different folder.** To store subsequent images in a different existing folder, use the touch screen or multi-controller to highlight the label for the folder you want to use. When a folder that already has photos is selected, two thumbnails representing images in that folder are displayed at the right side of the screen.

4. **Confirm the folder.** Choose SET to confirm your choice of an existing folder.

5. **Create new folder.** If you'd rather create a new folder, highlight Create Folder in the Select Folder screen and choose SET. The name of the folder that will be created is displayed, along with a choice to Cancel or OK creating the folder. Choose SET to confirm your choice.

6. **Exit.** Press MENU to return to the Set-up 1 menu.

The folders your 70D create always follow the *nnn*CANON convention. You can also use your computer to create folders with names that depart from this arrangement, as long as you adhere to the camera's general rules for memory card folder names. Here's how to create folders with personalized names:

1. Access the memory card from your computer. There are two ways to do this.

   a. **USB link.** Plug the USB cable into the port on the left side of the 70D and connect to a USB connector on your computer. In Windows, the 70D will appear as a generic digital camera icon. A similar icon will appear on the Mac OS X desktop.

   b. **Use a card reader.** Remove the card from the 70D and insert it in a card reader attached to your computer. A typical card reader is shown in Figure 9.2.

2. **Open the camera/memory card in your computer.** A folder called DCIM will appear at the top level. All the folders your 70D can access must be located inside the DCIM folder.

3. **Create a new folder within the DCIM folder.** Although you're not limited to the *nnn*CANON arrangement, you must adhere to the rules in the steps that follow.

4. **Type in a three-digit folder number.** You can use any three numbers from 100 to 999, as long as those numbers are not already in use on that memory card. In other words, you can't have folders named 101CANON and 101SPAIN.

5. **Add a five-character description of your choice.** You can use any uppercase or lowercase letters from A to z, plus the underscore character (to represent a space). You cannot use an actual space, nor any other characters, even if your computer allows them in a file name. An invalid folder name will end up being "invisible" to the 70D, even if it actually exists on your memory card.

Figure 9.1
The Set-up 1 menu.

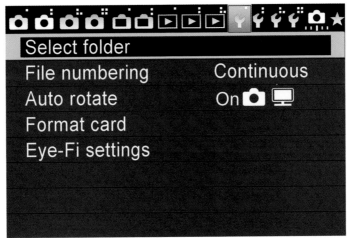

Figure 9.2
Access your memory cards using a card reader.

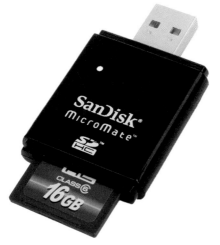

With a little imagination (and caution, to avoid creating "bad" folder names), you can develop some useful folder names, and switch among them at will. I find this capability especially useful when working with very large (32GB or 64GB) cards, because I can do a great deal of organizing right on the card itself. Perhaps I have some images in a particular folder that I use as a "slide show" for display on my 70D's back panel LCD. Or, I might want to sort images by location or date. For example, I could use 104_USA_, 105SPAIN, 106FRANC, or 107GBRIT to indicate the location where the images were shot.

File Number

The EOS 70D will automatically apply a file number to each picture you take, using consecutive numbering for all your photos over a long period of time, spanning many different memory cards, starting over from scratch when you insert a new card, or when you manually reset the numbers. Numbers are applied from 0001 to 9999, at which time the camera creates a new folder on the card

(100, 101, 102, and so forth), so you can have 0001 to 9999 in folder 100, then numbering will start over in folder 101.

The camera keeps track of the last number used in its internal memory. That can lead to a few quirks you should be aware of. For example, if you insert a memory card that had been used with a different camera, the 70D may start numbering with the next number after the highest number used by the previous camera. (I once had a brand new 70D start numbering files in the 8,000 range.) I'll explain how this can happen next.

On the surface, the numbering system seems simple enough: In the menu, you can choose Continuous, Automatic Reset, or Manual Reset. Here is how each works:

- **Continuous.** If you're using a blank/reformatted memory card, the 70D will apply a number that is one greater than the number stored in the camera's internal memory. If the card is not blank and contains images, then the next number will be one greater than the highest number on the card *or* in internal memory. (In other words, if you want to use continuous file number-ing consistently, you must always use a card that is blank or freshly formatted.) Here are some examples.

    - You've taken 4,235 shots with the camera, and you insert a blank/reformatted memory card. The next number assigned will be 4,236, based on the value stored in internal memory.

    - You've taken 4,235 shots with the camera, and you insert a memory card with a picture numbered 2,728. The next picture will be numbered 4,236.

    - You've taken 4,235 shots with the camera, and you insert a memory card with a picture numbered 8,281. The next picture will be numbered 8,282, and that value will be stored in the camera's menu as the "high" shot number (and will be applied when you next insert a blank card).

- **Automatic reset.** If you're using a blank/reformatted memory card, the next photo taken will be numbered 0001. If you use a card that is not blank, the next number will be one greater than the highest number found on the memory card. Each time you insert a memory card, the next number will either be 0001 or one higher than the highest already on the card.

- **Manual reset.** The 70D creates a new folder numbered one higher than the last folder created, and restarts the file numbers at 0001. Then, the camera uses the numbering scheme that was previously set, either Continuous or Automatic Reset, each time you subsequently insert a blank or non-blank memory card.

Auto Rotate

You can turn this feature On or Off. When activated, the EOS 70D rotates pictures taken in verti-cal orientation on the LCD screen so you don't have to turn the camera to view them comfortably. However, this orientation also means that the longest dimension of the image is shown using the shortest dimension of the LCD, so the picture is reduced in size. (You have three options, shown in Figure 9.3.) The image can be autorotated when viewing in the camera *and* on your computer screen using your image editing/viewing software. The image can be marked to autorotate *only* when

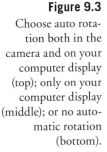

Figure 9.3
Choose auto rotation both in the camera and on your computer display (top); only on your computer display (middle); or no automatic rotation (bottom).

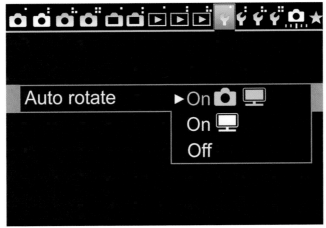

reviewing your image in your image editor or viewing software. This option allows you to have rotation applied when using your computer, while retaining the ability to maximize the image on your LCD in the camera. The third choice is Off. The image will not be rotated when displayed in the camera or with your computer. Note that if you switch Auto Rotate off, any pictures shot while the feature is disabled will not be automatically rotated when you turn Auto Rotate back on; information embedded in the image file when the photo *is taken* is used to determine whether autorotation is applied.

Format Card

Use this item to erase everything on your memory card and set up a fresh file system ready for use. When you select Format Card, you'll see a display like Figure 9.4, showing the capacity of the card, how much of that space is currently in use, and two choices at the bottom of the screen to Cancel or OK (proceed with the format). Press the Trash button if you'd like to do a low-level format. That's a more basic format that removes all sectors from the card and creates new ones, which can

Figure 9.4
You must confirm the format step before the camera will erase a memory card.

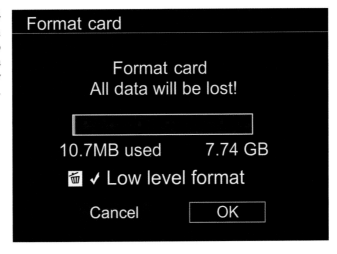

help speed up a card that seems to be slow (because the camera must skip over "bad" sectors left behind from previous uses). An orange bar appears on the screen to show the progress of the formatting step.

Eye-Fi Settings

This menu item appears when you have an Eye-Fi card inserted in the camera. You can enable and disable Eye-Fi wireless functions, and view connection information. I explained the 70D's Eye-Fi options in detail in Chapter 7. The pair of entries allows you to Enable or Disable the card, and view current connection information. Because the Eye-Fi card draws power from the camera even when it's switched off, you might want to Disable the card (or remove it from the camera) when you don't need to use its features.

Auto Power Off

This setting, the first in the Set-up 2 menu (see Figure 9.5), allows you to determine how long the EOS 70D remains active before shutting itself off. As you can see in Figure 9.6, you can select 30 seconds, 1, 2, 4, 8, or 15 minutes, or Disable, which leaves the camera turned on indefinitely. However, even if the camera has shut itself off, if the power switch remains in the On position, you can bring the camera back to life by pressing the shutter button.

LCD Brightness

Choose this menu option and a thumbnail image with a grayscale strip appears on the LCD, as shown in Figure 9.7. You can use the touch screen, multi-controller pad, or the Main Dial to adjust the brightness to a comfortable viewing level. Use the gray bars as a guide; you want to be able to see both the lightest and darkest steps at top and bottom, and not lose any of the steps in the middle. Brighter settings use more battery power, but can allow you to view an image on the LCD outdoors in bright sunlight. When you have the brightness you want, select SET to lock it in and return to the menu.

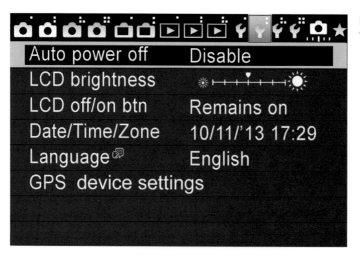

Figure 9.5
The Set-up 2 menu.

Figure 9.6
Select an automatic shut-off period to save battery power.

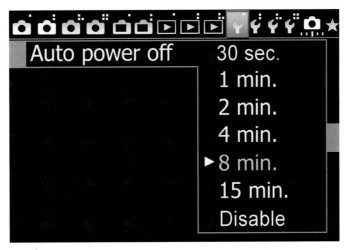

Figure 9.7
Adjust LCD brightness for easier viewing under varying ambient lighting conditions.

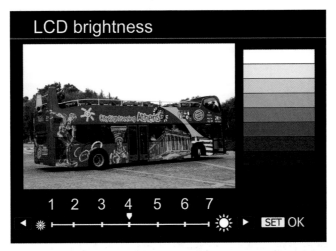

LCD On/Off Button

When composing images in shooting mode, the shooting settings display on the LCD monitor remains on until you turn it off by pressing the INFO. button. This entry allows you to switch from the default Remains On setting to the Shutter Btn option, which turns off the monitor display when you press the shutter button halfway, and switches it back on when you release the button.

Some prefer to have the settings screen shown all the time, or until they turn it off or on manually using the INFO. button; the Remains On option provides that behavior. But, ordinarily, when you're pressing the shutter release halfway, you're peering through the viewfinder and can't see or don't need the shooting settings display, anyway, so the Shutter Btn option may be a good choice. For example, if you're shooting under reduced light levels, having the LCD monitor display switch off automatically as you make an exposure (eliminating a potential distraction), then reappear between shots.

Date/Time/Zone

Use this option to set the date and time, which will be embedded in the image file along with exposure information and other data. As first outlined in Chapter 1, you can set the date and time by following these steps:

1. Access this menu entry from the Set-up 2 menu.

2. Rotate the QCD to move the highlighting down to the Date/Time entry.

3. Press the SET button in the center of the QCD to access the Date/Time setting screen, shown in Figure 9.8.

4. Rotate the QCD to select the value you want to change. When the gold box highlights the month, day, year, hour, minute, or second format you want to adjust, press the SET button to activate that value. A pair of up/down pointing triangles appears above the value.

5. Rotate the QCD to adjust the value up or down. Press the SET button to confirm the value you've entered.

6. Repeat steps 4 and 5 for each of the other values you want to change. The date format can be switched from the default mm/dd/yy to yy/mm/dd or dd/mm/yy; you can turn Daylight Saving Time on or off, and choose an appropriate time zone.

7. When finished, rotate the QCD to select either OK (if you're satisfied with your changes) or Cancel (if you'd like to return to the Set-up 2 menu without making any changes). Press SET to confirm your choice.

8. When finished setting the date and time, press the MENU button to exit, or just tap the shutter release.

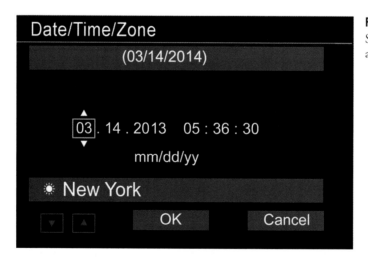

Figure 9.8
Set the date, time, and time zone here.

Language

Choose from 25 languages for menu display, rotating the multi-controller pad until the language you want to select is highlighted. Press the SET button to activate. Your choices include English, German, French, Dutch, Danish, Portuguese, Finnish, Italian, Ukrainian, Norwegian, Swedish, Spanish, Greek, Russian, Polish, Czech, Magyar, Romanian, Turkish, Arabic, Thai, Simplified Chinese, Traditional Chinese, Korean, and Japanese.

If you accidentally set a language you don't read and find yourself with incomprehensible menus, don't panic. Just choose the fifth option from the top of the Set-up 2 menu, and select the idioma, sprache, langue, or kieli of your choice. English is the first selection in the list.

GPS Device Settings

This entry allows you to adjust the settings of the optional Canon GP-E2 GPS device (a roughly $400 add-on). Or, you can disable GPS functions entirely. This menu option is available only when the device is mounted on your camera. A Set-up entry appears that allows you to access four different parameters:

- **Auto time setting.** The 70D can use time data embedded in the GPS signal to set the camera's internal clock accurately. You can choose Auto Update to set the time automatically whenever the camera is powered up and GPS data is available; Disable this function; or Set Now to update immediately.
- **Position update timing.** Use this to specify the interval the GPS device uses to update position information. Choose from every 1, 5, 10, 15, 30 seconds, or every 1, 2, or 5 minutes. Select a shorter interval when you are moving and/or accuracy is critical, or a longer interval to save power, when GPS reception is not optimal, or you are shooting from one position for a longer period.
- **GPS information display.** This entry simply displays a screen of current GPS information, including latitude, longitude, elevation, UTC time (essentially Greenwich Mean Time), and Satellite reception strength/status.
- **GPS logger.** Allows you to enable or disable tracking of GPS position data, transfer log data to your memory card for later manipulation by an appropriate software program, or to delete the camera's current GPS log.

Video System

This setting, the first on the Set-up 3 menu, controls the output of the 70D through the AV cable when you're displaying images on an external monitor. You can select either NTSC, used in the United States, Canada, Mexico, many Central, South American, and Caribbean countries, much of Asia, and other countries, or PAL, which is used in the UK, much of Europe, Africa, India, China, and parts of the Middle East.

VIEWING ON A TELEVISION

Canon makes it quite easy to view your images on a standard television screen, and not much more difficult on a high-definition television (HDTV). (You have to buy a separate cable for HDTV.) For regular TV, just open the port cover on the left side of the camera, plug in the optional AVC-DC400ST cable into the socket labeled A/V-digital, and connect the other end to the yellow VIDEO RCA composite jack on your television or monitor.

For HDTV display, purchase the optional HDMI Cable HTC-100 and connect it to the HDMI OUT terminal just below the microphone input on the left side of the camera.

Connect the other end to an HDMI input port on your television or monitor (my 42-inch HDTV has three of them; my 26-inch monitor has just two). Then turn on the camera and press the Playback button. The image will appear on the external TV/HDTV/monitor and will not be displayed on the camera's LCD. HDTV systems automatically show your images at the appropriate resolution for that set.

Feature Guide

The Feature Guide is an easy pop-up description of a function or option that appears when you change the shooting mode or use the Quick Control screen to select a function, switch to live view, Movie mode, or playback. The instructional screen quickly vanishes in a few seconds. You can use this setting to enable or disable the Feature Guide.

Touch Control

Use this entry to adjust the LCD touch screen feature. If you find yourself accidentally triggering commands by touching the screen or frequently touch the wrong settings and want to turn it off, you can do so. I often disable touch screen control when I am wearing gloves. Choose from Standard or Sensitive response, or Disable.

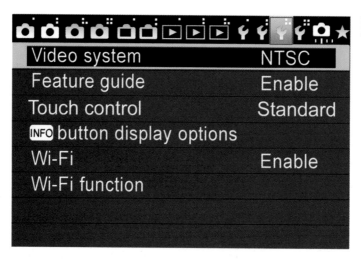

Figure 9.9
The Set-up 3 menu.

INFO. Button Display Options

The INFO. button on the back panel of the Canon EOS 70D by default alternates between the Camera Settings, Shooting Functions, and Electronic Level information displays. If one is shown, press the INFO. button to see the other. If you'd rather have only one or two of those screens shown, choose INFO. button from the Set-up 3 menu and change from the default Normal Disp. to either Camera Set. or Shoot. Func. After that, only the display you specified will be shown. Follow these steps:

1. When you select the menu entry, the INFO. button display options screen appears with three choices (described next). Use the Quick Control Dial or multi-controller to highlight any of the three and press SET to mark or unmark that option.

2. Always mark at least one of the three: Camera Settings, Electronic Level, or Shooting Functions. The 70D won't allow you to disable all of the display options.

3. When finished, press the SET button to confirm your changes.

4. Press SET to OK or Cancel and exit the screen. (If you exit in any other way, your changes will not be entered.) Once you've left this options screen, you can press MENU or tap the shutter release to return to shooting mode.

5. Thereafter, the 70D will cycle among the choices you've activated, plus a blank screen, each time you press the INFO. button.

Wi-Fi

Use this entry to enable or disable the EOS 70D's built-in Wi-Fi capabilities. Turning Wi-Fi off will save power if you don't need the feature. You'll also need to turn off Wi-Fi if you want to shoot movies, or need to connect your camera to a computer using the USB/Digital terminal, as those features are not possible when Wi-Fi is turned on.

Wi-Fi Function

This entry allows you to activate Wi-Fi features, including:

■ Transferring images between the camera and a computer.

■ Connecting to a smart phone.

■ Linking to your computer using the EOS Utility.

■ Printing directly from a Wi-Fi-compatible printer.

■ Uploading images to web pages on the Internet.

■ Viewing images on a DLNA (Digital Living Network Alliance) device, such as your smart TV, home media server, or even a smart phone that can connect through your home network.

You can select a nickname (such as "Canon 70D") for your Wi-Fi device, or clear your current Wi-Fi settings. I explained all the Wi-Fi features in detail in Chapter 6.

Sensor Cleaning

This is the first entry on the Set-up 4 menu. (See Figure 9.10.) One of the Canon EOS 70D's most useful features is the automatic sensor cleaning system that reduces or eliminates the need to clean your camera's sensor manually. Canon has applied anti-static coatings to the sensor and other portions of the camera body interior to counter charge build-ups that attract dust. A separate filter over the sensor vibrates ultrasonically each time the 70D is powered on or off, shaking loose any dust, which is captured by a sticky strip beneath the sensor.

Use this menu entry (see Figure 9.11) to enable or disable automatic sensor cleaning on power up (select Auto Cleaning to choose) or to activate automatic cleaning during a shooting session (select Clean Now). You can also choose the Clean Manually option to flip up the mirror and clean the sensor yourself with a blower, brush, or swab, as described in Chapter 14. If the battery level is too low to safely carry out the cleaning operation, the 70D will let you know and refuse to proceed, unless you use the optional AC Adapter Kit ACK-E6.

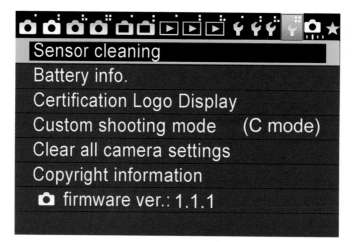

Figure 9.10
The fourth Set-up menu page.

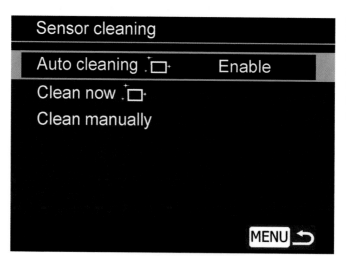

Figure 9.11
Use this menu choice to activate automatic sensor cleaning or enable/ disable it on power up.

Battery Info.

This entry is an exceptionally useful feature that allows you to view battery condition information and performance, and track the data among several different batteries. Your EOS 70D can keep track of multiple LP-E6 batteries because each of them is given a unique serial number (which is printed on an included sticker you can affix to the battery). The camera reads this serial number and stores information about each of the batteries that you use and have "registered" separately. I always recommend owning at least two and, preferably three or more batteries. That's especially true if you use the Battery Grip BG-E14, which holds two battery packs itself. I also own the 5D Mark III, which uses the same battery, so I'm able to justify four batteries to shuttle between my two cameras.

This feature makes it possible to see exactly how each battery you own is performing, allows you to rotate them to even out the usage, and helps you know when it's time to replace a battery. When you select this menu choice, a Battery info screen appears, with a wealth of information (if you use two LP-E6 packs in a BG-E14 grip, information about both packs will appear):

- **Battery position.** The second line of the screen includes an icon that shows where the battery currently being evaluated is installed (usually the hand grip if you're not using the BG-E6).

- **Power type.** Next to the position icon is an indicator that shows the model number of the battery installed, or shows that the DC power adapter is being used instead.

- **Remaining capacity.** The Battery check icon appears showing the remaining capacity visually, along with a percentage number that reads out in 1% increments. You can use this as a rough gauge of how much power you have remaining. If you're in the middle of an important shooting session, you might want to switch to a fully charged battery at the 25-33% level to avoid interruptions at the worst probable time. (If you're using six AA batteries in the BG-E13 grip instead of LP-E6 packs, only this battery capacity notice will appear; the other indicators are not shown.)

- **Shutter count.** Displays how many times the shutter has been actuated with the current charged battery. This info can help you learn just how much certain features cost you in terms of power. For example if a battery has only 50 percent of its power remaining, but you've taken only a few dozen photos, you know that your power is being sapped by picture review, lots of autofocus, frequent image stabilization because of lower shutter speeds, or (a major culprit) that flip-up flash you've been using. While in most cases knowledge is power, in this instance knowledge can help you *save* power, with a tip-off to use fewer juice-sapping features if the current battery pack must be stretched as far as possible.

- **Recharge performance.** This indicator shows how well your battery pack is accepting and holding a charge. Three green bars mean that the pack's performance is fine; two bars show that recharge performance is degraded a little. A red bar indicates that your pack is on its last legs and should be replaced soon. To lengthen the service time of your batteries, you might want to rotate usage among several different packs, so they all "age" at roughly the same rate.

Registering Your Battery Packs

The EOS 70D can "remember" information about up to six LP-E6 battery packs, and provide readouts of their status individually. To register the battery currently in your camera, follow these steps:

1. Access the Battery Info. screen from the Set-up 3 menu.

2. Press the INFO. button, located to the left of the LCD screen.

3. Information about the current battery, including its serial number and the current date will be shown on a new screen.

4. Choose Register to log the battery; if the pack has already been registered, you can choose Delete Info. to remove the battery from the list. (You'd want to do this if you already had registered the limit of six batteries and want to add another one.)

5. Press SET to add the battery to the registry.

6. If you're deleting a battery, the 70D shows you a Battery Info. delete screen instead. (You can delete a battery pack without having that battery installed in the camera—which could come in handy if you lose one.) Just select the battery (by serial number) and delete.

7. Press MENU to back out of any of the Battery Info. screens.

8. Once a battery has been registered, you can check on its remaining capacity at any time (even if it isn't currently installed in the 70D) from the Battery info page. The camera remembers and updates the status of each registered battery whenever it is inserted in the 70D. The date the battery was last used is also shown.

Tip

Use this info with caution, however, as a given battery may have self-discharged slightly during storage and, of course, you may have fully recharged it since the last time it was inserted in the camera. However, this data can be useful in tracking the remaining capacity of several different battery packs during a single shooting session, or over the course of several days when you're not recharging the packs at the conclusion of each session.

Certification Logo Display

This cryptic entry is used by Canon to display the logos of some of the certification organizations that have approved the 70D's specifications. You'll find others on the bottom of the camera itself. As a camera user, you don't really care about certifications, but Canon added this entry as a way of updating any new credentials through a firmware update, thus avoiding the need to change the labels/engravings on the camera body itself. So now you know.

Custom Shooting Mode (C Mode)

This entry allows you to register your EOS 70D's current camera shooting settings and file them away in the C position on the Mode Dial. Doing this overwrites any settings previously stored at the Camera user position. You can also clear the settings for the C "slot," returning them to their factory default values.

Table 9.1 shows the settings you can store:

Register your favorite settings for use in a particular situation. Keep in mind that individualized My Menu settings are not stored in the C user slot. You can have only one roster of My Menu entries available for all of the Mode Dial's positions, including C.

This menu choice has only two options: Register (which stores your current settings in the C slot) and Clear settings (which erases the settings). Note that you must use this menu entry to clear your settings; when using C mode, the Clear Settings option in the Set-up 4 menu is disabled. The Clear all Custom Func. (C.Fn) option in the Custom Functions menu is disabled as well.

To perform either of these tasks, just follow these steps:

1. **Make your settings.** Set the EOS 70D to an exposure mode other than Scene Intelligent Auto.

2. **Access camera user settings.** Navigate to the Custom Shooting Mode (C mode) option in Set-up 4 menu, and press SET.

3. **Choose function.** Rotate the Quick Control Dial to choose Register if you want to store your 70D's current settings in C; or select Clear Settings if you want to erase the settings. Press SET to access the settings screen for your choice.

4. **Store/Clear settings.** The individual screens for storing/clearing are virtually identical. Use the QCD to highlight Mode Dial: C, and press SET to store or clear the settings for that position. (You'll be given a choice to proceed or cancel first.)

5. **Auto update.** Keep in mind that if you change a setting while using the custom shooting mode and want to retain the new settings, your stored settings can be automatically updated to reflect the modifications. Select Auto Update Set. and choose Enable to activate this option. If you'd rather retain your custom settings until you manually decide to update, select Disable instead.

6. **Exit.** When you confirm, you'll be returned to the Set-up 4 menu. Press the MENU button or tap the shutter release button to exit the menu system entirely.

Clear All Camera Settings

This menu choice resets all the settings to their default values. Regardless of how you've set up your EOS 70D, it will be adjusted for One-Shot AF mode, Automatic AF point selection, Evaluative metering, JPEG Fine Large image quality, automatic ISO, sRGB color mode, automatic white balance, and Standard Picture Style. Any changes you've made to exposure compensation, flash exposure compensation, and white balance will be canceled, and any bracketing for exposure or white

Table 9.1 Stored Camera User Settings

Mode/Menu	Settings
Shooting settings	Shooting mode; ISO speed; exposure compensation; flash exposure compensation; AF operation; AF point; drive mode; metering mode
Shooting menu	Shooting 1: Image quality; VF grid display; Viewfinder level; Beep; Release shutter without card; Image review
	Shooting 2: Lens aberration correction; Flash control; E-TTL II metering; Flash sync. speed in Av mode; Red-eye reduction; Mirror lockup
	Shooting 3: Exposure compensation/AEB; ISO speed settings; Auto Lighting Optimizer; All white balance settings; Color space
	Shooting 4: Picture Style; Long exposure noise reduction; High ISO speed noise reduction; Highlight tone priority; Multiple exposure options; HDR mode options
	Live View 1: Live view shooting; AF method; Continuous AF; Grid display; Aspect Ratio; Exposure simulation
	Live View 2: Silent live view shooting; metering timer
Movie Shooting menu	Movie 1: AF method; Movie Servo AF; Silent live view shooting; metering timer
	Movie 2: Grid display; Movie Recording size; Digital Zoom; Sound recording; Movie Recording Count; Movie Play count; Video snapshot
Playback menu	Playback 2: Slide show options; Image Jump with Main Dial
	Playback 3: Highlight alert; AF point display; Playback grid; Histogram display; Movie play count
Set-up menu	Set-up 1: File numbering; Auto rotate
	Set-up 2: Auto power off; LCD brightness; LCD off/on button
	Set-up 3: Touch control; INFO. button display options
	Set-up 4: Auto cleaning option
Custom Functions	Custom I: Exposure: Exposure level increments; ISO speed setting increments; Bracketing auto cancel; Bracketing sequence; Number of bracketed shots; Safety shift
	Custom II: Autofocus: Tracking sensitivity; Acceleration/deceleration tracking; AI Servo 1st Image Priority; AI Servo 2nd Image Priority; AF-assist beam firing; Lens drive when AF impossible; Orientation-linked AF point; Superimposed display; AF Micro adjustment
	Custom III: Operation/Others: Dial direction during Tv/Av; Multi function lock; Custom controls

balance nullified. Custom white balances and Dust Delete Data will be erased. Remember, Custom Functions and Camera User Settings will *not* be cleared. If you want to cancel those, as well, you'll need to use the Camera User Setting option (described previously) and the Custom Functions clearing option.

Copyright Information

You can embed your name (as "author" or *auteur* of the image) and copyright information in the Exif (Exchangeable Image File format) data appended to each photo that you take. When you choose this menu entry (see Figure 9.12), you have four options:

- **Display copyright info.** Shows the current author and copyright data.

- **Enter author's name.** Produces a text entry screen like the one shown in Figure 9.13. See "Entering Text" for instructions on how to type in text for this screen and the Copyright Details screen.

- **Enter copyright details.** Produces the same text entry screen, allowing you to enter copyright details. Oddly enough, no copyright symbol is available (although the @ sign is provided so you can type in your e-mail address!). Many just use the parentheses and a lowercase c: (c). However, you should know that this is, strictly speaking, not legal. The legit substitute for the actual copyright symbol are the characters *Copr.* or the full term *Copyright*.

- **Delete copyright information.** Removes the current copyright information (both author and copyright data). Once you delete the data, or if you haven't entered it yet, this option and the Display Copyright Info. option are grayed out and unavailable.

Figure 9.12
Access text entry screens for entering the name of the photographer and copyright details here.

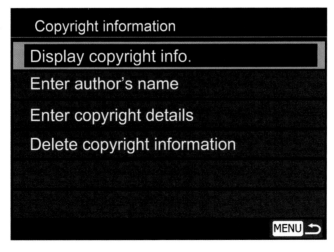

Entering Text

Entering text into the Author's Name or Copyright Details screens is done in the same way, using a screen like the one shown in Figure 9.13. Just use these instructions:

- **Choose areas.** Either the text area (at top left) or available characters area (bottom half of the screen) will be highlighted with a blue outline. Switch between them by pressing the Q button on the right side of the back of the camera.

- **Scroll among text.** When the text area is highlighted, you can scroll among the text using the multi-controller pad. Up to 63 alphanumeric characters can be entered/displayed.

- **Enter characters.** When the available characters list is highlighted, use the touch screen, or the multi-controller pad to move among the alphanumeric characters shown. Press the SET button to enter that character at the cursor position in the text area above. You can delete the current character by pressing the Delete/Trash button.

- **Finish/Cancel.** When finished entering text, press the MENU button to confirm your choice, or press the INFO. button to cancel and return to the Copyright Information screen.

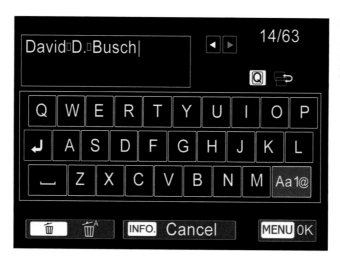

Figure 9.13
Select the alphanumeric characters for your text entry.

Firmware Version

You can see the current firmware release in use in the menu listing. If you want to update to a new firmware version for either the camera or a lens, press the SET button to select which type of firmware you want to upgrade. Then insert a memory card containing the binary file, and press the SET button to begin the process. You can read more about firmware updates in Chapter 14.

Custom Functions Menu

Custom Functions let you customize the behavior of your camera using three function groups: C.Fn I: Exposure, C.Fn II: Autofocus, and C.Fn III: Operation/Others. There is also a Clear All choice in the Custom Functions menu. If you don't like the default way the camera carries out certain tasks, you just may be able to do something about it. The Roman numeral divisions within a single screen with a single line of choices seem odd until you realize that some other more upscale Canon EOS models separate each of these groups into separate screens (with larger numbers of options). For example, my 5D Mark III has four separate C.Fn menus with a total of 14 different adjustable functions.

Each of the Custom Functions is set in exactly the same way, so I'm not going to bog you down with a bunch of illustrations showing how to make this setting or that. One quick run-through using Figure 9.14 should be enough. Here are the key parts of the Custom Functions screen.

■ **Custom Functions category.** At the top of the settings screen is a label that tells you which category that screen represents.

■ **Current Function name.** Use the touch screen or left/right multi-controller pad to select the function you want to adjust. The name of the function currently selected appears at the top of the screen, and its number is marked with an overscore in the row of numbers at the bottom of the screen. You don't need to memorize the function numbers.

■ **Function currently selected.** The function number appears in two places. In the upper-right corner you'll find a box with the current function clearly designated. In the lower half of the screen are two lines of numbers. The top row has numbers from 1 to 13, representing the Custom Function. The second row shows the number of the current setting. If the setting is other than the default value (a zero), it will be colored blue, so you can quickly see which Custom Functions have been modified. The currently selected function will have a gold line above it.

■ **Available settings.** Within the alternating medium gray/dark gray blocks appear numbered setting options. The current setting is highlighted in blue. You can use the up/down multi-controller pad to scroll to the option you want and then choose SET to select it; then press MENU to back out of the Custom Functions menus.

Figure 9.14
Custom Functions menu.

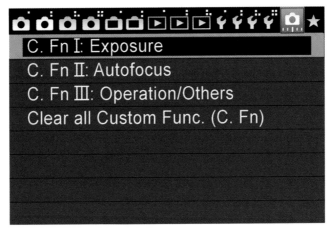

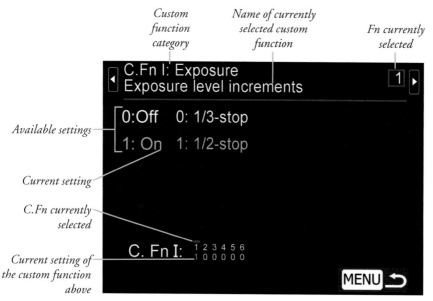

Custom function category · *Name of currently selected custom function* · *Fn currently selected*

Figure 9.15
Each C.Fn screen has two to four settings, represented by the numbers at the bottom of the screen. The currently selected function has a gold line above it.

Available settings

Current setting

C.Fn currently selected

Current setting of the custom function above

- **Current setting.** Underneath each Custom Function is a number from 0 to 4 that represents the current setting for that function.
- **Option selection.** When a function is selected, the currently selected option appears in a highlighted box. As you scroll up and down the option list, the setting in the box changes to indicate an alternate value.

C.Fn I-01: Exposure Level Increments

This setting tells the 70D the size of the "jumps" it should use when making exposure adjustments—either one-third or one-half stop. The increment you specify here applies to f/stops, shutter speeds, EV changes, and autoexposure bracketing.

- **0: 1/3 stop.** Choose this setting when you want the finest increments between shutter speeds and/or f/stops. For example, the 70D will use shutter speeds such as 1/60th, 1/80th, 1/100th, and 1/125th second, and f/stops such as f/5.6, f/6.3, f/7.1, and f/8, giving you (and the autoexposure system) maximum control.
- **1: 1/2 stop.** Use this setting when you want larger and more noticeable changes between increments, as when you're shooting HDR images. The 70D will apply shutter speeds such as 1/60th, 1/125th, 1/250th, and 1/500th second, and f/stops including f/5.6, f/6.7, f/8, f/9.5, and f/11. These coarser adjustments are useful when you want more dramatic changes between different exposures.

C.Fn I-02: ISO Speed Setting Increments

This setting determines the size of the "jumps" made when adjusting ISO—either one-third or one full stop. The larger increment can help you leap from one ISO setting to one that's twice (or half) as sensitive with one click.

- **0: 1/3 stop.** Choose this setting when you want the finest increments between shutter speeds and/or f/stops. For example, the 70D will use typical ISO values such as 100, 125, 160, 200, and so forth.

- **1: 1 stop.** Use this setting when you want larger and more noticeable changes between increments. The 70D will apply speeds such as 100, 200, 400, 800, and so forth. These coarser adjustments are useful when you want more dramatic changes between different exposures.

C.Fn I-03: Bracketing Auto Cancel

Here you can specify whether you want automatic bracketing to continue until you deactivate it, or you want it to be cancelled when the camera is switched off or perform any of several other functions.

- **0: On.** When Auto Cancel is activated (the default), AEB (Auto Exposure Bracketing) and WB-BKT (White Balance Bracketing) are cancelled when you turn the 70D off, change lenses, use the flash, or change memory cards; when Auto Cancel is deactivated, bracketing remains in effect until you manually turn it off or use the flash.

- **1: Off.** When Auto Cancel is switched off, the AEB and WB-BKT settings will be kept even when the power switch is turned to the OFF position. The flash still cancels autoexposure bracketing, but your settings are retained.

C.Fn I-04: Bracketing Sequence

You can define the sequence in which AEB and WB-BKT series are exposed. For exposure bracketing, you can determine whether the order is metered exposure, decreased exposure, increased exposure or decreased exposure, metered exposure, increased exposure. Or with white balance bracketing, if your bias preference is set to Blue/Amber in the WB SHIFT/BKT adjustments in the Shooting 3 menu, the white balance sequence when option 0 is selected will be current WB, more blue, more amber. If your bias preference is set to Magenta/Green, then the sequence for option 0 will be current WB, more magenta, more green.

- **0: 0 - +.** Exposure sequence is metered exposure, decreased exposure, increased exposure (0, -, +). White balance sequence is current WB, more blue/more magenta (depending on how your bias is set), more amber/more green (ditto).

- **1: - 0 +.** The sequence is decreased exposure, metered exposure, increased exposure (-, 0, +). White balance sequence is more blue/more magenta, current WB, more amber/more green.

- **2: + 0 -.** The sequence is increased exposure, metered exposure, decreased exposure (+, 0, -). White balance sequence is more amber/more green, current WB, more blue/more magenta.

C.Fn I-05: Number of Bracketed Shots

Choose how many shots will be exposed in a bracket sequence.

- **0: 3 shots.** With this default value, three shots will be exposed in the sequence. This is the best general-purpose setting, and often used when one-third, two-thirds, or one full stop bracketing is specified in the Expo. Comp./AEB entry in the Shooting 3 menu.

- **1: 2 shots.** If you feel you need just one alternate exposure, two shots might be enough. I use this setting when I'm confident that the metered exposure will be fine, but I'd like one extra shot that's slightly underexposed or slightly overexposed by, say, one-third to two-thirds stops.

- **2: 5 shots.** Five or more shots in a bracketed set are most useful when you're venturing into HDR territory and need a broad range of exposures to merge. The 70D's bracketing flexibility means that you can expose the bracketed set of five over a narrow range of 1 2/3 stops (using a 1/3 stop increment) or as wide as 6 stops (with a 3 stop increment between exposures). Some scenes suitable for HDR manipulation can benefit from such a broad range of exposures.

- **3: 7 shots.** Although a seven shot bracketed sequence will slow down your 70D if you're shooting continuously (and fill up your memory card quickly), this option allows extremely fine-tuning of exposure, or, when capturing images for HDR processing, covering a very broad range of exposure variations.

C.Fn I-06: Safety Shift

Ordinarily, both Aperture-priority and Shutter-priority modes work fine, because you'll select an f/stop or shutter speed that allows the 70D to produce a correct exposure using the other type of setting (shutter speed for Av; aperture for Tv). However, when lighting conditions change, it may not be possible to select an appropriate setting with the available exposure options, and the camera will be unable to take a picture at all.

For example, you might be at a concert shooting the performers and, to increase your chances of getting a sharp image, you've selected Tv mode and a shutter speed of 1/250th second. Under bright lights and with an appropriate ISO setting, the 70D might select f/5.6, f/4, or even f/2.8. Then, in a dramatic moment, the stage lights are dimmed significantly. An exposure of 1/250th second at f/2 is called for, but your lens has an f/2.8 maximum aperture. If you've used this Custom Function to allow the 70D to override your selection, the camera will automatically switch to 1/125th second to allow the picture to be taken at f/2.8.

Safety Shift will make similar adjustments if your scene suddenly becomes too bright; although, in practice, you'll find that the override will be needed most often when using Tv mode. It's easier to "run out of" f/stops, which generally range no smaller than f/22 or f/32, than to deplete the available supply of shutter speeds, which can be as brief as 1/8,000th second. For example, if you're shooting at ISO 400 in Tv mode at 1/1,000th second, an extra-bright beach scene could easily call for an f/stop smaller than f/22, causing overexposure. However, Safety Shift would bump your shutter speed up to 1/2,000th second with no problem.

On the other hand, if you were shooting under the same illumination in Av mode with the preferred aperture set to f/16, the EOS 70D could use 1/1,000th, 1/2,000th, or 1/4,000th second shutter speeds to retain that f/16 aperture under conditions that are 2X, 4X, or 8X as bright as normal daylight. No Safety Shift would be needed, even if the ISO were (for some unknown reason) set much higher than the ISO 400 used in this example. These are your options:

- **0: Disable.** Turn off Safety Shift. Your specified shutter speed or f/stop remains locked in, even if conditions are too bright or too dim for an appropriate exposure. Use this option if you'd prefer to have the shot taken at the shutter speed, aperture, or ISO you've selected under all circumstances, even if it means an improperly exposed photo. You might be able to salvage the photo in your image editor.

- **1: Shutter speed/Aperture.** Safety Shift is activated for Tv and Av modes. The 70D will adjust the preferred shutter speed or f/stop to allow a correct exposure. If you don't mind having your camera countermand your orders, this option can save images that otherwise might be incorrectly exposed. Use when working with a shutter speed or aperture that are *preferable,* but aren't critical.

- **2: ISO speed.** This option operates in Program AE (P) mode as well as Tv and Av modes. Think of it as an "emergency" Auto ISO option. You can manually select your preferred ISO setting, and the 70D will generally stick with that, but can adjust the ISO setting if required to produce an acceptable exposure. If you've selected a minimum and maximum allowable ISO range in the ISO Speed Settings entry of the Shooting 3 menu, this setting will honor those limits *unless* your current manually selected ISO is outside those boundaries.

  For example, if you've chosen a minimum and maximum auto ISO range of ISO 200-800, this setting will stay within that range when adjusting ISO (even though you have Auto ISO off), but if your camera is currently manually set to ISO 100 or a value higher than ISO 800, it will go ahead and use the extra values, too.

C.Fn II-01: Tracking Sensitivity

The Autofocus Custom functions are used to set important AF parameters, including those that cover speed of operation, focus or release priority during continuous shooting, and fine-tuning the focus characteristics of individual lenses. This first entry determines how quickly the AF system switches to a new subject entering the focus area when using AI Servo autofocus. Unlike the other Custom Functions described to this point, the Tracking Sensitivity parameter uses a sliding scale with five positions, from –2 (Locked On) to +2 (Responsive). (See Figure 9.16.) Negative numbers allow you to retain focus on the original subject even if it briefly leaves the area covered by the focus points, making tracking easier. The drawback is that if the camera selects the wrong subject, there is a longer delay before the correct subject is captured. Positive numbers cause the AF system to more quickly switch to a new subject. However, such quick response can cause the camera to focus on the wrong subject. You should use each setting extensively to get a feeling for how it operates before making any changes. Each of these settings will show a hyphen mark when unset or a blue asterisk when the slider has been moved.

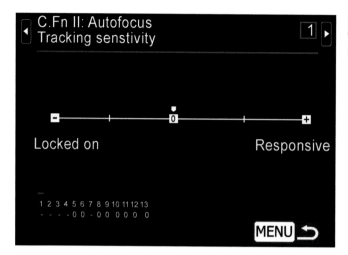

Figure 9.16
Tracking sensitivity uses a sliding scale.

- **0: Versatile multi purpose setting.** Use this default setting most of the time, as it works well with many moving subjects (and moving subject matter is why you selected AI Servo AF, isn't it?). Use with any type of action that isn't one of the special cases described next. It's good for some motor sports, many track meet events, and action that's moving toward or away from the camera.

- **-1: For subjects that accelerate or decelerate quickly.** This setting is better for basketball and soccer, because you can have players racing toward you one instant, and crossing your field of view the next. (See Figure 9.17.)

- **-2: Continue to track subject, ignoring possible obstacles.** This setting could be your mainstay for football games, because you can track a running back, receiver, or another player of interest without having focus disrupted when a referee, coach, or another player passes between you. The camera will delay refocusing on the new object long enough to resume following the original subject.

- **+1: For erratic subjects moving quickly in any direction.** This is my choice for hockey games and anything that involves skates—as well as small children and pets. It's also excellent for that most difficult of subjects: birds in flight (often abbreviated to just BIF because photographers talk about the challenges of photographing pesky avians so frequently). (See Figure 9.18.)

- **+2: Instantly focus on subjects suddenly entering the AF point areas.** This setting is ideal when you're photographing a relatively static scene in anticipation of a moving subject, such as a runner, skier, or bicyclist entering the frame. You could, for example, frame the finish line of a horse race, and the 70D would instantly lock focus on the winning steed as it crosses the line (or perhaps several horses if one wins "by a nose"). It's also excellent for subjects that change speed and move erratically. I use this on children and small pets.

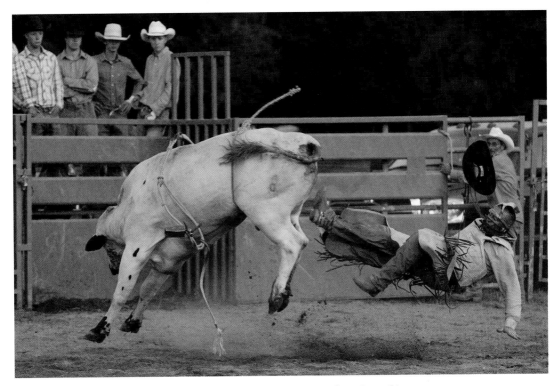

Figure 9.17 Focus tracking can be fined tuned for various types of moving subjects.

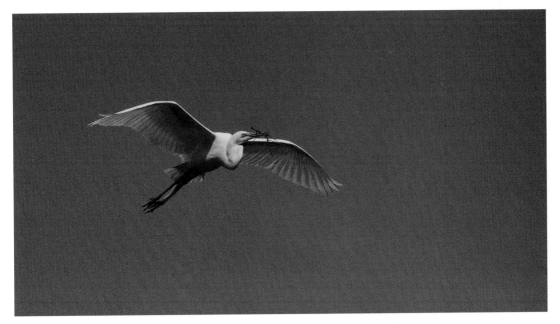

Figure 9.18 Birds in flight are one of the most difficult types of subjects to track.

C.Fn II-02: Accel/Decel Tracking

This parameter determines how the AF system responds to sudden acceleration, deceleration, or stopping. Your choices are 0 (for subjects that move at a constant speed) to 2 (for faster reactions to subjects that suddenly change speed). Lower values can cause the camera to be "fooled" if a subject that was moving consistently suddenly stops; focus may change to the position where the subject *would* have been if it'd kept moving. A higher value may cause inconsistent focus with subjects that move at a constant speed. Each of these settings will show a hyphen mark when unset or a blue asterisk when the slider has been moved.

- **0.** Use this setting for subjects that move at a constant speed, without sudden acceleration, deceleration, or unexpected stops, such as relay racers at a track meet.

- **1.** This setting is better for basketball and other sports where the pace remains fairly constant, but players do slow down or stop when they reach their destination on the field or court.

- **2.** Very erratic movements can be tracked effectively with this setting. I use it for small children in conjunction with a +2 tracking sensitivity.

C.Fn II-03: AI Servo 1st Image Priority

This setting determines the point at which the 70D locks in focus when you push the shutter button all the way down when taking a series of photographs. Remember that if you're using a small f/stop with extended depth-of-field, your chances of getting a shot with acceptable depth-of-field are improved at any of these settings. Use the Quick Control Dial to move the indicator to any of three positions (see Figure 9.19). Each of these settings will show a hyphen mark when unset or a blue asterisk when the slider has been moved.

- **Release priority.** The shutter will fire immediately, even if sharp focus has not yet been achieved. Use this setting when getting the shot—any shot—is crucial, and a slightly out-of-focus image would be preferable to none at all. Whether you're a photojournalist or a proud parent snapping Baby's first steps, you'd probably prefer not to miss the shot because the camera is still fine-tuning focus. The 70D focuses so quickly that, unless your subject is low in contrast or otherwise problematic, release priority will probably give you a good shot nearly all the time. Remember that if you're using a small f/stop with extended depth-of-field, your chances of getting a shot with acceptable depth-of-field are improved even though you're using release priority.

- **Equal priority.** If focus is important to you, try out this balanced setting that will give the camera a little extra time—but not too much—and improve your chances of getting a precisely focused image without inordinate delay.

- **Focus priority.** Sometimes, accurate focus is all-important, and with a leisurely shooting pace you might not mind waiting an extra fraction of a second while the AF system "hunts" to achieve precise autofocus when faced with the occasional more difficult subject. I tend to use this setting for everything except action shots and birds-in-flight, because my speedy 70D usually doesn't introduce much of a delay as it autofocuses.

Figure 9.19
Set first image priority.

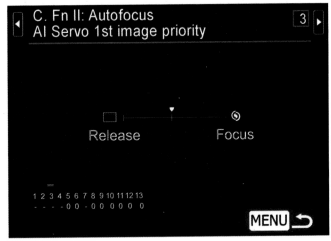

C.Fn II-04: AI Servo 2nd Image Priority

Most of us have an itchy trigger finger, so the first photograph in a series may not capture the decisive moment. When shooting bursts, the 70D can continue to fine-tune focus for the second and subsequent images in the series, using the priority you set here. The parameters are similar to those of the previous setting. Each of these settings will show a hyphen mark when unset or a blue asterisk when the slider has been moved.

- **Shooting speed priority.** Since this is the second (or ongoing) shot, the shutter has already fired at least once, so this setting tells the camera to keep the same focus setting and continue capturing images. Note that you can select this option regardless of what parameter you've specified for the *first* shot. So, if you've chosen focus priority for the initial image, selecting this setting is a safe bet *if your subject is not moving* quickly enough to require additional focus fine-tuning. But if you selected release priority for the first image, using this setting may mean that the first and all subsequent images may be a little (or a lot) out of focus.

- **Equal priority.** This balanced setting allows you to express your trust that the 70D will provide a reasonable compromise between speed and focus for all images captured after the first.

- **Focus priority.** Selecting this option can slow down the continuous shooting speed of your camera, but will almost ensure getting a series of shots that are in optimum focus.

C.Fn II-05: AF-Assist Beam Firing

This setting determines when bursts from an electronic flash are used to emit a pulse of light that helps provide enough contrast for the EOS 70D to focus on a subject. You can select Enable to use an attached Canon Speedlite to produce a focus assist beam. Use Disable to turn this feature off if you find it distracting. Keep in mind that if you select Enable and the Speedlite's own AF-Assist

Beam Firing is set to Disable, the AF-assist beam will not be emitted (the flash's setting takes precedence).

- **0: Enable.** The AF-assist light is emitted by the camera's external flash whenever light levels are too low for accurate focusing using the ambient light.

- **1: Disable.** The AF-assist illumination is disabled. You might want to use this setting when shooting at concerts, weddings, or darkened locations where the light might prove distracting or discourteous.

- **2: Enable external flash only.** The assist beam of the external flash is used exclusively.

- **3: IR AF Assist beam only.** Some Canon flash units, such as the Speedlite 600EX-RT, have a near-infrared pattern assist beam. Select this option to disable visible light flashes and activate only the less-obtrusive IR beam.

C.Fn II-06: Lens Drive When AF Impossible

When a scene has little inherent contrast (say, a blank wall or the sky) or if there isn't enough illumination to allow determining contrast accurately (in low light levels, or with lenses having maximum apertures of less than f/5.6), a lens may be unable to achieve autofocus. Very long telephoto lenses suffer from this syndrome because their depth-of-field is so shallow that the correct point of focus may zip past during the AF process before the AF system has a chance to register it.

Use this setting to tell the 70D either to keep trying to focus if AF seems to be impossible or to stop seeking focus. Your choices are as follows:

- **0: Continue Focus Search.** The 70D will keep trying to focus, even if the effort causes the lens to become grossly out of focus. Use this default setting if you'd prefer that the lens keep trying. Sometimes you can point the lens at an object with sufficient contrast at approximately the same distance to let the AF system lock on, then reframe your original subject with the hope that accurate focus will now be achieved.

- **1: Stop Focus Search.** When this option is selected, the camera will stop trying to focus uselessly, allowing you to attempt to manually bring the subject into focus. This setting is best for very long telephoto lenses (around 400mm and up), because they encounter AF difficulties more than most lenses, and are less likely to benefit from extended "hunting."

C.Fn II-07: Select AF Area Selection Mode

Specify which of the AF area selection modes (discussed in Chapter 5) you want to be available. You can place a checkmark next to one, two, or all three of the modes.

- **Manual selection: 1 pt AF.** You can manually select a single AF point. Note that this option is mandatory and cannot be unchecked.

- **Manual select.: Zone AF.** You can select one of five zones for focusing.

- **Auto selection: 19 pt. AF.** The 70D selects focus points from the full 19 AF points available.

C.Fn II-08: AF Area Selection Method

This setting allows you to choose the control used for changing the AF Area Selection method.

- **0: AF Area Selection button→AF Area Selection Mode button.** Press the AF Area Selection button (at the upper-right corner of the back panel of the camera) *or* the AF Area Selection Mode button (located just northwest of the Main Dial). Subsequently, pressing the AF Area Selection Mode button changes the AF area selection mode.

- **1: AF Area Selection button→Main Dial.** Press the AF Area Selection button (at the upper-right corner of the back panel of the camera) *or* the AF Area Selection Mode button (located just northwest of the Main Dial). Subsequently, rotating the Main Dial changes the AF area selection mode. When the Main Dial's behavior is defined this way, use the multi-controller pad to adjust the AF point horizontally.

C.Fn II-09: Orientation Linked AF Point

One outstanding new feature of the EOS 70D is the ability to specify different AF area selection modes for horizontal and vertically oriented scenes. This ability is useful because the kinds of things we shoot in each orientation tend to be different. In horizontal mode, we may be shooting landscapes and other scenes where the emphasis is on the middle or lower half of the frame. With the camera rotated to vertical orientation (in my case for, say, basketball games, portraits, or fashion photography), we may prefer to concentrate focus on a different zone, such as the upper half of the frame. Custom Function C.Fn II-09 allows you to do that. You can elect to use the same manually selected AF point/zone for vertically and horizontally composed shots—or to select a different point/zone for vertical and horizontal shots.

- **0: Same for both vertic./horiz.** The manually selected AF point that you specify is used for any camera orientation.

- **1: Select different AF points.** The focus point you select will be memorized for each of three camera orientations: horizontal, vertical with the camera grip upward, and vertical with the camera grip pointing downward. The 70D will switch to that selected point whenever you rotate the camera to one of those positions, until you manually select a different focus point when using a particular orientation. For example, you might want a focus point in the upper third of the frame when shooting a portrait, but prefer a more centrally located focus point when capturing close-up images of flowers.

C.Fn II-10: Manual AF Point Selection Pattern

Used in Single Point AF (Manual Selection) and 19-point Automatic Selection with AI Servo AF. As you move the selected AF point manually, you can specify that the selection either stops at the outer edge of the frame or wraps around to the opposite AF point.

- **0: Stops at AF area edges.** Use this if you frequently set the AF point at an edge of the frame and you don't want the selection to "jump" to the opposite side if you move it too far.

- **1: Continuous.** Use this if you simply want to speed up AF point selection movement.

C.Fn II-11: AF Point Display During Focus

This setting simply allows you to specify whether you want the selected AF point to be highlighted in red.

- **0: Selected (constant).** The AF point selected by you or the camera is always displayed. You'll use this default setting most of the time, because it's useful to be able to see exactly which part of the frame is being used to calculate focus.
- **1: All (constant).** All 19 AF points are displayed, all the time.
- **2: Selected (pre-AF, focused).** Selected AF points are displayed only when selecting AF points, when the camera is ready to shoot before AF operation, and when focus is achieved (except when AI Servo AF is being used).
- **3: Selected (focused).** The selected AF points are displayed only when selecting AF points or when focus is achieved (except when AI Servo AF is being used).
- **4: Disable display.** I often use this setting when the AF point highlighting is distracting, or when I'm photographing a scene with lots of red and the highlighting won't be readily visible, anyway.

C.Fn II-12: VF Display Illumination

Tells the 70D to highlight the AF points and alignment grid in red in the viewfinder when focus is achieved. With all three options, there is no illumination when AI Servo AF is used. In addition, pressing the AF Area Selection Button or AF Area Selection Mode button illuminates the AF points and grid regardless of which of these options you have chosen.

- **0: Auto.** AF points and grid are illuminated under low light when focus is achieved.
- **1: Enable.** AF points and grid are illuminated when focus is achieved under all lighting conditions.
- **2: Disable.** AF points and grid are not illuminated when focus is achieved.

C.Fn II-13: AF Microadjustment

This setting makes it possible to fine-tune the focus of individual lenses, or all your lenses, as described in more detail in Chapter 5. Your options are as follows:

- **0: Disable.** You can turn off AF microadjustment, effectively canceling any adjustments you've made for your lenses.
- **1: All by same amount.** Set a front/back focus amount from –20 to +20, and it will be applied to all your lenses when AF Microadjustment is enabled.
- **2: Adjust by Lens.** The EOS 70D is able to electronically recognize which Canon EF lens is mounted on the camera, and apply a specific amount of adjustment to each particular lens. I showed you how to use this feature in Chapter 5.

C.Fn III-01: Dial Direction During Tv/Av

The C.Fn III: Operation/Others category includes the settings that you can use to set other parameters, such as viewfinder warnings. This first setting reverses the result when rotating the Quick Control Dial and Main Dial when using Shutter-priority or Aperture-priority (Tv and Av). That is, rotating the Main Dial to the right will decrease the shutter speed rather than increase it; f/stops will become larger rather than smaller. Use this if you find the default rotation scheme in Tv and Av modes are not to your liking. Activating this option also reverses the dial direction in Manual exposure mode. In other shooting modes, only the Main Dial's direction will be reversed.

- **0: Normal.** The Main Dial and Quick Control Dial change shutter speed and aperture normally.
- **1: Reverse direction.** The dials adjust shutter speed and aperture in the reverse direction when rotated.

C.Fn III-02: Multi Function Lock

Your 70D includes a Lock switch just south of the Quick Control Dial. Slide it upward when you want to prevent the use of the Quick Control Dial, Main Dial, or multi-controller pad in the center of the QCD from accidentally changing a setting. You can select any or all three of the controls to lock, while freeing the others (or none) to act normally. I use this sometimes when I am using manual exposure, especially when I'm fumbling around in a darkened environment, and don't want to unintentionally manipulate my settings. The Multi Function Lock screen has one option for each control; highlight the control and press SET to lock or unlock it. A check mark appears next to the control's name when it's locked, and an L/Lock indicator appears in the viewfinder, top-panel LCD, and shooting settings display. Even if you've locked the QCD, its touchpad functions can still be used during movie shooting even if Silent Control has been activated in the Movie 2 menu.

- **Main Dial.** Locks the Main Dial only.
- **Quick Control Dial.** Locks the QCD only.
- **Multi-controller.** Locks the multi-controller pad in the center of the QCD only.

C.Fn III-03: Warnings in Viewfinder

This useful function lets you individually enable or disable four different viewfinder warnings, allowing you to reduce the amount of clutter in your field of view as you frame an image, while retaining the warnings that you really, really want to remain in effect. Mark any or all with a check mark by highlighting the option and pressing SET. Your choices include warnings for the following:

- **Monochrome Picture Style.** If you shoot JPEG most of the time, you might want a tip-off that you've set the camera in black-and-white mode, because color information cannot be added in post-processing. If you generally shoot RAW or RAW+JPEG, you won't care, because the RAW image retains the color information.

- **WB Correction.** It's easy to dial in some white balance correction, and easier to forget that you've done so. This warning will let you know—again, very important when shooting JPEG only.

- **ISO Expansion.** The 70D makes you manually enable the highest high and low ISO settings through ISO expansion, as discussed in Chapter 8. While the availability of these extreme settings isn't normally a problem, if you feel you're likely to need a tip-off, you can activate this warning.

- **Spot metering.** Most users rely on the intelligence of Evaluative metering, and use Spot metering only occasionally. Because exposure results can vary so much when Spot metering is in effect, this warning can be helpful.

C.Fn III-04: Custom Controls

If you're eager to totally confuse any poor soul who is not equipped to deal with a custom-configured 70D (or, perhaps, even yourself), Canon allows you to redefine the behavior of no less than ten different controls in interesting, and potentially hilarious ways. Just highlight any of the nine options, press SET to view the functions you can assign, and make your choice. You can truly manipulate your camera to work in a way that's fastest and most efficient for you. There are dozens of combinations of control possibilities. Press the Trash button from the Custom Controls screen to return all your settings to the default values shown in Table 9.2.

Clear All Custom Func. (C.Fn)

Select this entry and choose Cancel (if you chicken out) or OK to return all your Custom Functions to their default values. But don't panic—your matrix of Custom Controls is retained. If you want to zero out those settings, you'll need to do it within the Custom Controls Custom Function, using the Trash button.

My Menu

The Canon EOS 70D has a great feature that allows you to define your own menu, with just the items listed that you want. Remember that the 70D always returns to the last menu and menu entry accessed when you press the MENU button. So you can set up My Menu to include just the items you want, and jump to those items instantly by pressing the MENU button. Or, you can set your camera so that My Menu appears when the MENU button has been pressed, regardless of what other menu entry you accessed last.

To create your own My Menu, you have to *register* the menu items you want to include. Just follow these steps:

1. Press the MENU button and use the touch screen or Main Dial to select the My Menu tab. When you first begin, the personalized menu will be empty except for the My Menu Settings entry. Choose SET to select it. You'll then see a screen like the one shown in Figure 9.20.

Table 9.2 Assignable Controls

Control	Default	Assignable Functions
Shutter button half-press	Metering and AF start	Metering Start (only), AE lock
AF-On button	Metering and AF start	AF stop, AE/AF lock, AE lock (hold), AE lock (only), FE lock (only), Off
AE Lock button	AE/FE Lock	Metering and AF start, AF stop, AE lock (hold), AE lock (only), FE lock (only), Off
DOF Preview button	Depth-of-field preview	AF stop, AE/FE lock, Toggle One Shot/AI Servo, IS start, Viewfinder electronic level, AE lock (hold), AE lock (only), FE lock (only), Off
Lens AF stop button (if available on lens)	AF stop	Metering and AF start, AE/FE lock, Toggle One Shot/AI Servo, IS start, AE lock (hold), AE lock (only), FE lock (only)
SET button	No additional function	Image quality, Picture Style, MENU, ISO speed (with Main Dial), Flash exposure compensation
Main Dial	Shutter speed setting in Tv and Manual Mode	Tv, Av
Quick Control Dial	Aperture setting in Av and Manual Mode	Tv, Av
Multi-controller	No additional function	AF point direct selection

Figure 9.20
In the My Menu Settings screen you can add menu items, delete them, and specify whether My Menu always pops up when the MENU button is pressed.

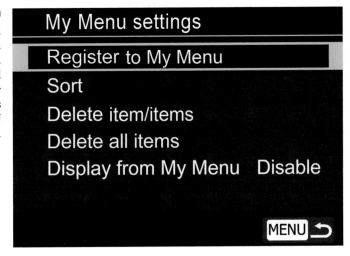

2. Use the touch screen or multi-controller pad to select Register; then press SET.

3. Use the touch screen or multi-controller pad to scroll down through the continuous list of menu entries to find one you would like to add. Choose SET.

4. Confirm your choice by selecting OK in the next screen and choosing SET again.

5. Continue to select up to six menu entries for My Menu.

6. When you're finished, press the MENU button twice to return to the My Menu screen to see your customized menu, which might look like Figure 9.21.

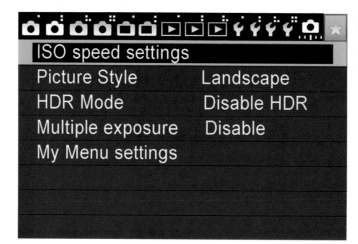

Figure 9.21
You can add one to six menu entries to My Menu.

In addition to registering menu items, you can perform other functions at the My Menu Settings screen:

- **Changing the order.** Choose Sort to reorder the items in My Menu. Select the menu item and choose SET. Rotate the multi-controller pad to move the item up and down within the menu list. When you've placed it where you'd like it, press MENU to lock in your selection and return to the previous screen.

- **Delete/Delete All Items.** Use these to remove an individual menu item or all menu items you've registered in My Menu.

- **Display from My Menu.** As I mentioned earlier, the 70D (almost) always shows the last menu item accessed. That's convenient if you used My Menu last, but if you happen to use another menu, then pressing the MENU button will return to that item instead. If you enable the Display from My Menu option, pressing the MENU button will *always* display My Menu first. You are free to switch to another menu tab if you like, but the next time you press the MENU button, My Menu will come up again. Use this option if you work with My Menu a great deal and make settings with other menu items less frequently.

Part IV

Enhancing Your Canon EOS 70D

The next five chapters are devoted to helping you dig deeper into the capabilities of your Canon EOS 70D, so you can exploit all those cool features that your previous camera may have lacked. Here's what you can expect:

- **Chapter 10, "Working with Lenses":** Working with lenses is the goal of this chapter, where I'll show you how to select the best lenses for the kinds of photography you want to do, with my recommendations for starter lenses as well as more advanced optics for specialized applications.

- **Chapter 11, "Working with Light":** This chapter is devoted to the magic of light—your fundamental tool in creating any photograph. There are entire books devoted to working with electronic flash, but I hope to get you started with plenty of coverage of the EOS 70D's capabilities. I'll show you how to master your camera's built-in flash—and avoid that "built-in flash" look, and offer an introduction to the use of external flash units.

- **Chapter 12, "Working with Wireless Flash":** This chapter goes a little more deeply into the use of flash, and covers working with the 70D's wireless flash capabilities.

- **Chapter 13, "Downloading, Editing, and Printing Your Images":** This chapter covers downloading and editing your images and will help you understand the software tools available to you.

- **Chapter 14, "Troubleshooting and Prevention":** Troubleshooting, updating your firmware, and cleaning your sensor are all covered in this chapter.

Working with Lenses

In mid-2013, Canon announced that it had produced its 90 millionth EF-series lens. Considering that it took 11 years for Canon to sell its first 10 million copies of its EF lens line, but only nine months to peddle its most recent 10 million lenses, it's easy to see that the digital photography revolution can take credit for the most recent explosion.

With nearly six dozen lenses in its current lineup, Canon is catering to the wide-ranging needs of a broad user base, from novice photo enthusiasts to advanced amateur and professional photographers. It's this mind-bending assortment of high-quality lenses available to enhance the capabilities of cameras like the Canon EOS 70D that make the product line so appealing. Thousands of current and older lenses introduced by Canon and third-party vendors since 1987 can be used to give you a wider view, bring distant subjects closer, let you focus closer, shoot under lower-light conditions, or provide a more detailed, sharper image for critical work. Other than the sensor itself, the lens you choose for your dSLR is the most important component in determining image quality and perspective of your images.

The most exciting development in recent months has been the introduction of Canon's first STM (Stepper Motor) lenses, which, when coupled with a new diaphragm mechanism, provides especially fast and quiet autofocus that's perfect for video capture (where camera noises can be recorded while shooting).

This chapter explains how to select the best lenses for the kinds of photography you want to do.

But Don't Forget the Crop Factor

From time to time you've heard the term *crop factor*, and you've probably also heard the term *lens multiplier factor*. Both are misleading and inaccurate terms used to describe the same phenomenon: the fact that cameras like the 70D (and most other affordable digital SLRs) provide a field of view that's smaller and narrower than that produced by certain other (usually much more expensive) cameras, when fitted with exactly the same lens.

Figure 10.1 quite clearly shows the phenomenon at work. The outer rectangle, marked 1X, shows the field of view you might expect with a 28mm lens mounted on a Canon EOS 5D Mark III camera, a so-called "full-frame" model. The rectangle marked 1.3X shows the effective field of view from the same vantage point with the exact same lens mounted on the discontinued Canon EOS 1D Mark III camera, while the area marked 1.6X shows the field of view you'd get with that 28mm lens installed on a 70D. It's easy to see from the illustration that the 1X rendition provides a wider, more expansive view, while the other two are, in comparison, *cropped*.

The cropping effect is produced because the sensors of the latter two cameras are smaller than the sensors of the 5D Mark III. The "full-frame" camera has a sensor that's the size of the standard 35mm film frame, 24mm × 36mm. Your 70D's sensor does *not* measure 24mm × 36mm; instead, it specs out at 22.5mm × 15mm, or about 62.5 percent of the area of a full-frame sensor, as shown by the yellow boxes in the figure. You can calculate the relative field of view by dividing the focal length of the lens by .625. Thus, a 100mm lens mounted on a 70D has the same field of view as a 160mm lens on the 5D Mark III. We humans tend to perform multiplication operations in our heads more easily than division, so such field of view comparisons are usually calculated using the reciprocal of .625—1.6—so we can multiply instead. (100 / .625=160; 100 × 1.6=160)

This translation is generally useful only if you're accustomed to using full-frame cameras (usually of the film variety) and want to know how a familiar lens will perform on a digital camera. I strongly prefer *crop factor* over *lens multiplier*, because nothing is being multiplied; a 100mm lens doesn't "become" a 160mm lens—the depth-of-field and lens aperture remain the same. (I'll explain more about these later in this chapter.) Only the field of view is cropped. But *crop factor* isn't much

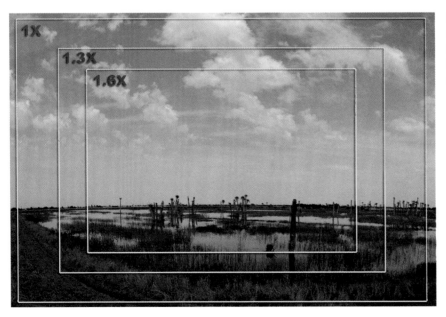

Figure 10.1
Canon offers digital SLRs with full-frame (1X) crops, as well as 1.3X and 1.6X crops.

better, as it implies that the 24mm × 36mm frame is "full" and anything else is "less." I get e-mails all the time from photographers who point out that they own full-frame cameras with 36mm × 48mm sensors (like the Mamiya 645ZD or Hasselblad H3D-39 medium-format digitals). By their reckoning, the "half-size" sensors found in cameras like the 1Ds Mark III and 5D Mark II are "cropped."

If you're accustomed to using full-frame film cameras, you might find it helpful to use the crop factor "multiplier" to translate a lens's real focal length into the full-frame equivalent, even though, as I said, nothing is actually being multiplied. Throughout most of this book, I've been using actual focal lengths and not equivalents, except when referring to specific wide-angle or telephoto focal length ranges and their fields of view.

Your First Lens

Back in ancient times (the pre-zoom, pre-autofocus era before the mid-1980s), choosing the first lens for your camera was a no-brainer: you had few or no options. Canon cameras (which used a different lens mount in those days) were sold with a 50mm f/1.4, a 50mm f/1.8, or, if you had deeper pockets, a super-fast 50mm f/1.2 lens. It was also possible to buy a camera as a body alone, which didn't save much money back when a film SLR like the Canon A-1 sold for $435—*with lens.* (Thanks to the era of relatively cheap optics, I still own a total of *eight* 50mm f/1.4 lenses; I picked one up each time I purchased a new or used body.)

Today, your choices are more complicated, and Canon lenses, which now include zoom, autofocus, and, more often than not, built-in image stabilization (IS) features, tend to cost a lot more compared to the price of a camera. (Adjusted for inflation, that $435 A-1 cost $879 in today's dollars.)

The Canon EOS 70D is frequently purchased with a lens, even now. I could have purchased mine as a body-only rather than in a kit, because I already own a nice collection of Canon lenses, but I wanted to try out the new Canon EF-S 18-55mm f/3.5-5.6 IS STM autofocus lens. It adds only about $100 to the price tag of the body alone, and is thus an irresistible bargain. You might opt instead for the EF-S 18-135mm f/3.5-5.6 IS STM lens, which adds about $350 to the price of the body. Those looking for a longer zoom range might opt to pay an additional $700 for the older Canon EF-S 18-200mm f/3.5-5.6 IS lens, which provides a very useful 11X zoom range. Some buyers don't need quite that zoom range, and save a few dollars by purchasing the Canon EF 28-135mm f/3.5-5.6 IS USM lens ($480). The latter lens has one advantage. *EF* lenses like the 28-135mm zoom can also be used with any *full-frame* camera you add/migrate to at a later date. You'll learn the difference later in this chapter.

So, depending on which category you fall into, you'll need to make a decision about what kit lens to buy, or decide what other kind of lenses you need to fill out your existing complement of Canon optics. This section will cover "first lens" concerns, while later in the chapter we'll look at "add-on lens" considerations.

When deciding on a first lens, there are several factors you'll want to consider:

- **Cost.** You might have stretched your budget a bit to purchase your 70D, so you might want to keep the cost of your first lens fairly low. Fortunately, as I've noted, there are excellent lenses available that will add from $100 to $600 to the price of your camera if purchased at the same time.

- **Zoom range.** If you have only one lens, you'll want a fairly long zoom range to provide as much flexibility as possible. Fortunately, the two most popular basic lenses for the 70D have 3X to 5X zoom ranges, extending from moderate wide-angle/normal out to medium telephoto. These are fine for everyday shooting, portraits, and some types of sports.

- **Adequate maximum aperture.** You'll want an f/stop of at least f/3.5 to f/4 for shooting under fairly low-light conditions. The thing to watch for is the maximum aperture when the lens is zoomed to its telephoto end. You may end up with no better than an f/5.6 maximum aperture. That's not great, but you can often live with it.

- **Image quality.** Your starter lens should have good image quality, befitting a camera with 20MP of resolution, because that's one of the primary factors that will be used to judge your photos. Even at a low price, the several different lenses sold with the 70D as a kit include extra-low dispersion glass and aspherical elements that minimize distortion and chromatic aberration; they are sharp enough for most applications. If you read the user evaluations in the online photography forums, you know that owners of the kit lenses have been very pleased with their image quality.

- **Size matters.** A good walking-around lens is compact in size and light in weight.

- **Fast/close focusing.** Your first lens should have a speedy autofocus system (which is where the ultrasonic motor/USM and new STM system found in nearly all moderately priced lenses is an advantage). Close focusing (to 12 inches or closer) will let you use your basic lens for some types of macro photography.

You can find comparisons of the lenses discussed in the next section, as well as third-party lenses from Sigma, Tokina, Tamron, and other vendors, in online groups and websites. I'll provide my recommendations, but obtaining more information from these additional sources is always helpful when making a lens purchase, because, while camera bodies come and go, lenses may be a lifetime addition to your kit.

Buy Now, Expand Later

The 70D is commonly available with several good, basic lenses that can serve you well as a "walk-around" lens (one you keep on the camera most of the time, especially when you're out and about without your camera bag). The number of options available to you is actually quite amazing, even if your budget is limited to about $100-$500 for your first lens. One other vendor, for example, offers only 18-70mm and 18-55mm kit lenses in that price range, plus a 24-85mm zoom. Two popular starter lenses Canon offers are shown in Figures 10.2 and 10.3. Canon's best-bet first lenses are in the list that follows, which includes some lenses that have been discontinued or otherwise require some hunting on sites like www.keh.com to find:

- **Canon EF-S 18-55mm f/3.5-5.6 IS STM autofocus lens.** This lens, shown in Figure 10.2, replaces the old "II" version, and is a bit larger than the older optic. It boasts the new STM stepper motor technology that Canon video fans have found to be so useful. It has image stabilization that can counter camera shake by providing the vibration-stopping capabilities of a shutter speed four stops faster than the one you've dialed in. That is, with image stabilization activated, you can shoot at 1/30th second and eliminate camera shake as if you were using a shutter speed of 1/250th second. (At least, that's what Canon claims; I usually have slightly less impressive results.) Of course, IS doesn't freeze subject motion—that basketball player driving for a layup will still be blurry at 1/30th second, even though the effects of camera shake will be effectively nullified. But this lens is an all-around good choice if your budget is tight.

- **Canon EF-S 18-135mm f/3.5-5.6 IS STM autofocus lens.** This one, priced at about $550 when purchased in a kit, is an upgrade from a similar earlier lens without the stepper motor technology. It's also light, compact (you can see it mounted on the 70D in Figure 10.3), and covers a useful range from true wide-angle to intermediate telephoto. As with Canon's other affordable zoom lenses, image stabilization partially compensates for the slow f/5.6 maximum aperture at the telephoto end, by allowing you to use longer shutter speeds to capture an image under poor lighting conditions. I'll explain the advantages of the STM autofocus later in this chapter.

- **Canon EF-S 18-200mm f/3.5-5.6 IS autofocus lens.** This one, priced at about $700, has been popular as a basic lens for the 70D, because it's light, compact, and covers a full range from true wide-angle to long telephoto. Image stabilization keeps your pictures sharp at the long end of the zoom range, allowing the longer shutter speeds that the f/5.6 maximum

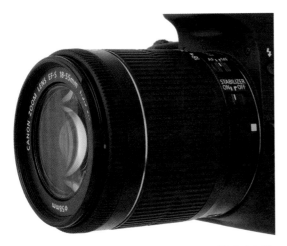

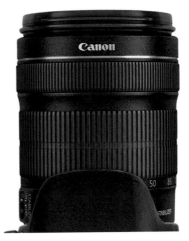

Figure 10.2 The Canon EF-S 18-55mm f/3.5-5.6 IS STM autofocus lens ships as a basic kit lens for entry-level Canon cameras.

Figure 10.3 The new EF-S 18-135 f/3.5-5.6 IS STM lens is affordable and features near-silent autofocus that's perfect for video shooting.

aperture demands at 200mm. Automatic panning detection turns the IS feature off when panning in both horizontal and vertical directions. An improved "Super Spectra Coating" minimizes flare and ghosting, while optimizing color rendition.

- **Canon EF-S 17-85mm f/4-5.6 IS USM autofocus lens.** This older lens (introduced in 2004 with the EOS 20D) is a very popular "basic" lens still sold for the 70D. The allure here with this $700 lens is the longer telephoto range, coupled with the built-in image stabilization, which allows you to shoot rock-solid photos at shutter speeds that are at least two or three notches slower than you'd need normally (say, 1/8th second instead of 1/30th or 1/60th second), as long as your subject isn't moving. It also has a quiet, fast, reliable ultrasonic motor (more on that later, too). This is another lens designed for the 1.6X crop factor; all but one of the remaining lenses in this list can also be used on full-frame cameras. (I'll tell you why later in this chapter.) This lens is shown in Figure 10.4.

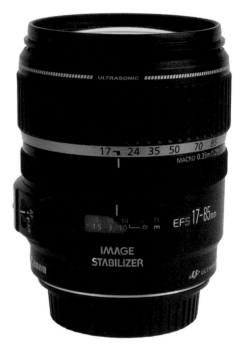

- **Canon EF 55-200mm f/4.5-5.6 II USM autofocus lightweight compact telephoto zoom lens.** If you bought the 18-55mm kit lens, this one picks up where that one leaves off, going from short telephoto to medium long (88mm-320mm full-frame equivalent). It features a desirable ultrasonic motor. Best of all, it's very affordable at around $300. If you can afford only two lenses, the 18-55mm and this one make a good basic set.

- **EF-S 55-250mm f/4-5.6 IS telephoto zoom lens.** This is an image-stabilized EF-S lens (which means it can't be used with Canon's 1.3X and 1.0X crop-factor pro cameras), providing the longest focal range in the EF-S range to date, and that 4-stop

Figure 10.4 The Canon EF-S 17-85mm f/4-5.6 IS USM autofocus lens is another popular starter lens for the 70D.

Image Stabilizer. It's about $300, but it's worth the cost for the stabilization.

- **Canon EF 24-85mm f/3.5-4.5 USM autofocus wide-angle telephoto zoom lens.** If you can get by with normal focal length to medium telephoto range, Canon offers four affordable lenses, plus one more expensive killer lens that's worth the extra expenditure. All of them can be used on full-frame or cropped-frame digital Canons, which is why they include "wide angle" in their product names. They're really wide-angle lenses only when mounted on a full-frame camera. This one, priced in the $300 range if you can find one for sale, offers a useful range of focal lengths, extending from the equivalent of 38mm to 136mm.

- **Canon EF 28-105mm f/3.5-4.5 II USM autofocus wide-angle telephoto zoom lens.** If you want to save about $100 and gain a little reach compared to the 24-85mm zoom, this 45mm-168mm (equivalent lens) might be what you are looking for.

- **Canon EF 28-200mm f/3.5-5.6 USM autofocus wide-angle telephoto zoom lens.** If you want one lens to do everything except wide-angle photography, this 7X zoom lens costs less than $400 and takes you from the equivalent of 45mm out to a long 320mm.

- **Canon EF 24-70mm f/2.8L II USM autofocus zoom wide-angle-telephoto lens.** I couldn't leave this premium lens out of the mix, even though it costs well over $2,000. As part of Canon's L-series (Luxury) lens line, it offers the best sharpness over its focal range than any of the other lenses in this list. Best of all, it's fast (for a zoom), with an f/.2.8 maximum aperture that *doesn't change* as you zoom out. Unlike the other lenses, which may offer only an f/5.6 maximum f/stop at their longest zoom setting, this is a *constant aperture* lens, which retains its maximum f/stop. The added sharpness, constant aperture, and ultra-smooth USM motor are what you're paying for with this lens. Another version with an f/4 maximum aperture with image stabilization can be purchased for less than $1,500.

What Lenses Can You Use?

The previous section helped you sort out what lens you need to buy with your 70D (assuming you already didn't own any Canon lenses). Now, you're probably wondering what lenses can be added to your growing collection (trust me, it will grow). You need to know which lenses are suitable and, most importantly, which lenses are fully compatible with your 70D.

With the Canon 70D, the compatibility issue is a simple one: It accepts any lens with the EF or EF-S designation, with full availability of all autofocus, autoaperture, autoexposure, and image-stabilization features (if present). It's comforting to know that any EF (for full-frame or cropped sensors) or EF-S (for cropped sensor cameras only) will work as designed with your camera. As I noted at the beginning of the chapter, that's more than 70 million lenses!

But wait, there's more. You can also attach Nikon F mount, Leica R, Olympus OM, and M42 ("Pentax screw mount") lenses with a simple adapter, if you don't mind losing automatic focus and aperture control. If you use one of these lenses, you'll need to focus manually (even if the lens operates in Autofocus mode on the camera it was designed for), and adjust the f/stop to the aperture you want to use to take the picture. That means that lenses that don't have an aperture ring (such as Nikon G-series lenses) must be used only at their maximum aperture if you use them with a simple adapter. However, Novoflex makes expensive adapter rings (the Nikon-Lens-on-Canon-Camera version is called EOS/NIK NT) with an integral aperture control that allows adjusting the aperture of lenses that do not have an old-style aperture ring. Expect to pay as much as $300 for an adapter of this type. Should you decide to pick up a new Canon EOS-M mirrorless camera, you'll be able to get double-duty with your EF and EF-S lenses, too, with an adapter that will allow you to use the same lenses on your 70D and companion EOS-M cameras.

Because of the limitations imposed on using "foreign" lenses on your 70D, you probably won't want to make extensive use of them, but an adapter can help you when you really, really need to use a particular focal length but don't have a suitable Canon-compatible lens. For example, I occasionally use an older 400mm lens that was originally designed for the Nikon line on my 70D. The lens needs to be mounted on a tripod for steadiness, anyway, so its slower operation isn't a major pain. Another good match is the 105mm Micro-Nikkor I sometimes use with my Canon 70D. Macro photos, too, are most often taken with the camera mounted on a tripod, and manual focus makes a lot of sense for fine-tuning focus and depth-of-field. Because of the contemplative nature of close-up photography, it's not much of an inconvenience to stop down to the taking aperture just before exposure.

The restrictions on use of lenses within Canon's own product line (as well as lenses produced for earlier Canon SLRs by third-party vendors) are fairly clear-cut. The 70D cannot be used with any of Canon's earlier lens mounting schemes for its film cameras, including the immediate predecessor to the EF mount, the FD mount (introduced with the Canon F1 in 1964 and used until the Canon T60 in 1990), FL (1964-1971), or the original Canon R mount (1959-1964). That's really all you need to know. While you'll find FD-to-EF adapters for about $40, you'll lose so many functions that it's rarely worth the bother.

WHY SO MANY LENS MOUNTS?

Four different lens mounts in 40-plus years (five, if you count the EF-M mount for the new EOS-M cameras) might seem like a lot of different mounting systems, especially when compared to the Nikon F mount of 1959, which retained quite a bit of compatibility with that company's film and digital camera bodies during that same span. However, in digital photography terms, the EF mount itself is positively ancient, having remained reasonably stable for more than 25 years. Lenses designed for the EF system work reliably with every EOS film and digital camera ever produced.

However, at the time, yet another lens mount switch, especially a change from the traditional breech system to a more conventional bayonet-type mount, was indeed a daring move by Canon. One of the reasons for staying with a particular lens type is to "lock" current users into a specific camera system. By introducing the EF mount, Canon in effect cut loose every photographer in its existing user base. If they chose to upgrade, they were free to choose another vendor's products and lenses. Only satisfaction with the previous Canon product line and the promise of the new system would keep them in the fold.

In retrospect, the switch to the EF mount seems like a very good idea, as the initial EOS film cameras can now be seen as the beginning of Canon's rise to eventually become the leader in film and (later) digital SLR cameras. By completely revamping its lens mounting system, the company was able to take advantage of the latest advances in technology without compromise.

For example, when the original EF bayonet mount was introduced in 1987, the system incorporated new autofocus technology (EF actually stands for "electro focus") in a more rugged and less complicated form. A tiny motor was built into the lens itself, eliminating the need for mechanical linkages with the camera. Instead, electrical contacts are used to send power and the required focusing information to the motor. That's a much more robust and resilient system that made it easier for Canon to design faster and more accurate autofocus mechanisms just by redesigning the lenses.

EF vs. EF-S

Today, in addition to its EF lenses, Canon offers lenses that use the EF-S (the S stands for "short back focus") mount, with the chief difference being (as you might expect) lens components that extend farther back into the camera body of some of Canon's latest digital cameras (specifically those with smaller than full-frame sensors), such as the 70D. As I'll explain next, this refinement allows designing more compact, less-expensive lenses especially for those cameras, but not for models that include current cameras like the EOS 5D Mark III, 1D X, or 1D Mark III (even though the latter camera does have a sensor that is slightly smaller than full frame).

Canon's EF-S lens mount variation was born in 2003, when the company virtually invented the consumer-oriented digital SLR category by introducing the original EOS 300D/Digital Rebel, a dSLR that cost less than $1,000 *with lens* at a time when all other interchangeable lens digital cameras (including the 70D's "grandparent," the original EOS 10D) were priced closer to $2,000 with a basic lens. Like the EOS 10D, the EOS 70D features a smaller than full-frame sensor with a 1.6X crop factor (Canon calls this format APS-C). But the EOS Digital accepted lenses that took advantage of the shorter mirror found in APS-C cameras, with elements of shorter focal length lenses (wide angles) that extended *into* the camera, space that was off limits in other models because the mirror passed through that territory as it flipped up to expose the shutter and sensor. (Canon even calls its flip-up reflector a "half mirror.")

In short (so to speak), the EF-S mount made it easier to design less-expensive wide-angle lenses that could be used *only* with 1.6X-crop cameras, and featured a simpler design and reduced coverage area suitable for those non-full-frame models. The new mount made it possible to produce lenses like the ultra-wide EF-S 10-22mm f/3.5-4.5 USM lens, which has the equivalent field of view as a 16mm-35mm zoom on a full-frame camera. (See Figure 10.5.)

Suitable cameras for EF-S lenses include all recent non-full-frame models. The EF-S lenses cannot be used on the APS-C-sensor EOS 10D, the 1D Mark II N/Mark III (which have a 28.7mm × 19.1mm APS-H sensor with a 1.3X crop factor), or any of the full-frame digital or film EOS models, such as the EOS 1D X, EOS 1Ds Mark III, or EOS 5D Mark III. It's easy to tell an EF lens from an EF-S lens: The latter incorporate EF-S into their name! Plus, EF lenses have a raised red dot on the barrel that is used to align the lens with a matching dot on the camera when attaching the lens. EF-S lenses and compatible bodies use a white square instead. Some EF-S lenses also have a rubber ring at the attachment

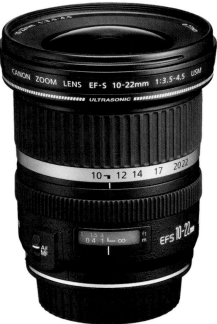

Figure 10.5 The EF-S 10-22mm ultra-wide lens was made possible by the shorter back focus difference offered by the original Digital and subsequent Canon 1.6X "cropped sensor" models.

end that provides a bit of weather/dust sealing and protects the back components of the lens if a user attempts to mount it on a camera that is not EF-S compatible.

Ingredients of Canon's Alphanumeric Soup

The actual product names of individual Canon lenses are fairly easy to decipher; they'll include either the EF or EF-S designation, the focal length or focal length range of the lens, its maximum aperture, and some other information. Additional data may be engraved or painted on the barrel or ring surrounding the front element of the lens, as shown in Figure 10.6. Here's a decoding of what the individual designations mean:

- **EF/EF-S.** If the lens is marked EF, it can safely be used on any Canon EOS camera, film or digital. If it is an EF-S lens, it should be used only on an EF-S compatible camera.

- **Focal length.** Given in millimeters or a millimeter range, such as 60mm in the case of a popular Canon macro lens, or 17-55mm, used to describe a medium-wide to short-telephoto zoom.

- **Maximum aperture.** The largest f/stop available with a particular lens is given in a string of numbers that might seem confusing at first glance. For example, you might see 1:1.8 for a fixed-focal length (prime) lens, and 1:4.5-5.6 for a zoom. The initial 1: signifies that the f/stop given is actually a ratio or fraction (in regular notation, f/ replaces the 1:), which is why a 1:2 (or f/2) aperture is larger than an 1:4 (or f/4) aperture—just as 1/2 is larger than 1/4. With most zoom lenses, the maximum aperture changes as the lens is zoomed to the telephoto position, so a range is given instead: 1:4.5-5.6. (Some zooms, called *constant aperture* lenses, keep the same maximum aperture throughout their range.)

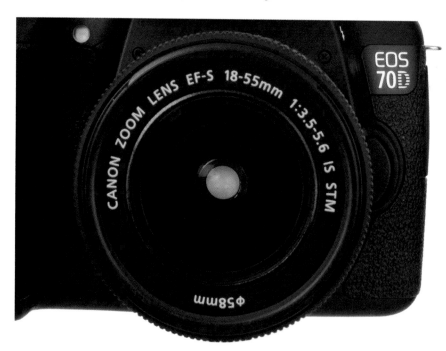

Figure 10.6
Most of the key specifications of the lens are marked on the ring around the front element.

■ **Autofocus type.** Most newer Canon lenses that aren't of the bargain-basement type use Canon's *ultrasonic motor* autofocus system (more on that later) and are given the USM designation. Several of the company's newest optics use the Stepper Motor (STM) technology. If USM or STM does not appear on the lens or its model name, the lens uses the less sophisticated AFD (arc-form drive) autofocus system or the micromotor (MM) drive mechanism.

■ **Series.** Canon adds a Roman numeral to many of its products to represent an updated model with the same focal length or focal length range, so some lenses will have a II or III added to their name.

■ **Pro quality.** Canon's more expensive lenses with more rugged construction and higher optical quality, intended for professional use, include the letter L (for "luxury") in their product name. You can further differentiate these lenses visually by a red ring around the lens barrel and the off-white color of the metal barrel itself in virtually all telephoto L-series lenses. (Some L-series lenses have shiny or textured black plastic exterior barrels.) Internally, every L lens includes at least one lens element that is built of ultra-low dispersion glass, is constructed of expensive fluorite crystal, or uses an expensive ground (not molded) aspheric (non-spherical) lens component.

■ **Filter size.** You'll find the front lens filter thread diameter in millimeters included on the lens, preceded by a Ø symbol, as in Ø67 or Ø72.

■ **Special-purpose lenses.** Some Canon lenses are designed for specific types of work, and they include appropriate designations in their names. For example, close-focusing lenses such as the Canon EF-S 60mm f/2.8 Macro USM lens incorporate the word *Macro* into their name. Lenses with perspective control features preface the lens name with T-S (for tilt-shift). Lenses with built-in image-stabilization features, such as the nifty EF 28-300mm f/3.5-5.6L IS USM telephoto zoom include *IS* in their product names.

SORTING THE MOTOR DRIVES

Incorporating the autofocus motor inside the lens was an innovative move by Canon, and this allowed the company to produce better and more sophisticated lenses as technology became available to upgrade the focusing system. As a result, you'll find four different types of motors in Canon-designed lenses, each with cost and practical considerations. Most newer lenses use only the latest USM motor, and incorporate that designation in their names.

■ **AFD (Arc-form drive)** and **Micromotor (MM)** drives are built around tiny versions of electromagnetic motors, which generally use gear trains to produce the motion needed to adjust the focus of the lens. Both are slow, noisy, and not particularly effective with larger lenses. Manual focus adjustments are possible only when the motor drive is disengaged.

■ **Micromotor ultrasonic motor (USM)** drives use high-frequency vibration to produce the motion used to drive the gear train, resulting in a quieter operating system at a cost that's not much more than that of electromagnetic motor drives. With the exception of a couple lenses that have a slipping clutch mechanism, manual focus with this kind of system is possible only when the motor drive is switched off and the lens is set in manual mode. This is the kind of USM system you'll find in lower-cost lenses.

- **Ring ultrasonic motor (USM)** drives, available in two different types (*electronic focus ring USM* and *ring USM*), also use high-frequency movement, but generate motion using a pair of vibrating metal rings to adjust focus. Both variations allow a feature called Full Time Manual (FTM) focus, which lets you make manual adjustments to the lens's focus even when the autofocus mechanism is engaged. With electronic focus ring USM, manual focus is possible only when the lens is mounted on the camera and the camera is turned on; the focus ring of lenses with ring USM can be turned at any time.

- **Stepper motor (STM) drives.** In autofocus mode, the precision motor of STM lenses, along with a new aperture mechanism, allows lenses equipped with this technology to focus quickly, accurately, silently, and with smooth continuous increments. If you think about video capture, you can see how these advantages pay off. Silent operation is a plus, especially when noise from autofocusing can easily be transferred to the camera's built-in microphones through the air or transmitted through the body itself. In addition, because autofocus is often done *during* capture, it's important that the focus increments are continuous. USM motors are not as smooth, but are better at jumping quickly to the exact focus point. You can adjust focus manually, using a focus-by-wire process. As you rotate the focus ring, that action doesn't move the lens elements; instead, your rotation of the ring sends a signal to the motor to change the focus. Figure 10.7 shows the new Canon EF-S 40mm f/2.8 STM lens.

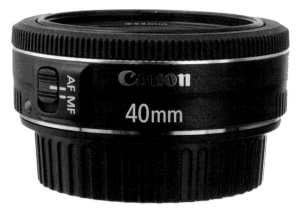

Figure 10.7
Canon's 40mm f/2.8 lens, with an STM motor, is designed for video capture.

Your Second (and Third...) Lens

There are really only two advantages to owning just a single lens. One of them is creative. Keeping one set of optics mounted on your 70D all the time forces you to be especially imaginative in your approach to your subjects. I once visited Europe with only a single camera body and a 35mm f/2 lens. The experience was actually quite exciting, because I had to use a variety of techniques to allow that one lens to serve for landscapes, available light photos, action, close-ups, portraits, and other kinds of images. Canon makes an excellent 35mm f/2 lens (which focuses down to 9.6 inches) that's perfect for that kind of experiment; although, today, my personal choice would be the sublime (and expensive) Canon Wide-Angle EF 35mm f/1.4L USM autofocus lens. I also own the Canon EF 50mm f/1.8 II lens, which I favor as a very compact and light walkaround/short telephoto/portrait lens, especially indoors. It makes a great close-up/macro lens, too, and, at less than $125, is my choice as a very good second lens.

Of course, it's more likely that your "single" lens is actually a zoom, which is, in truth, many lenses in one, taking you from, say, 17mm to 85mm (or some other range) with a rapid twist of the zoom ring. You'll still find some creative challenges when you stick to a single zoom lens's focal lengths.

The second advantage of the unilens camera is only a marginal technical benefit since the introduction of the 70D. If you don't exchange lenses, the chances of dust and dirt getting inside your 70D and settling on the sensor is reduced (but *not* eliminated entirely). Although I've known some photographers who minimized the number of lens changes they made for this very reason, reducing the number of lenses you work with is not a productive or rewarding approach for most of us. The 70D's automatic sensor cleaning feature has made this "advantage" much less significant than it was in the past.

It's more likely that you'll succumb to the malady known as *Lens Lust*, which is defined as an incurable disease marked by a significant yen for newer, better, longer, faster, sharper, anything-er optics for your camera. (And, it must be noted, this disease can *cost* you significant yen—or dollars, or whatever currency you use.) In its worst manifestations, sufferers find themselves with lenses that have overlapping zoom ranges or capabilities, because one or the other offers a slight margin in performance or suitability for specific tasks. When you find yourself already lusting after a new lens before you've really had a chance to put your latest purchase to the test, you'll know the disease has reached the terminal phase.

What Lenses Can Do for You

A saner approach to expanding your lens collection is to consider what each of your options can do for you and then choosing the type of lens that will really boost your creative opportunities. Here's a general guide to the sort of capabilities you can gain by adding a lens to your repertoire.

■ **Wider perspective.** Your 18-55mm f/3.5-5.6 or 17-85mm f/4-5.6 or 18-200mm lens has served you well for moderate wide-angle shots. Now you find your back is up against a wall and you *can't* take a step backward to take in more subject matter. Perhaps you're standing on the rim of the Grand Canyon, and you want to take in as much of the breathtaking view as you can. You might find yourself just behind the baseline at a high school basketball game and want an interesting shot with a little perspective distortion tossed in the mix. There's a lens out there that will provide you with what you need, such as the EF-S 10-22mm f/3.5-4.5 USM zoom. If you want to stay in the sub-$800 price category, you'll need something like the Sigma Super Wide-Angle 10-20mm f/4-5.6 EX DC HSM autofocus lens. The two lenses provide the equivalent of a 16mm to 32/35mm wide-angle view. For a distorted view, there is the Canon Fisheye EF 15mm f/2.8 autofocus, with a similar lens available from Sigma, which offers an extra-wide circular fisheye, and the Sigma Fisheye 8mm f/3.5 EX DG Circular Fisheye. Your extra-wide choices may not be abundant, but they are there. Figure 10.8 shows the perspective you get from an ultra-wide-angle, non-fisheye lens.

■ **Bring objects closer.** A long lens brings distant subjects closer to you, offers better control over depth-of-field, and avoids the perspective distortion that wide-angle lenses provide. They compress the apparent distance between objects in your frame. In the telephoto realm, Canon is second to none, with a dozen or more offerings in the sub-$650 range, including the Canon EF 100-300mm f/4.5-5.6 USM autofocus and Canon EF 70-300mm f/4-5.6 IS USM autofocus telephoto zoom lenses, and a broad array of zooms and fixed-focal length optics if you're willing to spend up to $1,000 or a bit more. Don't forget that the 70D's crop factor narrows the field of view of all these lenses, so your 70-300mm lens looks more like a 112mm-480mm zoom through the viewfinder. Figures 10.9 and 10.10 were taken from the same position as Figure 10.8, but with an 85mm and 500mm lens, respectively.

■ **Bring your camera closer.** Macro lenses allow you to focus to within an inch or two of your subject. Canon's best close-up lenses are all fixed focal length optics in the 50mm to 180mm range (including the well-regarded Canon EF-S 60mm f/2.8 compact and Canon EF 100mm f/2.8 USM macro autofocus lenses). But you'll find macro zooms available from Sigma and others. They don't tend to focus quite as close, but they provide a bit of flexibility when you want to vary your subject distance (say, to avoid spooking a skittish creature).

■ **Look sharp.** Many lenses, particularly Canon's luxury "L" line, are prized for their sharpness and overall image quality. While your run-of-the-mill lens is likely to be plenty sharp for most applications, the very best optics are even better over their entire field of view (which means no fuzzy corners), are sharper at a wider range of focal lengths (in the case of zooms), and have better correction for various types of distortion.

■ **More speed.** Your Canon EF 100-300mm f/4.5-5.6 telephoto zoom lens might have the perfect focal length and sharpness for sports photography, but the maximum aperture won't cut it for night baseball or football games, or, even, any sports shooting in daylight if the weather is cloudy or you need to use some unusually fast shutter speed, such as 1/4,000th second. You might be happier with the Canon EF 100mm f/2 medium telephoto for close-range stuff, or even the pricier Canon EF 135mm f/2L. If money is no object, you can spring for Canon's 400mm f/2.8 and 600mm f/4 L-series lenses (both with image stabilization and priced in the four- and five-figure stratosphere). Or, maybe you just need the speed and can benefit from an f/1.8 or f/1.4 lens in the 20mm-85mm range. They're all available in Canon mounts (there's even an 85mm f/1.2 and 50mm f/1.2 for the real speed demons). With any of these lenses you can continue photographing under the dimmest of lighting conditions without the need for a tripod or flash.

Figure 10.8
An ultra-wide-angle lens provided this view of a castle in Prague, Czech Republic.

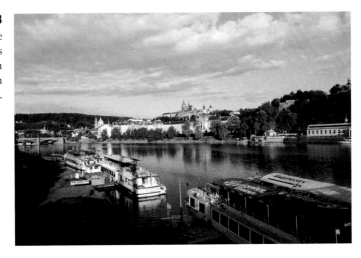

Figure 10.9
This photo, taken from roughly the same distance, shows the view using a short telephoto lens.

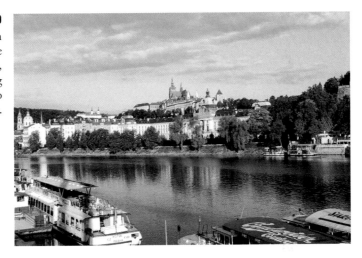

Figure 10.10
A longer telephoto lens captured this closer view of the castle from approximately the same shooting position.

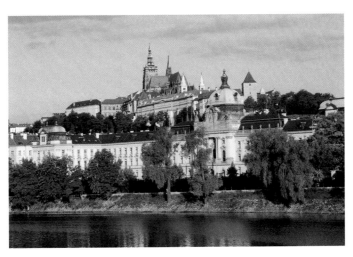

- **Special features.** Accessory lenses give you special features, such as tilt/shift capabilities to correct for perspective distortion in architectural shots. Canon offers four of these TS-E lenses in 17mm, 24mm, 45mm, and 90mm focal lengths, at more than $1,300-$2,000 (and up) each. You'll also find macro lenses, including the MP-E 65mm f/2.8 1-5x macro photo lens, a manual focus lens which shoots *only* in the 1X to 5X life-size range. If you want diffused images, check out the EF 135mm f/2.8 with two soft-focus settings. The fisheye lenses mentioned earlier and all IS (image-stabilized) lenses also count as special-feature optics. The recent Canon EF 8-15mm f/4L Fisheye USM ultra-wide zoom lens is highly unusual in offering a *zoomable* fisheye range. Tokina's 10-17mm fisheye zoom is its chief competitor; I've owned one and it is not in the same league in terms of sharpness and speed.

Zoom or Prime?

Zoom lenses have changed the way serious photographers take pictures. One of the reasons that I own 12 SLR film bodies is that in ancient times it was common to mount a different fixed focal length prime lens on various cameras and take pictures with two or three cameras around your neck (or tucked in a camera case) so you'd be ready to take a long shot or an intimate close-up or wide-angle view on a moment's notice, without the need to switch lenses. It made sense (at the time) to have a half dozen or so bodies (two to use, one in the shop, one in transit, and a couple backups). Zoom lenses of the time had a limited zoom range, were heavy, and not very sharp (especially when you tried to wield one of those monsters handheld).

That's all changed today. Lenses like the razor-sharp Canon EF 28-300mm f/3.5-5.6L IS USM can boast 10X or longer zoom ranges, in a package that's about 7 inches long, and while not petite at 3.7 pounds, it is quite usable handheld (especially with IS switched on). Although such a lens might seem expensive at $2,600-plus, it's actually much less costly than the six or so lenses it replaces.

When selecting between zoom and prime lenses, there are several considerations to ponder. Here's a checklist of the most important factors. I already mentioned image quality and maximum aperture earlier, but those aspects take on additional meaning when comparing zooms and primes.

- **Logistics.** As prime lenses offer just a single focal length, you'll need more of them to encompass the full range offered by a single zoom. More lenses mean additional slots in your camera bag, and extra weight to carry. Just within Canon's line alone you can select from about a dozen general-purpose prime lenses in 28mm, 35mm, 50mm, 85mm, 100mm, 135mm, 200mm, and 300mm focal lengths, all of which are overlapped by the 28-300mm zoom I mentioned earlier. Even so, you might be willing to carry an extra prime lens or two in order to gain the speed or image quality that lens offers.

- **Image quality.** Prime lenses usually produce better image quality at their focal length than even the most sophisticated zoom lenses at the same magnification. Zoom lenses, with their shifting elements and f/stops that can vary from zoom position to zoom position, are in general more complex to design than fixed focal length lenses. That's not to say that the very best prime lenses can't be complicated as well. However, the exotic designs, aspheric elements, low-dispersion glass, and Canon's diffraction optics (DO) technology (a three-layer diffraction grating to better control how light is captured by a lens) can be applied to improving the quality of the lens, rather than wasting a lot of it on compensating for problems caused by the zoom process itself.

■ **Maximum aperture.** Because of the same design constraints, zoom lenses usually have smaller maximum apertures than prime lenses, and the most affordable zooms have a lens opening that grows effectively smaller as you zoom in. The difference in lens speed verges on the ridiculous at some focal lengths. For example, the 18mm-55mm basic zoom gives you a 55mm f/5.6 lens when zoomed all the way out, while prime lenses in that focal length commonly have f/1.8 or faster maximum apertures. Indeed, the fastest f/2, f/1.8, f/1.4, and f/1.2 lenses are all primes, and if you require speed, a fixed focal length lens is what you should rely on. Figure 10.11 shows an image taken with a Canon 85mm f/1.8 Series EF USM telephoto lens.

Figure 10.11
An 85mm f/1.8 lens was perfect for this handheld photo of a musician.

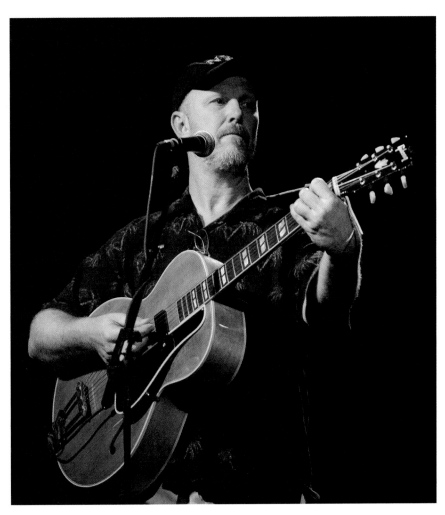

- **Speed.** Using prime lenses takes time and slows you down. It takes a few seconds to remove your current lens and mount a new one, and the more often you need to do that, the more time is wasted. If you choose not to swap lenses, when using a fixed focal length lens you'll still have to move closer or farther away from your subject to get the field of view you want. A zoom lens allows you to change magnifications and focal lengths with the twist of a ring and generally saves a great deal of time.

- **Special features.** Prime lenses often have special features not found in zoom lenses. For example, the new EF 40mm f/2.8 STM lens boasts that smooth, silent autofocus motor described earlier in this chapter. It functions as a wide-angle lens on a full-frame camera like the 5D Mark III, and as a short telephoto, portrait lens on cameras like the 70D. You'll also find close-focusing capabilities and perspective control features on prime lenses.

TIP

Early copies of the EF 40mm f/2.8 STM lens (including the one I purchased) had suffered from a defect that caused autofocusing to cease functioning when pressure was applied to the lens barrel. In my case, gripping the barrel while removing the UV filter I use as a lens cap was enough. Until Canon issued a product advisory, I was really puzzled by this phenomenon. When I removed the lens and tried it on my 5D Mark III to see if the problem was in the lens or the camera body, it went away (temporarily). Before a firmware fix was issued in August, 2012, Canon advised the workaround of removing and reattaching the lens, or removing and reinserting the battery. If you own this lens, make sure your 70D firmware updates are all current.

Categories of Lenses

Lenses can be categorized by their intended purpose—general photography, macro photography, and so forth—or by their focal length. The range of available focal lengths is usually divided into three main groups: wide-angle, normal, and telephoto. Prime lenses fall neatly into one of these classifications. Zooms can overlap designations, with a significant number falling into the catch-all, wide-to-telephoto zoom range. This section provides more information about focal length ranges, and how they are used.

Any lens with an equivalent focal length of 10mm to 20mm is said to be an *ultra-wide-angle lens*; from about 20mm to 40mm (equivalent) is said to be a *wide-angle lens*. *Normal lenses* have a focal length roughly equivalent to the diagonal of the film or sensor, in millimeters, and so fall into the range of about 45mm to 60mm (on a full-frame camera). *Telephoto lenses* usually fall into the 75mm and longer focal lengths, while those from about 300mm to 400mm and longer often are referred to as *super-telephotos*.

Using Wide-Angle and Wide-Zoom Lenses

To use wide-angle prime lenses and wide zooms, you need to understand how they affect your photography. Here's a quick summary of the things you need to know.

■ **More depth-of-field.** Practically speaking, wide-angle lenses offer more depth-of-field at a particular subject distance and aperture. (But see the sidebar below for an important note.) You'll find that helpful when you want to maximize sharpness of a large zone, but not very useful when you'd rather isolate your subject using selective focus (telephoto lenses are better for that).

■ **Stepping back.** Wide-angle lenses have the effect of making it seem that you are standing farther from your subject than you really are. They're helpful when you don't want to back up, or can't because there are impediments in your way.

■ **Wider field of view.** While making your subject seem farther away, as implied above, a wide-angle lens also provides a larger field of view, including more of the subject in your photos. Table 10.1 shows the diagonal field of view offered by an assortment of lenses, taking into account the crop factor introduced by the 70D's smaller-than-full-frame sensor.

■ **More foreground.** As background objects retreat, more of the foreground is brought into view by a wide-angle lens. That gives you extra emphasis on the area that's closest to the camera. Photograph your home with a normal lens/normal zoom setting, and the front yard probably looks fairly conventional in your photo (that's why they're called "normal" lenses). Switch to a wider lens and you'll discover that your lawn now makes up much more of the photo. So, wide-angle lenses are great when you want to emphasize that lake in the foreground, but problematic when your intended subject is located farther in the distance.

Table 10.1 Field of View at Various Focal Lengths

Diagonal Field of View	Focal Length at 1X Crop	Focal Length Needed to Produce Same Field of View at 1.6X Crop
107 degrees	16mm	10mm
94 degrees	20mm	12mm
84 degrees	24mm	15mm
75 degrees	28mm	18mm
63 degrees	35mm	22mm
47 degrees	50mm	31mm
28 degrees	85mm	53mm
18 degrees	135mm	85mm
12 degrees	200mm	125mm
8.2 degrees	300mm	188mm

■ **Super-sized subjects.** The tendency of a wide-angle lens to emphasize objects in the foreground, while de-emphasizing objects in the background can lead to a kind of size distortion that may be more objectionable for some types of subjects than others. Shoot a bed of flowers up close with a wide angle, and you might like the distorted effect of the larger blossoms nearer the lens. Take a photo of a family member with the same lens from the same distance, and you're likely to get some complaints about that gigantic nose in the foreground.

■ **Perspective distortion.** When you tilt the camera so the plane of the sensor is no longer perpendicular to the vertical plane of your subject, some parts of the subject are now closer to the sensor than they were before, while other parts are farther away. So, buildings, flagpoles, or NBA players appear to be falling backward, as you can see in Figure 10.12. While this kind of apparent distortion (it's not caused by a defect in the lens) can happen with any lens, it's most apparent when a wide angle is used.

■ **Steady cam.** You'll find that you can handhold a wide-angle lens at slower shutter speeds, without need for image stabilization, than you can with a telephoto lens. The reduced magnification of the wide-lens or wide-zoom setting doesn't emphasize camera shake like a telephoto lens does.

■ **Interesting angles.** Many of the factors already listed combine to produce more interesting angles when shooting with wide-angle lenses. Raising or lowering a telephoto lens a few feet probably will have little effect on the appearance of the distant subjects you're shooting. The same change in elevation can produce a dramatic effect for the much-closer subjects typically captured with a wide-angle lens or wide-zoom setting.

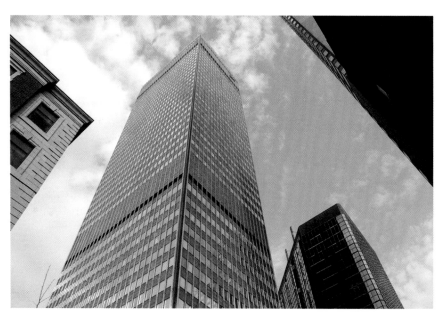

Figure 10.12
Tilting the camera back produces this "falling back" look in architectural photos.

The crop factor strikes again! You can see from this table that wide-angle lenses provide a broader field of view, and that, because of the 70D's 1.6 crop factor, lenses must have a shorter focal length to provide the same field of view. If you like working with a 28mm lens with your full-frame camera, you'll need an 18mm lens for your 70D to get the same field of view. (Some focal lengths have been rounded slightly for simplification.)

DOF IN DEPTH

The depth-of-field (DOF) advantage of wide-angle lenses is diminished when you enlarge your picture; believe it or not, a wide-angle image enlarged and cropped to provide the same subject size as a telephoto shot would have the *same* depth-of-field. Try it: take a wide-angle photo of a friend from a fair distance, and then zoom in to duplicate the picture in a telephoto image. Then, enlarge the wide shot so your friend is the same size in both. The wide photo will have the same DOF (and will have much less detail, too).

Avoiding Potential Wide-Angle Problems

Wide-angle lenses have a few quirks that you'll want to keep in mind when shooting so you can avoid falling into some common traps. Here's a checklist of tips for avoiding common problems:

- **Symptom: converging lines.** Unless you want to use wildly diverging lines as a creative effect, it's a good idea to keep horizontal and vertical lines in landscapes, architecture, and other subjects carefully aligned with the sides, top, and bottom of the frame. That will help you avoid undesired perspective distortion. Sometimes it helps to shoot from a slightly elevated position so you don't have to tilt the camera up or down.

- **Symptom: color fringes around objects.** Lenses are often plagued with fringes of color around backlit objects, produced by *chromatic aberration*, which comes in two forms: *longitudinal/axial*, in which all the colors of light don't focus in the same plane; and *lateral/transverse*, in which the colors are shifted to one side. Axial chromatic aberration can be reduced by stopping down the lens, but transverse chromatic aberration cannot. Both can be reduced by using lenses with low diffraction index glass (or UD elements, in Canon nomenclature) and by incorporating elements that cancel the chromatic aberration of other glass in the lens. For example, a strong positive lens made of low-dispersion crown glass (made of a soda-lime-silica composite) may be mated with a weaker negative lens made of high-dispersion flint glass, which contains lead.

- **Symptom: lines that bow outward.** Some wide-angle lenses cause straight lines to bow outward, with the strongest effect at the edges. In fisheye (or *curvilinear*) lenses, this defect is a feature, as you can see in Figure 10.13. When distortion is not desired, you'll need to use a lens that has corrected barrel distortion. Manufacturers like Canon do their best to minimize or eliminate it (producing a *rectilinear* lens), often using *aspherical* lens elements (which are not cross-sections of a sphere). You can also minimize less severe barrel distortion simply by framing your photo with some extra space all around, so the edges where the defect is most obvious can be cropped out of the picture.

- **Symptom: dark corners and shadows in flash photos.** The Canon EOS 70D's built-in electronic flash is designed to provide even coverage for lenses as wide as 17mm. If you use a wider lens, you can expect darkening, or *vignetting*, in the corners of the frame. At wider focal lengths, the lens hood of some lenses (my 17mm-85mm lens is a prime offender) can cast a semi-circular shadow in the lower portion of the frame when using the built-in flash. Sometimes removing the lens hood or zooming in a bit can eliminate the shadow. Mounting an external flash unit, such as the mighty Canon 580EX II or 600EX-RT, can solve both problems, as it has zoomable coverage up to 114 degrees with the included adapter, sufficient for a 15mm rectilinear lens. Its higher vantage point eliminates the problem of lens hood shadow, too.

- **Symptom: light and dark areas when using polarizing filter.** If you know that polarizers work best when the camera is pointed 90 degrees away from the sun and have the least effect when the camera is oriented 180 degrees from the sun, you know only half the story. With lenses having a focal length of 10mm to 18mm (the equivalent of 16mm-28mm), the angle of view (107 to 75 degrees diagonally, or 97 to 44 degrees horizontally) is extensive enough to cause problems. Think about it: when a 10mm lens is pointed at the proper 90-degree angle from the sun, objects at the edges of the frame will be oriented at 135 to 41 degrees, with only the center at exactly 90 degrees. Either edge will have much less of a polarized effect. The solution is to avoid using a polarizing filter with lenses having an actual focal length of less than 18mm (or 28mm equivalent).

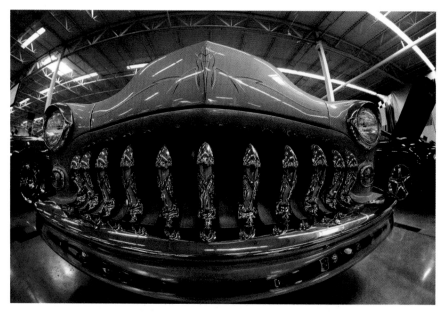

Figure 10.13

Many wide-angle lenses cause lines to bow outward toward the edges of the image; with a fisheye lens, this tendency is especially useful for creating special effects, as in this shot.

Using Telephoto and Tele-Zoom Lenses

Telephoto lenses also can have a dramatic effect on your photography, and Canon is especially strong in the long-lens arena, with lots of choices in many focal lengths and zoom ranges. You should be able to find an affordable telephoto or tele-zoom to enhance your photography in several different ways. Here are the most important things you need to know. In the next section, I'll concentrate on telephoto considerations that can be problematic—and how to avoid those problems.

- **Selective focus.** Long lenses have reduced depth-of-field within the frame, allowing you to use selective focus to isolate your subject. You can open the lens up wide to create shallow depth-of-field (see Figure 10.14), or close it down a bit to allow more to be in focus. The flip side of the coin is that when you *want* to make a range of objects sharp, you'll need to use a smaller f/stop to get the depth-of-field you need. Like fire, the depth-of-field of a telephoto lens can be friend or foe.

- **Getting closer.** Telephoto lenses bring you closer to wildlife, sports action, and candid subjects. No one wants to get a reputation as a surreptitious or "sneaky" photographer (except for paparazzi), but when applied to candids in an open and honest way, a long lens can help you capture memorable moments while retaining enough distance to stay out of the way of events as they transpire.

Figure 10.14
A wide f/stop helped isolate the lemur from its background.

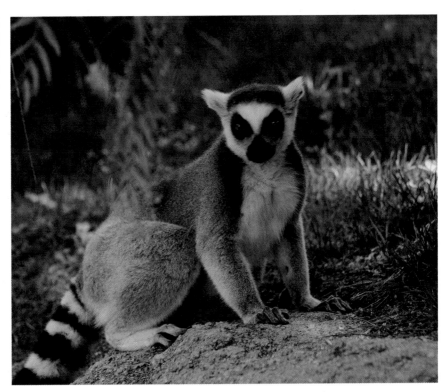

- **Reduced foreground/increased compression.** Telephoto lenses have the opposite effect of wide angles: they reduce the importance of things in the foreground by squeezing everything together. This compression even makes distant objects appear to be closer to subjects in the foreground and middle ranges. You can use this effect as a creative tool.

- **Accentuates camera shakiness.** Telephoto focal lengths hit you with a double-whammy in terms of camera/photographer shake. The lenses themselves are bulkier, more difficult to hold steady, and may even produce a barely perceptible see-saw rocking effect when you support them with one hand halfway down the lens barrel. Telephotos also magnify any camera shake. It's no wonder that image stabilization is popular in longer lenses.

- **Interesting angles require creativity.** Telephoto lenses require more imagination in selecting interesting angles, because the "angle" you do get on your subjects is so narrow. Moving from side to side or a bit higher or lower can make a dramatic difference in a wide-angle shot, but raising or lowering a telephoto lens a few feet probably will have little effect on the appearance of the distant subjects you're shooting.

Avoiding Telephoto Lens Problems

Many of the "problems" that telephoto lenses pose are really just challenges and not that difficult to overcome. Here is a list of the seven most common picture maladies and suggested solutions.

- **Symptom: flat faces in portraits.** Head-and-shoulders portraits of humans tend to be more flattering when a focal length of 50mm to 85mm is used. Longer focal lengths compress the distance between features like noses and ears, making the face look wider and flat. A wide angle might make noses look huge and ears tiny when you fill the frame with a face. So stick with 50mm to 85mm focal lengths, going longer only when you're forced to shoot from a greater distance, and wider only when shooting three-quarters/full-length portraits, or group shots.

- **Symptom: blur due to camera shake.** Use a higher shutter speed (boosting ISO if necessary), consider an image-stabilized lens, or mount your camera on a tripod, monopod, or brace it with some other support. Of those three solutions, only the first will reduce blur caused by *subject* motion; an IS lens or tripod won't help you freeze a race car in mid-lap.

- **Symptom: color fringes.** Chromatic aberration is the most pernicious optical problem found in telephoto lenses. There are others, including spherical aberration, astigmatism, coma, curvature of field, and similarly scary-sounding phenomena. The best solution for any of these is to use a better lens that offers the proper degree of correction, or stop down the lens to minimize the problem. But that's not always possible. Your second-best choice may be to correct the fringing in your favorite RAW conversion tool or image editor. Photoshop's Lens Correction filter offers sliders that minimize both red/cyan and blue/yellow fringing.

- **Symptom: lines that curve inward.** Pincushion distortion is found in many telephoto lenses. You might find after a bit of testing that it is worse at certain focal lengths with your particular zoom lens. Like chromatic aberration, it can be partially corrected using tools like Photoshop's Lens Correction filter and Photoshop Elements' Correct Camera Distortion filter.

- **Symptom: low contrast from haze or fog.** When you're photographing distant objects, a long lens shoots through a lot more atmosphere, which generally is muddied up with extra haze and fog. That dirt or moisture in the atmosphere can reduce contrast and mute colors. Some feel that a skylight or UV filter can help, but this practice is mostly a holdover from the film days. Digital sensors are not sensitive enough to UV light for a UV filter to have much effect. So you should be prepared to boost contrast and color saturation in your Picture Styles menu or image editor if necessary.

- **Symptom: low contrast from flare.** Lenses are furnished with lens hoods for a good reason: to reduce flare from bright light sources at the periphery of the picture area, or completely outside it. Because telephoto lenses often create images that are lower in contrast in the first place, you'll want to be especially careful to use a lens hood to prevent further effects on your image (or shade the front of the lens with your hand).

- **Symptom: dark flash photos.** Edge-to-edge flash coverage isn't a problem with telephoto lenses as it is with wide angles. The shooting distance is. A long lens might make a subject that's 50 feet away look as if it's right next to you, but your camera's flash isn't fooled. You'll need extra power for distant flash shots, and probably more power than your 70D's built-in flash provides. The shoe-mount Canon 580EX II or 600EX-RT Speedlites, for example, can automatically zoom their coverage down to that of a medium telephoto lens, providing a theoretical full-power shooting aperture of about f/8 at 50 feet and ISO 400. (Try *that* with the built-in flash!)

Telephotos and Bokeh

Bokeh describes the aesthetic qualities of the out-of-focus parts of an image and whether out-of-focus points of light—circles of confusion—are rendered as distracting fuzzy discs or smoothly fade into the background. *Boke* is a Japanese word for "blur," and the h was added to keep English speakers from rendering it monosyllabically to rhyme with *broke*. Although bokeh is visible in blurry portions of any image, it's of particular concern with telephoto lenses, which, thanks to the magic of reduced depth-of-field, produce more obviously out-of-focus areas.

Bokeh can vary from lens to lens, or even within a given lens depending on the f/stop in use. Bokeh becomes objectionable when the circles of confusion are evenly illuminated, making them stand out as distinct discs, or, worse, when these circles are darker in the center, producing an ugly "doughnut" effect. A lens defect called spherical aberration may produce out-of-focus discs that are brighter on the edges and darker in the center, because the lens doesn't focus light passing through the edges of the lens exactly as it does light going through the center. (Mirror or *catadioptric* lenses also produce this effect.)

Other kinds of spherical aberration generate circles of confusion that are brightest in the center and fade out at the edges, producing a smooth blending effect, as you can see at right in Figure 10.15. Ironically, when no spherical aberration is present at all, the discs are a uniform shade, which, while better than the doughnut effect, is not as pleasing as the bright center/dark edge rendition. The shape of the disc also comes into play, with round smooth circles considered the best, and nonagonal or some other polygon (determined by the shape of the lens diaphragm) considered less desirable.

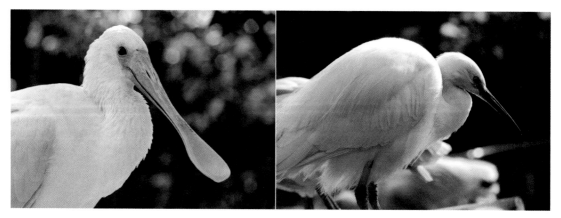

Figure 10.15 Bokeh is less pleasing when the discs are prominent (left), and less obtrusive when they blend into the background (right).

If you plan to use selective focus a lot, you should investigate the bokeh characteristics of a particular lens before you buy. Canon user groups and forums will usually be full of comments and questions about bokeh, so the research is fairly easy.

Add-ons and Special Features

Once you've purchased your telephoto lens, you'll want to think about some appropriate accessories for it. There are some handy add-ons available that can be valuable. Here are a couple of them to think about.

Lens Hoods

Lens hoods are an important accessory for all lenses, but they're especially valuable with telephotos. As I mentioned earlier, lens hoods do a good job of preserving image contrast by keeping bright light sources outside the field of view from striking the lens and, potentially, bouncing around inside that long tube to generate flare that, when coupled with atmospheric haze, can rob your image of detail and snap. In addition, lens hoods serve as valuable protection for that large, vulnerable, front lens element. It's easy to forget that you've got that long tube sticking out in front of your camera and accidentally whack the front of your lens into something. It's cheaper to replace a lens hood than it is to have a lens repaired, so you might find that a good hood is valuable protection for your prized optics.

When choosing a lens hood, it's important to have the right hood for the lens, usually the one offered for that lens by Canon or the third-party manufacturer. You want a hood that blocks precisely the right amount of light: neither too much light nor too little. A hood with a front diameter that is too small can show up in your pictures as vignetting. A hood that has a front diameter that's too large isn't stopping all the light it should. Generic lens hoods may not do the job.

When your telephoto is a zoom lens, it's even more important to get the right hood, because you need one that does what it is supposed to at both the wide-angle and telephoto ends of the zoom range. Lens hoods may be cylindrical, rectangular (shaped like the image frame), or petal shaped (that is, cylindrical, but with cut-out areas at the corners which correspond to the actual image area). Lens hoods should be mounted in the correct orientation (a bayonet mount for the hood on the front of the lens usually takes care of this).

Telephoto Extenders

Telephoto extenders (often called teleconverters outside the Canon world) multiply the actual focal length of your lens, giving you a longer telephoto for much less than the price of a lens with that actual focal length. These extenders fit between the lens and your camera and contain optical elements that magnify the image produced by the lens. Available in 1.4X and 2.0X configurations from Canon, an extender transforms, say, a 200mm lens into a 280mm or 400mm optic, respectively. Given the 70D's crop factor, your 200mm lens now has the same field of view as a 448mm or 640mm lens on a full-frame camera. At around $500 each, they're quite a bargain, aren't they?

Actually, there are some downsides. While extenders retain the closest focusing distance of your original lens, autofocus is maintained only if the lens's original maximum aperture is f/4 or larger (for the 1.4X extender) or f/2.8 or larger (for the 2X extender). The components reduce the effective aperture of any lens they are used with, by one f/stop with the 1.4X extender, and 2 f/stops with the 2X extender. So, your EF 200mm f/2.8L II USM becomes a 280mm f/4 or 400mm f/5.6 lens. Although Canon extenders are precision optical devices, they do cost you a little sharpness, but that improves when you reduce the aperture by a stop or two. Each of the extenders is compatible only with a particular set of lenses of 135mm focal length or greater, so you'll want to check Canon's compatibility chart to see if the component can be used with the lens you want to attach to it.

If your lenses are compatible and you're shooting under bright lighting conditions, the Canon Extender EF 1.4x III, and Canon Extender EF 2x III make handy accessories.

Macro Focusing

Some telephotos and telephoto zooms available for the 70D have particularly close focusing capabilities, making them *macro* lenses. Of course, the object is not necessarily to get close (get too close and you'll find it difficult to light your subject). What you're really looking for in a macro lens is to magnify the apparent size of the subject in the final image. Camera-to-subject distance is most important when you want to back up farther from your subject (say, to avoid spooking skittish insects or small animals). In that case, you'll want a macro lens with a longer focal length to allow that distance while retaining the desired magnification.

Canon makes 50mm, 60mm, 65mm, 100mm, and 180mm lenses with official macro designations. You'll also find macro lenses, macro zooms, and other close-focusing lenses available from Sigma, Tamron, and Tokina. If you want to focus closer with a macro lens, or any other lens, you can add an accessory called an *extension tube*, shown in Figure 10.16. These add-ons move the lens farther from the focal plane, allowing it to focus more closely. Canon also sells add-on close-up lenses, which look like filters, and allow lenses to focus more closely.

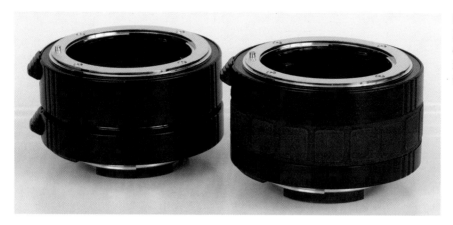

Figure 10.16
Extension tubes enable any lens to focus more closely to the subject.

Image Stabilization

Canon has a burgeoning line of more than a dozen lenses with built-in image stabilization (IS) capabilities. This feature uses lens elements that are shifted internally in response to the motion of the lens during handheld photography, countering the shakiness the camera and photographer produce and which telephoto lenses magnify. However, IS is not limited to long lenses; the feature works like a champ at the 17mm zoom position of Canon's EF-S 17-85mm f/4-5.6 IS USM and EF-S 17-55mm f/2.8 IS USM lenses. Other Canon IS lenses provide stabilization with zooms that are as wide as 24-28mm.

Image stabilization provides you with camera steadiness that's the equivalent of at least two or three shutter speed increments. (Canon claims four, which I feel may be optimistic.) This extra margin can be invaluable when you're shooting under dim lighting conditions or handholding a long lens for, say, wildlife photography. Perhaps that shot of a foraging deer calls for a shutter speed of 1/1,000th second at f/5.6 with your EF 100-400mm f/4.5-5.6L IS USM lens. Relax. You can shoot at 1/250th second at f/11 and get virtually the same results, as long as the deer doesn't decide to bound off.

Or, maybe you're shooting a high school play without a tripod or monopod, and you'd really, really like to use 1/15th second at f/4. Assuming the actors aren't flitting around the stage at high speed, your 17-85mm IS lens can grab the shot for you at its wide-angle position. However, keep these facts in mind:

- **IS doesn't stop action.** Unfortunately, no IS lens is a panacea to replace the action-stopping capabilities of a higher shutter speed. Image stabilization applies only to camera shake. You still need a fast shutter speed to freeze action. IS works great in low light, when you're using long lenses, and for macro photography. It's not always the best choice for action photography (unless you're willing to let subject motion become part of your image, as in Figure 10.17). In other situations, you may need enough light to allow a sufficiently high shutter speed. But in that case, IS can make your shot even sharper.

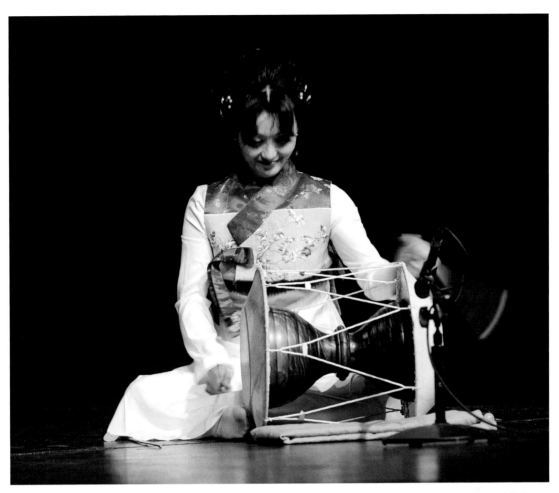

Figure 10.17 Image stabilization made it possible to shoot this concert photo with a 200mm lens at 1/60th second. Note that the drummer's hands are still a blur, but her beautiful costume is vividly sharp.

- **IS slows you down.** The process of adjusting the lens elements takes time, just as autofocus does, so you might find that IS adds to the lag between when you press the shutter and when the picture is actually taken. That's another reason why image stabilization might not be a good choice for sports.

- **Use when appropriate.** Some IS lenses produce worse results if you use them while you're panning, although newer Canon IS lenses have a mode that works fine when the camera is deliberately moved from side to side (or up and down) during exposure. Older lenses can confuse the motion with camera shake and overcompensate. You might want to switch off IS when panning or when your camera is mounted on a tripod.

- **Do you need IS at all?** Remember that an inexpensive monopod might be able to provide the same additional steadiness as an IS lens, at a much lower cost. If you're out in the field shooting wild animals or flowers and think a tripod isn't practical, try a monopod first.

IMAGE STABILIZATION: IN THE CAMERA OR IN THE LENS?

Sony's acquisition of Konica Minolta's dSLR assets and the introduction of an improved in-camera image-stabilization system has revived an old debate about whether IS belongs in the camera or in the lens. Perhaps it's my Canon bias showing, but I am quite happy not to have image stabilization available in the body itself. Here are some reasons:

■ Should in-camera IS fail, you have to send the whole camera in for repair, and camera repairs are generally more expensive than lens repairs. I like being able to simply switch to another lens if I have an IS problem.

■ IS in the camera doesn't steady your view in the viewfinder, whereas an IS lens shows you a steadied image as you shoot.

■ You're stuck with the IS system built into your camera. If an improved system is incorporated into a lens and the improvements are important to you, just trade in your old lens for the new one.

■ Optimized stabilization. Canon claims that it is able to produce the best possible image stabilization for each lens it introduces, something that would not be possible if a "one size fits all lenses" stabilization scheme had to be built into the camera.

Using the Lensbaby

I'm going to depart from my Canon-only regimen to include the wonderful Lensbaby line of optics, because Canon doesn't offer anything similar, nor as delightfully affordable. The Lensbaby comes in several varieties (including Edge 80, a shift-tilt model for about $300, and the Composer Pro shown in Figure 10.18), and uses distortion-heavy glass elements mounted on a system that allows you to bend, twist, and distort the lens's alignment to produce transmogrified images unlike anything else you've ever seen. Like the legendary cheap-o Diana and Holga cameras, the pictures are prized expressly because of their plastic image quality. Jack and Meg White (formerly of the White Stripes) have, in fact, sold personalized Diana and Holga cameras on their website for wacky *lomography* (named after the Lomo, another low-quality/high-concept camera). The various Lensbaby models are for more serious photographers, if you can say that about anyone who yearns to take pictures that look like they were shot through a glob of corn syrup.

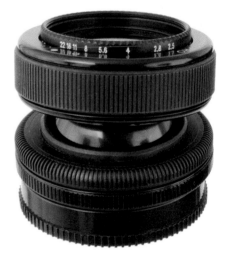

Figure 10.18 Lensbaby optics are specialized lens replacements with some special soft-focus features.

Lensbaby optics are capable of creating all sorts of special effects. You use a Lensbaby by shifting the front mount to move the lens's sweet spot to a particular point in the scene. This is basically a selective focus lens that gets very soft outside the sweet spot. There are several different types, which can be interchanged using the system's Optic Swap technology.

- **Macro.** A Lensbaby accessory makes it possible to use this tool for macro photography.

- **Wide-angle/telephoto conversion.** Add-on lenses convert the basic Lensbaby into a wide-angle or telephoto version.

- **Edge 80.** This is an 80mm f/2.8 lens with a flat field of focus—ideal for portraits. It has a 12-blade adjustable aperture, focuses as close as 17 inches, and functions as a tilt-shift lens. When canted, the Edge 80 delivers a slice of tack sharp focus through the image, bordered by a soft blur. When pointed straight ahead, Edge 80 can be used like a conventional lens. You can also use it in any of the traditional selective focus applications you'd use one of Canon's PC-E lenses for—but *not* for perspective correction. (It tilts, but does not shift from side to side.)

- **Creative aperture kit.** Various shaped cutouts can be used in place of the regular aperture inserts that control depth-of-field. These shapes can include things like hearts, stars, and other shapes.

- **Optic swap kit.** This three-lens accessory kit provides different adapters that include a pinhole lens, plastic lens, and single glass lens.

Among the interchangeable components are the Sweet 35, Fisheye, Soft Focus, Double Glass, Single Glass, and Pinhole lenses. Models include the Composer Pro, Composer, Muse, Control Freak, and Scout, each with varying amounts of adjustments. (The Scout does not bend at all, making it ideal for use with the fisheye component.)

The other Lensbaby models, like the Composer Pro, have the same tilting lens configuration as previous editions, but are designed for easier and more precise distorting movements. Hold the camera with your finger gripping the knobs as you bend the camera to move the central "sweet spot" (sharp area) to any portion of your image. With two (count 'em) multicoated optical glass lens elements, you'll get a blurry image, but the amount of distortion is under your control. F/stops from f/2 to f/22 are available to increase/decrease depth-of-field and allow you to adjust exposure. The 50mm lens focuses down to 12 inches and is strictly manual focus/manual exposure in operation. At up to $300 or so, these lenses are not cheap accessories, but there is really no other easy way to achieve the kind of looks you can get with a Lensbaby.

Figures 10.19 and 10.20 are examples of the type of effect you can get, in photographs crafted by Cleveland photographer Nancy Balluck. She also produced the back cover photography of yours truly, and one of her specialties is Lensbaby effects.

Nancy regularly gives demonstrations and classes on the use of these optics, and you can follow her work at www.nancyballuckphotography.com.

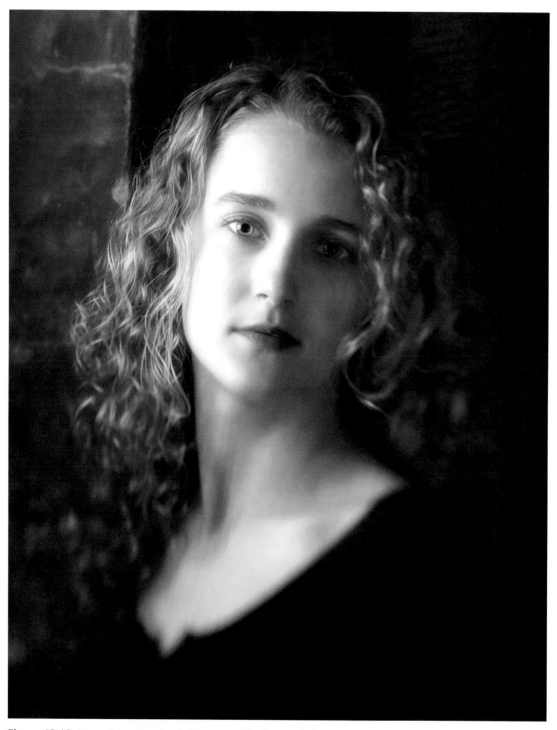

Figure 10.19 Everything is uniquely blurry outside the Lensbaby's "sweet spot," but you can move that spot around within your frame at will.

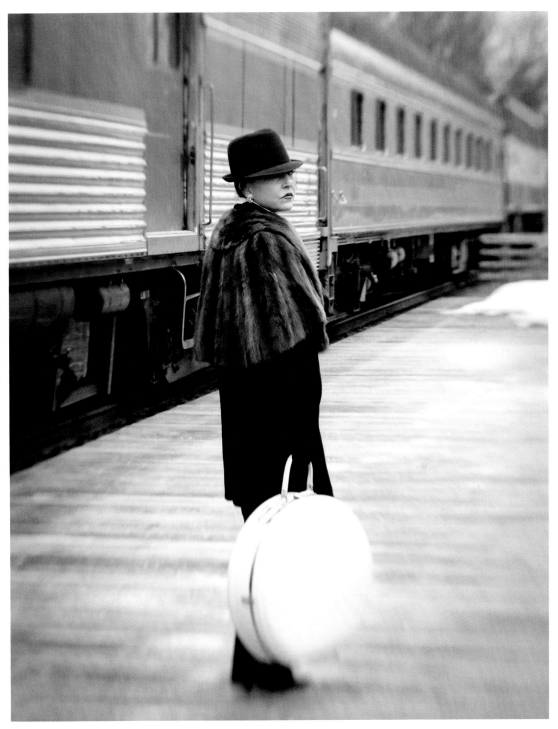

Figure 10.20 They can be used for selective focus effects, and can simulate the dreamy look of some old-style cameras.

11

Working with Light

Unless you're extraordinarily lucky, or supremely observant, great lighting, like most things of artistic value, doesn't happen by accident. It's entirely possible that you'll randomly encounter a scene or subject that's bathed in marvelous lighting, illumination that perfectly sculpts an image in highlights and shadows. But how often can you count on such luck? Ansel Adams is often quoted as saying (although he probably didn't) that "The harder I work, the luckier I get."

The great photographer *was* known for his patience in seeking out the best lighting for a composition, and he *did* actually say, "A good photograph is knowing where to stand." My own take on excellence in illumination is that you have to possess the ability to *recognize* effective lighting when it is already present, and have the skill to manipulate the light when it is not.

All successful photographers and artists have an intimate understanding of the importance of light in shaping an image. Rembrandt was a master of using light to create moods and reveal the character of his subjects. The late artist Thomas Kinkade's official tagline was "Painter of Light." Dean Collins, co-founder of Finelight Studios, revolutionized how a whole generation of photographers learned and used lighting. Photo guru Ed Pierce has a popular seminar called "Captivated by the Light." It's impossible to underestimate how the use of light adds to—and how misuse can detract from—your photographs.

All forms of visual art use light to shape the finished product. Sculptors don't have control over the light used to illuminate their finished work, so they must create shapes using planes and curved surfaces so that the form envisioned by the artist comes to life from a variety of viewing and lighting angles. Painters, in contrast, have absolute control over both shape and light in their work, as well as the viewing angle, so they can use both the contours of their two-dimensional subjects and the qualities of the "light" they use to illuminate those subjects to evoke the image they want to produce.

Photography is a third form of art. The photographer may have little or no control over the subject (other than posing human subjects) but can often adjust both viewing angle *and* the nature of the light source to create a particular compelling image. The direction and intensity of the light sources create the shapes and textures that we see. The distribution and proportions determine the contrast and tonal values: whether the image is stark or high key, or muted and low in contrast. The colors of the light (because even "white" light has a color balance that the sensor can detect), and how much of those colors the subject reflects or absorbs, paint the hues visible in the image.

As a 70D photographer, you must learn to be a painter and sculptor of light if you want to move from *taking* a picture to *making* a photograph. This chapter introduces using the two main types of illumination: *continuous* lighting (such as daylight, incandescent, or fluorescent sources) and the brief, but brilliant snippets of light we call *electronic flash.*

Continuous Illumination versus Electronic Flash

Continuous lighting is exactly what you might think: uninterrupted illumination that is available all the time during a shooting session. Daylight, moonlight, and the artificial lighting encountered both indoors and outdoors count as continuous light sources (although all of them can be "interrupted" by passing clouds, solar eclipses, a blown fuse, or simply by switching off a lamp). Indoor continuous illumination includes both the lights that are there already (such as incandescent lamps or overhead fluorescent lights indoors) and fixtures you supply yourself, including photoflood lamps or reflectors used to bounce existing light onto your subject.

Electronic flash is notable because it can be much more intense than continuous lighting, lasts only a brief moment, and can be much more portable than supplementary incandescent sources. It's a light source you can carry with you and use anywhere. Indeed, your 70D has a flip-up electronic flash unit built in.

But you can also use an external flash, either mounted on the 70D's accessory shoe or used off-camera and linked with a cable or triggered by a slave light (which sets off a flash when it senses the firing of another unit). Studio flash units are electronic flash, too, and aren't limited to "professional" shooters, as there are economical "monolight" (one-piece flash/power supply) units available in the $200 price range. You can buy a couple to store in a closet and use to set up a home studio, or use as supplementary lighting when traveling away from home.

There are advantages and disadvantages to each type of illumination. Here's a quick checklist of pros and cons:

- **Lighting preview—Pro: continuous lighting.** With continuous lighting, you always know exactly what kind of lighting effect you're going to get and, if multiple light sources are used, how they will interact with each other, as shown in Figure 11.1, where the main light was the sun, but a bit of fill was provided by a gold reflector held up a few feet off-camera to her left. With electronic flash, the general effect you're going to see may be a mystery until you've built some experience, and you may need to review a shot on the LCD, make some adjustments, and then reshoot to get the look you want. (In this sense, a digital camera's review capabilities replace the Polaroid test shots pro photographers relied on in decades past.)

- **Lighting preview—Con: electronic flash.** With flash, the general effect you're going to see may be a mystery until you've built some experience, and you may need to review a shot on the LCD monitor, make some adjustments, and then reshoot to get the look you want. (In this sense, a digital camera's review capabilities replace the Polaroid test shots pro photographers relied on in decades past.) An image like the one in Figure 11.1 would have been difficult to achieve with an off-camera battery-powered flash unit, because it would be tricky to preview exactly how the shadows would fall without a true continuous modeling light.

- **Exposure calculation—Pro: continuous lighting.** Your 70D has no problem calculating exposure for continuous lighting, because the illumination remains constant and can be measured through a sensor that interprets the light reaching the viewfinder. The amount of light available just before the exposure will, in almost all cases, be the same amount of light present when the shutter is released. The 70D's Spot metering mode can be used to measure and compare the proportions of light in the highlights and shadows, so you can make an adjustment (such as using more or less fill light) if necessary. You can even use a handheld light meter to measure the light yourself.

Figure 11.1
You always know how the lighting will look when using continuous illumination.

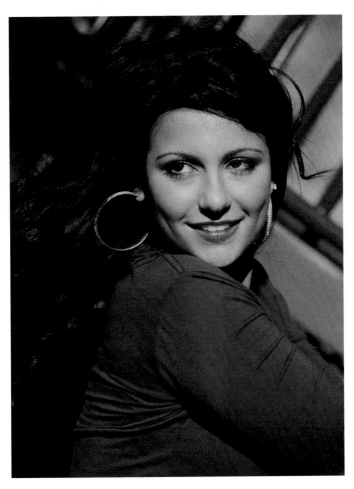

- **Exposure calculation—Con: electronic flash.** Electronic flash illumination doesn't exist until the flash fires and so can't be measured by the 70D's exposure sensor when the mirror is flipped up during the exposure. Instead, the light must be measured metering the intensity of a pre-flash triggered an instant before the main flash, as it is reflected back to the camera and through the lens. An alternative is to use a sensor built into an external flash itself and measure reflected light that has not traveled through the lens. If you have a do-it-yourself bent, there are handheld flash meters, too, including models that measure both flash and continuous light.

- **Evenness of illumination—Pro/con: continuous lighting.** Of continuous light sources, daylight, in particular, provides illumination that tends to fill an image completely, lighting up the foreground, background, and your subject almost equally. Shadows do come into play, of course, so you might need to use reflectors or fill-in light sources to even out the illumination further, but barring objects that block large sections of your image from daylight, the light is spread fairly evenly. Indoors, however, continuous lighting is commonly less evenly distributed. The average living room, for example, has hot spots and dark corners. But on the plus side, you can *see* this uneven illumination and compensate with additional lamps.

- **Evenness of illumination—Con: electronic flash.** Electronic flash units (like continuous light sources such as lamps that don't have the advantage of being located 93 million miles from the subject) suffer from the effects of their proximity. The *inverse square law*, first applied to both gravity and light by Sir Isaac Newton, dictates that as a light source's distance increases from the subject, the amount of light reaching the subject falls off proportionately to the square of the distance. In plain English, that means that a flash or lamp that's 12 feet away from a subject provides only one-quarter as much illumination as a source that's 6 feet away (rather than half as much). (See Figure 11.2.) This translates into relatively shallow "depth-of-light."

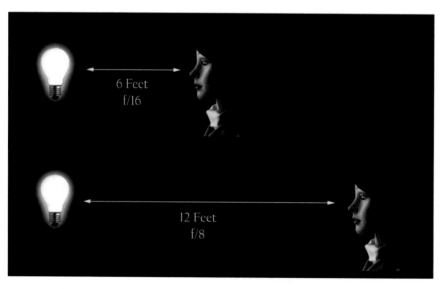

6 Feet
f/16

12 Feet
f/8

Figure 11.2
A light source that is twice as far away provides only one-quarter as much illumination.

■ **Action stopping—Pro: electronic flash.** When it comes to the ability to freeze moving objects in their tracks, the advantage goes to electronic flash. The brief duration of electronic flash serves as a very high "shutter speed" when the flash is the main or only source of illumination for the photo. Your 70D's shutter speed may be set for 1/250th second during a flash exposure, but if the flash illumination predominates, the *effective* exposure time will be the 1/1,000th to 1/50,000th second or less duration of the flash, as you can see in Figure 11.3, because the flash unit reduces the amount of light released by cutting short the duration of the flash. The only fly in the ointment is that, if the ambient light is strong enough, it may produce a secondary, "ghost" exposure, as I'll explain later in this chapter.

Figure 11.3
Electronic flash can freeze almost any action.

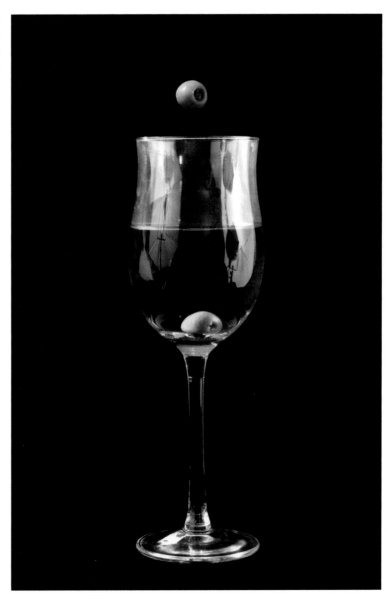

- **Action stopping—Con: continuous lighting.** Action stopping with continuous light sources is completely dependent on the shutter speed you've dialed in on the camera. And the speeds available are dependent on the amount of light available and your ISO sensitivity setting. Outdoors in daylight, there will probably be enough sunlight to let you shoot at 1/2,500th second and f/6.3 with a non-grainy sensitivity setting of ISO 400. That's a fairly useful combination of settings if you're not using a super-telephoto with a small maximum aperture. But inside, the reduced illumination quickly has you pushing your 70D to its limits. For example, if you're shooting indoor sports, there probably won't be enough available light to allow you to use a 1/2,000th second shutter speed (although I routinely shoot indoor basketball with my 70D at ISO 1600 and 1/500th second at f/4). In many indoor sports situations, you may find yourself limited to 1/500th second or slower.

- **Cost—Pro: continuous lighting.** Incandescent or fluorescent lamps are generally much less expensive than electronic flash units, which can easily cost several hundred dollars. I've used everything from desktop high-intensity lamps to reflector flood lights for continuous illumination at very little cost. There are lamps made especially for photographic purposes, too, priced up to $50 or so. Maintenance is economical, too: many incandescent or fluorescents use bulbs that cost only a few dollars.

- **Cost—Con: electronic flash.** Electronic flash units aren't particularly cheap. The lowest-cost dedicated flash designed specifically for the Canon dSLRs is about $150. Such units are limited in features, however, and intended for those with entry-level cameras. Plan on spending some money to get the features that a sophisticated electronic flash offers.

- **Flexibility—Pro: electronic flash.** Electronic flash's action-freezing power allows you to work without a tripod in the studio (and elsewhere), adding flexibility and speed when choosing angles and positions. Flash units can be easily filtered, and, because the filtration is placed over the light source rather than the lens, you don't need to use high-quality filter material. Roscoe or Lee lighting gels, which may be too flimsy to use in front of the lens, can be mounted or taped in front of your flash with ease.

- **Flexibility—Con: continuous lighting.** Because incandescent and fluorescent lamps are not as bright as electronic flash, the slower shutter speeds required (see Action stopping, above) mean that you may have to use a tripod more often, especially when shooting portraits. The incandescent variety of continuous lighting gets hot, especially in the studio, and the side effects range from discomfort (for your human models) to disintegration (if you happen to be shooting perishable foods like ice cream). The heat also makes it more difficult to add filtration to incandescent sources.

Continuous Lighting Basics

While continuous lighting and its effects are generally much easier to visualize and use than electronic flash, there are some factors you need to take into account, particularly the color temperature of the light. (Color temperature concerns aren't exclusive to continuous light sources, of course, but the variations tend to be more extreme and less predictable than those of electronic flash.)

Living with Color Temperature

Canon and vendors with equipment compatible with the 70D have been valiant in their efforts to help us tame the color balance monster. One popular color balancing technology lives on in the form of ExpoDisc filter/caps (see Figure 11.4) and their ilk (www.expoimaging.com), which allow the camera's built-in custom white balance measuring feature to evaluate the illumination that passes through the disc/cap/filter/Pringle's can lid, or whatever neutral-color substitute you employ. (A white or gray card also works.)

Color temperature, in practical terms, is how "bluish" or how "reddish" the light appears to be to the digital camera's sensor. Indoor illumination is quite warm, comparatively, and appears reddish to the sensor. Daylight, in contrast, seems much bluer to

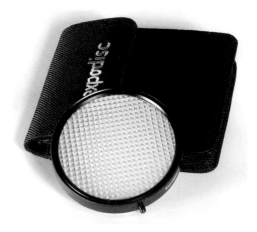

Figure 11.4 The ExpoDisc is placed on a lens and used as a neutral subject for measuring white balance.

the sensor. Our eyes (our brains, actually) are quite adaptable to these variations, so white objects don't appear to have an orange tinge when viewed indoors, nor do they seem excessively blue outdoors in full daylight. Yet, these color temperature variations are real and the sensor is not fooled. To capture the most accurate colors, we need to take the color temperature into account in setting the color balance (or *white balance*) of the 70D—either automatically using the camera's smarts or manually, using our own knowledge and experience.

Color temperature can be confusing, because of a seeming contradiction in how color temperatures are named: warmer (more reddish) color temperatures (measured in degrees Kelvin) are the *lower* numbers, while cooler (bluer) color temperatures are *higher* numbers. It might not make sense to say that 3,400K is warmer than 6,000K, but that's the way it is. If it helps, think of a glowing red ember contrasted with a white-hot welder's torch, rather than fire and ice.

The confusion comes from physics. Scientists calculate color temperature from the light emitted by a mythical object called a black body radiator, which absorbs all the radiant energy that strikes it, and reflects none at all. Such a black body not only *absorbs* light perfectly, but it *emits* it perfectly when heated (and since nothing in the universe is perfect, that makes it mythical).

At a particular physical temperature, this imaginary object always emits light of the same wavelength or color. That makes it possible to define color temperature in terms of actual temperature in degrees on the Kelvin scale that scientists use. Incandescent light, for example, typically has a color temperature of 3,200K to 3,400K. Daylight might range from 5,500K to 6,000K. Each type of illumination we use for photography has its own color temperature range—with some cautions. The next sections will summarize everything you need to know about the qualities of these light sources.

Daylight

Daylight is produced by the sun, and so is moonlight (which is just reflected sunlight). Daylight is present, of course, even when you can't see the sun. When sunlight is direct, it can be bright and harsh. If daylight is diffused by clouds, softened by bouncing off objects such as walls or your photo reflectors, or filtered by shade, it can be much dimmer and less contrasty.

Daylight's color temperature can vary quite widely. It is highest (most blue) at noon when the sun is directly overhead, because the light is traveling through a minimum amount of the filtering layer we call the atmosphere. The color temperature at high noon may be 6,000K. At other times of day, the sun is lower in the sky and the particles in the air provide a filtering effect that warms the illumination to about 5,500K for most of the day. Starting an hour before dusk and for an hour after sunrise, the warm appearance of the sunlight is even visible to our eyes when the color temperature may dip below 4,500K, as shown in Figure 11.5.

Because you'll be taking so many photos in daylight, you'll want to learn how to use or compensate for the brightness and contrast of sunlight, as well as how to deal with its color temperature. I'll provide some hints later in this chapter.

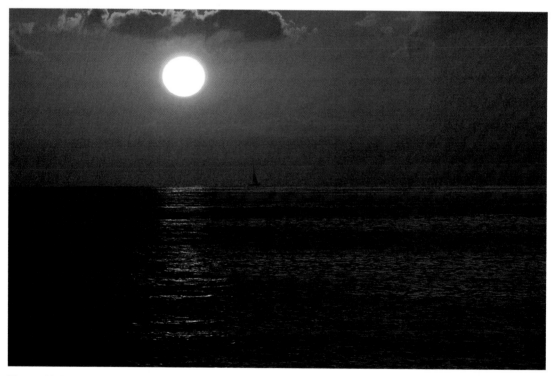

Figure 11.5 At dawn and dusk, the color temperature of daylight may dip below 4,500K, providing this reddish rendition.

Incandescent/Tungsten Light

The term incandescent or tungsten illumination is usually applied to the direct descendents of Thomas Edison's original electric lamp. Such lights consist of a glass bulb that contains a vacuum, or is filled with a halogen gas, and contains a tungsten filament that is heated by an electrical current, producing photons and heat. Tungsten-halogen lamps are a variation on the basic light bulb, using a more rugged (and longer lasting) filament that can be heated to a higher temperature, housed in a thicker glass or quartz envelope, and filled with iodine or bromine ("halogen") gases. The higher temperature allows tungsten-halogen (or quartz-halogen/quartz-iodine, depending on their construction) lamps to burn "hotter" and whiter. Although popular for automobile headlamps today, they are also popular for photographic illumination. Although incandescent illumination isn't a perfect black body radiator, it's close enough that the color temperature of such lamps can be precisely calculated and used for photography without concerns about color variation (at least, until the very end of the lamp's life).

Fluorescent Light/Other Light Sources

Fluorescent light has some advantages in terms of illumination, but some disadvantages from a photographic standpoint, especially when it comes to CFLs. This type of lamp generates light through an electro-chemical reaction that emits most of its energy as visible light, rather than heat, which is why the bulbs don't get as hot. The type of light produced varies depending on the phosphor coatings and type of gas in the tube. So, the illumination fluorescent bulbs produce can vary widely in its characteristics.

That's not great news for photographers. Different types of lamps have different "color temperatures" that can't be precisely measured in degrees Kelvin, because the light isn't produced by heating. Worse, fluorescent lamps have a discontinuous spectrum of light that can have some colors missing entirely, producing that substandard Color Rendering Index, discussed next. A particular type of tube can lack certain shades of red or other colors (see Figure 11.6), which is why fluorescent lamps and other alternative technologies such as sodium-vapor illumination can produce ghastly looking human skin tones. Their spectra can lack the reddish tones we associate with healthy skin and emphasize the blues and greens popular in horror movies.

Adjusting White Balance

I showed you how to adjust white balance bracketing in Chapter 4 (there's more on bracketing in Chapter 8, too). In most cases, however, the 70D will do a good job of calculating white balance for you, so Auto can be used as your choice most of the time. Use the preset values or set a custom white balance that matches the current shooting conditions when you need to. The only really problematic light sources are likely to be fluorescents. Vendors, such as GE and Sylvania, may actually provide a figure known as the *color rendering index* (or CRI), which is a measure of how accurately a particular light source represents standard colors, using a scale of 0 (some sodium-vapor lamps) to 100 (daylight and most incandescent lamps). Daylight fluorescents and deluxe cool white fluorescents might have a CRI of about 79 to 95, which is perfectly acceptable for most

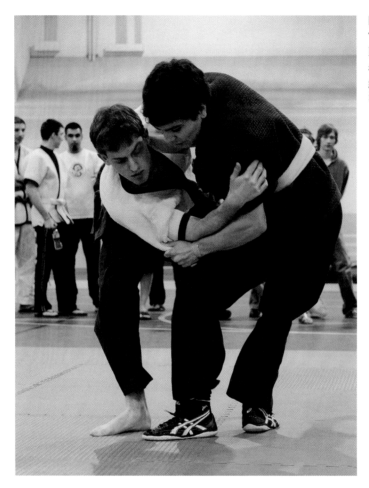

photographic applications. Warm white fluorescents might have a CRI of 55. White deluxe mercury vapor lights are less suitable with a CRI of 45, while low-pressure sodium lamps can vary from CRI 0-18.

Remember that if you shoot RAW, you can specify the white balance of your image when you import it into Photoshop, Photoshop Elements, or another image editor using your preferred RAW converter. While color-balancing filters that fit on the front of the lens exist, they are primarily useful for film cameras, because film's color balance can't be tweaked as extensively or as easily as that of a sensor.

Electronic Flash Basics

Until you delve into the situation deeply enough, it might appear that serious photographers have a love/hate relationship with electronic flash. You'll often hear that flash photography is less natural looking, and that the built-in flash in most cameras should never be used as the primary source of illumination because it provides a harsh, garish look. Indeed, most "pro" cameras like the Canon EOS 1D X, Ds Mark III, 6D, and 5D Mark III don't have a built-in flash at all. Available ("continuous") lighting is praised, and built-in flash photography seems to be roundly denounced.

In truth, however, the bias is against *bad* flash photography. Indeed, flash has become the studio light source of choice for pro photographers, because it's more intense (and its intensity can be varied to order by the photographer), freezes action, frees you from using a tripod (unless you want to use one to lock down a composition), and has a snappy, consistent light quality that matches daylight. (While color balance changes as the flash duration shortens, some Canon flash units can communicate to the camera the exact white balance provided for that shot.) And even pros will cede that the built-in flash of the 70D has some important uses as an adjunct to existing light, particularly to illuminate dark shadows using a technique called *fill flash*.

But electronic flash isn't as inherently easy to use as continuous lighting. As I noted earlier, electronic flash units are more expensive, don't show you exactly what the lighting effect will be (unless you use a second source called a *modeling light* for a preview), and the exposure of electronic flash units is more difficult to calculate accurately.

Fire When Ready!

Once the capacitor is charged, the burst of light that produces the main exposure can be initiated by a signal from the 70D that commands the internal or connected flash units to fire. External strobes can be linked to the camera in several different ways:

- **Camera mounted/hardwired external dedicated flash.** Units offered by Canon or other vendors that are compatible with Canon's lighting system can be clipped onto the accessory "hot" shoe on top of the camera or linked through a wired system such as the Canon Off Shoe Camera Cord OC-E3.

- **Wireless dedicated flash.** A compatible unit can be triggered by signals produced by a preflash (before the main flash burst begins), which offers two-way communication between the camera and flash unit. The triggering flash can be the 70D's built-in unit, an external flash unit in Master mode, or a wireless non-flashing accessory, such as the Canon Speedlite Transmitter ST-E2 and new radio-controlled wireless trigger, the Speedlite Transmitter ST-E3-RT, which each do nothing but "talk" to the external flashes. You'll find more on this mode in Chapter 12.

- **Wired, non-intelligent mode.** If you use a third-party adapter for the hot shoe that has a PC/X connector, you can connect non-dedicated flash units, including studio strobes, through a non-intelligent camera/flash link that sends just one piece of information, one way: it tells a connected flash to fire. There is no other exchange of information between the camera and flash. The PC/X adapter connector can be used to link the 70D to studio flash units, manual flash, flash units from other vendors that can use a PC cable, or even Canon brand Speedlites that you elect to connect to the 70D in "unintelligent" mode.

■ **Infrared/radio transmitter/receivers.** Another way to link flash units to the 70D is through third-party wireless infrared or radio *transmitters*, like a Pocket Wizard, Radio Popper, or the Paul C. Buff CyberSync trigger shown in Figure 11.7. These are generally mounted on the accessory shoe of the camera, and emit a signal when the 70D sends a command to fire through the hot shoe. The simplest of these function as a wireless PC/X connector, with no other communication between the camera and flash (other than the instruction to fire). However, sophisticated units have their own built-in controls and can send additional commands to the receivers when connected to compatible flash units. I use one to adjust the power output of my Alien Bees studio flash from the camera, without the need to walk over to the flash itself.

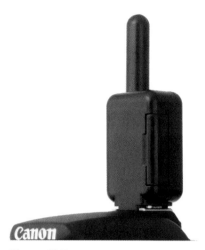

Figure 11.7 A wireless trigger can command external flash units to fire.

■ **Simple slave connection.** In the days before intelligent wireless communication, the most common way to trigger off-camera, non-wired flash units was through a *slave* unit. These can be small external triggers connected to the remote flash (or built into the flash itself), and set off when the slave's optical sensor detects a burst initiated by the camera itself. When it "sees" the main flash (from the 70D's built-in flash, or another flash), the slave flash units are triggered quickly enough to contribute to the same exposure. The main problem with this type of connection—other than the lack of any intelligent communication between the camera and flash—is that the slave may be fooled by any pre-flashes that are emitted by the other strobes, and fire too soon. Modern slave triggers have a special "digital" mode that ignores the pre-flash and fires only from the main flash burst.

How Electronic Flash Works

The bursts of light we call electronic flash are produced by a flash of photons generated by an electrical charge that is accumulated in a component called a *capacitor* and then directed through a glass tube containing xenon gas, which absorbs the energy and emits the brief flash. For the pop-up flash built into the 70D, the full burst of light lasts about 1/1,000th of a second and provides enough illumination to shoot a subject 10 feet away at f/4 using the ISO 100 setting. In a more typical situation, you'd use ISO 200, f/5.6 to f/8 and photograph something 8 to 10 feet away. As you can see, the built-in flash is somewhat limited in range; you'll see why external flash units are often a good idea later in this chapter.

An electronic flash (whether built in or connected to the 70D through an adapter's PC terminal or a cable plugged into a hot shoe adapter) is triggered at the instant of exposure, during a period when the sensor is fully exposed by the shutter. As I mentioned earlier in this book, the 70D has a vertically traveling shutter that consists of two curtains. The first curtain opens and moves to the opposite side of the frame, at which point the shutter is completely open. The flash can be triggered at this point (so-called *1st curtain sync*), making the flash exposure. Then, after a delay that can vary from 30 seconds to 1/250th second (with the 70D; other cameras may sync at a faster or slower speed), a second curtain begins moving across the sensor plane, covering up the sensor again. If the flash is triggered just before the second curtain starts to close, then *2nd curtain sync* is used. In both cases, though, a shutter speed of 1/250th second is the maximum that can be used to take a photo.

Figure 11.8 illustrates how this works. At upper left, you can see a fanciful illustration of a generic shutter (your 70D's shutter does *not* look like this), with both curtains tightly closed. At upper right, the first curtain begins to move downward, starting to expose a narrow slit that reveals the sensor behind the shutter. At lower left, the first curtain moves downward farther until, as you can see at lower right in the figure, the sensor is fully exposed.

Ghost Images

The difference between triggering the flash when the shutter just opens, or just when it begins to close might not seem like much. But whether you use 1st curtain sync (the default setting) or 2nd curtain sync (an optional setting) can make a significant difference to your photograph *if the ambient light in your scene also contributes to the image.* You can set either of these sync modes in the Shooting 2 menu, under Flash Control and the Built-in Flash Setting and External Flash Func. Setting options.

At faster shutter speeds, particularly 1/250th second, there isn't much time for the ambient light to register, unless it is very bright. It's likely that the electronic flash will provide almost all the illumination, so 1st curtain sync or 2nd curtain sync isn't very important. However, at slower shutter

Figure 11.8
A focal plane shutter has two curtains, the upper, or front curtain, and a lower, second curtain.

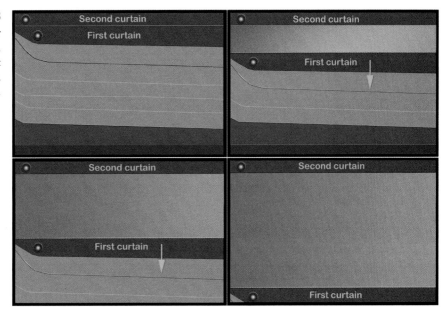

speeds, or with very bright ambient light levels, there is a significant difference, particularly if your subject is moving, or the camera isn't steady.

In any of those situations, the ambient light will register as a second image accompanying the flash exposure, and if there is movement (camera or subject), that additional image will not be in the same place as the flash exposure. It will show as a ghost image and, if the movement is significant enough, as a blurred ghost image trailing in front of or behind your subject in the direction of the movement.

As I noted, when you're using 1st curtain sync, the flash's main burst goes off the instant the shutter opens fully (a pre-flash used to measure exposure in auto flash modes fires *before* the shutter opens). This produces an image of the subject on the sensor. Then, the shutter remains open for an additional period (30 seconds to 1/250th second, as I said). If your subject is moving, say, toward the right side of the frame, the ghost image produced by the ambient light will produce a blur on the right side of the original subject image, making it look as if your sharp (flash-produced) image is chasing the ghost. For those of us who grew up with lightning-fast superheroes who always left a ghost trail *behind them*, that looks unnatural (see Figure 11.9).

So, Canon uses 2nd curtain sync to remedy the situation. In that mode, the shutter opens, as before. The shutter remains open for its designated duration, and the ghost image forms. If your subject moves from the left side of the frame to the right side, the ghost will move from left to right, too. *Then*, about 1.5 milliseconds before the second shutter curtain closes, the flash is triggered, producing a nice, sharp flash image *ahead* of the ghost image. Voilà! We have monsieur *Speed Racer* out-driving his own trailing image.

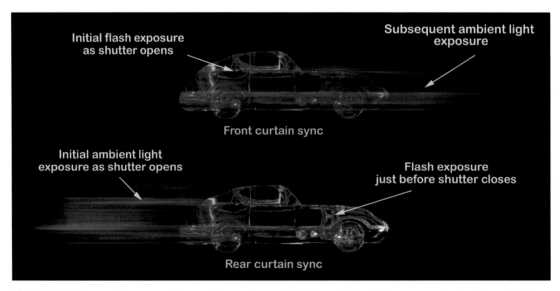

Figure 11.9 1st curtain sync produces an image that trails in front of the flash exposure (top), whereas 2nd curtain sync creates a more "natural looking" trail behind the flash image.

Avoiding Sync Speed Problems

Using a shutter speed faster than 1/250th second can cause problems. Triggering the electronic flash only when the shutter is completely open makes a lot of sense if you think about what's going on. To obtain shutter speeds faster than 1/250th second, the 70D exposes only part of the sensor at one time, by starting the second curtain on its journey before the first curtain has completely opened, as shown in Figure 11.10. That effectively provides a briefer exposure as a slit, narrower than the full height of the sensor, passes over the surface of the sensor. If the flash were to fire during the time when the first and second curtains partially obscured the sensor, only the slit that was actually open would be exposed.

You'd end up with only a narrow band, representing the portion of the sensor that was exposed when the picture is taken. For shutter speeds *faster* than 1/250th second, the second curtain begins moving *before* the first curtain reaches the bottom of the frame. As a result, a moving slit, the distance between the first and second curtains, exposes one portion of the sensor at a time as it moves from the top to the bottom. Figure 11.10 shows three views of our typical (but imaginary) focal plane shutter. At left is pictured the closed shutter; in the middle version you can see the first curtain has moved down about 1/4 of the distance from the top; and in the right-hand version, the second curtain has started to "chase" the first curtain across the frame toward the bottom.

If the flash is triggered while this slit is moving, only the exposed portion of the sensor will receive any illumination. You end up with a photo like the one shown in Figure 11.11. Note that a band across the bottom of the image is black. That's a shadow of the second shutter curtain, which had started to move when the flash was triggered. Sharp-eyed readers will wonder why the black band is at the *bottom* of the frame rather than at the top, where the second curtain begins its journey. The answer is simple: your lens flips the image upside down and forms it on the sensor in a reversed position. You never notice that, because the camera is smart enough to show you the pixels that make up your photo in their proper orientation. But this image flip is why, if your sensor gets dirty and you detect a spot of dust in the upper half of a test photo, if cleaning manually, you need to look for the speck in the *bottom* half of the sensor.

I generally end up with sync speed problems only when shooting in the studio, using studio flash units rather than my 70D's built-in flash or a Canon-dedicated Speedlite. That's because if you're using either type of "smart" flash, the camera knows that a strobe is attached, and remedies any

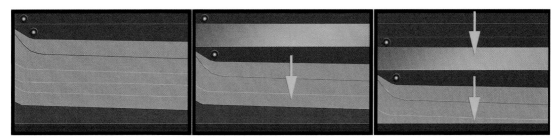

Figure 11.10 A closed shutter (left); partially open shutter as the first curtain begins to move downward (middle); only part of the sensor is exposed as the slit moves (right).

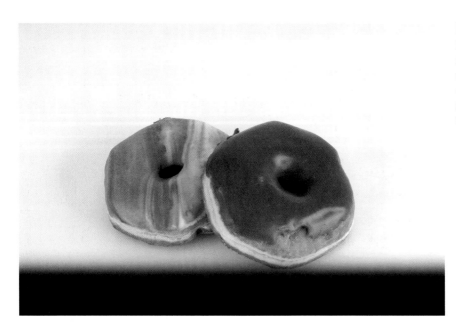

Figure 11.11
If a shutter speed faster than 1/250th second is used, you can end up photographing only a portion of the image.

unintentional goof in shutter speed settings. If you happen to set the 70D's shutter to a faster speed in Tv or M mode, the camera will automatically adjust the shutter speed down to 1/250th second. In Av, P, or any of the automatic modes, where the 70D selects the shutter speed, it will never choose a shutter speed higher than 1/250th second when using flash. In P mode, shutter speed is automatically set between 1/60th to 1/250th second when using flash.

But when using a non-dedicated flash, such as a studio unit plugged into an adapter with a PC/X connector, the camera has no way of knowing that a flash is connected, so shutter speeds faster than 1/250th second can be set inadvertently. Note that the 70D can use a feature called *high-speed sync* that allows shutter speeds faster than 1/250th second with certain external dedicated Canon flash units. When using high-speed sync, the flash fires a continuous serious of bursts at reduced power for the entire duration of the exposure, so that the illumination is able to expose the sensor as the slit moves. High-speed sync is set using the controls on the attached and powered-up compatible external flash.

Determining Exposure

Calculating the proper exposure for an electronic flash photograph is a bit more complicated than determining the settings by continuous light. The right exposure isn't simply a function of how far away your subject is (which the 70D can figure out based on the autofocus distance that's locked in just prior to taking the picture). Various objects reflect more or less light at the same distance so, obviously, the camera needs to measure the amount of light reflected back and through the lens. Yet, as the flash itself isn't available for measuring until it's triggered, the 70D has nothing to measure.

The solution is to fire the flash twice. The initial shot is a pre-flash that can be analyzed, then followed by a main flash that's given exactly the calculated intensity needed to provide a correct exposure. As a result, the primary flash may be longer for distant objects and shorter for closer subjects, depending on the required intensity for exposure. This through-the-lens evaluative flash exposure system is called E-TTL II, and it operates whenever the pop-up internal flash is used, or you have attached a Canon dedicated flash unit to the 70D.

Guide Numbers

Guide numbers, usually abbreviated GN, are a way of specifying the power of an electronic flash in a way that can be used to determine the right f/stop to use at a particular shooting distance and ISO setting. In fact, before automatic flash units became prevalent, the GN was actually used to do just that. A GN is usually given as a pair of numbers for both feet and meters that represent the range at ISO 100. For example, the 70D's built-in flash has a GN of 12/39 (meters/feet) at ISO 100. To calculate the right exposure at that ISO setting, you'd divide the guide number by the distance to arrive at the appropriate f/stop.

Using the 70D's built-in flash as an example, at ISO 100 with its GN of 43, if you wanted to shoot a subject at a distance of 10 feet, you'd use f/3.9 (39 divided by 10; round to f/4 for simplicity's sake). At 8 feet, an f/stop of f/5.3 (round up to f/5.6) would be used. Some quick mental calculations with the GN will give you any particular electronic flash's range. You can easily see that the built-in flash would begin to peter out at about 15 feet, where you'd need an aperture of roughly f/2.8 at ISO 100. Of course, in the real world you'd probably bump the sensitivity up to a setting of ISO 400 so you could use a more practical f/5.6 at that distance.

Today, guide numbers are most useful for comparing the power of various flash units. You don't need to be a math genius to see that an electronic flash with a GN of, say, 190 would be *a lot* more powerful than your built-in flash (at ISO 100, you could use f/13 instead of f/2.8 at 15 feet).

Getting Started with the Built-In Flash

The Canon 70D's built-in flash is a handy accessory because it is available as required, without the need to carry an external flash around with you constantly. The next sections explain how to use the flip-up flash in the various Basic Zone and Creative Zone modes.

Basic Zone Flash

When the 70D is set to one of the Basic Zone modes (except for Landscape, Sports, or Flash Off modes), the built-in flash will pop up when needed to provide extra illumination in low-light situations, or when your subject matter is backlit and could benefit from some fill flash. The flash doesn't pop up in Landscape mode because the flash doesn't have enough reach to have much effect for pictures of distant vistas in any case; nor does the flash pop up automatically in Sports mode, because you'll often want to use shutter speeds faster than 1/250th second and/or be shooting subjects that are out of flash range. Pop-up flash is disabled in Flash Off mode for obvious reasons.

If you happen to be shooting a landscape photo and do want to use flash (say, to add some illumination to a subject that's closer to the camera), or you want flash with your sports photos, or you *don't* want the flash popping up all the time when using one of the other Basic Zone modes, switch to an appropriate Creative Zone mode and use that instead.

Creative Zone Flash

When you're using a Creative Zone mode, you'll have to judge for yourself when flash might be useful, and flip it up yourself by pressing the Flash button on the side of the pentamirror housing. The behavior of the internal flash varies, depending on which Creative Zone mode you're using.

- **P.** In this mode, the 70D fully automates the exposure process, giving you subtle fill flash effects in daylight, and fully illuminating your subject under dimmer lighting conditions. The camera selects a shutter speed from 1/60th to 1/250th second and sets an appropriate aperture.

- **Av.** In Aperture-priority mode, you set the aperture as always, and the 70D chooses a shutter speed from 30 seconds to 1/250th second. Use this mode with care, because if the camera detects a dark background, it will use the flash to expose the main subject in the foreground, and then leave the shutter open long enough to allow the background to be exposed correctly, too. If you're not using an image-stabilized lens, you can end up with blurry ghost images even of non-moving subjects at exposures longer than 1/30th second, and if your camera is not mounted on a tripod, you'll see these blurs at exposures longer than about 1/8th second even if you are using IS.

  To disable use of a slow shutter speed with flash, access Flash Sync Speed in Av Mode in the Flash Control screen found in the Shooting 2 menu, and change from the default setting Auto to either 1/250-1/60sec. Auto or 1/250sec. (fixed), as described in Chapter 8.

- **Tv.** When using flash in Tv mode, you set the shutter speed from 30 seconds to 1/250th second, and the 70D will choose the correct aperture for the correct flash exposure. If you accidentally set the shutter speed higher than 1/250th second, the camera will reduce it to 1/250th second when you're using the flash.

- **M/B.** In Manual or Bulb exposure modes, you select both shutter speed (30 seconds to 1/250th second) and aperture. The camera will adjust the shutter speed to 1/250th second if you try to use a faster speed with the internal flash. The E-TTL II system will provide the correct amount of exposure for your main subject at the aperture you've chosen (if the subject is within the flash's range, of course). In Bulb mode, the shutter will remain open for as long as the release button on top of the camera is held down, or the release of your remote control is activated.

Flash Range

The illumination of the 70D's built-in flash varies with distance, focal length, and ISO sensitivity setting.

- **Distance.** The farther away your subject is from the camera, the greater the light fall-off, thanks to the inverse square law discussed earlier. Keep in mind that a subject that's twice as far away receives only one-quarter as much light, which is two f/stops' worth.

- **Focal length.** The built-in flash "covers" only a limited angle of view, which doesn't change. So, when you're using a lens that is wider than the default focal length, the frame may not be covered fully, and you'll experience dark areas, especially in the corners. As you zoom in using longer focal lengths, some of the illumination is outside the area of view and is "wasted." (This phenomenon is why some external flash units, such as the 580EX II or 600EX-RT, "zoom" to match the zoom setting of your lens to concentrate the available flash burst onto the actual subject area.)

- **ISO setting.** The higher the ISO sensitivity, the more photons captured by the sensor. So, doubling the sensitivity from ISO 100 to 200 produces the same effect as, say, opening up your lens from f/8 to f/5.6.

Red-Eye Reduction and Autofocus Assist

When Red-Eye Reduction is turned on in the Shooting 2 menu (as described in Chapter 8), and you are using flash with any shooting mode except for Flash Off, Landscape, Sports, or Movie, the red-eye reduction lamp on the front of the camera will illuminate for about 1.5 seconds when you press down the shutter release halfway, theoretically causing your subjects' irises to contract (if they are looking toward the camera), and thereby reducing the red-eye effect in your photograph. Red-eye effects are most frequent under low light conditions, when the pupils of your subjects' eyes open to admit more light, thus providing a larger "target" for your flash's illumination to bounce back from the retinas to the sensor.

Another phenomenon you'll encounter under low light levels may be difficulty in focusing. Canon's answer to that problem is an autofocus assist beam emitted by the 70D's built-in flash, or by any external dedicated flash unit that you may have attached to the camera (and switched on). In dim lighting conditions, the built-in flash will emit a burst of reduced-intensity flashes when you press the shutter release halfway, providing additional illumination for the autofocus system. Here are some things you need to know about the AF assist beam:

- **Basic Zone activation.** When using a Basic Zone exposure mode other than Flash Off, Landscape, Sports, or Movie, if AF-assist is required, the 70D's built-in flash will pop up automatically.

- **Creative Zone activation.** If you're working with a Creative Zone exposure mode, you must pop up the built-in flash manually using the Flash button to enable AF assist.

■ **Focus mode.** The AF-assist beam will fire only if you are using One-Shot AF (single autofocus) or AI Focus AF (automatic autofocus). The beam is disabled if the camera is set to AI Servo AF (continuous autofocus) mode.

■ **Distance.** The beam provides autofocus assistance only for subjects closer than roughly 13 feet from the camera. The illumination is too dim at great distances to improve autofocus performance. If you need more of an assist, an external flash such as the 580EX II and 600EX-RT can provide a focusing aid for subjects as far as 32.8 feet away.

■ **Live View.** The AF-assist flash is disabled when using live view's Live mode and Face Detection focusing modes, for both the built-in flash and external flash. However, if a Canon Speedlite with an LED light is used (such as the 320EX), the beam will illuminate to provide autofocus assistance. The AF-Assist beam functions normally when using Quick mode autofocus in live view.

■ **Enabling/Disabling AF-assist.** You can specify how the AF-assist beam is fired using C.Fn II-05, as described below.

AF-Assist with Flash Disabled

You can still use the Autofocus Assist Beam function even when you don't want the flash to contribute to the exposure by disabling flash while enabling autofocus assist, using one of the Flash Control options in the Shooting 2 menu. Just follow these steps:

1. Press the MENU button and navigate to the Shooting 2 menu.
2. Use the multi-controller to select the Flash Control entry.
3. Select Flash Firing, press SET, and choose Disable. That option disables both the built-in flash and any external dedicated flash you may have attached. However, the AF-assist beam will still fire as described earlier.
4. Press the MENU button twice to exit. (Or just tap the shutter release button.)

Enabling/Disabling AF-Assist

Use C.Fn II-05 to choose whether the AF-assist beam is emitted by the built-in flash or the external Speedlite. You can disable the feature, activate it for both built-in flash and an external Speedlite, specify only external flash assist, or use only the infrared AF-assist beam included with some Canon flash units, such as the 580EX II and 600EX-RT. That option eliminates the obtrusive visible flashes, but still allows autofocus assistance using IR signals.

Using FE Lock and Flash Exposure Compensation

If you want to lock flash exposure for a subject that is not centered in the frame, you can use the FE Lock button (*) to lock in a specific flash exposure. Just depress and hold the shutter button halfway to lock in focus, then center the viewfinder on the subject you want to correctly expose and press the * button. The pre-flash fires and calculates exposure, displaying the FEL (flash exposure lock) message in the viewfinder. Then, recompose your photo and press the shutter down the rest of the way to take the photo.

Figure 11.12
Set flash exposure
compensation in the
Quick Control
screen.

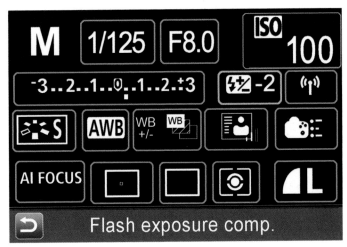

You can also manually add or subtract exposure to the flash exposure calculated by the 70D when using a Creative Zone mode. The easiest way is to use the Quick Control menu. Press the Q button and the screen shown in Figure 11.12 appears. Navigate to the flash exposure compensation box (it's highlighted in orange in the figure), and rotate the Main Dial to set flash compensation.

You can also specify flash compensation using the menus, which can be easy when working with the touch screen, even though there are a few extra steps. Just choose the Flash Control entry in Shooting 2 menu, then the Built-in Flash function setting, and choose Flash Exp. Comp. Then use the multi-controller or touch screen to enter flash exposure compensation plus or minus two f/stops. The exposure index scale on the LCD and in the viewfinder will indicate the change you've made, and a flash exposure compensation icon will appear to warn you that an adjustment has been made. As with non-flash exposure compensation, the compensation you make remains in effect for the pictures that follow, and even when you've turned the camera off, remember to cancel the flash exposure compensation adjustment by reversing the steps used to set it when you're done using it.

A third way to access flash exposure compensation is to assign that feature to the SET button, using C.Fn III-04, as described in Chapter 9. Thereafter, you can press the SET button when in Shooting mode, and rotate the Main Dial to adjust flash exposure compensation from the screen that pops up on the LCD. Flash exposure compensation can also be adjusted using the controls on your attached and active external flash unit. Those settings (any setting other than 0 dialed in with the external flash) will override any flash exposure compensation you've specified in the camera.

Tip

If you've enabled the Auto Lighting Optimizer in the Shooting 3 menu, as described in Chapter 8, it may cancel out any EV you've subtracted using flash exposure compensation. Disable the Auto Lighting Optimizer if you find your images are still too bright when using flash exposure compensation.

More on Flash Control Settings

I introduced the Shooting 2 menu's Flash Control settings in Chapter 8. This next section offers additional information for using the Flash Control menu. The menu includes six options (see Figure 11.13): Flash Firing, E-TTL II Metering, Flash Sync in AV Mode, Built-in Flash Settings, External Flash Function Settings, and External Flash C.Fn Settings.

Flash Firing

This menu entry has two options: Enable and Disable. It can be used to activate or deactivate the built-in electronic flash and any attached external electronic flash unit. When disabled, the flash cannot fire even if you accidentally elevate it, or have an accessory flash attached and turned on. However, you should keep in mind that the AF-assist beam can still be used. If you want to disable that, too, you'll need to turn it off using C.Fn II-05. Disabling the flash here does so for all exposure modes, and so is a better choice than using the Basic Zone Flash Off setting of the Mode Dial.

Here are some applications where I always disable my flash and AF-assist beam, even though my 70D won't pop up the flash and fire without my intervention anyway. Some situations are too important to take chances. (Who knows, maybe I've accidentally set the Mode Dial to Creative Auto?)

- **Venues where flash is forbidden.** I've discovered that many No Photography signs actually mean "No Flash Photography," either because those who make the decisions feel that flash is distracting or they fear it may potentially damage works of art. Tourists may not understand the difference between flash and available light photography, or may be unable to set their camera to turn off the flash. One of the first phrases I learn in any foreign language is "Is it permitted to take photos if I do not use flash?" A polite request, while brandishing an advanced camera like the 70D (which may indicate you know what you are doing), can often result in permission to shoot away.

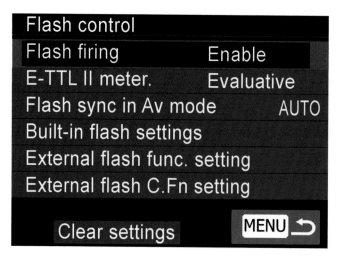

Figure 11.13
Six entries are available from the Flash Control menu.

■ **Venues where flash is ineffective anyway.** We've all seen the concert goers who stand up in the last row to shoot flash pictures from 100 yards away. I tend to not tell friends that their pictures are not going to come out, because they usually come back to me with a dismal, grainy shot (actually exposed by the dim available light) that they find satisfactory, just to prove I was wrong.

■ **Venues where flash is annoying.** If I'm taking pictures in a situation where flash is permitted, but mostly supplies little more than visual pollution, I'll disable or avoid using it. Concerts or religious ceremonies may *allow* flash photography, but who needs to add to the blinding bursts when you have a camera that will take perfectly good pictures at ISO 3200? Of course, I invariably see one or two people flashing away at events where flash is not allowed, but that doesn't mean I am eager to join in the festivities.

E-TTL II Metering

The second choice in the Flash Control menu allows you to choose the type of exposure metering the 70D uses for electronic flash. You can select the default Evaluative metering, which selectively interprets the 63 metering zones in the viewfinder to intelligently classify the scene for exposure purposes. Alternatively, you can select Average, which melds the information from all the zones together as an average exposure. You might find this mode useful for evenly lit scenes, but, in most cases, exposure won't be exactly right and you may need some flash exposure compensation adjustment.

Flash Sync Speed in Av Mode

You can select the flash synchronization speed that will be used when working in Aperture-priority mode; choose from Auto (the 70D selects the shutter speed from 30 seconds to 1/250th second) to a range embracing only the speeds from 1/250th to 1/60th second, or fixed at 1/250th second.

Normally, in Aperture-priority mode when using flash, you specify the f/stop to be locked in. The exposure is then adjusted by varying the output of the electronic flash. Because the primary exposure comes from the flash, the main effects of the shutter speed selected is on the secondary exposure from the ambient light on the scene. Your choices include:

■ **Auto.** This is your best choice under most conditions. The 70D will analyze your scene and choose a shutter speed that balances flash exposure and available light. For example, if the camera determines that a flash exposure requires an aperture of f/5.6, and then determines that the background illumination is intense enough to produce an exposure of 1/30th second at f/5.6, it might choose that slow shutter speed to provide a balanced exposure. As you might guess, the chief problem with Auto is that the 70D can choose a shutter speed that is slow enough to cause ghost images, as discussed earlier in this chapter. Don't use Auto if the ambient light is bright and your subject is far from the camera—that combination can lead to large f/stops and slow shutter speeds. (Use a tripod in such situations.) On the other hand, if your subject is fairly close to the camera—10 feet or closer—Auto will rarely get you into trouble. (See Figure 11.14.)

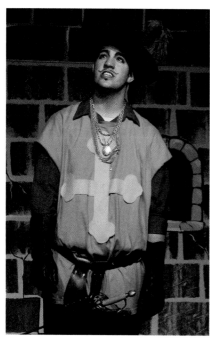
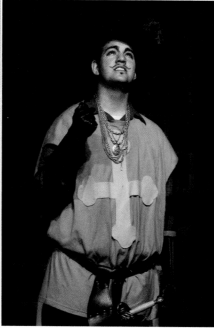

Figure 11.14
At left, a shutter speed of 1/60th second was used, allowing ambient illumination to brighten the background. At right, a 1/250th second shutter speed produced a black background.

- **1/250-1/60 sec auto.** If you want to ensure that a slow shutter speed won't be used, activate this option to lock out shutter speeds slower than 1/60th second.

- **1/250 sec (fixed).** This setting ensures that the 70D will always select 1/250th second. You'll end up with pitch-black backgrounds much of the time, but won't have to worry about ghost images.

Built-in Flash Settings

There are four main choices for this menu choice, which normally appears as shown in Figure 11.15. You cannot select Built-in Flash Settings if an external flash is attached to the accessory shoe. A message will pop up explaining that this menu option has been disabled.

However, that does not mean that you can't use an external flash; your add-on flash unit must be used off-camera and not attached to the 70D's accessory shoe. Indeed, this menu entry has additional settings that apply when using an off-camera wireless external flash, such as Channel and Firing Group (see Figure 11.16), which I'll address in the sections on external flash. Here's a quick summary of the main built-in flash selections, plus additional options that appear when you change the Built-in Flash setting to one of the two wireless flash modes. I'll explain each in more detail in the sections that follow this one, and in Chapter 12.

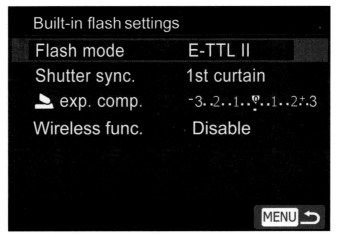

Figure 11.15
Four entries are available from the Built-in Flash Functions menu.

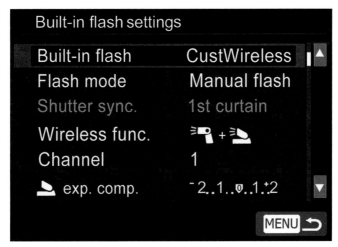

Figure 11.16
Choose Wireless Flash settings and additional options appear.

- **Flash mode.** This entry allows you to choose automatic exposure calculation (E-TTL II).
- **Shutter sync.** Available only in Normal Firing mode, you can choose 1st curtain sync, which fires the pre-flash used to calculate the exposure before the shutter opens, followed by the main flash as soon as the shutter is completely open. This is the default mode, and you'll generally perceive the pre-flash and main flash as a single burst. Alternatively, you can select 2nd curtain sync, which fires the pre-flash as soon as the shutter opens, and then triggers the main flash in a second burst at the end of the exposure, just before the shutter starts to close. (If the shutter speed is slow enough, you may clearly see both the pre-flash and main flash as separate bursts of light.) This action allows photographing a blurred trail of light of moving objects with sharp flash exposures at the beginning and the end of the exposure. This type of flash exposure is slightly different from what some other cameras produce using 2nd curtain sync.

If you have an external compatible Speedlite attached, you can also choose High-speed sync, which allows you to use shutter speeds faster than 1/250th second, using the External Flash Function Setting menu.

- **Flash exposure compensation.** You can use the Quick Control screen (press the Q button) and enter flash exposure compensation. If you'd rather adjust flash exposure using a menu, you can do that here. Select this option with the SET button, then dial in the amount of flash EV compensation you want using the multi-controller. The EV that was in place before you started to make your adjustment is shown as a blue indicator, so you can return to that value quickly. Press SET again to confirm your change, then press the MENU button twice to exit.

- **Wireless functions.** These choices appear when you've selected Custom Wireless, and include Mode, Channel, Firing Group, and other options used only when you're working in wireless mode to control an external flash. If you've disabled wireless functions, the other options don't appear on the menu. I'm going to leave the explanation of these options for Chapter 12, which is an entire chapter dedicated to using the 70D's wireless shooting capabilities, first introduced in the EOS 7D.

Using Flash Mode

As I noted, Flash Mode is grayed out and unavailable when the 70D is set to Normal Firing or Easy Wireless. If you select Custom Wireless, you can select Flash Mode and choose one of two options: E-TTL II and Manual Flash.

E-TTL II

You'll leave Flash Mode at this setting most of the time. In this mode, the camera fires a pre-flash prior to the exposure, and measures the amount of light reflected to calculate the proper settings. As noted earlier, when you've selected the E-TTL II Flash mode, you can also choose either Evaluative or Average metering methods. If you select Manual Flash or MULTI Flash (which are only available when using an external flash), that option is removed from the Built-in Flash Setting menu.

Manual Flash

Use this setting when you want to specify exactly how much light is emitted by the flash units, and don't want the 70D's E-TTL II exposure system to calculate the f/stop for you. When you activate this option, the two flash exposure compensation entries are replaced by internal and external flash output scales (the built-in and external flash units are represented by icons). You can select from 1/4 to 1/128th power for the built-in flash, and 1/1 to 1/128th power for the external flash. A blue indicator appears under the previous setting, and a white indicator under your new setting, a reminder that you've chosen reduced power. Click on External flash func. setting, then click ETTL and select M or Multi with the multi-controller.

Here are some situations where you might want to use manual flash settings:

■ **Close-ups.** You're shooting macro photos and the E-TTL II exposure is not precisely what you'd like. You can dial in exposure compensation, or set the output manually. Close-up photos are problematic, because the power of the built-in flash may be too much (choose 1/128 power to minimize the output), or the reflected light may not be interpreted accurately by the through-the-lens metering system. Manual flash gives you greater control.

■ **Fill flash.** Although E-TTL II can be used in full daylight to provide fill flash to brighten shadows, using manual flash allows you to tweak the amount of light being emitted in precise steps. Perhaps you want just a little more illumination in the shadows to retain a dramatic lighting effect without the dark portions losing all detail. Again, you can try using exposure compensation to make this adjustment, but I prefer to use manual flash settings. (See Figure 11.17.)

■ **Action stopping.** The lower the power of the flash, the shorter the effective exposure. Use 1/128th power in a darkened room (so that there is no ambient light to contribute to the exposure and cause a "ghost" image, like that seen in Figure 11.18) and you can end up with a "shutter speed" that's the equivalent of 1/50,000th second! Of course, with such a minimal amount of flash power, you need to be very close to your subject.

Figure 11.17
You can fine-tune fill illumination by adjusting the output of your camera's built-in flash manually.

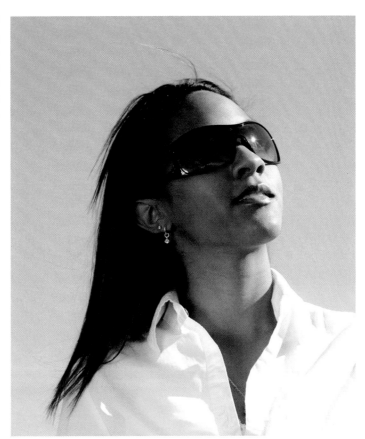

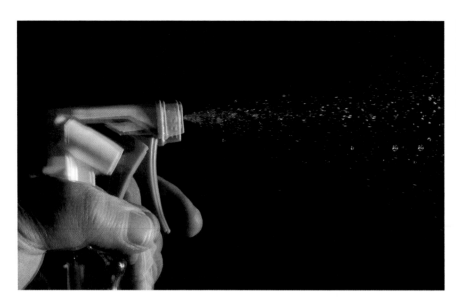

Figure 11.18 At 1/128th power, the duration of the flash is very brief, producing the same effect as a fast shutter speed.

External Flash Function Setting

You can access this menu only when you have a compatible electronic flash attached and switched on. The settings available are shown in Figure 11.19.

- **Flash mode.** This entry allows you to set the flash mode for the external flash, from E-TTL II, Manual flash, and MULTI flash.

- **Wireless functions.** These functions are available when using wireless flash, and will be explained in Chapter 12. This setting allows you to enable or disable wireless functions. You can choose Wireless: Off, Wireless: On (Optical Transmission), or Wireless: On (Radio Transmission). The last choice is shown and available only when using a radio-capable triggering device or flash, such as the 600EX-RT.

- **Flash Zoom.** Some flash units can vary their coverage to better match the field of view of your lens at a particular focal length. You can allow the external flash to zoom automatically, based on information provided, or manually, using a zoom button on the flash itself. This setting is disabled when using a flash like the Canon 270EX II, which does not have zooming capability. You can select Auto, in which case the camera will tell the flash unit the focal length of the lens, or choose individual focal lengths including 24mm, 28mm, 35mm, 50mm, 70mm, 80mm, and 105mm. The 600EX-RT offers an additional setting of 200mm.

- **Shutter synchronization.** As with the 70D's internal flash, you can choose 1st curtain sync, which fires the flash as soon as the shutter is completely open (this is the default mode). Alternatively, you can select 2nd curtain sync, which fires the flash as soon as the shutter opens, and then triggers a second flash at the end of the exposure, just before the shutter starts to close. If a compatible Canon flash, such as the Speedlite 580EX II or 600EX-RT is attached and turned on, you can also select High-speed sync. and shoot using shutter speeds faster than 1/250th second. HSS does not work in wireless mode, as I'll explain in Chapter 12.

- **Flash exposure compensation.** You can add/subtract exposure compensation for the external flash unit, in a range of –2 to +2 EV. Dial in the amount of flash EV compensation you want using the multi-selector. The EV that was in place before you started to make your adjustment is shown as a blue indicator, so you can return to that value quickly.

- **Flash exposure bracketing.** Flash Exposure Bracketing (FEB) operates similarly to ordinary exposure bracketing, providing a series of different exposures to improve your chances of getting the exact right exposure, or to provide alternative renditions for creative purposes.

If you enable wireless flash, additional options appear in this menu. I'll cover these in more detail in Chapter 12:

- **Channel.** All flashes used wirelessly can communicate on one of four channels. This setting allows you to choose which channel is used. Channels are especially helpful when you're working around other Canon photographers; each can select a different channel so one photographer's flash units don't trigger those of another photographer.

- **Master flash.** You can enable or disable use of the external flash as the master controller for the other wireless flashes. When set to enable, the attached external flash is used as the master; when disabled, the external flash becomes a slave unit triggered by the 70D's built-in flash.

- **Flash Firing Group.** Multiple flash units can be assigned to a group. This choice allows specifying which groups are triggered, A/B, A/B plus C, or All. The 600EX-RT offers additional groups when using radio control mode, Groups D and E.

- **A:B fire ratio.** If you select A/B or A/B plus C, this option appears, and allows you to set the proportionate outputs of Groups A and B, in ratios from 8:1 to 1:8 as explained in Chapter 12.

- **Group C exposure compensation.** If you select A/B plus C, this option appears, too, allowing you to set flash exposure compensation separately for Group C flashes.

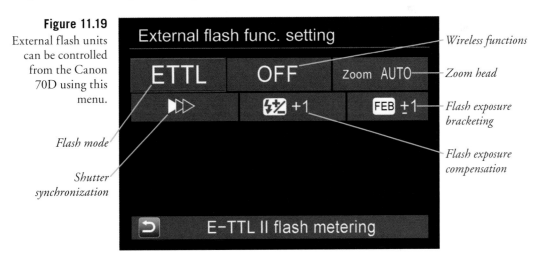

Figure 11.19
External flash units can be controlled from the Canon 70D using this menu.

Learning about MULTI Flash

The MULTI flash setting, if it's available with your flash unit, makes it possible to shoot cool stroboscopic effects, with the flash firing several times in quick succession. You can use the capability to produce multiple images of moving objects, to trace movement (say, your golf swing). When you've activated MULTI flash, three parameters appear on the External Flash Function Setting menu, as shown in Figure 11.20. They include:

- **Frequency/Times per second.** This figure specifies the number of bursts per second. With the built-in flash, you can choose (theoretically) 1 to 199 bursts per second. The actual number of flashes produced will be determined by your flash count (which turns off the flash after the specified number of flashes), flash output (higher output levels will deplete the available energy in your flash unit), and your shutter speed.

- **Flash count/number of shots.** This setting determines the number of flashes in a given burst, and can be set from 1 to 50 flashes.

- **Power level.** Adjust the output of the flash for each burst, from 1/4 to 1/128th power.

These factors work together to determine the maximum number of flashes you can string together in a single shot. The exact number will vary, depending on your settings.

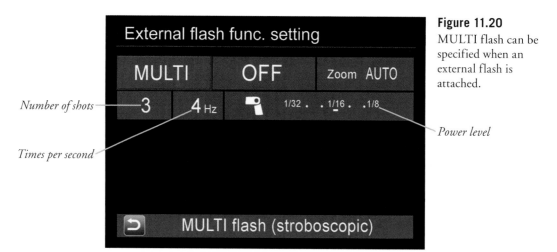

Figure 11.20
MULTI flash can be specified when an external flash is attached.

High-Speed Sync

High-speed sync is a special mode that allows you to synchronize an *external* flash (but not the built-in flash) at all shutter speeds, rather than just 1/250th second and slower. The entire frame is illuminated by a series of continuous bursts as the shutter opening moves across the sensor plane, so you do *not* end up with a horizontal black band, as shown earlier in Figure 11.11.

HSS is especially useful in three situations, all related to problems associated with high ambient light levels:

- **Eliminate "ghosts" with moving images.** When shooting with flash, the primary source of illumination may be the flash itself. However, if there is enough available light, a secondary image may be recorded by that light (as described under "Ghost Images" earlier in this chapter). If your main subject is not moving, the secondary image may be acceptable or even desirable. Indeed, the 70D has a provision for slow sync in its Basic Mode Night Portrait setting that allows using a slow shutter speed to record the ambient light and help illuminate dark backgrounds. But if your subject is moving, the secondary image creates a ghost image.

  High-speed sync gives you the ability to use a higher shutter speed. If ambient light produces a ghost image at 1/250th second, upping the shutter speed to 1/500th or 1/1,000th second may eliminate it.

  Of course, HSS *reduces* the amount of light the flash produces. If your subject is not close to the camera, the waning illumination of the flash may force you to use a larger f/stop to capture the flash exposure. So, while shifting from 1/250th second at f/8 to 1/500th second at f/8 *will* reduce ghost images, if you switch to 1/500th second at f/5.6 (because the flash is effectively less intense), you'll end up with the same ambient light exposure. Still, it's worth a try.

- **Improved fill flash in daylight.** The 70D can use the built-in flash or an attached unit to fill in inky shadows—both automatically and using manually specified power ratios, as described earlier in this chapter. However, both methods force you to use a 1/250th second (or slower) shutter speed. That limitation can cause three complications.

  First, in very bright surroundings, such as beach or snow scenes, it may be difficult to get the correct exposure at 1/250th second. You might have to use f/16 or a smaller f/stop to expose a given image, even at ISO 100. If you want to use a larger f/stop for selective focus, then you encounter the second problem—1/250th second won't allow apertures wider than f/8 or f/5.6 under many daylight conditions at ISO 100. (See the discussion of fill flash with Aperture-priority in the next bullet.)

  Finally, if you're shooting action, you'll probably want a shutter speed faster than 1/250th second, if at all possible under the current lighting. That's because, in fill flash situations, the ambient light (often daylight) provides the primary source of illumination. For many sports and fast-moving subjects, 1/500th second, or faster, is desirable. HSS allows you to increase your shutter speed and still avail yourself of fill flash. This assumes that your subject is close enough to your camera that the fill flash has some effect; forget about using fill and HSS with subjects a dozen feet away or farther. The flash won't be powerful enough to have much effect on the shadows.

- **When using fill flash with Aperture-priority.** The difficulties of using selective focus with fill flash, mentioned earlier, become particularly acute when you switch to Av exposure mode. Selecting f/5.6, f/4, or a wider aperture when using flash is guaranteed to create problems when photographing close-up subjects, particularly at ISO settings higher than ISO 100. If you own an external flash unit, HSS may be the solution you are looking for.

ALL HSS, ALL THE TIME

If you are using a compatible flash unit, it's safe to enable high-speed sync *all the time*. That's because if you set the camera for 1/250th second or slower, the flash will fire normally at its set power output, just as if HSS were not enabled. But once you venture past 1/250th second to a faster shutter speed, the camera/flash combination is smart enough to use HSS. However, it's your responsibility to remember that you've enabled high-speed sync, and realize that as you increase the shutter speed, the effective range of the flash is reduced. At 1/1000th second, the 600EX-RT is "good" out to about two feet from the camera. (Remember, HSS does not work in wireless mode, so the flash must be attached to the camera's hot shoe.) At 1/8000th second, the flash will illuminate subjects no more than about one foot from the flash/camera.

To activate HSS using the 580EX II or 600EX-RT, just follow these steps:

1. **Attach the flash.** Mount/connect the external flash on the 70D, using the hot shoe or a cable. (HSS cannot be used in wireless mode, nor with a flash linked through an adapter that provides a PC/X terminal.)

2. **Power up.** Turn the flash and camera on.

3. **Select HSS in the camera.** Set the External Flash Function Setting in the camera to HSS as the 70D's sync mode.

   a. Choose Flash Control in the Shooting 2 menu.

   b. Select External Flash Func. Setting.

   c. Navigate to the Shutter Sync. Entry, press SET, and choose High-Speed (at the far right of the list). Press SET again to confirm.

4. **Choose HSS on the flash.** Activate HSS (FP flash) on your attached external flash. With the 580EX II, press the High-speed sync button on the back of the flash unit (it's the second from the right under the LCD). (See Figure 11.21.) With the 600EX-RT, press Function Button 4 (Sync), located at the far right of the row of four buttons just under the LCD.

5. **Confirm HSS is active**. The HSS icon will be displayed on the flash unit's LCD (at the upper-left side with the 580EX II), and at bottom left in the 70D's viewfinder. If you choose a shutter speed of 1/250th second or slower, the indicator will not appear in the viewfinder, as HSS will not be used at slower speeds.

6. **View minimum/maximum shooting distance.** Choose a distance based on the maximum shown in the line at the bottom of the flash's LCD display (from 0.5 to 18 meters).

7. **Shoot.** Take the picture. To turn off HSS, press the button on the flash again. Remember that you can't use MULTI flash or Wireless flash when working with High-speed sync.

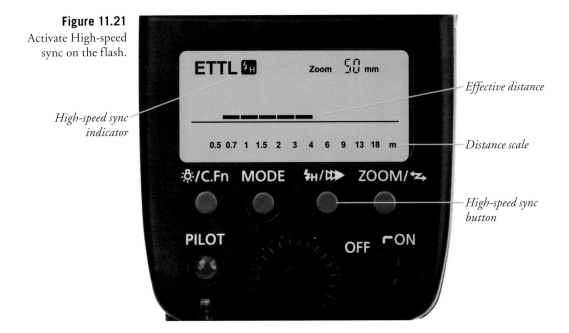

Figure 11.21
Activate High-speed sync on the flash.

High-speed sync indicator

Effective distance

Distance scale

High-speed sync button

External Flash Custom Function Setting

Some external Speedlites from Canon include their own list of Custom Functions, which can be used to specify things like flash metering mode and flash bracketing sequences, as well as more sophisticated features, such as modeling light/flash (if available), use of external power sources (if attached), and functions of any slave unit attached to the external flash. This menu entry allows you to set an external flash unit's Custom Functions from your 70D's menu. The settings available in the 70D for the Speedlite 580EX II are shown later in the section that describes that flash.

Clear External Flash Custom Function Setting

This entry allows you to zero-out any changes you've made to your external flash's Custom Functions, and return them to their factory default settings.

Using External Electronic Flash

Canon offers a broad range of accessory electronic flash units for the 70D. They can be mounted to the flash accessory shoe, or used off-camera with a dedicated cord that plugs into the flash shoe to maintain full communications with the camera for all special features. (Non-dedicated flash units, such as studio flash, can be connected using a PC terminal adapter mounted in the accessory shoe.) They range from the Speedlite 600EX-RT and Speedlite 580EX II, which can correctly expose subjects up to 24 feet away at f/11 and ISO 200, to the 270EX, which is good out to 19 feet at f/11 and ISO 200. (You'll get greater ranges at even higher ISO settings, of course.) There are also two electronic flash units specifically for specialized close-up flash photography.

I power my Speedlites with Sanyo Eneloop AA nickel metal hydride batteries, seen in Figure 11.22. These are a special type of rechargeable battery with a feature that's ideal for electronic flash use. The Eneloop cells, unlike conventional batteries, don't self-discharge over relative short periods of time. Once charged, they can hold onto their juice for a year or more. That means you can stuff some of these into your Speedlite, along with a few spares in your camera bag, and not worry about whether the batteries have retained their power between uses. There's nothing worse than firing up your strobe after not using it for a month, and discovering that the batteries are dead.

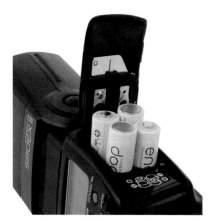

Figure 11.22 Sanyo's Eneloop AA batteries are a perfect power source for Canon Speedlites.

Speedlite 600EX-RT

This flagship of the Canon accessory flash line (and most expensive at about $550) is the most powerful unit the company offers, with a GN of 197, and a manual/automatic zoom flash head that covers the full frame of lenses from 24mm wide angle to 200mm telephoto. (There's a flip-down, wide-angle diffuser that spreads the flash to cover a 14mm lens's field of view, too.) All angle specifications given by Canon refer to full-frame sensors, but this flash unit automatically converts its field of view coverage to accommodate the crop factor of the 70D and the other 1.6X crop Canon dSLRs. The 600EX-RT shares its basic features with the 580EX II, described next, so I won't repeat them here, because the typical 70D owner is more likely to own one of the less expensive Speedlites.

The killer feature of this unit (see Figure 11.23) is the new wireless two-way radio communication between the camera and this flash (or ST-E3-RT wireless controller and the flash) at distances of up to 98 feet. You can link up to 15 different flash units with radio control, using *five* groups (A, B, C, D, and E), and no line-of-sight connection is needed. (You can hide the flash under a desk or in a potted plant.) With the latest Canon cameras having a revised "intelligent" hot shoe (which includes the 70D), a second 600EX-RT can be used to trigger a *camera* that also has a 600EX-RT mounted, from a remote location. That means you can set up multiple cameras equipped with multiple flash units to all fire simultaneously! For example, if you were shooting a wedding, you could photograph the bridal couple from two different angles, with the second camera set up on a tripod, say, behind the altar. A pro shooter might find the 70D to be an excellent, affordable second (or third) camera to use in such situations.

The 600EX-RT maintains backward compatibility with optical transmission used by earlier cameras. However, it's a bit pricey for the average EOS 70D owner, who is unlikely to be able to take advantage of all its features. If you're looking for a high-end flash unit and don't need radio control, I still recommend the Speedlite 580EX II (described next), which remains in the line.

600EX (NON-RADIO)

If you see references to a 600EX model (non-RT), you'll find that a version with the radio control crippled is sold only outside the USA in countries where obtaining permission to use the relevant radio spectrum is problematic.

Remember that with the 600EX-RT, you can't use radio control and some other features unless you own at least *two* of these Speedlites, or one 600EX-RT plus the ST-E3-RT, which costs half as much. Radio control is possible only between a camera that has a 600EX-RT or ST-E3-RT in the hot shoe, and an additional 600EX-RT flash or ST-E3-RT.

Some 18 Custom Functions of the 600EX-RT can be set using the 70D's External Flash C.Fn Setting menu. Additional Personal Functions can be specified on the flash itself. The 70D-friendly functions include:

C.Fn-00   Distance indicator display (Meters/Feet)

C.Fn-01   Auto power off (Enabled/Disabled)

C.Fn-02   Modeling flash (Enabled-DOF preview button/Enabled-test firing button/Enabled-both buttons/Disabled)

C.Fn-03   FEB Flash exposure bracketing auto cancel (Enabled/Disabled)

C.Fn-04   FEB Flash exposure bracketing Sequence (Metered > Decreased > Increased Exposure/Decreased > Metered > Increased Exposure)

C.Fn-05   Flash metering mode (E-TTL II-E-TTL/TTL/External metering: Auto/External metering: Manual)

C.Fn-06   Quickflash with continuous shot (Disabled/Enabled)

C.Fn-07   Test firing with autoflash (1/32/Full power)

C.Fn-08   AF-assist beam firing (Enabled/Disabled)

C.Fn-09   Auto zoom adjusted for image/sensor size (Enabled/Disabled)

C.Fn-10   Slave auto power off timer (60 minutes/10 minutes)

C.Fn-11   Cancellation of slave unit auto power off by master unit (Within 8 Hours/Within 1 Hour)

C.Fn-12   Flash recycling on external power (Use internal and external power/Use only external power)

C.Fn-13   Flash exposure metering setting button (Speedlite button and dial/Speedlite dial only)

C.Fn-20   Beep (Enable/Disable)

C.Fn-21   Light Distribution (Standard, Guide Number Priority, Even Coverage)

C.Fn-22   LCD panel illumination (On for 12 seconds, Disable, Always On)

C.Fn-23   Slave Flash Battery Check (AF-assist beam/Flash Lamp, Flash Lamp only)

The Personal Functions available include the following. Note that you can set the LCD panel color to differentiate at a glance whether a given flash is functioning in Master or Slave mode.

P.Fn-01 LCD panel display contrast (Five levels of contrast)

P.Fn-02 LCD panel illumination color: Normal (Green, Orange)

P.Fn-03 LCD panel illumination color: Master (Green, Orange)

P.Fn-04 LCD panel illumination color: Slave (Green, Orange)

P.Fn-05 Color filter auto detection (Auto, Disable)

P.Fn-06 Wireless button toggle sequence (Normal>Radio>Optical, Normal< >Radio, Normal< >Optical)

P.Fn-07 Flash firing during linked shooting (Disabled, Enabled)

Speedlite 580EX II

This deposed flagship of the Canon accessory flash line (and still available new or used from some sources) is the second-most powerful unit the company offered, with a GN of 190, and a manual/automatic zoom flash head that covers the full frame of lenses from 24mm wide angle to 105mm telephoto, as well as 14mm optics with a flip-down diffuser.

Like the 600EX-RT, this unit offers full-swivel, 180-degrees in either direction, and has its own built-in AF-assist beam and an exposure system that's compatible with the nine focus points of the 70D. Powered by economical AA-size batteries, the unit recycles in 0.1 to 6 seconds, and can squeeze 100 to 700 flashes from a set of alkaline batteries.

The 580EX II, shown in Figure 11.23, automatically communicates white balance information to your camera, allowing it to adjust WB to match the flash output. You can even simulate a modeling light effect: When you press the depth-of-field preview button on the 70D, the 580EX II emits a one-second burst of light that allows you to judge the flash effect. If you're using multiple flash units with Canon's wireless E-TTL system, this model can serve as a master flash that controls the slave units you've set up (more about this later) or function as a slave itself.

It's easy to access all the features of this unit, because it has a large backlit LCD panel on the back that provides information about all flash

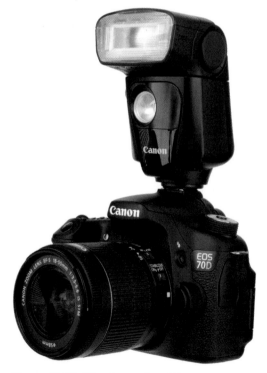

Figure 11.23 The Canon Speedlite 580EX II is the second-most powerful shoe-mount flash Canon offers.

settings. There are 14 Custom Functions that can be controlled from the flash, numbered from 00 to 13. These functions are (the first setting is the default value):

C.Fn-00   Distance indicator display (Meters/Feet)

C.Fn-01   Auto power off (Enabled/Disabled)

C.Fn-02   Modeling flash (Enabled-DOF preview button/Enabled-test firing button/Enabled-both buttons/Disabled)

C.Fn-03   FEB Flash exposure bracketing auto cancel (Enabled/Disabled)

C.Fn-04   FEB Flash exposure bracketing sequence (Metered > Decreased > Increased Exposure/Decreased > Metered > Increased Exposure)

C.Fn-05   Flash metering mode (E-TTL II-E-TTL/TTL/External metering: Auto/External metering: Manual)

C.Fn-06   Quickflash with continuous shot (Disabled/Enabled)

C.Fn-07   Test firing with autoflash (1/32/Full power)

C.Fn-08   AF-assist beam firing (Enabled/Disabled)

C.Fn-09   Auto zoom adjusted for image/sensor size (Enabled/Disabled)

C.Fn-10   Slave auto power off timer (60 minutes/10 minutes)

C.Fn-11   Cancellation of slave unit auto power off by master unit (Within 8 Hours/Within 1 Hour)

C.Fn-12   Flash recycling on external power (Use internal and external power/Use only external power)

C.Fn-13   Flash exposure metering setting button (Speedlite button and dial/Speedlite dial only)

Speedlite 430EX II

This less pricey electronic flash (available for less than $300) has automatic and manual zoom coverage from 24mm to 105mm, and the same wide-angle pullout panel found on the 580EX II that covers the area of a 14mm lens on a full-frame camera, and automatic conversion to the cropped frame area of the 70D and other 1.6X crop Canon dSLRs. The 430EX II also communicates white balance information with the camera, and has its own AF-assist beam. Compatible with Canon's wireless E-TTL system, it makes a good slave unit, but cannot serve as a master flash. It, too, uses AA batteries, and offers recycle times of 0.1 to 3.7 seconds for 200 to 1,400 flashes, depending on subject distance.

The Canon Speedlite 430EX II offers a sophisticated set of features, including an LCD panel that allows you to navigate the unit's menu and view its status. These features, along with powerful output and automatic zoom means this unit has more in common with Canon's high-end Speedlites than it does with the 320EX or the 270EX II. The Speedlite 430EX II is compatible with E-TTL

II and earlier flash technologies. It can serve as a slave unit in an optical wireless configuration. The Speedlite 430EX II has a Guide Number of 43/141 (meters/feet) at ISO 100, at 105mm focal length.

This is another aging unit, dating from mid-2008, and possibly due for replacement. It's a bit more powerful than the just-introduced Speedlite 320EX (described next), which is roughly in the same price range. So, I'm guessing that there will be a slightly more powerful 400-series Speedlite unveiled in the near future with a roughly $325 price point.

Speedlite 320EX

One of two new flash units (with the Speedlite 270EX II, described next) introduced early in 2011, this $249 flash has a GN of 105. Lightweight and more pocket-sized than the 430EX II or 580EX II, this bounceable (both horizontally and vertically) flash has some interesting features, including a built-in LED video light that can be used for shooting movies with the 70D, or as a modeling light or even AF-assist beam when shooting with live view. Canon says that this efficient LED light can provide up to four hours of illumination with a set of AA batteries. It can be used as a wireless slave unit, and has a new flash release function that allows the shutter to be triggered remotely with a two-second delay.

Speedlite 270EX II

The Canon Speedlite 270EX II is designed to work with compatible EOS cameras utilizing E-TTL II and E-TTL automatic flash technologies. This flash unit is entirely controlled from the camera, making it as simple to use as a built-in flash. Its options can be selected and set via the camera's menu system. The 270EX II can also be used as an off-camera slave unit when controlled by a master Speedlite, transmitter unit, or a camera with an integrated Speedlite transmitter. One interesting feature of this unit is that it is also a remote control transmitter, allowing you to wirelessly release the shutter on cameras compatible with certain remote controller units. The Speedlite 270EX II has a Guide Number of 27/89 (meters/feet) at ISO 100, with the flash head pulled forward.

This $170 ultra-compact unit is Canon's entry-level Speedlite, and suitable for 70D owners who want a simple strobe for occasional use, without sacrificing the ability to operate it as a wireless slave unit. With its modest guide number, it provides a little extra pop for fill flash applications. It has vertical bounce capabilities of up to 90 degrees, and can be switched between Tele modes to Normal (28mm full-frame coverage) at a reduced guide number of 72.

The 270EX II functions as a wireless slave unit triggered by any Canon EOS unit or flash (such as the 580EX II) with a Master function. It also has the new flash release function with a two-second delay that lets you reposition the flash. There's a built-in AF-assist beam, and this 5.5-ounce, 2.6 × 2.6 × 3-inch unit is powered by just two AA-size batteries.

Ring Lites

Canon has offered two ring lites, the Macro Ring Lite MR-14EX, and Macro Twin Ring Lite flash MT-24EX. As you might guess from their names, ring lites are especially suitable for close-up, or macro photography, because they provide a relatively shadowless illumination. It's always tricky photographing small subjects up close, because there often isn't room enough between the camera lens and the subject to position lights effectively. Ring lites, especially those with their own modeling lamps to help you visualize the illumination you're going to get, mount around the lens at the camera position, and help solve many close-up lighting problems.

But, in recent years, the ring lite has gone far beyond the macro realm and is now probably even more popular as a light source for fashion and glamour photography. The right ring lite, properly used, can provide killer illumination for glamour shots, while eliminating the need to move and reset lights for those shots that lend themselves to ring lite illumination. As you, the photographer, move around your subject, the ring lite moves with you.

One of the key drawbacks to ring lites (whether used for macro or glamour photography) is that they are somewhat bulky and clumsy to use (they must be fastened around the camera lens itself, or the photographer must position the ring lite, and then shoot "through" the opening or ring). That means that you might not be moving around your subject as much as you thought and will, instead, mount the ring lite and camera on a tripod, studio stand, or other support.

Another drawback is the cost. The MR-14EX and MR-24EX are priced in the $550 and $800 range, respectively. You have to be planning a *lot* of macro or fashion work to pay for one of those. Specialists take note. I tend to favor a third-party substitute, the Alien Bees ABR800 Ringflash, shown in Figure 11.24. It's priced at about $400, and, besides, it integrates very well with my other Alien Bees studio flash units.

Figure 11.24
This Alien Bees ringflash is a more economical alternative to Canon's own units.

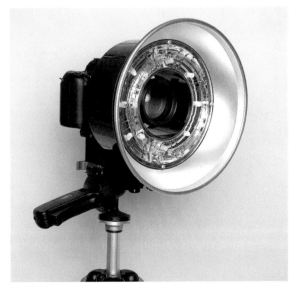

More Advanced Lighting Techniques

As you advance in your Canon 70D photography, you'll want to learn more sophisticated lighting techniques, using more than just straight-on flash, or using just a single flash unit. Check out *David Busch's Guide to Canon Flash Photography* if you want to delve further. I'm going to provide a quick introduction to some of the techniques you should be considering.

Diffusing and Softening the Light

Direct light can be harsh and glaring, especially if you're using the flash built into your camera, or an auxiliary flash mounted in the hot shoe and pointed directly at your subject. The first thing you should do is stop using direct light (unless you're looking for a stark, contrasty appearance as a creative effect). There are a number of simple things you can do with both continuous and flash illumination.

- **Use window light.** Light coming in a window can be soft and flattering, and a good choice for human subjects. Move your subject close enough to the window that its light provides the primary source of illumination. You might want to turn off other lights in the room, particularly to avoid mixing daylight and incandescent light (see Figure 11.25).

- **Use fill light.** Your 70D's built-in flash makes a perfect fill-in light for the shadows, brightening inky depths with a kicker of illumination (see Figure 11.17, earlier in the chapter).

- **Bounce the light.** External electronic flash units mounted on the 70D usually have a swivel that allows them to be pointed up at a ceiling for a bounce light effect. You can also bounce the light off a wall. You'll want the surface to be white or have a neutral gray color to avoid a color cast.

- **Use reflectors.** Another way to bounce the light is to use reflectors or photo umbrellas that you can position yourself to provide a greater degree of control over the quantity and direction of the bounced light. Good reflectors can be pieces of foamboard, Mylar, or a reflective disk held in place by a clamp and stand. Although some expensive photo umbrellas and reflectors are available, spending a lot isn't necessary. A simple piece of white foamboard does the job beautifully. Umbrellas have the advantage of being compact and foldable, while providing a soft, even kind of light. They're relatively cheap, too, with a good 40-inch umbrella designed specifically for photographic applications available for as little as $20.

- **Use diffusers.** Sto-Fen and some other vendors offer clip-on diffusers like the one shown in Figures 11.26 (furnished with the 580EX II) and 11.27 (an after market unit), that fit over your electronic flash head and provide a soft, flattering light. These add-ons are more portable than umbrellas and other reflectors, yet provide a nice diffuse lighting effect.

Using Multiple Light Sources

Once you gain control over the qualities and effects you get with a single light source, you'll want to graduate to using multiple light sources. Using several lights allows you to shape and mold the illumination of your subjects to provide a variety of effects, from backlighting to side lighting to

Figure 11.25
Window light makes
the perfect diffuse
illumination for
informal soft-focus
portraits like
this one.

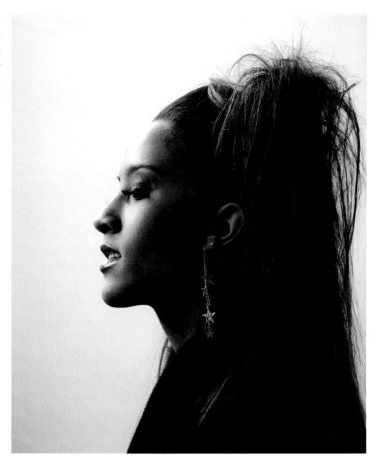

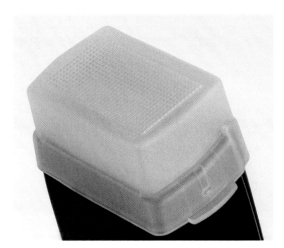

Figure 11.26 The Sto-Fen OmniBounce is a clip-on diffuser that softens the light of an external flash unit.

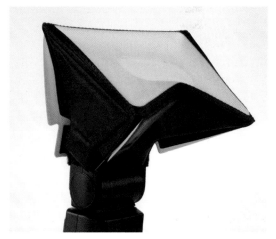

Figure 11.27 Soft boxes use Velcro strips to attach them to third-party flash units (like the one shown) or any Canon external flash.

more formal portrait lighting. You can start simply with several incandescent light sources, bounced off umbrellas or reflectors that you construct. Or you can use more flexible multiple electronic flash setups.

Effective lighting is the one element that differentiates great photography from candid or snapshot shooting. Lighting can make a mundane subject look a little more glamorous. Make subjects appear to be soft when you want a soft look, or bright and sparkly when you want a vivid look, or strong and dramatic if that's what you desire. As you might guess, having control over your lighting means that you probably can't use the lights that are already in the room. You'll need separate, discrete lighting fixtures that can be moved, aimed, brightened, and dimmed on command.

Selecting your lighting gear will depend on the type of photography you do, and the budget you have to support it. It's entirely possible for a beginning 70D photographer to create a basic, inexpensive lighting system capable of delivering high-quality results for a few hundred dollars, just as you can spend megabucks ($1,000 and up) for a sophisticated lighting system.

Basic Flash Setups

If you want to use multiple electronic flash units, the Canon Speedlites described earlier will serve admirably. The two higher-end models can be used with Canon's wireless E-TTL feature, which allows you to set up to three separate groups of flash units (several flashes can be included in each group) and trigger them using a master flash (such as the 580EX II) and the camera. Just set up one master unit (there's a switch on the unit's foot that sets it for master mode) and arrange the compatible slave units around your subject. You can set the relative power of each unit separately, thereby controlling how much of the scene's illumination comes from the main flash, and how much from the auxiliary flash units, which can be used as fill flash, background lights, or, if you're careful, to illuminate the hair of portrait subjects. You'll find more about wireless flash in Chapter 12.

Studio Flash

If you're serious about using multiple flash units, a studio flash setup might be more practical. The traditional studio flash is a multi-part unit, consisting of a flash head that mounts on your light stand, and is tethered to an AC (or sometimes battery) power supply. A single power supply can feed two or more flash heads at a time, with separate control over the output of each head.

When they are operating off AC power, studio flash don't have to be frugal with the juice, and are often powerful enough to illuminate very large subjects or to supply lots and lots of light to smaller subjects. The output of such units is measured in watt seconds (ws), so you could purchase a 200ws, 400ws, or 800ws unit, and a power pack to match.

Their advantages include greater power output, much faster recycling, built-in modeling lamps, multiple power levels, and ruggedness that can stand up to transport, because many photographers pack up these kits and tote them around as location lighting rigs. Studio lighting kits can range in price from a few hundred dollars for a set of lights, stands, and reflectors, to thousands for a high-end lighting system complete with all the necessary accessories.

A more practical choice these days are *monolights* (see Figure 11.28), which are "all-in-one" studio lights that sell for about $200-$400. They have the flash tube, modeling light, and power supply built into a single unit that can be mounted on a light stand. Monolights are available in AC-only and battery-pack versions, although an external battery eliminates some of the advantages of having a flash with everything in one unit. They are very portable, because all you need is a case for the monolight itself, plus the stands and other accessories you want to carry along. Because these units are so popular with photographers who are not full-time professionals, the lower-cost monolights are often designed more for lighter duty than professional studio flash. That doesn't mean they aren't rugged; you'll just need to handle them with a little more care, and, perhaps, not expect them to be used eight hours a day for weeks on end. In most other respects, however, monolights are the equal of traditional studio flash units in terms of fast recycling, built-in modeling lamps, adjustable power, and so forth.

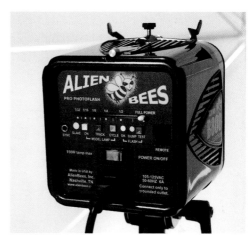

Figure 11.28 All-in-one "monolights" contain flash, power supply, and a modeling light in one compact package (umbrella not included).

Other Lighting Accessories

Once you start working with light, you'll find there are plenty of useful accessories that can help you. Here are some of the most popular that you might want to consider.

Soft Boxes

Soft boxes are large square or rectangular devices that may resemble a square umbrella with a front cover, and produce a similar lighting effect. They can extend from a few feet square to massive boxes that stand five or six feet tall—virtually a wall of light. With a flash unit or two inside a soft box, you have a very large, semi-directional light source that's very diffuse and very flattering for portraiture and other people photography.

Soft boxes are also handy for photographing shiny objects. They not only provide a soft light, but if the box itself happens to reflect in the subject (say you're photographing a chromium toaster), the box will provide an interesting highlight that's indistinct and not distracting.

You can buy soft boxes (like the one shown in Figure 11.29) or make your own. Some lengths of friction-fit plastic pipe and a lot of muslin cut and sewed just so may be all that you need.

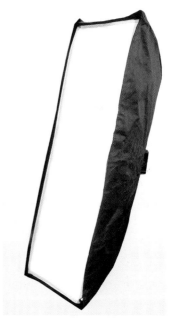

Figure 11.29 Soft boxes provide an even, diffuse light source.

Light Stands

Both electronic flash and incandescent lamps can benefit from light stands. These are lightweight, tripod-like devices (but without a swiveling or tilting head) that can be set on the floor, tabletops, or other elevated surfaces and positioned as needed. Light stands should be strong enough to support an external lighting unit, up to and including a relatively heavy flash with soft box or umbrella reflectors. You want the supports to be capable of raising the lights high enough to be effective. Look for light stands capable of extending six to seven feet high. The nine-foot units usually have larger, steadier bases, and extend high enough that you can use them as background supports. You'll be using these stands for a lifetime, so invest in good ones. I bought the light stand shown in Figure 11.30 when I was in college, and I have been using it for decades.

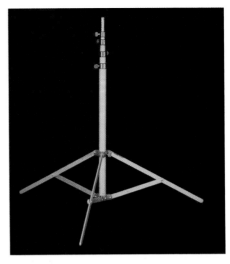

Figure 11.30 Light stands can hold lights, umbrellas, backdrops, and other equipment.

Backgrounds

Backgrounds can be backdrops of cloth, sheets of muslin you've painted yourself using a sponge dipped in paint, rolls of seamless paper, or any other suitable surface your mind can dream up. Backgrounds provide a complementary and non-distracting area behind subjects (especially portraits) and can be lit separately to provide contrast and separation that outlines the subject, or which helps set a mood.

I like to use plain-colored backgrounds for portraits, and white seamless backgrounds for product photography. You can usually construct these yourself from cheap materials and tape them up on the wall behind your subject, or mount them on a pole stretched between a pair of light stands.

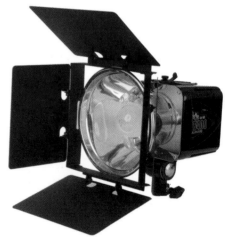

Snoots and Barn Doors

These fit over the flash unit and direct the light at your subject. Snoots are excellent for converting a flash unit into a hair light, while barn doors give you enough control over the illumination by opening and closing their flaps that you can use another flash as a background light, with the capability of feathering the light exactly where you want it on the background. A barn door unit is shown in Figure 11.31.

Figure 11.31 Barn doors allow you to modulate the light from a flash or lamp, and they are especially useful for hair lights and background lights.

12

Working with Wireless Flash

As I mentioned in the last chapter, one of the chief objections to the use of electronic flash is the stark, flat look of direct/on-camera flash. But as flash wizard Joe McNally, author of *The Hotshoe Diaries*, has proven, small flash units can produce amazingly creative images when used properly.

The key to effective flash photography is to get the flash off the camera, so its illumination can be used to paint your subject in interesting and subtle ways from a variety of angles. But, sometimes, using a cable to liberate your flash from the accessory shoe isn't enough. Nor is the use of just a single electronic flash always the best solution. What we really have needed is a way to trigger one—or more—flash units wirelessly, giving us the freedom to place the electronic flash anywhere in the scene and, if our budgets and time allow, to work in this mode with multiple flashes.

Wireless Evolution

For all Canon cameras prior to the introduction of the Canon EOS 7D, wireless operation was an add-on option. The built-in flash of those earlier cameras was not capable of triggering any off-camera Canon Speedlite with full E-TTL exposure automation. (And, of course, cameras like EOS 5D Mark III, which do not have any built-in flash at all, were in the same boat.)

Because wireless triggering was not built into the camera itself, to control other flash units it was necessary to use either a Canon Speedlite Transmitter ST-E2 (a $350 accessory that uses hard-to-find and expensive 2CR5 batteries) or mount a "master" flash on the camera. Dedicating a flash meant sinking another $400 or more into a unit like the Speedlite 580EX II, or, more recently, a 600EX-RT (at a cost north of $500) to your camera just to trigger your wireless strobes. It was especially frustrating when you did not want to use the on-camera flash to contribute to the exposure. Your "triggering" device was invariably an expensive accessory. This, of course, led to the popularity of third-party triggers, like the Pocket Wizard and Radio Popper product lines.

The situation changed dramatically when the Canon EOS 7D was introduced as the first camera to offer built-in wireless triggering capabilities using the built-in flash. This feature was subsequently matched by the EOS 60D, T3i, T4i, the T5i and other mid-level cameras with a built-in flash that followed, including the 70D. Of course, while Canon shooters who owned cameras introduced *before* the 7D have long had access to wireless flash capabilities using add-ons, I was very pleased when Canon introduced the built-in wireless flash control through the pop-up flash. It's an improvement many photographers have welcomed. Any time a new feature eliminates the need to carry a costly accessory and its unusual batteries, the manufacturer has made life simpler and easier for the photographer.

It's not possible to cover every aspect of wireless flash in one chapter. There are too many permutations involved. For example, you can use the 70D's built-in flash, an external flash, or the ST-E2 optical transmitter (or ST-E3-RT radio transmitter) as the master. You may have one external "slave" flash, or use several. It's possible to control all your wireless flash units as if they were one multi-headed flash, or you can allocate them into "groups" that can be managed individually. You may select one of several "channels" to communicate with your strobes (or any of multiple wireless IDs when using radio controlled units like the 600EX-RT). These are all aspects that you'll want to explore as you become used to working with the 70D's amazing wireless capabilities.

What I hope to do in this chapter is provide the introduction to the basics that you won't find in the other guidebooks, so you can learn how to operate the 70D's wireless capabilities quickly, and then embark on your own exploration of the possibilities. Canon has taken a giant step forward by making this "pro" feature more accessible to owners of a mid-entry-level camera like yours. You'll find more complete information in *David Busch's Guide to Canon Flash Photography.*

This chapter builds on the information in Chapter 11 and shows how to take advantage of the 70D's built-in wireless controller. While it may seem complicated at first, it really isn't. Learning the 70D's controls doesn't take a lot of effort, and once you get the hang of it, you'll be able to make changes quickly.

YOUR STEPS MAY VARY

This chapter is intended to teach you the basics of wireless flash: why to use it, how the 70D or another dedicated flash can be used to trigger and control additional units, and what lighting ratios, channels, and groups are. I'm going to provide instructions on getting set up with wireless flash, but, depending on what flash unit you're working with (and how many you have), your specific steps may vary. The final authority on working with wireless flash has to be the manual furnished with your flash unit.

Elements of Wireless Flash

Here are some of the key concepts to electronic flash and wireless flash that I'll be describing in this chapter. Learn what these are, and you'll have gone a long way toward understanding how to use wireless flash. You need to understand the various combinations of flashes that can be used, how they can be controlled individually and together, and why you might want to use multiple and off-camera flash units. I'm going to address all these points in this section.

Flash Combinations

Your 70D has a built-in flash unit, which can be used alone, or in combination with other, external flash units. Here's a quick summary of the permutations available to you.

- **Built-in flash used alone.** Your built-in flash can function as the only flash illumination used to take a picture. In that mode, the flash can provide the primary illumination source (the traditional "flash photo") with the ambient light in the scene contributing little to the overall exposure. (See Figure 12.1, left.) Or, the built-in flash can be used in conjunction with the scene's natural illumination to provide a balanced lighting effect. (Figure 12.1, center.) In this mode, the flash doesn't overpower the ambient light, but, instead, serves to supplement it. Finally, the built-in flash can be used as a "fill" light in scenes that are illuminated predominantly by a natural main light source, such as daylight. In this mode, the flash serves to brighten dark shadows created by the primary illumination, such as the glaring daylight in Figure 12.1, right. I covered the use of the pop-up flash alone in Chapter 11.

- **Built-in flash used simultaneously with off-camera flash.** You can use the off-camera flash as a *main light* and supply *fill light* from the built-in flash to produce interesting effects and pleasing portraits.

- **Built-in flash used as a trigger only for off-camera flash.** Use the 70D's built-in wireless flash controller to command single or multiple Speedlites for studio-like lighting effects, without having the pop-up flash contribute to the exposure itself.

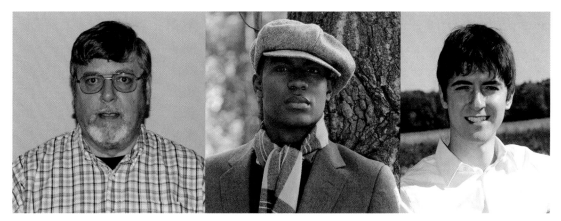

Figure 12.1 Built-in flash alone (left), as a supplement (center), and for fill flash (right).

Controlling Flash Units

There are multiple ways of controlling flash units, both through direct or wired connections and wirelessly. Here are the primary methods used:

- **Direct connection.** The built-in flash, of course, is directly connected to the 70D, and triggered electronically when a picture is taken. External flash units can also be controlled directly, either by plugging them into the accessory shoe on top of the camera or by linking them to a camera with a dedicated flash cord that in turn attaches to the accessory hot shoe. When used in these modes, the camera has full communication with the flash, which can receive information about zoom lens position, correct exposure required, and the signals required to fire the flash. There also exist accessory shoe adapters that provide a PC/X connection, allowing non-dedicated strobes, such as studio flash units, to be fired by the camera. These connections are "dumb" and convey no information other than the signal to fire.

- **Dedicated wireless signals.** In this mode, external flash units communicate with the camera through a pre-flash, which is used to measure exposure prior to the "real" flash burst an instant later. The pre-flash can also wirelessly send information from the camera to the flash unit, used to adjust zoom head position (if the flash has that), and required flash duration to produce the desired exposure. In the case of Canon flash units, the pre-flash information is sent and received as pulses of illumination—much like the remote control of your television. (And, also like your TV remote, the optical signal can bounce around the room somewhat, but you more or less need a line-of-sight connection for the communication to work properly.)

- **Dedicated wireless infrared signals.** Some devices, such as the Canon ST-E2 Speedlite Transmitter, can communicate with dedicated flash units through their own infrared signals. The transmitter attaches to the accessory shoe or is connected to the accessory shoe through a dedicated cable. It was an option for wireless flash for Canon cameras prior to the EOS 7D (and later models with a built-in wireless controller), as well as for Canon cameras that have no flash unit at all (such as the EOS 1D, 1Ds, and 5D series). Although the ST-E2 costs about $350, it's still less expensive than using a unit like the 580EX II or 600EX II as a master controller, particularly when on-camera flash is not desired.

- **Canon and third-party IR and radio transmitters.** The 600EX-RT and ST-E3-RT units from Canon can communicate using radio signals as well as infrared. In addition, some excellent wireless flash controllers that use IR or radio signals to operate external flash units are available from sources like PocketWizard and RadioPopper. One advantage some of these third-party units have is the ability to dial in exposure/output adjustments from the transmitter mounted on the accessory shoe of the camera.

- **Optical slave units.** A relatively low-tech/low-versatility option is to use optical slave units that trigger the off-camera flash units when they detect the firing of the main flash. Slave triggers are inexpensive, but dumb: they don't allow making any adjustments to the external flash units, and are not compatible with the 70D's E-TTL II exposure system. Moreover, you should make sure that the slave trigger responds to the *main* flash burst only, rather than a pre-flash, using a so-called *digital* mode. Otherwise, your slave units will fire before the main flash, and not contribute to the exposure.

Why Use Wireless Flash?

Canon's wireless flash system gives you a number of advantages that include the ability to use directional lighting, which can help bring out detail or emphasize certain aspects of the picture area. It also lets you operate multiple strobes; with the 580EX II that's as many as four flash units in each of three groups, or twelve in all (although most of us won't own 12 Canon Speedlites). With the 600EX-RT, which also has radio control in addition to optical transmission, you can control many more flash units optically, but only 15 radio-controlled Speedlites, in five different groups.

You can set up complicated portrait or location lighting configurations. Since the two top Canon Speedlites pump out a lot of light for a shoe mount flash, a set of these units can give you near studio-quality lighting. Of course, the cost of these high-end Speedlites approaches or exceeds that of some studio monolights—but the Canon battery-powered units are more portable and don't require an external AC or DC power source.

Key Wireless Concepts

There are three key concepts you must understand before jumping into wireless flash photography: channels, groups, and flash ratios. Here is an explanation of each:

- **Channel controls.** Canon's wireless flash system offers users the ability to determine on which of four possible channels the flash units can communicate. (The pilots, ham radio operators, or scanner listeners among you can think of the channels as individual communications frequencies.) When using optical transmission, the channels are numbered 1, 2, 3, and 4, and each flash must be assigned to one of them. Moreover, in general, each of the flash units you are working with should be assigned to the *same* channel, because the slave Speedlites will respond *only* to a master flash that is on the same channel.

    When using the 600EX-RT in radio control mode, there are 15 different channels, plus an Auto setting that allows the flash to select a channel. In addition, you can assign a four-digit Wireless Radio ID that further differentiates the communications channel your flashes use.

    The channel ability is important when you're working around other photographers who are also using the same system. Photojournalists, including sports photographers, encounter this situation frequently. At any event populated by a sea of "white" lenses you'll often find photographers who are using Canon flash units triggered by Canon's own optical or (now) radio control. Third-party triggers from PocketWizard or RadioPopper are also popular, but Canon's technology remains a mainstay for many shooters.

    Each photographer sets flash units to a different channel so as to not accidentally trigger other users' strobes. (At big events with more than four photographers using Canon flash and optical transmission, you may need to negotiate.) I use this capability at workshops I conduct where we have two different setups. Photographers working with one setup use a different channel than those using the other setup, and can work independently even though we're at opposite ends of the same large room.

There is less chance of a channel conflict when working with radio control and all 600EX-RT flash units. With 15 channels to select from, and almost 10,000 wireless radio IDs to choose from, any overlap is unlikely. (It's smart not to use a radio ID like 0000, 1111, 2222, etc. to avoid increasing the chances of conflicts. I use the last four digits of my mother-in-law's Social Security Number.) Remember that you must use either all optical or all radio transmission for all your flash units; you can't mix and match.

- **Groups.** Canon's wireless flash system lets you designate multiple flash units in separate groups. There can be as many as three groups with the 70D's built-in controller and Speedlites like the 580EX II, labeled A, B, and C.

With the 600EX-RT and ST-E3-RT, up to five groups (A, B, C, D, and E) can be used with as many as 15 different flash units. All the flashes in all the groups use the exact same *channel* and all respond to the same master controller, but you can set the output levels of each group separately. So, Speedlites in Group A might serve as the main light, while Speedlites in Group B might be adjusted to produce less illumination and serve as a fill light. It's convenient to be able to adjust the output of all the units within a given group simultaneously. This lets you create different styles of lighting for portraits and other shots.

TIP

It's often smart to assign flash units that will reside to the left of the camera to the A group, and flashes that will be placed to the right of the camera to the B group. It's easier to adjust the comparative power ratios because you won't have to stop and think where your groups are located. That's because the adjustment controls in the *menus* are always arranged in the same A-B-C left-to-right alignment.

For example, if your A group is used as a main light on the left, and the B group as fill on the right, you intuitively know to specify more power to the A group, and less output to the B group. Reserve the C group (if used) to some other purpose, such as background or hair lights.

- **Flash ratios.** This ability to control the output of one flash (or set of flashes) compared to another flash or set allows you to produce lighting *ratios*. You can control the power of multiple off-camera Speedlites to adjust each unit's relative contribution to the image, for more dramatic portraits and other effects.

Which Flashes Can Be Operated Wirelessly?

A particular Speedlite can have one of two functions. It can serve as a *master* flash that's capable of triggering other compatible Canon units that are on the same channel. Or, a Speedlite can be triggered wirelessly as a *slave unit* that's activated by a *master*, with full control over exposure through the 70D's eTTL flash system. The second function is easy: all current Canon shoe-mount flash, including the 600EX-RT, 580EX II, 430EX II, 320EX, and 270EX II can be triggered wirelessly. In addition, some Speedlites and the 70D's built-in flash have the ability to serve as a master flash.

I'm not going to discuss older, discontinued flash units in this chapter; if you own one, particularly a non-Canon unit, it may or may not function as a slave. For example, the early Speedlite 380EX lacked the wireless capabilities added with later models, such as the 420EX, 430EX, and 430EX II.

Here's a quick run-down of current flash capabilities:

- **Built-in flash.** The flash built into the Canon EOS 70D can serve as a master, triggering any of the other current flash units wirelessly. It shares that capability with the EOS 7D (which introduced wireless in-camera triggering to the Canon line), the T3i, T4i, T5i, and the Canon EOS 60D. At this writing, all other Canon cameras with a built-in flash, introduced *prior* to the 70D, can activate external flash units wirelessly *only* when physically connected to an external flash that has master capabilities, the Canon ST-E2/ST-E3-RT transmitter, or third-party transmitters. The Canon EOS Rebel SL1/100D is a newer camera that cannot function as a master flash. 70D's built-in flash (of course) cannot itself function as a slave unit. (It has no facility for receiving signals from a master flash.)

- **Canon Speedlite 600EX-RT.** This top of the line flash can function as a master flash when physically attached to any Canon EOS model, using either optical or radio transmission, and can be triggered wirelessly by another master flash (a 7D/60D/T3i/T4i/T5i/70D camera, another 600EX-RT or 580EX II, or the ST-E2/ST-E3-RT transmitters).

- **Canon Speedlite 580EX II.** This flash can function as a master flash when physically attached to any Canon EOS model, and can be triggered wirelessly by an optical (not radio) transmission from another master flash (a 7D/60D/T3i/T4i/T5i/70D camera, another 580EX II, a 600EX-RT, the ST-E2 transmitter, or ST-E3-RT transmitter in optical mode).

- **Canon Speedlite 430EX II.** This flash cannot function as a master, but can be triggered wirelessly by a master flash (a 7D/60D/T3i/T4i/T5i/70D camera, a Speedlite 600EX-RT/580EX II, or the ST-E-2 and ST-E3-RT transmitters in optical mode).

- **Canon Speedlite 320EX.** This flash can be triggered wirelessly by a master flash (a 7D/60D/T3i/T4i/T5i/70D camera, a 600EX-RT/580EX II, or the ST-E-2 and ST-E3-RT transmitters in optical mode).

- **Canon Speedlite 270EX II.** This flash can be triggered wirelessly by a master flash (a 7D/60D/T3i/T4i/T5i/70D camera, a 600EX-RT/580EX II, or the ST-E-2 and ST-E3-RT transmitters in optical mode).

You can use any combination of compatible flash units in your wireless setup. The 70D can serve as the master, or you can use an attached 600EX-RT, 580EX II, or ST-E2/ST-E3-RT as a master, with any number of 600EX-RT, 580EX II, 430EX II, 320EX, or 270EX II units (or older compatible Speedlites not discussed in this chapter) as wireless slaves. I'll get you started assigning these flash to groups and channels later on.

Getting Started

The EOS 70D has an easy wireless flash mode,. Since it's necessary to set up both the camera and the strobes for wireless operation, this guide will help you with both, starting with prepping the camera and flash. To configure your equipment for wireless flash, just follow these steps. (I'm going to condense them a bit, because many of these settings have been introduced in previous chapters.)

We're going to begin by assuming that you want to use the 70D's built-in flash as the master controller flash. If that's the case, you need to follow these steps with your external flash units first:

1. **Set the wireless off-camera Speedlite to slave mode.** Any of the flash units listed earlier can be used as a slave flash. The first step is to set the off-camera flash to slave mode. The procedure differs for each individual flash model. Check your manual for exact instructions. I'll use the 580EX II as a typical example: Press the Zoom button for two seconds until the display flashes, then rotate the control dial on the flash until the Slave indicator blinks on the LCD. Press the control dial's center button to confirm your choice.

2. **Assign a channel.** All units must use the same channel. The default channel is 1. If you need to change to a different communications channel, do so using the instructions for your particular flash unit. With the 580EX II, press the Zoom button several times until the CH indicator flashes. Then rotate the control dial on the flash until the channel you want appears on the LCD. Press the control dial center button to confirm your choice.

3. **Assign slave to a group.** If you want to use a flash ratio to adjust the output of some slave units separately, you'll want to assign the slave flash to a group, either Group A (the default) or Group B. All units within a particular group fire at the same proportionate level. If you've set Group B to fire at half power, *all* the Speedlites that have been assigned to Group B will fire at half power.

   And remember that all flash units on a particular channel are controlled by the same master flash, regardless of the group they belong to. Set the group according to the instructions for your particular flash. For the 580EX II, press the Zoom button until the A flashes on the LCD. Then rotate the control dial on the flash to choose B. Press the control dial center button to confirm your choice.

4. **Position the off-camera flash units, with the Speedlite's wireless sensor facing the camera/master flash.** Indoors, you can position the external flash up to 33 feet from the master unit; outdoors, keep the distance to 23 feet or less. Your ability to use a flash wirelessly can depend on whether the Speedlite's sensor can receive communication from the master flash. Factors can include the direction the slave flash is pointed, and whether light can bounce off walls or other surfaces to reach the sensor. When working with the 600EX-RT's radio controls, Canon guarantees "reception" up to 98 feet from the master flash/trigger, but many shooters report no problems at distances of 150 to 200 feet (and no line-of-sight required!).

If you want to use more than one slave unit, follow these instructions. All additional units using the same communications channel will fire at once, regardless of the slave ID (Group) assignment.

Wireless Flash Shooting

The procedures for using this mode are basically the same as for Easy Wireless Flash shooting, except that you have more options for adjusting things like flash ratios. Just follow these steps:

1. **Using the built-in flash as a wireless flash controller.** Start by using a Creative Zone mode and popping up the camera's built-in flash. You can use this flash in conjunction with your remote, off-camera strobes (adding some illumination to your photos), or just to control them (with no illumination from your pop-up flash contributing to the exposure). The built-in flash needs to be in the up position to use the 70D's wireless flash controller either way.

2. **Enable internal flash.** Press the MENU button and navigate to the Shooting 2 menu. Choose the Flash Control entry (see Figure 12.2), as described in Chapter 11, and press the SET button. This brings up the Flash Control menu (which is at the bottom of the menu). Press the SET button to enter the Flash Control menu. Next, select the Flash Firing setting and set the camera to Enable. This activates the built-in flash, which makes wireless flash control with the 70D possible.

3. **Confirm/Enable E-TTL II exposure.** While you can use wireless flash techniques and manual flash exposure, you're better off learning to use wireless features with the EOS 70D set to automatic exposure. So, from the Flash Control menu, choose E-TTL II metering and select Evaluative exposure.

4. **Enable wireless functions.** Next, choose Built-in Flash Settings and select Wireless Func. Press SET to confirm and return to the Built-in Flash Settings menu.

Figure 12.2
The Flash Control menu.

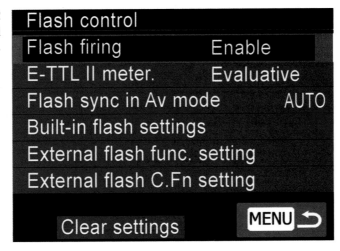

5. **Access wireless configuration.** In the Built-in Flash Setting menu, scroll down to Wireless Func. (see Figure 12.3) and press SET.

6. **Select wireless configuration.** Choose the External Flash:Built-in Flash icon at the top of the list of choices. Press SET to confirm. The colon between the two flash icons indicates that in this mode you can set a flash *ratio* between the units.

7. **Choose a channel.** Scroll down to Channel, press SET, and select the channel you want to use (generally that will be Channel 1).

8. **Set flash ratio.** Scroll down to the Ratio Setting entry (it's directly under the Flash Exp. Comp entry) and set a flash ratio between 1:1 (equal output) and 8:1 (external flash 8X the output of the internal flash, or, three stops). Ratios where the internal flash is *more* powerful than the external flash (i.e., 1:2, 1:4, etc.) are not possible.

9. **Take photos.** You're all set! You can now take photos wirelessly.

10. **Exit wireless mode.** When you're finished using wireless flash, navigate to the Built-in Flash Settings in the Flash Control menu and select NormalFiring. Wireless flash is deactivated.

Once you've completed the steps above, your 70D is set up to begin using wireless flash using your camera's built-in flash and one external off-camera flash. Additional options are available for the brave. I'll show you each of these one at a time.

WIRELESS SETTING FOR EXTERNAL FLASH

As noted, you must switch your external flash from normal to wireless modes. The procedure will vary, depending on your flash unit. With the 580EX II, press and hold the Zoom button for two seconds or longer until the display blinks. Then rotate the flash's control dial until either Master or Slave appears on the flash's LCD. Press the dial's center button to confirm your choice of Master or Slave wireless operation.

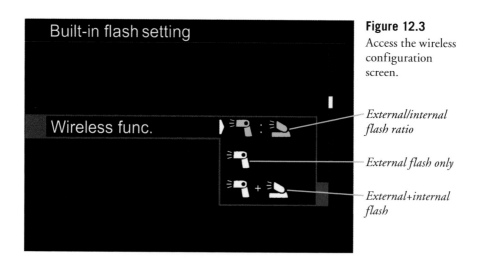

Figure 12.3
Access the wireless configuration screen.

External/internal flash ratio

External flash only

External+internal flash

REMINDER

Keep in mind that when the Canon Speedlite 580EX II and most other Canon units are ready to fire as a slave, the AF-assist beam will blink at one-second intervals. The unit will *not* go into a sleep mode while it is waiting to be used as a slave, but the camera will shut off at the interval you've specified in the menus.

Setting Up an External Master Flash or Controller

The first step in using an external flash or controller as the master (instead of the built-in flash) is to set up one unit (either a flash or controller) as the external *master*. You can mount a Speedlite 580EX, 580EX II, or 600EX-RT to your camera, which can serve as the master unit, transmitting E-TTL II optical signals to one or more off-camera Speedlite *slave* units. The master unit can have its flash output set to "off" so that it controls the remote units without contributing any flash output of its own to the exposure. This is useful for images where you don't want noticeable flash illumination coming in from the camera position. The next sections explain your options for setting up a master unit for fully automatic, E-TTL II exposure.

WIRELESS MANUAL EXPOSURE

You can also use manual exposure instead of E-TTL II automatic exposure in wireless mode. Setting up your master flash for manual operation is beyond the scope of this book, but you'll find instructions in my Canon flash book, described earlier.

Using a Speedlite as the Master

Here are the steps to follow to set up and use a compatible Speedlite as a camera-mounted master unit for automatic exposure.

600EX-RT

1. Press the Wireless button repeatedly until the LCD panel indicates you are in optical wireless master mode.

2. Press Mode to cycle through the ETTL, M, and Multi modes.

3. Use the menu system to control and make changes to ratio, output, and other options on the master and slave units.

580EX II

1. Press and hold the Zoom button to bring up the wireless options. Use the Select dial to cycle through the Off, Master on, and Slave on options. Select and confirm Master on.

2. Press Mode to cycle through the ETTL, M, and Multi modes.

3. Press the Zoom button repeatedly to cycle through the following options: Flash zoom, Ratio, CH., flash emitter On/Off. Use the Select dial and Select/SET button to make any changes to these options.

4. Use the Select/SET button to select and confirm the output power settings when using Manual and Multi modes, or to use FEC or FEB when in ETTL mode.

580EX

1. Slide the Off/Master/Slave wireless switch near the base of the unit to Master.

2. Press Mode to cycle through the ETTL, M, and Multi modes.

3. Press the Zoom button repeatedly to cycle through the following options: Flash zoom, Ratio, CH., flash emitter On/Off. Use the Select dial and Select/SET button to make any changes to these options.

4. Use the Select/SET button to select and confirm the output power settings when using Manual and Multi modes, or to use FEC or FEB when in ETTL mode.

Using the ST-E2 Transmitter as Master

Canon's Speedlite Transmitter (ST-E2) is mounted on the camera's hot shoe and provides a way to control one or more Speedlites and/or units assigned to Groups A and B. The ST-E2 does not provide any flash output of its own and will not trigger units assigned to Group C. It has the following features and controls:

- **Transmitter.** Located on the top front of the unit, the transmitter emits E-TTL II pulses through an infrared filter.

- **AF-assist beam emitter.** Just below the transmitter, the AF-assist beam emitter works similarly to the Speedlite 430EX II and higher models.

- **Battery compartment.** The ST-E2 uses a 6.0V 2CR5 lithium battery. The battery compartment is accessed from the top of the unit.

- **Lock slider and mounting foot.** The lock slider is located on the right side of the unit when facing the front. Sliding it to the left lowers the lock pin in the mounting foot (located on the bottom of the unit) to secure it to the camera's hot shoe.

- **Back panel.** The rear of the unit features several indicators and controls:
  - **Ratio indicator.** A series of red LED lights indicating the current A:B ratio setting.
  - **Flash ratio control lamp.** A red LED that lights up when flash ratio is in use.
  - **Flash ratio setting button.** Next to the flash ratio control lamp. Press this button to activate flash ratio control.
  - **Flash ratio adjustment buttons.** Two buttons with raised arrows (same color as buttons) pointing left and right. Use these to change the A:B ratio setting.
  - **Channel indicator.** The channel number in use (1-4) glows red.
  - **Channel selector button.** Next to the channel indicator. Press this button to select the communication channel.
  - **High-speed sync (FP flash) indicator.** A red LED that glows when high-speed sync is in use.
  - **High-speed sync button.** Press this button to activate/deactivate high-speed sync.
  - **ETTL indicator.** A red LED that glows when E-TTL II is in use.
  - **Off/On/Hold switch.** Slide this switch to turn the unit off, on, or on with adjustments disabled (Hold). The ST-E2 will power off after approximately 90 seconds of idle time. It will turn back on when the shutter button or test transmission button is pressed.
  - **Pilot lamp/Test transmission button.** This lamp works similarly to the Speedlite pilot lamp/test buttons. The lamp glows red when ready to transmit. Press the lamp button to send a test transmission to the slave units.
  - **Flash confirmation lamp.** This lamp glows green for about three seconds when the ST-E2 detects a good flash exposure.

Here are the steps to follow to set up and use the ST-E2 transmitter as a camera-mounted master unit:

1. Mount the ST-E2 unit on your 70D.
2. Make sure both the ST-E2 unit and your camera are powered on.
3. Make sure the slave units are set to E-TTL II, assigned to the appropriate group(s), and that all units are operating on the same channel.
4. If you'd like to set a flash ratio between Groups A and B, press the flash ratio setting button and flash ratio adjustment buttons to select the desired ratio. Press the high-speed sync button to use high-speed sync (often helpful with outdoor shooting).

Using the Speedlite 600EX-RT as Radio Master

The Speedlite 600EX-RT can serve as the master unit when mounted to your camera, transmitting radio signals to one or more off-camera Speedlite 600EX-RT slave units. The master unit can have its flash output set to "off" so that it controls the remote units without contributing any flash output of its own to the exposure. This is useful for images where you don't want noticeable flash illumination coming in from the camera position.

Here are the steps to follow to set up and use a Speedlite 600EX-RT as a camera-mounted master unit for radio wireless E-TTL II operation.

1. Mount the Speedlite 600EX-RT to your 70D.
2. Make sure the 600EX-RT master units, slave units, and the camera are powered on.
3. Set the camera-mounted 600EX-RT to radio wireless Master mode. Press the Wireless button until the LCD panel indicates you are on radio wireless master mode.
4. Set the slave 600EX-RT units to radio wireless Slave mode. For each unit, press the Wireless button until the LCD panel indicates you are on radio wireless slave mode.
5. Confirm that all units are set to E-TTL II, assigned to the appropriate group(s), and that all units are operating on the same channel and ID number. The LINK lamps on all units should glow green.

Using the ST-E3-RT as Radio Master

The ST-E3-RT transmitter can be mounted to the camera's hot shoe and used as a master controller to one or more slave Speedlite 600EX-RT units. The ST-E3-RT and the 600EX-RT share essentially the same radio control capabilities except that the ST-E3-RT does not produce flash, provide AF-assist, or otherwise emit light, and is therefore incapable of optical wireless transmission.

The layout of the ST-E3-RT's control panel is virtually identical to the 600EX-RT. So is the menu system and operation, except that, as stated earlier, it will only operate as a radio wireless transmitter. Here are the steps to follow to set up and use the ST-E3-RT transmitter as a camera-mounted master unit for radio wireless E-TTL II operation:

1. Mount the ST-E3-RT unit on your 70D.
2. Make sure both the ST-E3-RT unit and your camera are powered on.
3. Set the slave 600EX-RT units to radio wireless Slave mode. For each unit, press the Wireless button until the LCD panel indicates you are on radio wireless slave mode.
4. Confirm that all units are set to E-TTL II, assigned to the appropriate group(s), and that all units are operating on the same channel and ID number. The Link lamps on all units should glow green.

The ST-E3-RT controls slave units as described earlier in the section, "Speedlite 600EX-RT as Radio Wireless Master Using E-TTL II."

Setting Up a Slave Flash

The whole point of working wirelessly is to have a master flash/controller trigger and adjust one or more slave flash units. So, once you've defined your master flash, the next step is to switch your remaining Speedlites into slave mode. That's done differently with each particular Canon Speedlite.

- **Speedlite 600EX-RT.** Press the Wireless button repeatedly until the LCD panel indicates that the unit is in optical wireless slave mode or radio wireless slave mode. In this mode, the 600EX-RT is assigned a flash mode by the master transmitter, either a flash or ST-E2 or ST-E3-RT.

- **Speedlite 580EX II.** Press and hold the Zoom button until the wireless setting options appear. Use the Select dial and Select/SET button to select and confirm that wireless is on and in slave mode.

- **Speedlite 430EX II.** Press and hold the Zoom button until the wireless setting options appear. Use the Select dial and Select/SET button to select and confirm that wireless is on and in slave mode.

- **Speedlite 320EX.** This flash has an On/Off/Slave switch at the lower left of the back panel. In Slave mode, you can use the flash's C.Fn 10 to tell the unit to power down after either 10 or 60 minutes of idle time. That can help preserve the 320EX's batteries. The unit's C.Fn 11 can be set to allow the master transmitter to "wake" a sleeping 320EX after your choice of within 1 hour or within 8 hours. Note that the C.Fn settings of the 320EX and 270EX II (described next) can be set only while the Speedlites are connected to the camera with the hot shoe.

- **Speedlite 270EX II.** This flash has an Off/Slave/On switch. If left on and idle, the 270EX II will power itself off after approximately 90 seconds. C.Fn 01 can be used to disable auto power off. As with the 320EX, in Slave mode, you can use the flash's C.Fn 10 to tell the unit to power down after either 10 or 60 minutes of idle time. The unit's C.Fn 11 can be set to allow the master transmitter to "wake" a sleeping unit after your choice of within 1 hour or within 8 hours.

More Wireless Options and Capabilities

If you're ready to immerse yourself even more deeply in wireless flash photography, the next sections will provide a little more detail on using some of the settings for ratios, channels, and groups.

Internal/External Flash Ratio Setting

Your built-in flash and your wireless flash units have their own individual *oomph*—how much illumination they put out. This option lets you choose the relationship between these units, a *power ratio* between your built-in flash and your wireless flash units—the relative strength of each—as we did in Step 8 in the last section. That ability can be especially useful if you want to use the built-in flash for just a little fill light (it's not very powerful, anyway), while letting your off-camera units do the heavy work. This setting is the top choice in the Wireless Function menu, designated with icons that show an external flash and a raised camera flash.

Having the ability to vary the power of each flash unit or group of flash units wirelessly gives you greater flexibility and control. Varying the light output of each flash unit makes it possible to create specific types of lighting (such as traditional portrait lighting which frequently calls for a 3:1 lighting ratio between main light and fill light) or to use illumination to highlight one part of the photo while reducing contrast in another.

Lighting ratios determine the contrast between the main (sometimes called a "key" light) and fill light. For portraiture, the main light is typically placed at a 45-degree angle to the subject (although there are some variations), with the fill-in light on the opposite side or closer to the camera position. Choosing the right lighting ratio can do a lot to create a particular look or mood. For instance, a 1:1 ratio produces what's known as "flat" lighting. While this is good for copying or documentation, it's not usually as interesting for portraiture. Instead, making the main light more powerful than the fill light creates interesting shadows for more dramatic images. (See Figure 12.4.)

By selecting the power ratio between the flash units, you can change the relative illumination between them. Figure 12.5 shows a series of four images with a single main flash located at a 45-degree angle off to the right and slightly behind the model. The built-in flash at the camera provided illumination to fill in the shadows on the side of the face closest to the camera. The ratio between the external and internal flash were varied using 2:1 (upper left), 3:1 (upper right), 4:1 (lower left), and 5:1 (lower right) ratios.

Here's how to set the lighting ratio between the internal flash and one external wireless flash unit:

1. **Choose Ratio Setting in Wireless Func. menu.** In the Built-in Flash Setting menu, highlight Wireless Func., press SET, and choose Ratio Setting. Press SET again to confirm and return to the previous menu.

2. **Access the Power Ratio entry.** Now you can set the power ratio by scrolling down just below Flash Exp. Comp., represented by a pair of icons corresponding to an external and internal flash unit.

3. **Set the control.** Press the SET button.

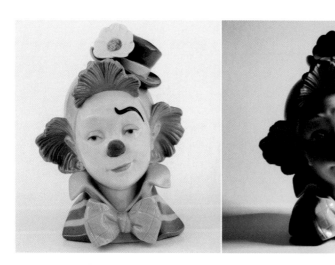

Figure 12.4
More dramatic lighting ratios produce more dramatic-looking illumination.

Figure 12.5

The main light (to the right and behind the model) and fill light (at the camera position) were varied using 2:1 and 3:1 (top row, left to right) as well as 4:1 and 5:1 (bottom row, left to right) ratios.

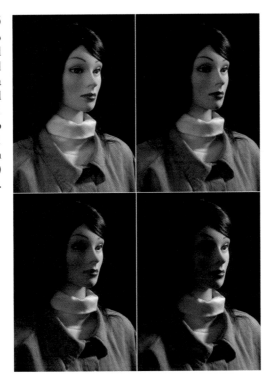

4. **Choose the desired ratio.** Then use the multi-controller to choose the setting you want. (See Figure 12.6.) Your choices range from 1:1 (the off-camera and built-in flash have equal output) to 8:1 (the off-camera flash supplies 8X output compared to the internal flash). Set the ratio to 4:1, for example, and the external flash will produce four times as much light as the on-camera flash, which is then used as fill illumination. For most subjects, ratios of 2:1 to 5:1 will produce the best results, as shown earlier in Figure 12.5.

5. **Confirm.** Press SET to confirm your ratio.

Figure 12.6

Select a ratio from 8:1 to 1:1.

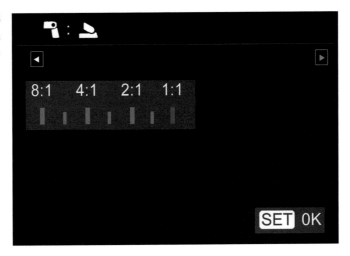

Wireless Flash Only

This setting, represented earlier in Figure 12.3 by an icon of a flash unit alone, allows you to turn off the flash output of your 70D's built-in flash, while allowing it to emit a wireless controller flash that signals the external flash units you're working with. You'll still see a burst from your camera's built-in flash, but that burst will not contribute to the exposure. It will only be used to tell the remote/slave flash units to fire.

This is the setting to choose if you only want to use the flash controller to operate your remote flashes. It's probably the most commonly used choice when you don't want to use the internal flash for fill light, since firing the built-in flash increases the risk of red-eye effects.

Photographers prefer this mode in part because Canon's portable shoe mount flash units are much more powerful than a camera's built-in flash. They want to avoid using a light source that is directly above the lens and close to the lens, since red-eye is caused by light from the flash unit reflecting off the subject's retinas and bouncing back into the lens.

Using off-camera flash lets the photographer precisely control light direction and effect. It also makes it possible for the photographer to move around within the constraints of the flash units' ability to illuminate a scene, without worrying about getting too far from the subject for the flash unit(s) to be effective. Only the camera to subject position changes and not the light to subject position and ratio. Once you've set up the flash units relative to your subject, you can move around freely.

Being able to control lighting direction is a very useful capability since it can lead to more dramatic images. In Figure 12.7 a single flash unit was used to light the model. A grid (a small light "concentrator") was placed on the flash head to restrict the light from the unit. In this case, the lighting effect is dramatic.

Here are the steps to follow when using wireless flash only (whether you're working with a single external flash, or multiple units).

1. **Choose wireless flash only.** Navigate to the Wireless Func. menu as you did earlier, but choose Wireless Flash Only (the single-flash icon in the middle of the list).

2. **Confirm.** Press the SET button to confirm the Wireless Flash Only setting.

3. **Set the Power Ratio (optional).** If you are using only one flash, or all the flash units are assigned to the same group, you don't need to do this; setting a power ratio won't make any difference. The Firing Group entry will read "All" and the fire ratio entry will not be visible. You can only select a power ratio if you've chosen A:B in the Firing Group entry. (Remember to change the power ratio back to normal when you are finished with a session; Canon's Speedlites retain the settings you make, even after a quick battery change.)

Figure 12.7
The subject was lit by a Canon 600EX-RT flash unit with a Honl Speed Grid. The flash unit was placed on a light stand positioned to the left of the model and angled slightly downward.

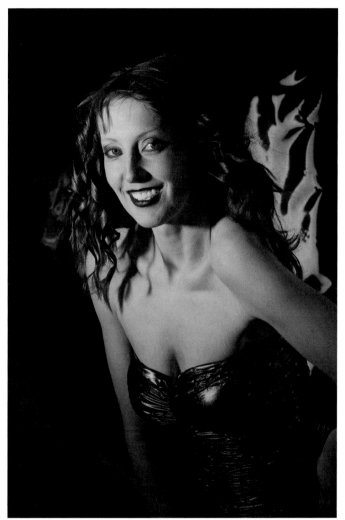

Using Wireless and Built-in Flash

This option in the Wireless Func. screen, represented by an icon of an external unit *plus* an icon of a raised camera flash, adds the built-in flash to whatever wireless groups you're using. You can then use the built-in flash in conjunction with whatever firing groups you've set up. In this case you're still using the external flash units as the main sources of light, but the built-in flash can either serve to provide some extra fill (such as to illuminate the face under the brim of a hat) or to provide a second light when you only have one off-camera flash available.

It is also possible to set up a two-light portrait using an off-camera flash as a main light (about 45 degrees to the model) and the built-in flash as the fill light, as discussed earlier. Use the External/Internal Flash Ratio Setting to adjust their relative contribution to the image.

Some photographers do like to position their fill light directly above the camera and straight toward the model. The lighting ratio for such a setup would have the built-in and external strobes set to 1:1 or 2:1. Keep in mind that if using such a configuration, the light from the built-in flash is striking the subject head on and needs to be added to your calculations for the main light. In other words, setting your lighting ratio to 1:1 would actually provide a 2:1 effective lighting ratio since you would have 1 part light from the main light and 1 part light from the built-in flash illuminating one side of the subject and just 1 part light from the built-in flash illuminating the other side. Setting your lighting ratio to 2:1 would effectively provide a 3:1 lighting ratio this way. If you have set the camera to E-TTL II exposure as recommended, the lighting you choose will be automatically accounted for in the exposure selected by the camera, so no calculations are necessary by the photographer.

Working with Groups

With what you've already learned, you can shoot wirelessly using your camera's built-in flash and one or more external flash units. All these strobes will work together with the 70D for automatic exposure using E-TTL II exposure mode. You can vary the power ratio between your built-in flash and the external units. As you become more comfortable with wireless flash photography, you can even switch the individual external flash units into manual mode, and adjust their lighting ratios manually.

But there's a lot more you can do if you've splurged and own two or more compatible external flash units (some photographers I know own five or six Speedlite 580EX II or 600EX-RT units). Canon wireless photography lets you collect individual strobes into *groups*, and control all the Speedlites within a given group together. You can operate as few as two strobes in two groups or three strobes in three groups, while controlling more units if desired. You can also have them fire at equal output settings (A+B+C mode) versus using them at different power ratios (A:B or A:B C modes). Setting each group's strobes to different power ratios gives you more control over lighting for portraiture and other uses.

This is one of the more powerful options of the EOS wireless flash system. I prefer to keep my Speedlites set to different groups normally. I can always set the power ratio to 1:1 if I want to operate the flash units all at the same power. If I change my mind and need to make adjustments, I can just change the wireless flash controller and then manipulate the different groups' output as desired.

Canon's wireless flash system works with a number of Canon flashes and even some third-party units. I routinely mix a 600EX-RT, 580EX II, 550EX, and 420EX plus sometimes add a Sigma EF-500 Super. I control these flash units either with the EOS 70D's built-in wireless capabilities or using a Canon ST-E2 Speedlite Transmitter.

The ST-E2 is a hot shoe mount device that offers wireless flash control for a wide variety of Canon wireless flash capable strobes and can even control flash units wirelessly for High-speed sync (HSS) photography. (HSS is described in Chapter 11.) The ST-E2 can only control three flash groups though and also can support flash exposure bracketing. Its range isn't as great as the 70D's though.

Canon flash units that can be operated wirelessly include: 580EX II, 580EX, 550EX, 430EX, 420EX, 320EX, MR-14EX, MT-24EX. The 270EX, 220EX, 380EX, and earlier Canon flash units cannot be operated wirelessly via Canon's wireless flash system. There are third-party flash units that can (such as the Sigma I use), but you must use one designed to work with Canon's wireless flash system only.

Here's how you set up groups:

1. **Determine lighting setup.** Decide whether you're using the built-in flash as part of your lighting scheme or just using the external flash units. If you do want the internal flash to contribute to the exposure, then you can scroll down in the Built-in Flash Setting entry to the External Flash/Built-in Flash Lighting Ratio Control (if you're using lighting ratios) and set that control (from 8:1 to 2:1, as noted earlier).

2. **Access lighting groups.** If you're not using the built-in flash (Wireless Func. is set to the external flash only icon), scroll down to the Firing Group entry that appears and press SET.

3. **Select the group configuration you want.** From top to bottom, the choices are as follows:

   ■ **All external.** Multiple external flash units functioning as one big flash.

   ■ **A:B.** Multiple external units in two groups.

   I'll explain exactly what these two configurations do next.

4. **Allocate flash units into groups.** You must do this at the flash unit itself. You'll need to tell each flash which group it "belongs" to, so it will respond, along with any other strobes (if any) in its group, to wireless commands directed at that particular group. The procedure for setting each flash unit's slave ID/group varies depending on what flash you are using, so consult your Speedlite's manual.

SETTING SLAVE/GROUP ID WITH THE 580EX II

1. Press the Zoom button for two seconds or longer until the display blinks.
2. Rotate the control dial until the Slave indicator blinks.
3. Press the control dial button to confirm Slave operation.
4. To change from Group A to another group, press the Zoom button until the Group A indicator blinks.
5. Rotate the control dial until the A indicator is replaced by the B or C indicators.
6. Press the control dial button to confirm the group ID.

Ratio Control

By default, all the flashes in each group will fire at full power. However, for more advanced lighting setups, you can select lighting ratios.

Here's how to set the lighting ratio between the internal flash and one external wireless flash unit:

1. **Navigate to the 70D's Flash Group selection option.** With wireless flash already activated, visit the Flash Control entry in the Shooting 2 menu, and navigate to the Flash Function Settings choice, Flash Functions. Navigate to the Flash Group choice at the lower left of the screen and choose SET.

2. **Choose Group Configuration.** You can select ALL, A:B, or A:B C. If you're using the 600EX-RT in radio transmission mode, you can also select Groups D and E. Press SET to confirm.

3. **Select Ratio.** If you've chosen A:B C, navigate to the A:B Ratio Control option, and select a ratio from 8:1 to 1:8. At 8:1, Group A supplies 8X output of Group B. At 1:8, the ratio is reversed.

4. **Confirm.** Press SET to confirm your ratio.

Here's how the various basic Group Configurations work:

- **ALL.** All groups will fire at the power level set at the flash unit itself. That may be full power, or you may have set individual flashes to fire at some other power level. It's usually simpler to set your flashes at full power and allow the master to control their output.

- **A:B.** In this configuration, you can specify the ratio of the power levels of Groups A and B, as described in Step 3 above.

Choosing a Channel

Canon's wireless flash system can work on any of four channels, so if more than one photographer is using the Canon system, each can set his gear to a different channel so they don't accidentally trigger each other's strobes. You need to be sure all of your gear is set to the same channel. Selecting a channel is done differently with each particular flash model.

The ability to operate flash units on one of four channels isn't really important unless you're shooting in an environment where other photographers are also using the Canon wireless flash system. If the system only offered one channel, then each photographer's wireless flash controller would be firing every Canon flash set for wireless operation. By having four channels available, the photographers can coordinate their use to avoid that problem. Such situations are common at sporting events and other activities that draw a lot of shooters.

It's always a good idea to double-check your flash units before you set them up to make sure they're all set to the same channel, and this should also be one of your first troubleshooting questions if a flash doesn't fire the first time you try to use it wirelessly.

You do this as follows:

1. **Set flash units to the channel you want to use for all your groups.** Each flash unit may use its own procedure for setting that strobe's channel. Consult your Speedlite's manual for instructions. With the 580EX II, press the Zoom button repeatedly until the CH. Indicator blinks, then rotate the control dial to select Channel 1, 2, 3, or 4. Press the control dial center button to confirm.

2. **Navigate to the 70D's channel selection option.** In the Built-in Flash Func. Settings screen, use the multi-controller to scroll down to the Channel Setting and push the SET button.

3. **Select the channel your flashes are set to.** You can then use the up/down multi-controller to advance the channel number from 1 to 4 or back down again (you have to reverse the multi-controller direction to get back to one; you can't just keep advancing it to get there—it doesn't "wrap around").

4. **Double-check to make sure your flash units are set to the appropriate channel.** Your wireless flash units must be set to the same channel as the 70D's wireless flash controller; otherwise, the Speedlites won't fire.

Flash Release Function

The Canon Speedlite 320EX and Speedlite 270EX II have a nifty feature called the Remote Release Function, which, as I write this, is completely novel in the Canon accessory flash line-up. The feature allows you to detach the Speedlite from certain EOS cameras (right now the 5D Mark II and Mark III, 6D, 7D, 60D, 70D, T4i, T3i, T2i, T1i, Xsi, Xti, XT, and 2003-era original Digital Rebel), and then use a button on the flash unit as a remote control to trigger the camera from up to 16 feet away. That's right, your 320EX and 270EX II can function as wireless remote controls, just like the Canon RC-6, RC-5, and RC-1 infrared controls!

As you can see from the list of cameras, it works with any EOS camera that can be triggered by an IR remote. There's a (mandatory) two-second delay after you press the flash's remote release, and the flash itself does not have to fire and contribute to the exposure. An invisible infrared signal emitted by the flash triggers the camera.

To use the feature with the 70D, use the Drive function, described earlier, and select the self-timer/infrared remote option. If you don't want the 70D's flash to fire, make sure it's set to P or a Creative Zone mode where the flash doesn't pop up automatically. With the 320EX or 270EX II turned on and detached from the camera, position the flash so it "sees" the remote control sensor on the front of the camera. Press the remote release button on the side of the flash, and the camera will fire two seconds later. If you're taking a picture of yourself, this delay allows you to stash the flash out of sight and grin. The flash will not fire.

If you prefer to have the flash fire and contribute to the exposure, move the On/Off switch on the back to the middle "slave" position. In this mode, the camera itself must serve as the master, or you must have another master unit physically attached to the camera. To use the camera in master mode, use the Built-in Flash Control menu entry to activate the 70D's master mode, as described previously. Or, you can connect a 580EX II, set to master mode, either by putting it in the accessory shoe or linked with a cable, such as the Off Camera Cord OC-E3. Alternatively, you can connect the Speedlite Transmitter ST-E2.

When you're ready, point the 320EX or 270EX II at the front of the camera/master flash within 16 feet of the camera, and press the remote control button on the side of the flash. During the two-second delay, you can then point the 320EX or 270EX II in a different direction (as is likely, because you're probably using this feature to illuminate the scene, not the camera). That's the real reason for the two-second delay, by the way: giving you the ability to reposition the "remote" release flash.

The 600EX-RT has its own remote release function, which allows you to use a slave unit to trigger your camera by remote control when using radio transmission mode. EOS cameras released since 2012 (including the 70D) can be triggered in this way through the intelligent hot shoe, using a 600EX-RT mounted on the camera as a receiver, and the slave 600EX-RT off camera as the remote trigger. Older cameras can still be used in this mode, but you'll need to connect the on-camera 600EX-RT to the camera's N3 remote control terminal using an optional Release Cable SR-N3. (If your camera uses a different type of remote release, you're out of luck.)

Using Wireless Flash Creatively

Getting the flash off the camera is fundamental to improving the quality of your lighting. Wireless flash lets you control the light's direction and allows you to use a number of light sources to create more interesting and attractive images.

These next sections look at some ways of using wireless flash to improve your photography. They break down into tips and tricks based on the number of flash units used to create an image. Keep in mind, even just one small flash unit, used creatively, can lead to a significant improvement in your photos, especially when you can use your external flash off camera and you're not tied down to the accessory shoe.

Single-Flash Unit Ideas

As you've seen, using a Canon Speedlite wirelessly is simple with the 70D. Many Canon flash units come with a handy table stand accessory that allows you to set up the flash as a freestanding light. Just configure the strobe for wireless connectivity to the camera, as described previously in this chapter, and then position it wherever you want. So long as the strobe and the camera can see each other (the wireless signal from the 70D can even be bounced off of walls to connect with the flash), they will communicate with each other.

Some handy uses for a single off-camera flash include moving it closer to the subject to increase its effectiveness (remember the inverse square law), placing it off to the side of the subject to show detail (or positioned alongside a reflective surface such as a white wall or reflector to provide main light and fill), or raised up high and angled to one side to get rid of harsh shadows.

While the number of possibilities is endless, here are some examples of things that can be done with a single off-camera flash. Some of these are done with just a basic flash unit, while others rely on light modifiers to create unusual effects.

Single-Flash Unit and Sunlight

When shooting outdoors you can often combine sunlight and an off-camera flash to create a more pleasing looking portrait. Position your subject so the sun is at a 45-degree angle to her and your off-camera flash is lighting her from the parallel 45-degree angle. You can either go with equal exposures (for flat portrait lighting) or expose the flashlit side brighter or darker than the sun's exposure for a more stylistic type of lighting.

You can improve the quality of the light by firing the flash unit into a soft box or umbrella, as in this photograph of a young model (shown in Figure 12.8). Placing the soft box and flash closer to the subject would soften the light even more (the larger the light source in relation to the subject, the softer the light) and make the flash unit's effective output even greater.

Figure 12.8
A Canon 600EX-RT Speedlite was mounted on a light stand and fired through a soft box to one side, while the sun illuminated the young lady from the other.

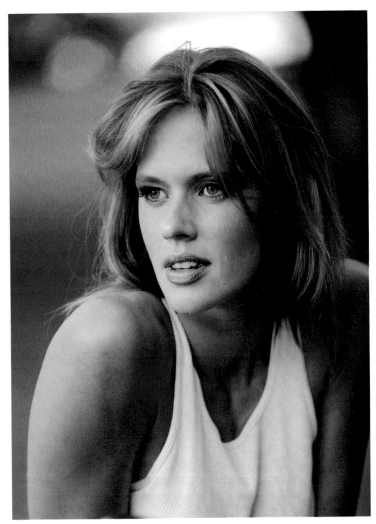

Single-Flash Unit with a Reflector

This is similar to the sun and flash combo shot, but this approach relies on the off-camera flash as the main light and uses reflected ("bounced") light from either a white wall or a reflector of some kind. Here the flash will be the stronger light source, and the distance the reflector is positioned from the light will determine the lighting ratio between the two light sources (flash and reflector). Generally, you want to have the reflector pretty close to the subject to keep the lighting ratio manageable. If it's too far away, one side of the face will end up in deep shadow.

Side Lighting for Effect

Lighting from the side is useful for showing texture and detail as the light fills in shadows on one side and emphasizes them on the other. It's also a more dramatic style of light, particularly if the light is restricted as this photo shows (see Figure 12.9).

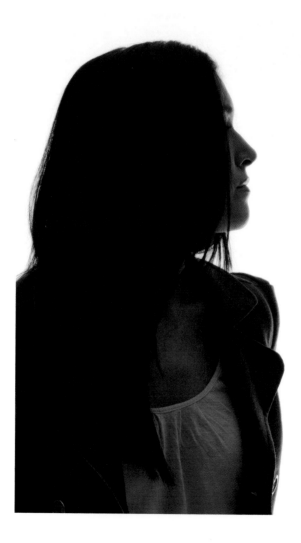

Figure 12.9
A Canon 600EX-RT mounted on a light stand set to the right and slightly behind the subject provided all the illumination in this portrait.

This is a very moody and dramatic style of lighting. Depending on how you modify the light it can produce a very dramatic effect (by restricting the light with a snoot, barn doors, or grids or by allowing the light to spread a bit by firing the flash directly from the side). You can even try bouncing it off a wall from the side to spread the light a bit more. Each technique can produce a compelling image.

Shooting Through Blinds

You can fire a flash unit through a set of window blinds to mimic the effect of sunlight streaming through a window. I even keep a set of blinds in my studio for this effect. Position the blinds and a flash unit on a light stand both angled to the side of your subject and fire the flash unit through the blinds.

There are even some interesting variations you can try with this idea. One is to attach a 1/4 or 1/2 yellow or orange gel to the flash head to add some color to the light. This will mimic the effect of early or late daylight streaming through the blinds. Another option is to add a second light or reflector to fill in some of the shadows.

Adding a Gel for a Special Effect

Gels are colored filters for your flash. Some units, such as the 580EX II and 600EX-RT are furnished with gel holders that fit over the flash head. You can also tape gels over the head using gaffer's tape. Gels are a convenient way to color the light from the flash. You can use a red, yellow, or orange gel to create a late day type of light. Or, you can use funkier colors to go for something on the wild side. I use the orange gel furnished with my 600EX-RT to balance the Speedlite with incandescent light indoors when I want to use both sources of illumination.

You can also put a gel on a background flash and use it to turn a white or gray background into a background of a different color. I know photographers who routinely use neutral backgrounds and then color them with flash as required.

Raising Your Flash Up High Via Monopod or Light Stand

Mounting your flash on a monopod, using one of the many available flash shoe/tripod adapters, gives you the option of positioning your light farther from your camera and allows you to direct its light where you need it (you may have to hold the camera with just one hand or talk someone else into holding the monopod flash combo for you). While it's common to raise it up to get rid of shadows, you can also position it to light from the side. If you're using a monopod with built-in legs (such as the Trek Tech Go! Pro, http://www.trek-tech.com/), you now have a freestanding light stand too. Or, if you have a portable light stand, you can do the same thing.

13

Downloading, Editing, and Printing Your Images

Taking the picture is only half the work and, in some cases, only half the fun. After you've captured some great images and have them safely stored on your Canon EOS 70D's memory card, you'll need to transfer them from your camera and memory card to your computer, where they can be organized, fine-tuned in an image editor, and prepared for web display, printing, or some other final destination.

Fortunately, there are lots of software utilities and applications to help you do all these things. This chapter will introduce you to a few of them.

Printing

You can print your images directly from some of the software applications and utilities described later in this chapter, but your EOS 70D can also be used to print from the camera, and to set up print "orders." These next sections will explain your options.

Direct Printing from the Camera

You can print photos stored on your camera's memory card directly to a PictBridge-compatible printer using the cable supplied with the 70D. Just follow these steps to get started:

1. **Set up your printer.** Follow the instructions for your PictBridge-compatible printer to load it with paper, and prepare it for printing.

2. **Connect the camera to the printer.** With the 70D and printer both powered down, open the port cover on the left side of the camera (the one closest to the back of the camera when it's held in shooting position), and plug the Interface Cable IFC-200U into the A/V Out/Digital port. Connect the other end to the PictBridge USB input port of your printer.

3. **Turn printer and camera on.** Flip the switch on the 70D, and power up your printer using its power switch.

4. **Press the Playback button on the camera.** Navigate to the image on your memory card that you want to print using the multi-selector. Press SET to select the image.

5. **Select options.** The image, overlaid with the current status for options like those shown in Figure 13.1, will appear when the camera and printer are connected with a cable. (The options will vary, depending on what printer you have.) I'll describe the options next.

The EOS 70D offers a surprising number of options when direct printing from your camera. You can choose effects, print date and time on your hardcopies, select the number of copies to be output, trim the image, and select paper settings—from your camera! While you can print using the current values as shown in the status screen, to adjust the settings, follow these steps, briefly summarized here with the camera connected to the printer:

- **Access the print options screen.** Press SET when the screen shown in Figure 13.1 is shown on your LCD. The PictBridge icon shows that the camera has successfully linked to the printer.

- **Use the multi-selector.** Highlight the options shown at right in Figure 13.2 in any order, and press SET to adjust that option. Within each option, use the SET button to confirm your entry, or the MENU button to back out of the option's screen.

- **Printing effects.** Use the multi-selector to choose Off (no effects), On (the printer's automatic corrections will be applied), Default (values stored in your printer, and which will vary depending on your printer), Vivid (higher saturation in blues and greens), or NR (noise reduction is applied). Three B/W choices are also available, for B/W (true blacks), B/W Cool tone (bluish blacks), and B/W Warm tone (yellowish blacks). Natural and Natural M choices are also available to provide true colors. If the INFO. icon appears, you can press it to make some adjustments to the printing effect, including image brightening, levels, and red-eye correction.

- **Date/File number imprint.** You can set this On or Off.

- **Copies.** Select 1 to 99 copies of the selected image.

- **Trimming.** Use this to crop your image. Your image appears on a trimming screen. Press the Magnify and Index/Reduce buttons to magnify or reduce the size of the cropping frame. Use the multi-selector to move the cropping frame around within the image. Rotate the Quick Control Dial to rotate the image. Press the INFO. button to toggle the cropping frame between horizontal and vertical orientations. When you've defined the crop for the image, press the SET button to apply your trimming to the image.

■ **Paper settings.** Choose the paper size, type, and layout. Use the multi-selector to select your paper size, with choices from credit card size through 8.5 × 11 inches. Press SET to confirm, and the screen changes to a Paper Type selection. After choosing Paper Type, press SET once more and choose a layout, from Borderless, Bordered, 2-up, 4-up, 9-up, 16-up, and 20-up (multiple copies of the image on a single sheet). When using Letter size (8.5 × 11-inch) paper, you can also elect to print 20-up and 35-up thumbnails of images you've chosen using the DPOF options described later in this chapter. The 20-up version will also include shooting information, such as camera and lens used, shooting mode, shutter speed, aperture, and other data. Another press of the SET button confirms Paper Type and returns to the settings screen.

■ **Cancel.** Returns to the status screen (seen in Figure 13.1).

■ **Print.** Starts the printing process with the selected options. The camera warns you not to disconnect the cable during printing. To print another photo using the same settings, just select it, highlight Print, and press the SET button.

Figure 13.1
You can print directly from the EOS 70D.

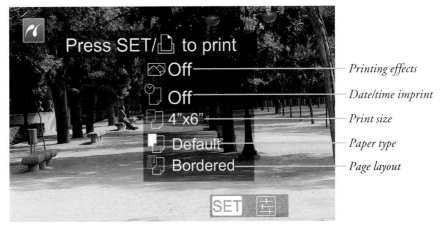

Printing effects
Date/time imprint
Print size
Paper type
Page layout

Figure 13.2
Choose the number of copies, crop the image, and apply other settings and preferences.

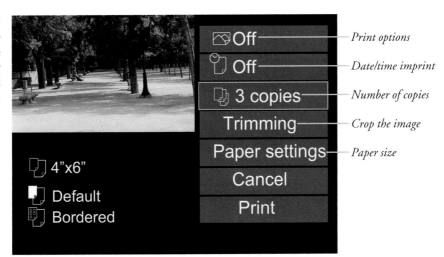

Print options
Date/time imprint
Number of copies
Crop the image
Paper size

Direct Print Order Format (DPOF) Printing

If you don't want to print directly from the camera, you can set some of the same options from the Playback 1 menu's Print Order entry, and designate single or multiple images on your memory card for printing. Once marked for DPOF printing, you can print the selected images, or take your memory card to a digital lab or kiosk, which is equipped to read the print order and make the copies you've specified. (You can't "order" prints of RAW images or movies.)

To create a DPOF print order, just follow these steps:

1. **Access Print Order screen.** In the Playback 1 menu, navigate to Print Order. (See Figure 13.3.) Press SET.
2. **Access Set up.** The Print Order screen will appear. (See Figure 13.4.) Use the multi-selector to highlight Set up. Press SET.

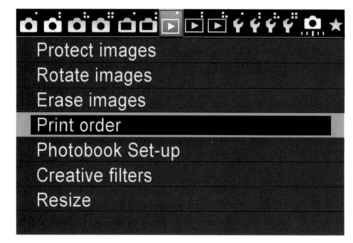

Figure 13.3
Print orders can be assembled from the Playback 1 menu.

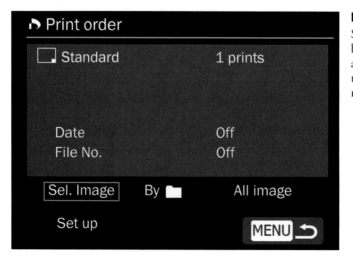

Figure 13.4
Select the images to be printed individually, by folder, or all the images on your memory card.

3. **Select Print type.** Choose Print Type (Standard, Index/Thumbnails print, or Both), and specify whether Date or File Number imprinting should be turned on or off. (You can turn one or the other on, but not both Date and File Number imprinting.) Press MENU to return to the Print Order screen.

4. **Choose selection method.** Highlight Sel. Image (choose individual images), By Folder (to select/deselect all images in a folder), or All Image (to mark/unmark all the images on your memory card). Press SET.

5. **Select individual images.** With Sel. Image, use the multi-selector to view the images, and press SET to mark or unmark an image for printing. If you'd rather view thumbnails of images, press the Index/Reduce button. Press the Magnify button to return to single-image view.

6. **Choose number of prints.** Once an image is selected, use the multi-selector to specify 1 to 99 prints for that image. (For Index prints, you can only specify whether the selected image is included in the index print, not the number of copies.) Press SET to confirm. You can then use the multi-selector to select additional images. Press MENU when finished selecting to return to the Print Order screen.

7. **Output your hardcopies.** If the camera is linked to a PictBridge-compatible printer, an additional option appears on the Print Order screen—Print. You can select that; optionally, adjust Paper Settings as described in the previous section, and start the printing process. Alternately, you can exit the Print Order screen by tapping the shutter release button. Then turn off the camera and printer, remove the memory card, and insert it in the memory card slot of a compatible printer, retailer kiosk, or digital minilab.

Using the Supplied Software

Your Canon EOS 70D came with software programs on CD for both Windows PCs and Macs. Pop the CD into your computer and it will self-install a selection of these useful applications and utilities. Manuals for all these programs are included on a separate CD, but here's a summary of what you get on the EOS Digital Solutions disc:

EOS Utility

Both Windows and Mac versions are provided for this useful program. It serves as command center for several useful functions, all available from the main control panel. Using the Control Camera panel, you can jump to modules that download images to either Digital Photo Professional or ZoomBrowser EX, change camera settings when your 70D is linked to your computer with the USB cable, shoot remotely with a live view image previewed on your computer screen, and monitor folders for new images.

The most-used of these options will probably be the download utility. But many will appreciate the Camera Settings/Remote Shooting module that allows you to link your computer with the 70D and use a dialog box to change camera settings and to control the camera for remote shooting. You can have access to many of the 70D's menus right from the software. The Settings feature is especially useful for changing Picture Styles quickly, while you'll find the remote shooting capabilities useful when you want to program a delay before the camera takes a picture, or do some interval (time-lapse) shooting. The updated version of the utility supports the 70D's Live View and Dust Delete Data functions. It includes many preferences you can use to tailor its operation.

The Accessories panel includes modules for working with the optional WFT-E3/E3A/B/C/D wireless communications link (for saving your pictures directly to external media over a Wi-Fi network). If you're using the OSK-E3 Data Security Kit, you can access the Original Data Security (ODS) Administrator tool and Utility, which are used to register and manage OS card verification information for image encryption and decryption, management of authorized users and cameras, verified card duplication, and other functions. There is also a link to the Picture Style Editor.

Digital Photo Professional

While far from a Photoshop replacement, Digital Photo Professional is a useful image-editing program that helps you organize, trim, correct, and print images. You can make RAW adjustments, and correct tonal curves, color tone, color saturation, sharpness, as well as brightness and contrast. Especially handy are the "recipes" that can be developed and saved so that a given set of corrections can be kept separate from the file itself, and, if desired, applied to other images.

Picture Style Editor

The Picture Style Editor allows you to create your own custom Picture Styles, or edit existing styles, including the Standard, Landscape, Faithful, and other predefined settings already present in your 70D. You can change sharpness, contrast, color saturation, and color tone—and a lot more—and then save the modifications as a PF2 file that can be uploaded to the camera, or used by Digital Photo Professional (described later in this chapter) to modify a RAW image as it is imported.

You can define your own color response using a color picker in a sample RAW photograph to choose a specific hue, which you can then modify using hue/saturation/luminance adjustments. The range of adjacent colors affected by your new settings can also be specified. Before/after views let you compare the Picture Style settings you've entered with standard settings using a sample image you upload.

ZoomBrowser/ImageBrowser

This is an image viewing and editing application for Windows PCs (the equivalent program for Macs is called ImageBrowser and performs the same functions). You can organize, sort, classify, and rename files, and convert JPEG files in batches. This utility is especially useful for printing index sheets of groups of images. It can also prepare images for e-mailing. It works with RAW Image Task for converting CR2 files to some other format for editing.

The simple image-editing facilities of ZoomBrowser/ImageBrowser allow red-eye correction, brightness/contrast and color correction, manipulating sharpness, trimming photos, and a few other functions. For more complex editing, you can transfer images directly from this application to Photoshop or another image editor. The software also includes applications for planning and editing movies, and for extracting still photos from video clips.

PhotoStitch

This Windows/Mac utility, available free from Canon, allows you to take several JPEG images and combine them to create a panorama in a single new file. You can choose the images to be merged in ZoomBrowser and then transfer them to PhotoStitch, or operate the utility as a standalone module and select the images using the standard File > Open commands.

Transferring Your Photos

While it's rewarding to capture some great images and have them ensconced in your camera, eventually you'll be transferring them to your laptop or PC, whether you're using a Windows or Macintosh machine. You have three options for image transfer: direct transfer over a USB cable, automated transfer using a card reader and transfer software such as the EOS Utility or Adobe Photoshop Elements Photo Downloader, or manual transfer using drag and drop from a memory card inserted in a card reader.

Using a Card Reader and Software

You can also use a memory card reader and software to transfer photos and automate the process using the EOS Utility, Photoshop Elements' Photo Downloader, or the downloading program supplied with some other third-party applications. This method is more frugal in its use of your 70D's battery and can be faster if you have a speedy USB 2.0/3.0 or FireWire card reader attached to an appropriate port.

The installed software automatically remains in memory as you work, and it recognizes when a memory card is inserted in your card reader; you don't have to launch it yourself. With Photoshop Elements's Photo Downloader, you can click Get Photos to begin the transfer of all images immediately or choose Advanced Dialog to produce a dialog box that allows you to select which images to download from the memory card by marking their thumbnails with a check. You can select the photos you want to transfer, plus options such as Automatically Fix Red Eyes. Start the download, and a confirmation dialog box shows the progress.

Dragging and Dropping

The final way to move photos from your memory card to your computer is the old-fashioned way: manually dragging and dropping the files from one window on your computer to another. The procedure works pretty much the same whether you're using a Mac or a PC.

1. Remove the memory card from the 70D and insert it in your memory card reader.

2. Using Windows Explorer, My Computer, or your Mac desktop, open the icon representing the memory card, which appears on your desktop as just another disk drive. (You can also link your camera directly to your computer with a USB cable, and it will appear as a disk drive, too.)

3. Open a second window representing the folder on your computer that you want to use as the destination for the files you are copying or moving.

4. Drag and drop the files from the memory card window to the folder on your computer. You can select individual files, press Ctrl/Command+A to select all the files, or Ctrl/Command+click to select multiple files.

Editing Your Photos

Image manipulation tasks fall into several categories. You might want to fine-tune your images, retouch them, change color balance, composite several images together, and perform other tasks we know as image editing, with a program like Adobe Photoshop, Photoshop Elements, or Corel Photo Paint.

You might want to play with the settings in RAW files, too, as you import them from their CR2 state into an image editor. There are specialized tools expressly for tweaking RAW files, ranging from Canon's own Digital Photo Professional to Adobe Camera Raw, and PhaseOne's Capture One Pro (C1 Pro). A third type of manipulation is the specialized task of noise reduction, which can be performed within Photoshop, Adobe Camera Raw, or tools like Bibble Professional. There are also specialized tools just for noise reduction, such as Noise Ninja (also included with Bibble) and Neat Image.

Each of these utilities and applications deserves a chapter of its own, so I'm simply going to enumerate some of the most popular image-editing and RAW conversion programs here and tell you a little about what they do.

Image Editors

Image editors are general-purpose photo-editing applications that can do color correction, tonal modifications, retouching, combining of several images into one, and usually include tools for working with RAW files and reducing noise. So, you'll find programs like those listed here good for all-around image manipulation.

The leading programs are as follows:

Adobe Photoshop/Photoshop Elements/Photoshop Elements Premiere. Photoshop is the serious photographer's number one choice for image editing, and Elements is an excellent option for those who need most of Photoshop's power, but not all of its professional-level features. Both editors use the latest version of Adobe's Camera Raw plug-in, which makes it easy to adjust things like color space profiles, color depth (either 8 bits or 16 bits per color channel), image resolution, white balance, exposure, shadows, brightness, sharpness, luminance, and noise reduction. One plus with the Adobe products is that they are available in identical versions for both Windows and Macs. Elements Premiere adds video editing features that 70D owners who shoot a lot of video will find useful.

Corel Photo Paint. This is the image-editing program that is included in the popular CorelDRAW Graphics suite. Although a Mac version was available in the past, this is primarily a Windows application today. It's a full-featured photo retouching and image-editing program with selection, retouching, and painting tools for manual image manipulations, and it also includes convenient automated commands for a few common tasks, such as red-eye removal. Photo Paint accepts Photoshop plug-ins to expand its assortment of filters and special effects.

Corel Paint Shop Pro. This is a general-purpose Windows-only image editor that has gained a reputation as the "poor man's Photoshop" for providing a substantial portion of Photoshop's capabilities at a fraction of the cost. It includes a nifty set of wizard-like commands that automate common tasks, such as removing red eye and scratches, as well as filters and effects, which can be expanded with other Photoshop plug-ins.

Corel Painter. Here's another image-editing program from Corel for both Mac and Windows. This one's strength is in mimicking natural media, such as charcoal, pastels, and various kinds of paint. Painter includes a basic assortment of tools that you can use to edit existing images, but the program is really designed for artists to use in creating original illustrations. As a photographer, you might prefer another image editor, but if you like to paint on top of your photographic images, nothing else really does the job of Painter.

Corel PhotoImpact. Corel finally brought one of the last remaining non-Adobe image editors into its fold when it acquired Ulead PhotoImpact. This is a general-purpose photo-editing program for Windows with a huge assortment of brushes for painting, retouching, and cloning, in addition to the usual selection, cropping, and fill tools. If you frequently find yourself performing the same image manipulations on a number of files, you'll appreciate PhotoImpact's batch operations. Using this feature, you can select multiple image files and then apply any one of a long list of filters, enhancements, or auto-process commands to all the selected files.

RAW Utilities

Your software choices for manipulating RAW files are broader than you might think. Camera vendors always supply a utility to read their cameras' own RAW files, but sometimes, particularly with those point-and-shoot cameras that can produce RAW files, the options are fairly limited. Other vendors, such as Nikon (with its Nikon Capture), offer RAW file handling that is much more flexible and powerful.

Because in the past digital camera vendors offered RAW converters that weren't very good (Canon's File View Utility comes to mind), there is a lively market for third-party RAW utilities available at extra cost. However, the EOS Utility and Digital Photo Professional do a good job and may be all that you need.

The third-party solutions are usually available as standalone applications (often for both Windows and Macintosh platforms), as Photoshop-compatible plug-ins, or both. Because the RAW plug-ins displace Photoshop's own RAW converter, I tend to prefer to use most RAW utilities in standalone mode. That way, if I choose to open a file directly in Photoshop, it automatically opens using Photoshop's fast and easy-to-use Adobe Camera Raw (ACR) plug-in. If I have more time or need the capabilities of another converter, I can load that, open the file, and make my corrections there. Most are able to transfer the processed file directly to Photoshop even if you aren't using plug-in mode.

This section provides a quick overview of the range of RAW file handlers, so you can get a better idea of the kinds of information available with particular applications. I'm going to include both high-end and low-end RAW browsers so you can see just what is available.

Digital Photo Professional

Digital Photo Professional, introduced earlier in this chapter, is preferred by many for Canon dSLR cameras like the 70D. DPP offers much higher-speed processing of RAW images than was available with the late, not lamented, sluggardly File Viewer Utility (as much as six times faster). Canon says this utility rivals third-party standalone and plug-in RAW converters in speed and features. It supports both Canon's original CRW format and the newer CR2 RAW format used by the 70D, along with TIFF, Exif TIFF, and JPEG.

You can save settings that include multiple adjustments and apply them to other images, and use the clever comparison mode to compare your original and edited versions of an image either side by side or within a single split image. The utility allows easy adjustment of color channels, tone curves, exposure compensation, white balance, dynamic range, brightness, contrast, color saturation, ICC Profile embedding, and assignment of monitor profiles. A new feature is the ability to continue editing images while batches of previously adjusted RAW files are rendered and saved in the background.

IrfanView

At the low (free) end of the price scale is IrfanView, a Windows freeware program you can download at www.irfanview.com. It can read many common RAW photo formats. It's a quick way to view RAW files (just drag and drop to the IrfanView window) and make fast changes to the unprocessed file. You can crop, rotate, or correct your image, and do some cool things like swap the colors around (red for blue, blue for green, and so forth) to create false color pictures.

The price is right, and IrfanView has some valuable capabilities. Check out www.irfanview.com.

Phase One Capture One Pro (C1 Pro)

If there is a Cadillac of RAW converters for Nikon and Canon digital SLR cameras, C1 Pro has to be it. This premium-priced program does everything, does it well, and does it quickly. If you can't justify the price tag of this professional-level software, there are "lite" versions for serious amateurs and cash-challenged professionals called Capture and Capture One Pro 6 at $299 and Capture One Express 6, which costs as little as $99.

Aimed at photographers with high-volume needs (that would include school and portrait photographers, as well as busy commercial photographers), C1 Pro is available for both Windows and Mac OS X, and supports a broad range of Canon digital cameras. Phase One is a leading supplier of megabucks digital camera backs for medium and larger format cameras, so they really understand the needs of photographers.

The latest features include individual noise reduction controls for each image, automatic levels adjustment, a "quick develop" option that allows speedy conversion from RAW to TIFF or JPEG formats, dual-image side-by-side views for comparison purposes, and helpful grids and guides that can be superimposed over an image. Photographers concerned about copyright protection will appreciate the ability to add watermarks to the output images. See www.phaseone.com.

BreezeBrowser

BreezeBrowser was long the RAW converter of choice for Canon dSLR owners who run Windows and who were dissatisfied with Canon's lame antique File Viewer Utility. It works quickly and has lots of options for converting CRW and CR2 files to other formats. You can choose to show highlights that will be blown out in your finished photo as flashing areas (so they can be more easily identified and corrected), use histograms to correct tones, add color profiles, auto rotate images, and adjust all those raw image parameters, such as white balance, color space, saturation, contrast, sharpening, color tone, EV compensation, and other settings.

You can also control noise reduction (choosing from low, normal, or high reduction), evaluate your changes in the live preview, and then save the file as a compressed JPEG or as either an 8-bit or 16-bit TIFF file. BreezeBrowser can also create HTML web galleries directly from your selection of images. See www.breezesys.com.

Photoshop, Lightroom, or Both?

I've been using Photoshop since Version 2.0, and as far back as the 1980s struggled with a variety of other programs with names like Digital Darkroom, Image Studio, Picture Publisher, SuperPaint, UltraPaint, Dr. Halo, and Gray F/X (believe it or not, many early image editors could not handle *color* photos). Over the years, Photoshop has grown from being a simple image-editing program that was difficult to learn to a complete suite with basic and "extended" versions, and the capability to satisfy everyone from photographers to graphic designers to 3D artists working on motion picture production. It's gone from being difficult to learn to something akin to quantum mechanics: nobody seems to know everything about it, and most of us could spend a lifetime adding little pieces of expertise in it to our repertoires.

Today Photoshop folds the capabilities of many other applications into its bulk. It does a decent job of assembling multiple RAW images into an HDR photograph. It retouches, it color corrects, it does an amazing job of compositing, and it can tame noise and create animations. My biggest relief when I upgraded to Photoshop CS6 was that, unlike some previous versions, the new edition was enough like the old one that I was able to use it comfortably from Day One. Drastic paradigm shifts are not as bad as they appear to be—but not when I'm trying to get work done. I'll probably be sticking with CS6 for a while, as Adobe has announced that it will be the last standalone version; all future upgrades will come as part of the Adobe Creative Cloud subscription program, which will be the only way you will be able to license future versions of this software.

Lightroom, on the other hand, will, according to Adobe, remain as a standalone program as well as part of the Creative Cloud subscription program. It is a newer tool that has some limited image-editing features similar to some of the pixel manipulation tools in Photoshop. However, the intent of Lightroom is to function as a workflow management application. Photoshop can do just about anything, except help you manage 100,000 different images effectively (even using its Bridge and Mini-Bridge organizing tools). Lightroom *can't* do everything, but it excels at giving you a way to manage tens or hundreds of thousands of images easily. In these days of inexpensive, huge hard drives, bracketing, and ridiculously fast continuous shooting rates, it's easy to amass that many photos. Two 3TB internal hard drives in my computer are dedicated to storing the images I shoot. (Don't worry, all those photos are safely backed up to a pair of 6TB RAID-like arrays, plus multiple duplicate hard drives stored off-site.) It would be impossible to manage all those images without something like Lightroom.

The secret behind Lightroom's image management prowess is a database it builds automatically from the EXIF data embedded in each image, with information that includes the camera model, date and time the image was captured, shutter speed, aperture, ISO, white balance, and other information. You can add more information to its catalog, including keywords that will help you retrieve a specific image later and star ratings.

Lightroom's Develop module includes correction using histograms, cropping/straightening, the ability to remove spots and correct red-eye problems, along with white balance. The exposure tools include recovery, fill light, blacks, brightness/contrast, clarity, vibrance, and saturation modules, similar to those found in Adobe Camera Raw. You can also adjust curves, perform sharpening and noise reduction, correct lens distortion, chromatic aberration, and vignetting from profiles specific for each lens. When you're done with your images, you can assemble them into slide shows or web galleries quickly.

Photoshop has all those image manipulation tools—many of them embedded in Adobe Camera Raw. Indeed, when a new release of ACR becomes available, the update fine-tunes both Lightroom and Camera Raw to offer the same functionality. But while Photoshop has more extensive image-editing features, including sophisticated selection (including Skin-Tone Selection), layering, and masking tools, its changes to your files are usually "destructive." You'll need to save snapshots as you work, or use a limited history of Undo steps to reverse your changes. Lightroom, in contrast, never applies permanent changes to the original file.

Which to choose? If you have large numbers of images to catalog and don't need the most advanced Photoshop editing tools, Lightroom may be your best bet for organizing your workflow. While Photoshop includes image management in its Bridge module, there is no database catalog system comparable to Lightroom available in Photoshop. Lightroom is also best for batch processing many files quickly. You'll probably find it easier to learn.

If you need to manipulate your images in complex ways, including compositing to combine objects from one image to another (or to move objects around within the same image), or to creatively *remove* unwanted image areas, dig in and learn Photoshop in more depth. My favorite capabilities are probably Photoshop's Content Aware editing tools, including the new Content Aware Move tool in CS6 that lets you seamlessly replace part of an image with a pattern that resembles the surrounding area. Should you be shooting a lot of movies with your 70D, Photoshop CS6 is a great deal more video-friendly than the last edition of the program.

Now, should you need *both* the most sophisticated editing tools available *and* comprehensive workflow/image management capabilities, you probably will want both Photoshop and Lightroom. Buying both—even if you qualify for upgrades for one or the other—isn't cheap. The full version of the basic Photoshop CS6 may be difficult to purchase as Adobe phases it out, but at this writing the program costs $700, or $199 for the Photoshop CS6 upgrade. Creative Cloud subscriptions vary from $20 to $49 per month, depending on how many of the CC applications you want to use. Lightroom 5 is $149 or around $80 for the Lightroom 5 update.

14

Troubleshooting and Prevention

One of the nice things about modern electronic cameras like the Canon EOS 70D is that they have fewer mechanical moving parts to fail, so they are less likely to "wear out." No film transport mechanism, no wind lever or motor drive, and no complicated mechanical linkages from camera to lens to physically stop down the lens aperture. Instead, tiny, reliable motors are built into each lens (and you lose the use of only that lens should something fail), and one of the few major moving parts in the camera itself is a lightweight mirror (its small size one of the results of the 70D's 1.6X crop factor) that flips up and down with each shot.

Of course, the camera also has a moving shutter that can fail, but the shutter is built rugged enough that you can expect it to last 100,000 shutter cycles or more. Unless you're shooting sports in continuous mode day in and day out, the shutter on your 70D is likely to last as long as you expect to use the camera.

The only other things on the camera that move are switches, dials, buttons, the flip-up electronic flash, and the door that slides open to allow you to remove and insert the memory card. Unless you're extraordinarily clumsy or unlucky or give your built-in flash a good whack while it is in use, there's not a lot that can go wrong mechanically with your EOS 70D.

On the other hand, one of the chief drawbacks of modern electronic cameras is that they are modern *electronic* cameras. Your 70D is fully dependent on two different batteries. Without them, the camera can't be used. There are numerous other electrical and electronic connections in the camera (many connected to those mechanical switches and dials), and components like the color LCD that can potentially fail or suffer damage. The camera also relies on its "operating system," or *firmware*, which can be plagued by bugs that cause unexpected behavior. Luckily, electronic components are generally more reliable and trouble-free, especially when compared to their mechanical counterparts from the pre-electronic film camera days. (Film cameras of the last 10 to 20 years have had almost as many electronic features as digital cameras, but, believe it or not, there were whole generations of film cameras that had *no* electronics or batteries.)

Digital cameras have problems unique to their breed, too; the most troublesome being the need to clean the sensor of dust and grime periodically. This chapter will show you how to diagnose problems, fix some common ills, and, importantly, learn how to avoid some of them in the future.

Updating Your Firmware

As I said, the firmware in your EOS 70D is the camera's operating system, which handles everything from menu display (including fonts, colors, and the actual entries themselves), what languages are available, and even support for specific devices and features. Upgrading the firmware to a new version makes it possible to add new features while fixing some of the bugs that sneak in.

Official Firmware

Official firmware for your 70D is given a version number that you can view by turning the power on, pressing the MENU button, and navigating to Firmware Ver. x.x.x in the Set-up 4 menu. As I write this, the current version is 1.1.1. The first number in the string represents the major release number, while the second and third represent less significant upgrades and minor tweaks, respectively. Theoretically, a camera should have a firmware version number of 1.0.0 when it is introduced, but vendors have been known to do some minor fixes during testing and unveil a camera with a 1.0.5 firmware designation. If a given model is available long enough, it can evolve into significant upgrades, such as 2.0.3.

Firmware upgrades are used for both cameras and certain lenses, most frequently to fix bugs in the software, and much less frequently to add or enhance features. For example, previous firmware upgrades for Canon cameras have mended things like incorrect color temperature reporting when using specific Canon Speedlites, or problems communicating with memory cards under certain conditions. The exact changes made to the firmware are generally spelled out in the firmware release announcement. You can examine the remedies provided and decide if a given firmware patch is important to you. If not, you can usually safely wait a while before going through the bother of upgrading your firmware—at least long enough for the early adopters to report whether the bug fixes have introduced new bugs of their own. Each new firmware release incorporates the changes from previous releases, so if you skip a minor upgrade you should have no problems.

Upgrading Your Firmware

If you're computer savvy, you might wonder how your EOS 70D is able to overwrite its own operating system—that is, how can the existing firmware be used to load the new version on top of itself? It's a little like lifting yourself by reaching down and pulling up on your bootstraps. Not ironically, that's almost exactly what happens: At your command (when you start the upgrade process), the 70D shifts into a special mode in which it is no longer operating from its firmware but, rather, from a small piece of software called a *bootstrap loader*, a separate, protected software program that functions only at startup or when upgrading firmware. The loader's function is to look for firmware to launch or, when directed, to copy new firmware from a memory card or your computer to the internal memory space where the old firmware is located. Once the new firmware has replaced the old, you can turn your camera off and then on again, and the updated operating system will be loaded.

Because the loader software is small in size and limited in function, there are some restrictions on what it can do. For example, the loader software isn't set up to go hunting through your memory card for the firmware file. It looks only in the top or root directory of your card, so that's where you must copy the firmware you download. Once you've determined that a new firmware update is available for your camera and that you want to install it, just follow these steps. (If you chicken out, any Canon service center can install the firmware upgrade for you.)

WARNING

Use a fully charged battery or Canon's optional ACK-E6 AC adapter kit to ensure that you'll have enough power to operate the camera for the entire upgrade. Moreover, you should not turn off the camera while your old firmware is being overwritten. Don't open the memory card door or do anything else that might disrupt operation of the 70D while the firmware is being installed.

1. Download the firmware from Canon (you'll find it in the Downloads section of the Support portion of Canon's website) and place it on your computer's hard drive. The firmware is contained in a self-extracting file for either Windows or Mac OS. It will have a name such as 70D000102.fir.

2. In your camera, format a memory card. Choose Format Card from the Set-up 1 menu, and initialize the card (make sure you don't have images you want to keep before you do this!).

3. You can copy the upgrade software to the card either using a memory card reader or by connecting the camera to your computer with a USB cable and using the EOS Utility application furnished with your camera (and described in the next section). The Firmware Version entry in the Set-up 4 menu will remind you that a memory card containing the firmware is required before you can proceed.

4. Insert the memory card in the camera and then turn the camera on. With the 70D set to any mode other than Creative Auto or Full Auto, press MENU and scroll to Firmware Ver. x.x.x in the Set-up 4 menu (see Figure 14.1) and press SET.

5. You'll see the current firmware version, and an option to update, as shown in Figure 14.2. (This is a "fictional" update, as no new firmware has been released for the 70D as I write this. As a result, the screens you see when you update your camera may be slightly different.) Choose OK and press the SET button to begin loading the update program.

6. A confirmation screen will appear (see Figure 14.3). Select OK and press SET to continue. As the Firmware Update Program loads, you'll see the screen shown in Figure 14.4.

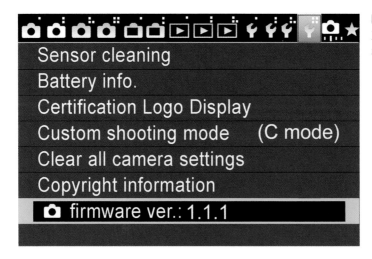

Figure 14.1
Determine the current version number.

7. Next, you'll get the opportunity to confirm that the version you're upgrading to is the one you want, as you can see in Figure 14.5. You can press the MENU button to cancel. (Yes, I know there are a lot of confirmation screens; Canon wants to make sure you don't upgrade your firmware by accident, or, possibly, intentionally.)

8. Finally, the very last confirmation screen is shown in Figure 14.6. Select OK, and press SET, and, I promise, the actual firmware update will really begin.

9. While the firmware updates, you'll be warned not to turn off the power switch or touch any of the 70D's buttons. (See Figure 14.7.)

10. When the update complete screen appears (Figure 14.8), you can turn off the EOS 70D, remove the AC adapter, if used, and replace or recharge the battery. Then turn the camera on to boot up your camera with the new firmware update.

11. Be sure to reformat the card before returning it to regular use to remove the firmware software.

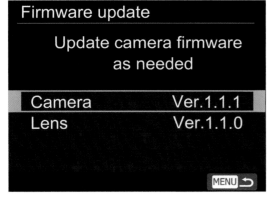

Figure 14.2

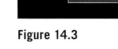

Figure 14.3

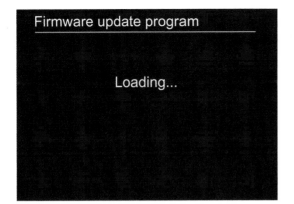

Figure 14.4

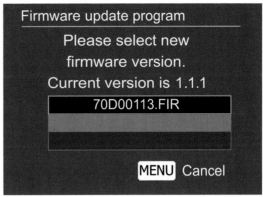

Figure 14.5

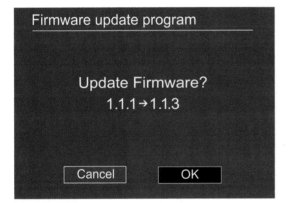

Figure 14.6

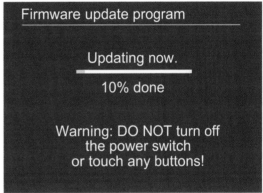

Figure 14.7

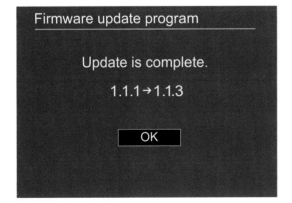

Figure 14.8

Using Direct Camera USB Link to Copy the Software

The procedure is slightly different (and a little more automated) if you choose to transfer the firmware software to the camera through a USB linkup. Follow these instructions to get started:

1. Connect the camera (with a freshly charged battery or attached to the AC Adapter) to the computer using the USB cable and turn it on.

2. Load the EOS Utility.

3. Click the Camera/Settings/Remote Shooting button.

4. Select the Firmware Update option. When the Update Firmware window appears at the bottom of the EOS Utility, choose OK.

5. Click Yes in the confirmation screen.

6. Follow the instructions in the dialog boxes that pop up next by pressing the SET button on the camera.

Protecting Your LCD

The color LCD on the back of your EOS 70D almost seems like a target for banging, scratching, and other abuse. Fortunately, it's quite rugged, and a few errant knocks are unlikely to shatter the protective cover over the LCD, and scratches won't easily mar its surface. However, if you want to be on the safe side, there are a number of protective products you can purchase to keep your LCD safe—and, in some cases, make it a little easier to view. I've found that the capacitive touch screen does continue to be responsive to touches and gestures with the protectors I've tried, but I haven't tried them all. Here's a quick overview of your options.

- **Plastic overlays.** The simplest solution (although not always the cheapest) is to apply a plastic overlay sheet or "skin" cut to fit your LCD. These adhere either by static electricity or through a light adhesive coating that's even less clingy than stick-it notes. You can cut down overlays made for PDAs (although these can be pricey at up to $19.95 for a set of several sheets), or purchase overlays sold specifically for digital cameras. Vendors such as Hoodman (www.hoodmanusa.com) offer overlays of this type. These products will do a good job of shielding your 70D's LCD screen from scratches and minor impacts, but will not offer much protection from a good whack. These are your best choice if you plan to reverse the LCD so it faces the camera; thicker shields may not allow the LCD panel to close completely in the reversed position.

- **Flip-up hoods.** These protectors slip on using the flanges around your 70D's eyepiece, and provide a cover that completely shields the LCD, but unfolds to provide a three-sided hood that allows viewing the LCD while minimizing the extraneous light falling on it and reducing contrast. They're sold by Delkin (www.delkin.com). If you want to completely protect your LCD from hard knocks and need to view the screen outdoors in bright sunlight, there is nothing better. However, I have a couple problems with these devices. First, with the cover closed, you can't peek down after taking a shot to see what your image looks like during picture review.

You must open the cap each time you want to look at the LCD. Moreover, with the hood unfolded, it's difficult to look through the viewfinder: Don't count on being able to use the viewfinder *and* the LCD at the same time with one of these hoods in place.

■ **Magnifiers.** If you look hard enough, you should be able to find an LCD magnifier that fits over the monitor panel and provides a 2X magnification. These often strap on clumsily, and serve better as a way to get an enlarged view of the LCD than as protection. Hoodman and other suppliers offer these specialized devices.

Troubleshooting Memory Cards

Sometimes good memory cards go bad. Sometimes good photographers can treat their memory cards badly. It's possible that a memory card that works fine in one camera won't be recognized when inserted into another. In the worst case, you can have a card full of important photos and find that the card seems to be corrupted and you can't access any of them. Don't panic! If these scenarios sound horrific to you, there are lots of things you can do to prevent them from happening, and a variety of remedies available if they do occur. You'll want to take some time—before disaster strikes—to consider your options.

All Your Eggs in One Basket?

The debate about whether it's better to use one large memory card or several smaller ones has been going on since even before there were memory cards. I can remember when computer users wondered whether it was smarter to install a pair of 200MB (not *gigabyte*) hard drives in their computer, or if they should go for one of those new-fangled 500MB models. By the same token, a few years ago the user groups were full of proponents who insisted that you ought to use 128MB memory cards rather than the huge 512MB versions. Today, most of the arguments involve 8GB cards versus 16GB or 32GB cards, and I expect that as prices for 64GB memory cards continue to drop, they'll find their way into the debate as well. Size is especially important when you're using a camera like the 70D that captures 20-megapixel images.

Why all the fuss? Are 16GB memory cards more likely to fail than 8GB cards? Are you risking all your photos if you trust your images to a larger card? Isn't it better to use several smaller cards, so that if one fails you lose only half as many photos? Or, isn't it wiser to put all your photos onto one larger card, because the more cards you use, the better your odds of misplacing or damaging one and losing at least some pictures?

In the end, the "eggs in one basket" argument boils down to statistics, and how you happen to use your 70D. The rationales can go both ways. If you have multiple smaller cards, you do increase your chances of something happening to one of them, so, arguably, you might be boosting the odds of losing some pictures. If all your images are important, the fact that you've lost 100 rather than 200 pictures isn't very comforting.

Also consider that the eggs/basket scenario assumes that the cards that are lost or damaged are always full. It's actually likely that your 16GB card might suffer a mishap when it's less than half-full (indeed, it's more likely that a large card won't be completely filled before it's offloaded to a computer), so you really might not lose any more shots with a single 16GB card than with multiple 8GB cards.

If you shoot photojournalist-type pictures, you probably change memory cards when they're less than completely full in order to avoid the need to do so at a crucial moment. (When I shoot sports, my cards rarely reach 80 to 90 percent of capacity before I change them.) Using multiple smaller cards means you have to change them that more often, which can be a real pain when you're taking a lot of photos. As an example, if you use tiny 2GB memory cards with an EOS 70D and shoot RAW+JPEG FINE, you may get only 68 pictures on the card. That's not even twice the capacity of a 36-exposure roll of film (remember those?). In my book, I prefer keeping all my eggs in one basket, and then making very sure that nothing happens to that basket.

There are only two really good reasons to justify limiting yourself to smaller memory cards when larger ones can be purchased at the same cost per-gigabyte. One of them is when every single picture is precious to you and the loss of any of them would be a disaster. If you're a wedding photographer, for example, and unlikely to be able to restage the nuptials if a memory card goes bad, you'll probably want to shoot no more pictures than you can afford to lose on a single card, and have an assistant ready to copy each card removed from the camera onto a backup hard drive or DVD onsite.

To be even safer, you'd want to alternate cameras or have a second photographer at least partially duplicating your coverage so your shots are distributed over several memory cards simultaneously. (Strictly speaking, the safest route of all is to spend some significant bucks on Canon's Wireless File Transmitter WFT-E5/WFT-E5A/B/C/D, and beam the images to a computer as you shoot them.)

If none of these options are available to you, consider *interleaving* your shots. Say you don't shoot weddings, but you do go on vacation from time to time. Take 50 or so pictures on one card, or whatever number of images might fill about 25 percent of its capacity. Then, replace it with a different card and shoot about 25 percent of that card's available space. Repeat these steps with diligence (you'd have to be determined to go through this inconvenience), and, if you use four or more memory cards, you'll find your pictures from each location scattered among the different memory cards. If you lose or damage one, you'll still have *some* pictures from all the various stops on your trip on the other cards. That's more work than I like to do (I usually tote around a portable hard disk and copy the files to the drive as I go), but it's an option.

What Can Go Wrong?

There are lots of things that can go wrong with your memory card, but the ones that aren't caused by human stupidity are statistically very rare. Yes, a memory card's internal bit bin or controller can suddenly fail due to a manufacturing error or some inexplicable event caused by old age. However, if your memory card works for the first week or two that you own it, it should work forever. There's really not a lot that can wear out.

The typical memory card is rated for a Mean Time Between Failures of 1,000,000 hours of use. That's constant use 24/7 for more than 100 years! According to the manufacturers, they are good for 10,000 insertions in your camera, and should be able to retain their data (and that's without an external power source) for something on the order of 11 years. Of course, with the millions of memory cards in use, there are bound to be a few lemons here or there.

Given the reliability of solid-state memory, compared to magnetic memory, though, it's more likely that your memory problems will stem from something that you do. Memory cards are small and easy to misplace if you're not careful. For that reason, it's a good idea to keep them in their original cases or a "card safe" offered by Gepe (www.gepecardsafe.com), Pelican (www.pelican.com), and others. Always placing your memory card in a case can provide protection from the second-most common mishap that befalls memory cards: the common household laundry. If you slip a memory card in a pocket, rather than a case or your camera bag often enough, sooner or later it's going to end up in the washing machine and probably the clothes dryer, too. There are plenty of reports of relieved digital camera owners who've laundered their memory cards and found they still worked fine, but it's not uncommon for such mistreatment to do some damage.

Memory cards can also be stomped on, accidentally bent, dropped into the ocean, chewed by pets, and otherwise rendered unusable in myriad ways. It's also possible to force a card into your 70D's memory card slot incorrectly if you're diligent enough. Or, if the card is formatted in your computer with a memory card reader, your 70D may fail to recognize it. Occasionally, I've found that a memory card used in one camera would fail if used in a different camera (until I reformatted it in Windows, and then again in the camera). Every once in a while, a card goes completely bad and—seemingly—can't be salvaged.

Another way to lose images is to do commonplace things with your memory card at an inopportune time. If you remove the card from the 70D while the camera is writing images to the card, you'll lose any photos in the buffer and may damage the file structure of the card, making it difficult or impossible to retrieve the other pictures you've taken. The same thing can happen if you remove the memory card from your computer's card reader while the computer is writing to the card (say, to erase files you've already moved to your computer). You can avoid this by *not* using your computer to erase files on a memory card but, instead, always reformatting the card in your 70D before you use it again.

What Can You Do?

Pay attention: If you're having problems, the *first* thing you should do is *stop* using that memory card. Don't take any more pictures. Don't do anything with the card until you've figured out what's wrong. Your second line of defense (your first line is to be sufficiently careful with your cards that you avoid problems in the first place) is to *do no harm* that hasn't already been done. Read the rest of this section and then, if necessary, decide on a course of action (such as using a data recovery service or software described later) before you risk damaging the data on your card further.

Now that you've calmed down, the first thing to check is whether you've actually inserted a card in the camera. If you've set the camera in the Shooting menu so that Shoot w/o Card has been turned on, it's entirely possible (although not particularly plausible) that you've been snapping away with no memory card to store the pictures to, which can lead to massive disappointment later on. Of course, the No Memory Card message appears on the LCD when the camera is powered up, and it is superimposed on the review image after every shot, but maybe you're inattentive, aren't using picture review, or have purchased one of those LCD fold-up hoods mentioned earlier in this chapter. You can avoid all this by turning the Shoot w/o Card feature off and leaving it off.

Things get more exciting when the card itself is put in jeopardy. If you lose a card, there's not a lot you can do other than take a picture of a similar card and print up some Have You Seen This Lost Flash Memory? flyers to post on utility poles all around town.

If all you care about is reusing the card, and have resigned yourself to losing the pictures, try reformatting the card in your camera. You may find that reformatting removes the corrupted data and restores your card to health. Sometimes I've had success reformatting a card in my computer using a memory card reader (this is normally a no-no because your operating system doesn't understand the needs of your 70D), and *then* reformatting again in the camera.

If your memory card is not behaving properly, and you *do* want to recover your images, things get a little more complicated. If your pictures are very valuable, either to you or to others (for example, a wedding), you can always turn to professional data recovery firms. Be prepared to pay hundreds of dollars to get your pictures back, but these pros often do an amazing job. You wouldn't want them working on your memory card on behalf of the police if you'd tried to erase some incriminating pictures. There are many firms of this type, and I've never used them myself, so I can't offer a recommendation. Use a Google search to turn up a ton of them. I use a software program called RescuePro, which came free with one of my SanDisk memory cards.

THE ULTIMATE IRONY

I recently purchased an 8GB Kingston memory card that was furnished with some nifty OnTrack data recovery software. The first thing I did was format the card to make sure it was okay. Then I hunted around for the free software, only to discover it was preloaded onto the memory card. I was supposed to copy the software to my computer before using the memory card for the first time.

Fortunately, I had the OnTrack software that would reverse my dumb move, so I could retrieve the software. No, wait. I *didn't* have the software I needed to recover the software I erased. I'd reformatted it to oblivion. Chalk this one up as either the ultimate irony or Stupid Photographer Trick #523.

A more reasonable approach is to try special data recovery software you can install on your computer and use to attempt to resurrect your "lost" images yourself. They may not actually be gone completely. Perhaps your memory card's "table of contents" is jumbled, or only a few pictures are damaged in such a way that your camera and computer can't read some or any of the pictures on the card. Some of the available software was written specifically to reconstruct lost pictures, while other utilities are more general-purpose applications that can be used with any media, including floppy disks and hard disk drives. They have names like OnTrack, Photo Rescue 2, Digital Image Recovery, MediaRecover, Image Recall, and the aptly named Recover My Photos. You'll find a comprehensive list and links, as well as some picture-recovery tips at www.ultimateslr.com/memory-card-recovery.php.

DIMINISHING RETURNS

Usually, once you've recovered any images on a memory card, reformatted it, and returned it to service, it will function reliably for the rest of its useful life. However, if you find a particular card going bad more than once, you'll almost certainly want to stop using it forever. See if you can get it replaced by the manufacturer, if you can, but, in the case of memory card failures, the third time is never the charm.

Cleaning Your Sensor

There's no avoiding dust. No matter how careful you are, some of it is going to settle on your camera and on the mounts of your lenses, eventually making its way inside your camera to settle in the mirror chamber. As you take photos, the mirror flipping up and down causes the dust to become airborne and eventually make its way past the shutter curtain to come to rest on the anti-aliasing filter atop your sensor. There, dust and particles can show up in every single picture you take at a small enough aperture to bring the foreign matter into sharp focus. No matter how careful you are and how cleanly you work, eventually you will get some of this dust on your camera's sensor. Some say that CMOS sensors, like the one found in the EOS 70D, "attract" less dust than CCD sensors found in cameras from other vendors. But even the cleanest-working photographers using Canon cameras are far from immune.

Fortunately, one of the EOS 70D's most useful features is the automatic sensor cleaning system that reduces or eliminates the need to clean your camera's sensor manually. Canon has applied anti-static coatings to the sensor and other portions of the camera body interior to counter charge build-ups that attract dust. A separate filter over the sensor vibrates ultrasonically each time the 70D is powered on or off, shaking loose any dust.

Although the automatic sensor-cleaning feature operates when you power the camera up or turn it off, you can activate it at any time. Choose Sensor Cleaning from the Set-up 4 menu, and select Clean Now. If you'd rather turn the feature on or off, choose Auto Cleaning instead, and then choose either Enable or Disable with the multi-selector. Press SET, then press the MENU button to return to the Set-up 4 menu (see Figure 14.9).

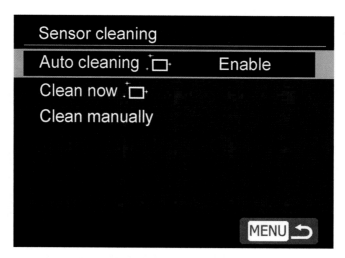

Figure 14.9
You can activate automatic sensor cleaning immediately or enable/disable the feature.

If some dust does collect on your sensor, you can often map it out of your images (making it invisible) using software techniques with the Dust Delete Data feature in the Shooting 4 menu. Operation of this feature is described in Chapter 8. Of course, even with the EOS 70D's automatic sensor cleaning/dust resistance features, you may still be required to manually clean your sensor from time to time. This section explains the phenomenon and provides some tips on minimizing dust and eliminating it when it begins to affect your shots. I also cover this subject in my book, *Digital SLR Pro Secrets*, with complete instructions for constructing your own sensor cleaning tools. However, I'll provide a condensed version here of some of the information in that book, because sensor dust and sensor cleaning are two of the most contentious subjects Canon EOS 70D owners have to deal with.

Dust the FAQs, Ma'am

Here are some of the most frequently asked questions about sensor dust issues.

Q. I see tiny specks in my viewfinder. Do I have dust on my sensor?

A. If you see sharp, well-defined specks, they are clinging to the underside of your focus screen and not on your sensor. They have absolutely no effect on your photographs, and are merely annoying or distracting.

Q. I can see dust on my mirror. How can I remove it?

A. Like focus screen dust, any artifacts that have settled on your mirror won't affect your photos. You can often remove dust on the mirror or focus screen with a bulb air blower, which will loosen it and whisk it away. Stubborn dust on the focus screen can sometimes be gently flicked away with a soft brush designed for cleaning lenses. I don't recommend brushing the mirror or touching it in any way. The mirror is a special front-surface-silvered optical device (unlike conventional mirrors, which are silvered on the back side of a piece of glass or plastic) and can be easily scratched. If you can't blow mirror dust off, it's best to just forget about it. You can't see it in the viewfinder, anyway.

Q. I see a bright spot in the same place in all of my photos. Is that sensor dust?

A. You've probably got either a "hot" pixel or one that is permanently "stuck" due to a defect in the sensor. A hot pixel is one that shows up as a bright spot only during long exposures as the sensor warms. A pixel stuck in the "on" position always appears in the image. Both show up as bright red, green, or blue pixels, usually surrounded by a small cluster of other improperly illuminated pixels, caused by the camera's interpolating the hot or stuck pixel into its surroundings, as shown in Figure 14.10. A stuck pixel can also be permanently dark. Either kind is likely to show up when they contrast with plain, evenly colored areas of your image.

Figure 14.10 A stuck pixel is surrounded by improperly interpolated pixels created by the 70D's demosaicing algorithm.

Finding one or two hot or stuck pixels in your sensor is unfortunately fairly common. They can be "removed" by telling the 70D to ignore them through a simple process called *pixel mapping*. If the bad pixels become bothersome, Canon can remap your sensor's pixels with a quick trip to a service center.

Bad pixels can also show up on your camera's color LCD panel, but, unless they are abundant, the wisest course is to just ignore them.

Q. I see an irregular out-of-focus blob in the same place in my photos. Is that sensor dust?

A. Yes. Sensor contaminants can take the form of tiny spots, larger blobs, or even curvy lines if they are caused by minuscule fibers that have settled on the sensor. They'll appear out of focus because they aren't actually on the sensor surface but, rather, a fraction of a millimeter above it on the filter that covers the sensor. The smaller the f/stop used, the more in-focus the dust becomes. At large apertures, it may not be visible at all.

Q. I never see any dust on my sensor. What's all the fuss about?

A. Those who never have dust problems with their EOS 70D fall into one of four categories: those for whom the camera's automatic dust removal features are working well; those who seldom change their lenses and have clean working habits that minimize the amount of dust that invades their cameras in the first place; those who simply don't notice the dust (often because they don't shoot many macro photos or other pictures using the small f/stops that makes dust evident in their images); and those who are very, very lucky.

Identifying and Dealing with Dust

Sensor dust is less of a problem than it might be because it shows up only under certain circumstances. Indeed, you might have dust on your sensor right now and not be aware if it. The dust doesn't actually settle on the sensor itself, but, rather, on a protective filter a very tiny distance above the sensor, subjecting it to the phenomenon of *depth-of-focus*. Depth-of-focus is the distance the focal plane can be moved and still render an object in sharp focus. At f/2.8 to f/5.6 or even smaller, sensor dust, particularly if small, is likely to be outside the range of depth-of-focus and blur into an unnoticeable dot.

However, if you're shooting at f/16 to f/22 or smaller, those dust motes suddenly pop into focus. Forget about trying to spot them by peering directly at your sensor with the shutter open and the lens removed. The period at the end of this sentence, about .33mm in diameter, could block a group of pixels measuring 40 × 40 pixels (160 pixels in all!). Dust spots that are even smaller than that can easily show up in your images if you're shooting large, empty areas that are light colored. Dust motes are most likely to show up in the sky, as in Figure 14.11, or in white backgrounds of your seamless product shots and are less likely to be a problem in images that contain lots of dark areas and detail.

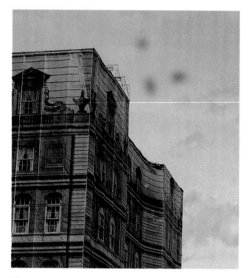

Figure 14.11 Only the dust spots in the sky are apparent in this shot.

To see if you have dust on your sensor, take a few test shots of a plain, blank surface (such as a piece of paper or a cloudless sky) at small f/stops, such as f/22, and a few wide open. Open Photoshop, copy several shots into a single document in separate layers, then flip back and forth between layers to see if any spots you see are present in all layers. You may have to boost contrast and sharpness to make the dust easier to spot.

Avoiding Dust

Of course, the easiest way to protect your sensor from dust is to prevent it from settling on the sensor in the first place. Some Canon lenses come with rubberized seals around the lens mounts that help keep dust from infiltrating, but you'll find that dust will still find a way to get inside. Here are my tips for eliminating the problem before it begins.

- **Clean environment.** Avoid working in dusty areas if you can do so. Hah! Serious photographers will take this one with a grain of salt, because it usually makes sense to go where the pictures are. Only a few of us are so paranoid about sensor dust (considering that it is so easily removed) that we'll avoid moderately grimy locations just to protect something that is, when you get down to it, just a tool. If you find a great picture opportunity at a raging fire, during a sandstorm, or while surrounded by dust clouds, you might hesitate to take the picture, but, with a little caution (don't remove your lens in these situations, and clean the camera afterwards!) you can still shoot. However, it still makes sense to store your camera in a clean environment. One place cameras and lenses pick up a lot of dust is inside a camera bag. Clean your bag from time to time, and you can avoid problems.

- **Clean lenses.** There are a few paranoid types that avoid swapping lenses in order to minimize the chance of dust getting inside their cameras. It makes more sense just to use a blower or brush to dust off the rear lens mount of the replacement lens first, so you won't be introducing dust into your camera simply by attaching a new, dusty lens. Do this before you remove the lens from your camera, and then avoid stirring up dust before making the exchange.

- **Work fast.** Minimize the time your camera is lens-less and exposed to dust. That means having your replacement lens ready and dusted off, and a place to set down the old lens as soon as it is removed, so you can quickly attach the new lens.

- **Let gravity help you.** Face the camera downward when the lens is detached so any dust in the mirror box will tend to fall away from the sensor. Turn your back to any breezes, indoor forced air vents, fans, or other sources of dust to minimize infiltration.

- **Protect the lens you just removed.** Once you've attached the new lens, quickly put the end cap on the one you just removed to reduce the dust that might fall on it.

- **Clean out the vestibule.** From time to time, remove the lens while in a relatively dust-free environment and use a blower bulb like the one shown in Figure 14.12 (*not* compressed air or a vacuum hose) to clean out the mirror box area. A blower bulb is generally safer than a can of compressed air, or a strong positive/negative airflow, which can tend to drive dust further into nooks and crannies.

- **Be prepared.** If you're embarking on an important shooting session, it's a good idea to clean your sensor *now*, rather than come home with hundreds or thousands of images with dust spots caused by flecks that were sitting on your sensor before you even started. Before I left on my recent trip to Spain, I put both cameras I was taking through a rigid cleaning regimen, figuring they could remain dust-free for a measly 10 days. I even left my bulky blower bulb at home. It was a big mistake, but my intentions were good.

Figure 14.12

Use a robust air bulb for cleaning your sensor.

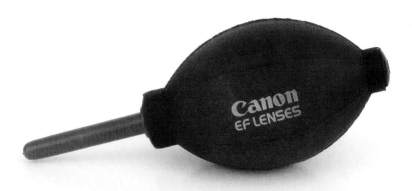

- **Clone out existing spots in your image editor.** Photoshop and other editors have a clone tool or healing brush you can use to copy pixels from surrounding areas over the dust spot or dead pixel. This process can be tedious, especially if you have lots of dust spots and/or lots of images to be corrected. The advantage is that this sort of manual fix-it probably will do the least damage to the rest of your photo. Only the cloned pixels will be affected.

- **Use filtration in your image editor.** A semi-smart filter like Photoshop's Dust & Scratches filter can remove dust and other artifacts by selectively blurring areas that the plug-in decides represent dust spots. This method can work well if you have many dust spots, because you won't need to patch them manually. However, any automated method like this has the possibility of blurring areas of your image that you didn't intend to soften.

Sensor Cleaning

Those new to the concept of sensor dust actually hesitate before deciding to clean their camera themselves. Isn't it a better idea to pack up your 70D and send it to a Canon service center so their crack technical staff can do the job for you? Or, at the very least, shouldn't you let the friendly folks at your local camera store do it?

Of course, if you choose to let someone else clean your sensor, they will be using methods that are more or less identical to the techniques you would use yourself. None of these techniques are difficult, and the only difference between their cleaning and your cleaning is that they might have done it dozens or hundreds of times. If you're careful, you can do just as good a job.

Of course vendors like Canon won't tell you this, but it's not because they don't trust you. It's not that difficult for a real goofball to mess up his camera by hurrying or taking a shortcut. Perhaps the person uses the "Bulb" method of holding the shutter open and a finger slips, allowing the shutter curtain to close on top of a sensor cleaning brush. Or, someone tries to clean the sensor using masking tape, and ends up with goo all over its surface. If Canon recommended *any* method that's mildly risky, someone would do it wrong, and then the company would face lawsuits from those who'd contend they did it exactly in the way the vendor suggested, so the ruined camera is not their fault. If you visit Canon's website, you'll find this recommendation: "If the image sensor needs cleaning, we recommend having it cleaned at a Canon service center, as it is a very delicate component."

You can see that vendors like Canon tend to be conservative in their recommendations, and, in doing so, make it seem as if sensor cleaning is more daunting and dangerous than it really is. Some vendors recommend only dust-off cleaning, through the use of reasonably gentle blasts of air, while condemning more serious scrubbing with swabs and cleaning fluids. However, these cleaning kits for the exact types of cleaning they recommended against are for sale in Japan only, where, apparently, your average photographer is more dexterous than those of us in the rest of the world. These kits are similar to those used by official repair staff to clean your sensor if you decide to send your camera in for a dust-up.

As I noted, sensors can be affected by dust particles that are much smaller than you might be able to spot visually on the surface of your lens. The filters that cover sensors tend to be fairly hard compared to optical glass. Cleaning the 22.5mm × 15.0mm sensor in your Canon 70D within the tight confines of the mirror box can call for a steady hand and careful touch. If your sensor's filter becomes scratched through inept cleaning, you can't simply remove it yourself and replace it with a new one.

There are four basic kinds of cleaning processes that can be used to remove dusty and sticky stuff that settles on your dSLR's sensor. All of these must be performed with the shutter locked open. I'll describe these methods and provide instructions for locking the shutter later in this section.

- **Air cleaning.** This process involves squirting blasts of air inside your camera with the shutter locked open. This works well for dust that's not clinging stubbornly to your sensor.

- **Brushing.** A soft, very fine brush is passed across the surface of the sensor's filter, dislodging mildly persistent dust particles and sweeping them off the imager.

- **Liquid cleaning.** A soft swab dipped in a cleaning solution such as ethanol is used to wipe the sensor filter, removing more obstinate particles.

- **Tape cleaning.** There are some who get good results by applying a special form of tape to the surface of their sensor. When the tape is peeled off, all the dust goes with it. Supposedly. I'd be remiss if I didn't point out right now that this form of cleaning is somewhat controversial; the other three methods are much more widely accepted. Now that Canon has equipped the front-sensor filter with a special anti-dust coating, I wouldn't chance damaging that coating by using any kind of adhesive tape.

Placing the Shutter in the Locked and Fully Upright Position for Cleaning

Make sure you're using a fully charged battery or the optional AC Adapter Kit ACK-E6.

1. Remove the lens from the camera and then turn the camera on.

2. Set the EOS 70D to any one of the non-fully automatic modes.

3. You'll find the Clean Manually menu choice in the Set-up 4 menu under Sensor Cleaning (see Figure 14.9, shown earlier). Press the SET button.

4. Select OK and press SET again. The mirror will flip up and the shutter will open.

5. Use one of the methods described below to remove dust and grime from your sensor. Be careful not to accidentally switch the power off or open the memory card or battery compartment doors as you work. If that happens, the shutter may be damaged if it closes onto your cleaning tool.

6. When you're finished, turn the power off, replace your lens, and switch your camera back on.

Air Cleaning

Your first attempts at cleaning your sensor should always involve gentle blasts of air. Many times, you'll be able to dislodge dust spots, which will fall off the sensor and, with luck, out of the mirror box. Attempt one of the other methods only when you've already tried air cleaning and it didn't remove all the dust.

Here are some tips for doing air cleaning:

- **Use a clean, powerful air bulb.** Your best bet is bulb cleaners designed for the job, like the Giottos Rocket. Smaller bulbs, like those air bulbs with a brush attached sometimes sold for lens cleaning or weak nasal aspirators, may not provide sufficient air or a strong enough blast to do much good.

- **Hold the EOS 70D upside down.** Then look up into the mirror box as you squirt your air blasts, increasing the odds that gravity will help pull the expelled dust downward, away from the sensor. You may have to use some imagination in positioning yourself. (See Figure 14.13.)

- **Never use air canisters.** The propellant inside these cans can permanently coat your sensor if you tilt the can while spraying. It's not worth taking a chance.

- **Avoid air compressors.** Super strong blasts of air are likely to force dust under the sensor filter.

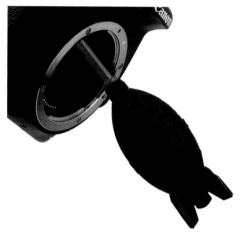

Figure 14.13 Hold the camera upside down when cleaning to allow dust to fall out.

Brush Cleaning

If your dust is a little more stubborn and can't be dislodged by air alone, you may want to try a brush, charged with static electricity, that can pick off dust spots by electrical attraction. One good, but expensive, option is the Sensor Brush sold at www.visibledust.com. A cheaper version can be purchased at www.copperhillimages.com. You need a 16mm version, like the one shown in Figure 14.14, that can be stroked across the short dimension of your 70D's sensor.

Ordinary artist's brushes are much too coarse and stiff and have fibers that are tangled or can come loose and settle on your sensor. A good sensor brush's fibers are resilient and described as "thinner than a human hair." Moreover, the brush has a wooden handle that reduces the risk of static sparks.

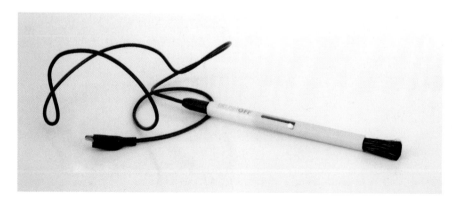

Figure 14.14
A proper brush, preferably with a grounding strap to eliminate static electricity, is required for dusting off your sensor.

Brush cleaning is done with a dry brush by gently swiping the surface of the sensor filter with the tip. The dust particles are attracted to the brush particles and cling to them. You should clean the brush with compressed air before and after each use, and store it in an appropriate air-tight container between applications to keep it clean and dust-free. Although these special brushes are expensive, one should last you a long time.

Liquid Cleaning

Unfortunately, you'll often encounter really stubborn dust spots that can't be removed with a blast of air or flick of a brush. These spots may be combined with some grease or a liquid that causes them to stick to the sensor filter's surface. In such cases, liquid cleaning with a swab may be necessary. During my first clumsy attempts to clean my own sensor, I accidentally got my blower bulb tip too close to the sensor, and some sort of deposit from the tip of the bulb ended up on the sensor. I panicked until I discovered that liquid cleaning did a good job of removing whatever it was that took up residence on my sensor.

You can make your own swabs out of pieces of plastic (some use fast food restaurant knives, with the tip cut at an angle to the proper size) covered with a soft cloth or Pec-Pad, as shown in Figures 14.15 and 14.16. However, if you've got the bucks to spend, you can't go wrong with good-quality commercial sensor cleaning swabs, such as those sold by Photographic Solutions, Inc. (www.photosol.com).

You want a sturdy swab that won't bend or break so you can apply gentle pressure to the swab as you wipe the sensor surface. Use the swab with methanol (as pure as you can get it, particularly medical grade; other ingredients can leave a residue), or the Eclipse solution also sold by Photographic Solutions. Eclipse is actually quite a bit purer than even medical-grade methanol. A couple drops of solution should be enough, unless you have a spot that's extremely difficult to remove. In that case, you may need to use extra solution on the swab to help "soak" the dirt off.

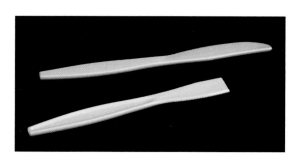

Figure 14.15 You can make your own sensor swab from a plastic knife that's been truncated.

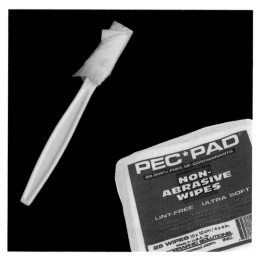

Figure 14.16 Carefully wrap a Pec-Pad around the swab.

Once you overcome your nervousness at touching your 70D's sensor, the process is easy. You'll wipe continuously with the swab in one direction, then flip it over and wipe in the other direction. You need to completely wipe the entire surface; otherwise, you may end up depositing the dust you collect at the far end of your stroke. Wipe; don't rub.

If you want a close-up look at your sensor to make sure the dust has been removed, you can pay $50-$100 for a special sensor "microscope" with an illuminator. (See Figure 14.17.) Or, you can do like I do and work with a plain old Carson MiniBrite PO-55 illuminated 5X magnifier, as seen in Figure 14.18. It has a built-in LED and, held a few inches from the lens mount with the lens removed from your 70D, provides a sharp, close-up view of the sensor, with enough contrast to reveal any dust that remains. You can read more about this great device at http://dslrguides.com/carson.

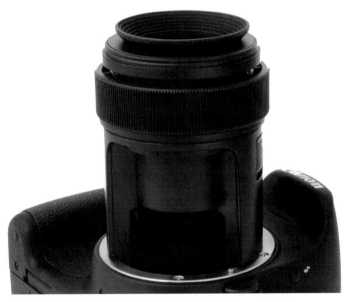

Figure 14.17
This SensorKlear magnifier provides a view of your sensor as you work.

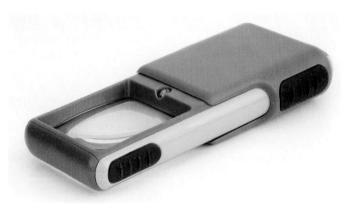

Figure 14.18
An illuminated magnifier like this Carson MiniBrite PO-55 can be used as a 'scope to view your sensor.

Index

C

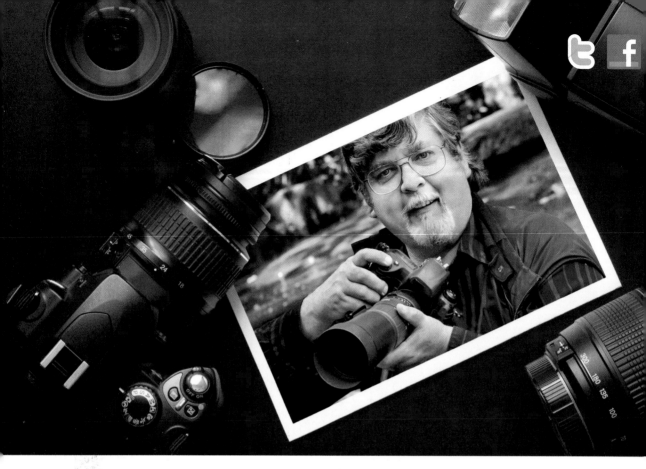
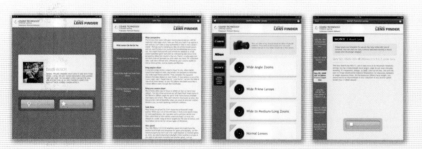

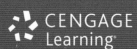